Traditions & Encounters

CONNECT WITH THE
Stories
OF HISTORY

Students will readily engage with the past when they see that history is the work of real people. Bentley and Ziegler enliven world history through the vivid tales of merchants, missionaries, monarchs, explorers, conquerors, and commoners across cultures:

> I n 629 . . . in defiance of the [Chinese] emperor [Tang Taizong], a young Buddhist monk slipped past imperial watchtowers under cover of darkness and made his way west. His name was Xuanzang, and his destination was India, homeland of Buddhism . . . [where he would] visit the holy sites of Buddhism, and . . . learn about Buddhism from the purest sources. Xuanzang could not have imagined the difficulties he would face. Immediately after his departure from China, his guide abandoned him in the Gobi desert. After losing his water bag and collapsing in the heat, Xuanzang made his way to the oasis town of Turpan on the silk roads . . . [Then] Xuanzang crossed three of the world's highest mountain ranges—the Tian Shan, Hindu Kush, and Pamir ranges—and lost one-third of his party. . . . Yet Xuanzang persisted and arrived in India in 630. By the time of his return [to Chang'an] in 645, Xuanzang had logged more than 16,000 kilometers (10,000 miles) on the road.

MAP 12.1

The silk roads, 200 B.C.E.–300 C.E.
Note the extent of the land and sea routes known collectively as the silk roads.

Consider the political and economic conditions that would be necessary for regular travel and trade across the silk roads.

- Vivid stories keep students involved and help them to get the most from their study of world history.

- Clear, vibrant, precise maps with extended captions—entirely redesigned for this edition—help students put the experiences of individual historical actors in geographical context.

CONNECT TO THE
Experience
OF HISTORY

Students will experience history interactively:

- With *Connect History*—a visual, auditory, and interactive online experience—students no longer skim a text passively for facts and dates to memorize. They engage with what they read through hands-on activities, and they expand upon and apply what they learn in the process.

- Through its features, *Traditions & Encounters* emphasizes the point that history is not just a collection of facts. It is rather a creative effort based on detective work of historians examining evidence from the past and the analysis of themes that cross cultural boundary lines.

- New "Thinking About Traditions" and "Thinking About Encounters" boxes pose critical-thinking questions about the ways these twin themes play out across cultures and time periods.

- Images—paintings, mosaics, photos, posters, sculptures, architecture, and the like—draw students into the related narrative, and extended captions help them learn how to analyze visual clues to the past.

thinking about TRADITIONS

Competing Christianities
The Byzantine empire and western Europe inherited the same Christianity from the late Roman empire. How did Christianity develop along distinct lines in the two regions? What influences contributed to the development of such different understandings of Christianity?

CONNECT TO
Success
IN HISTORY

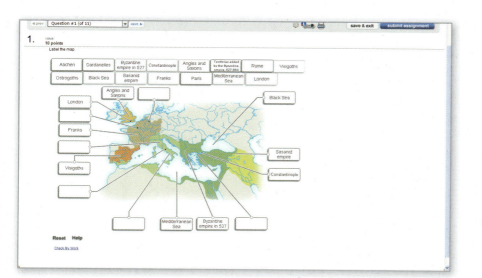

Connect History paves a path to student success:

- *Connect History,* a groundbreaking digital learning solution, helps students study more effectively—confirming what they know and pushing their learning further through engaging activities.

- *Connect History* works in tandem with questions accompanying image captions and primary sources in each chapter and builds a personalized study plan for each student.

- *Connect History* builds critical-thinking skills by placing students in a historical "critical mission" scenario and asking them to examine, evaluate, and analyze relevant data to support a recommended action.

- *Connect History* includes tools for understanding maps and geography, analyzing primary source documents, and writing a research paper (including documenting sources and avoiding plagiarism).

5 EDITION

Traditions & Encounters

A Global Perspective on the Past

Volume B: From 1000 to 1800

Jerry H. Bentley
University of Hawai`i

Herbert F. Ziegler
University of Hawai`i

McGraw Hill

Connect
Learn
Succeed™

Published by McGraw-Hill, an imprint of The McGraw-Hill Companies, Inc., 1221 Avenue of the Americas, New York, NY 10020. Copyright © 2011, 2008, 2006, 2003, 2000. All rights reserved. No part of this publication may be reproduced or distributed in any form or by any means, or stored in a database or retrieval system, without the prior written consent of The McGraw-Hill Companies, Inc., including, but not limited to, in any network or other electronic storage or transmission, or broadcast for distance learning.

This book is printed on acid-free paper.

2 3 4 5 6 7 8 9 0 DOW/DOW 9 8 7 6 5 4 3 2 1

ISBN: 978-0-07736798-5
MHID: 0-07-736798-7

Vice President Editorial: *Michael Ryan*
Publisher: *Christopher Freitag*
Sponsoring Editor: *Matthew Busbridge*
Executive Marketing Manager: *Stacy Best Ruel*
Executive Director of Development: *Lisa Pinto*
Senior Developmental Editor: *Mikola De Roo*
Editorial Coordinators: *Elena Mackawgy, Jaclyn Mautone*
Senior Production Editor: *Carey Eisner*
Art Editor: *Robin Mouat*
Cartography: *Mapping Specialists and Mary Swab*
Design Manager: *Jeanne Schreiber*
Interior Designer: *Amanda Kavanagh*
Cover Designer: *Kirk DouPonce, DogEared Design*
Manager, Photo Research: *Brian J. Pecko*
Buyer II: *Tandra Jorgensen*
Composition: *9/12 Garamond Book by Thompson Type*
Printing: *45# New Era Matte Thin, R.R. Donnelley & Sons*

Cover: 13th cent. illustration of a Muslim traveler passing a lively agricultural village on camel: © Art Resource, NY; Mosaic from San Vitale in Ravenne depicting Justinian and court officials in robes: © Scala/Art Resource, NY; Oseberg Viking vessel served as a royal tomb until its discovery in 1903: © Werner Foreman/Art Resource, NY; Drawing of Maori chief's son: © HIP/Art Resource, NY; Illustration of Dona Marina translating for Hernan Cortez entering an alliance with Tlaxcala ruler: Benson Latin American Collection, General Libraries, University of Texas at Austin; Maris Pacifici, detail of Magellan's ship Victory by Abraham Ortelius, 1589: © Royalty-Free/Corbis; Earth: © istockphoto.com/7nuit

Library of Congress Cataloging-in-Publication Data

Bentley, Jerry H., 1949–
   Traditions & encounters : a global perspective on the past / Jerry Bentley, Herbert Ziegler. — 5th ed.
      v. cm.
   Includes bibliographical references and index.
   ISBN-13: 978-0-07-736798-5 (softcover : alk. paper)
   ISBN-10: 0-07-736798-7 (softcover : alk. paper)

   1. World history. 2. Intercultural communication—History. I. Ziegler, Herbert F., 1949–
II. Title. III. Title: Traditions and encounters.
   D20.B42 2011
   909—dc22

                                                                2010036144

The Internet addresses listed in the text were accurate at the time of publication. The inclusion of a Web site does not indicate an endorsement by the authors or McGraw-Hill, and McGraw-Hill does not guarantee the accuracy of the information presented at these sites.

www.mhhe.com

brief contents

part 5

contents

part 3
The Postclassical Era, 500 to 1000 C.E. 256

part4
The Acceleration of Cross-Cultural Interaction, 1000 to 1500 C.E.   350

part5
The Origins of Global Interdependence,
1500 to 1800 462

maps

sources from the past

preface

Since its first edition, *Traditions & Encounters* has broken new ground. It has explored the grand scheme of world history as a product of real-life human beings pursuing their individual and collective interests. It has also offered a global perspective on the past by focusing on both the distinctive characteristics of individual societies and the connections that have linked the fortunes of different societies. It has combined a clear chronological framework with the twin themes of tradition and encounter, which help to make the unwieldy story of world history both more manageable and more engaging. From the beginning, *Traditions & Encounters* has offered an inclusive vision of the global past—one that is meaningful and appropriate for the interdependent world of contemporary times.

With this fifth edition, *Traditions & Encounters* takes another bold step and becomes the first truly interactive world history program by integrating an engaging text narrative with an innovative online learning platform, *Connect History*.* The narrative and analysis of world history presented in *Traditions & Encounters* are now married to *Connect History*'s hands-on online activities, an adaptive diagnostic, and additional pedagogy, primers, and resources. The result is a unique learning environment that promotes active student learning, student success, and better course results.

(*A fully integrated e-book is included in *Connect Plus History*.)

How does *Traditions & Encounters* help students comprehend what they read?

Traditions & Encounters connects students to the story of world history.

A Cohesive Organization that Frames Global History into Seven Eras. How is it possible to make sense of the entire human past? Given the diversity of human societies, gathering and organizing the sheer mass of information in a meaningful way is a daunting challenge for any world history survey course. *Traditions & Encounters* addresses this challenge through its seven-part chronological organization, which enables students to understand the development of the world through time while also exploring broader, big-picture thematic issues in world history.

Captivating Stories of World History, in Geographical Context. Chapter-opening "Eyewitness" vignettes and an engaging narrative of the people and processes that have shaped world history work together with a highly praised map program to lend a strong framework to historical knowledge—clearly connecting the *who* and the *what* of world history (individual human actors, networks of communication and exchange, significant events, and global processes) to the *when* and the *where* (the chronological and geographical context).

Online Activities in *Connect History* Turn Reading about World History into a Hands-On, Sensory Learning Experience. The activities in *Connect History,* a new Web-based assignment and assessment platform, are based on the narrative content of *Traditions & Encounters,* so they build on what students learn from reading the text and push them to explore that knowledge at greater depth. Making full use of the Web's flexibility as a learning platform, the activities in *Connect History* take a range of forms—textual, audio, and visual—and address multiple learning styles. Some exercises require students to interact with and analyze images and primary sources; others prompt students to compare and contrast the political structures or religious beliefs of different cultures they've been reading about; still others assess students' knowledge of chronology or geography. Across the board, these activities prompt active dialogue between student and text. As a result, students go beyond reading to engagement and interaction with the tools of world history.

How does *Traditions & Encounters* guide students from seeing history as an assortment of facts to a hands-on, interactive engagement with the past?

Traditions & Encounters connects students to the experience of world history.

A Pair of Themes Organize the Complexity of Global Human Experience. Since its first edition, *Traditions & Encounters* has used its title's twin themes to bring focus to the vastness of world history. The "tradition" theme draws attention to the distinctive political, social, economic, and cultural traditions that the world's peoples have devised to organize their societies and guide their affairs:

> *What forms of political leadership have different peoples devised?* • *How have the world's peoples exploited natural resources to provide themselves with food, shelter, and other necessities?* • *What forms of social organization have different peoples developed, on the basis of birth, class, wealth, gender, ethnicity, or other criteria?* • *What kinds of religious beliefs have the world's peoples espoused, which scientific and philosophical ideas have they explored, and what artistic and cultural practices have they pursued?*

The "encounter" theme directs attention to the networks of transportation, communication, and exchange that have linked individual societies to one another through processes of cross-cultural interaction:

> *Why have individuals left their own societies to explore the larger world?* • *What kinds of relationships did they establish with their counterparts in other societies?* • *What networks of transportation, communication, and exchange did they construct to sustain interactions among different societies?* • *What effects did these exchanges have on the societies that engaged in dealings with one another?*

Through new chapter-level and part-level features, the hallmark twin themes of *Traditions & Encounters* emerge in greater clarity than ever before in this fifth edition. As a result, students have resources that enable them to move beyond the facts of history and examine the past critically, analyze causes and effects, and recognize similarities and differences across world regions and time periods. By digging deeper into the implications of world history's stories—not just the *who,* the *what,* and the *where,* but also the *why* and the *how*—students can make sense of the human past.

***Connect History* Activities, Learning Scenarios, and Intellectual Tools that Hone Students' Analytical Skills.** *Connect History* offers a range of online resources and assignments designed to cultivate the skills that enable students to think like historians—from geography diagnostics and primary source tutorials to exercises in the critical analysis of historical images, artifacts, and primary sources. These tools help students read maps, understand geography, question primary sources and other historical evidence, and develop the skills of analysis and synthesis.

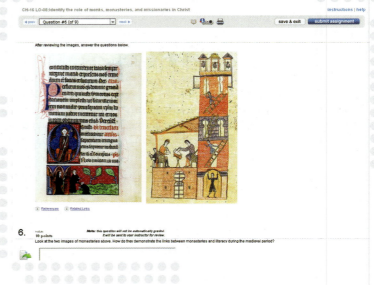

How does *Traditions & Encounters* enable students to comprehend reading assignments, think critically about important issues, and prepare for essays and exams?

Traditions & Encounters connects students to success in your world history course.

Comprehensive Chapter-Ending Pedagogy and Current Scholarship. Chronology boxes outline each chapter's most important dates and events. "In Perspective" sections, chapter-ending summaries, offer brief overviews of significant developments. "For Further Reading" sections, fully updated for the fifth edition, mention the most important works available about the chapter's topics and serve as a resource for further study or research projects. A running pronunciation guide appearing at the bottom of pages and an end-of-book glossary help students with unfamiliar names and terms.

Digital Assignments that Assess and Improve Students' Knowledge Base. The groundbreaking digital tools in *Connect History* enable students reading *Traditions & Encounters* to create a personalized study plan tailored to their own learning styles. By using the online diagnostics, exercises, and activities that *Connect History* provides for every chapter of *Traditions & Encounters,* students can clearly identify what they know well and what they need to study more carefully. The interactivity and assessment feedback of *Connect History* reinforces what students read, ensuring that they genuinely understand events and their sequence, key historical developments in chronological and geographical context, important concepts, and cause-and-effect relationships. As a result, students not only read more, but they also devote their studying time and energy to the most useful issues, and they are able to think and write critically about what they read.

CHANGES FOR THE FIFTH EDITION

PART 1: The Early Complex Societies, 3500 to 500 B.C.E.

CHAPTER 1: Before History
Revised discussions of early Homo sapiens *and* Homo erectus *use of language and communication, and expanded discussion on origins of agriculture*

CHAPTER 5: Early Society in East Asia
Expanded discussion of iron weapons in the Zhou dynasty

CHAPTER 6: Early Societies in the Americas and Oceania
Expanded discussion of migrations to the Americas and Oceania and revised discussion of Olmec influence in Mesoamerica

PART 2: The Formation of Classical Societies, 500 B.C.E. to 500 C.E.

CHAPTER 7: The Empires of Persia
Revised discussion of Xerxes' Persian rule in Mesopotamia and Egypt

CHAPTER 8: The Unification of China
Revised and expanded discussion of the Qin and Han emperors' bureaucracy and Ban Zhao's treatise

CHAPTER 9: State, Society, and the Quest for Salvation in India
New discussion of Ghandara-style art

CHAPTER 10: Mediterranean Society: The Greek Phase
Revised discussion of Socrates and new discussion of Greek contributions to the sciences and mathematics

CHAPTER 11: Mediterranean Society: The Roman Phase
New discussion of sea lanes and expanded discussion of Mediterranean trade

CHAPTER 12: Cross-Cultural Exchanges on the Silk Roads
Expanded discussion of the monsoon system and the spread of disease caused by maritime travel

PART 3: The Postclassical Era, 500 to 1000 C.E.

CHAPTER 13: The Expansive Realm of Islam
Revised and expanded discussion of Abbasid capital Baghdad and cultural adaptation
A brand-new "Sources from the Past," Al-Muqaddasi on Iraq in the late tenth century

CHAPTER 14: The Resurgence of Empire in East Asia
New discussion of Wu Zhao and the spread of Buddhism in China

CHAPTER 16: The Two Worlds of Christendom
A "Sources from the Past" included in Chapter 13 in the previous edition, Benjamin of Tudela on the Caliph's Court at Baghdad, now appears in this new chapter.

PART 4: The Acceleration of Cross-Cultural Interaction, 1000 to 1500 C.E.

CHAPTER 17: Nomadic Empires and Eurasian Integration
New discussion of nomadic pastoralists in Central Asia
A brand-new "Sources from the Past," William of Rubruck on Gender Relations among the Mongols

CHAPTER 18: States and Societies of Sub-Saharan Africa
New discussion of Jenne-jeno and revised discussion of the effects of the slave trade in sub-Saharan Africa

CHAPTER 19: The Increasing Influence of Europe
New discussion of the decline of the Byzantine empire and revised discussion of Christian influence during the High Middle Ages, the Bogomils and Cathars heresies, and the Crusades of 1095

PART 5: The Origins of Global Interdependence, 1500 to 1800

CHAPTER 22: Transoceanic Encounters and Global Connections
Revised discussion of the effects of the Columbian exchange of food crops, goods and animals, and world population growth

CHAPTER 23: The Transformation of Europe
New discussion of notable female scientists, including Émilie du Châtelet, and their contributions to the sciences during the sixteenth and seventeenth centuries
A brand-new "Sources from the Past," an excerpt from John Locke's An Essay Concerning Human Understanding

CHAPTER 24: New Worlds: The Americas and Oceania
New discussion of the effects of race and ethnicity on social hierarchy in colonial society

CHAPTER 27: The Islamic Empires
Revised discussion of the Ottoman Empire of early modern times and the three Islamic ruling empires

PART 6: An Age of Revolution, Industry, and Empire, 1750 to 1914

CHAPTER 28: Revolutions and National States in the Atlantic World
Revised and expanded discussion of revolutionary wars in America, France, and Haiti

CHAPTER 32: The Building of Global Empires

Expanded and revised discussion of the English East India Company and the Indian rebellion

A brand-new "Sources from the Past," The Royal Niger Company Mass-Produces Imperial Control in Africa

PART 7: Contemporary Global Realignments, 1914 to the Present

CHAPTER 33: The Great War: The World in Upheaval

A brand-new "Sources from the Past," Memorandum of the General Syrian Congress

CHAPTER 34: An Age of Anxiety

A brand-new "Sources from the Past," Joseph Stalin on the First Five-Year Plan

CHAPTER 36: New Conflagrations: World War II and the Cold War

New discussion of the medical mistreatment of POWs during the cold war

CHAPTER 38: A World without Borders

New discussion of the cold war, and revised discussion of globalization, developing economies, and climate change in the contemporary world

Two brand-new "Sources from the Past": an excerpt on climate change from Al Gore's An Inconvenient Truth, *and Aung San Suu Kyi's* Politics and Family: The Hope of and for Girl Children

NEW FEATURES AND CHANGES THROUGHOUT THE TEXT

"Thinking About" features. New "Thinking About Traditions" and "Thinking About Encounters" boxes focus on historical elements that highlight how the twin themes of traditions and encounters play out across cultures and time periods. Each box ends with related critical-thinking questions around these two forces that have shaped world history.

New primary sources. Eight brand-new "Sources from the Past," along with a wealth of resources in *Connect History* provide students with plenty of opportunities for critical analyses of primary sources. The primary sources new to this edition: Al-Muqaddasi, on Iraq in the Late Tenth Century; William of Rubruck on Gender Relations among the Mongols; an excerpt from John Locke's *An Essay Concerning Human Understanding;* The Royal Niger Company Mass-Produces Imperial Control in Africa; Memorandum from the General Syrian Congress; Joseph Stalin on the First Five-Year Plan; an excerpt on climate change from Al Gore's *An Inconvenient Truth,* and Aung San Suu Kyi's "Politics and Family: The Hope of and for Girl Children."

New part-ending features. "State of the World" assesses the global themes covered during the preceding chapters, giving students a thematic big-picture snapshot—both textually and visually using a combined global map and timeline—of the world during a particular period.

New map program. An entirely redesigned map program offers superior clarity, better topographical information, and greater global geographical precision and context with more vivid and distinct use of color and new globe locator icons within regional maps to better orient students. Extended captions with critical-thinking questions enrich students' understanding of the relationship between geography and history.

Fresh, inviting design for visual engagement and ease of use. An engaging, modern, and vivid design with new images and extended captions draws students into the narrative, provides visual cues for remembering content, and makes content easier to parse and digest.

Streamlined organization. Reorganization of content reduces the total number of chapters in the text, making the individual volumes more manageable to teach in one semester.

A new Chapter 16, "The Two Worlds of Christendom," combines elements of former Chapters 13 and 17 and places Europe in a more global perspective.

Elimination of the prior edition's Chapter 38 ("The Bipolar World") integrates the events of the cold war more seamlessly and clearly into coverage of World War II (Chapter 36, "New Conflagrations: World War II") and post–World War II decline of imperialist empires (Chapter 37, "The End of Empire").

Traditions & Encounters

FIFTH EDITION:

more emphasis on critical thinking and analysis

thinking about ENCOUNTERS

Trading-Post Empires

Trading-post empires provided the most prominent spaces for cross-cultural interactions between Europeans, Africans, and Asians. Trading posts also limited European intrusion into Africa and Asia, especially in contrast to the settlement empires of the Americas. What characterized the relations between, for example, the Portuguese and the inhabitants of the Indian Ocean basin? Why were Europeans confined to such posts?

thinking about TRADITIONS

Empires and Their Roads

All the classical empires invested resources in the building of roads and transportation networks that helped them to integrate their vast territories into manageable societies. Compare the road system of the Roman empire with those of the Persian, Han, and Mauryan empires. How did Roman roads complement Mediterranean sea lanes to link regions of the empire?

NEW

"Thinking About Traditions" and "Thinking About Encounters" boxes

These brief boxes—one of each in every chapter—spotlight instances in which the traditions and encounters themes arise in specific historical contexts. Each box ends with critical-thinking questions that prompt reflection about the roles of traditions and encounters in shaping the global past.

NEW

"Sources From the Past"

Every chapter showcases primary source documents—letters, journal entries, political tracts, philosophical reflections, religious writings, and other relevant primary sources. Each source concludes with a critical-thinking question that prompts students to explore the issues raised in the document. The fifth edition includes eight brand-new "Sources from the Past"—including Stalin's thoughts about his First Five-Year Plan and an excerpt from Al Gore's *An Inconvenient Truth*. Together with a wealth of resources in *Connect History*, students have numerous opportunities for critical analyses of primary sources.

sources from the past

The Royal Niger Company Mass-Produces Imperial Control in Africa

The 1880s proved a crucial time for sub-Saharan African societies and European imperial adventurers. European nations at the Berlin Conference set forth the rules by which they would partition and rule African states, and then those nations—such as Great Britain—commissioned companies like the Royal Niger Company to assert imperial prerogatives. To fend off French competitors in the Niger River delta, the British-controlled Royal Niger Company had local rulers sign its "standard treaty," a mass-produced, fill-in-the-blank treaty that essentially ceded trade and political control to the company, and thus to Britain, in what became the British colony of Nigeria.

We, the undersigned Chiefs of _____, with the view to the bettering of the condition of our country and our people, do this day cede to the Royal Niger Company, for ever, the whole of our territory from _____.

We also give to the said Royal Niger Company full power to settle all native disputes arising from any cause whatever, and we pledge ourselves not to enter into any war with other tribes without the sanction of the said Royal Niger Company.

We understand that the said Royal Niger Company have full power to mine, farm, and build in any portion of our country.

We bind ourselves not to have any intercourse with any strangers or foreigners except through the said Royal Niger Company.

In consideration of the foregoing, the said Royal Niger Company (Chartered and Limited) bind themselves not to interfere with any of the native laws or customs of the country, consistently with the maintenance of order and good government.

The said Royal Niger Company agree to pay native owners of land a reasonable amount for any portion they may require.

The said Royal Niger Company bind themselves to protect the said Chiefs from the attacks of any neighboring aggressive tribes.

The said Royal Niger Company also agree to pay the said Chiefs _____ measures native value.

We, the undersigned witnesses, do hereby solemnly declare that the _____ Chiefs whose names are placed opposite their respective crosses have in our presence affixed their crosses of their own free will and consent, and that the said _____ has in our presence affixed his signature.

Done in triplicate at _____, this _____ day of _____, 188__.

Declaration by interpreter   I, _____, of _____, do hereby solemnly declare that I am well acquainted with the language of the country, and that on the _____ day of _____, 188__, I truly and faithfully explained the above Agreement to all the Chiefs present, and that they understood its meaning.

For Further Reflection

■ What did this "standard treaty" promise to Nigerian leaders, and what was expected in return? Given language barriers and imperial greed, do you believe Nigerians received true and faithful explanations of the treaty's meaning?

Source: Alfred J. Andrea and James H. Overfield, eds. *The Human Record: Sources of Global History,* 3rd ed., vol. 2. Boston: Wadsworth, 1998, pp. 299–300.

stronger support for the main themes discussed in each era

part4

THE ACCELERATION OF CROSS-CULTURAL INTERACTION, 1000 TO 1500 C.E.

The half millennium from 1000 to 1500 c.e. differed markedly from earlier eras. During classical and post-classical times, large, regional societies situated in China, India, southwest Asia, and the Mediterranean basin dominated the eastern hemisphere. Peoples of these lands built extensive networks of trade and communication that spanned the eastern hemisphere and influenced the development of all its societies. From 1000 to 1500 c.e., however, nomadic Turkish and Mongol peoples overran settled societies and established vast transregional empires from China to eastern Europe.

Nomadic peoples toppled several postclassical states, most notably the Song empire in China and the Abbasid realm in southwest Asia. By building empires that transcended the boundaries of postclassical states, however, nomadic Turks and Mongols laid a political foundation for sharply increased trade and communication between peoples of different societies and cultural regions. Indeed, their empires prompted the peoples of the eastern hemisphere to forge closer links than ever before in history. By the mid-fourteenth century, merchants, diplomats, and missionaries traveled frequently between lands as far removed as Italy and China.

Increased trade in the Indian Ocean basin also promoted more intense cross-cultural communications. Maritime trade built on the political stability, economic expansion, and demographic growth of the postclassical era. By the fourteenth century, mariners called at ports throughout the Indian Ocean basin from southeast Asia to India, Ceylon, Arabia, and east Africa, while sea lanes through the South China Sea offered access to ports in the islands of southeast Asia, China, Japan, and Korea. Commercial goods traveled over the Indian Ocean in larger quantities than ever before. From the eleventh century forward, cargoes increasingly consisted of bulky commodities such as timber, coral, steel, building materials, grains, dates, and other foodstuffs. This trade in bulk goods indicated a movement toward economic integration as societies of the Indian Ocean basin concentrated increasingly on cultivating crops or producing goods for export while importing foods or goods that they could not produce very well themselves.

Demographic growth, increased agricultural production, and economic expansion helped to underwrite rapid political development in sub-Saharan Africa and western Europe. Powerful regional states and centralized empires

350

Part Openers

Seven brief part openers—newly designed for this edition—explain the coherence of each major era in human history by introducing the themes that run through all the chapters in each part. Taken together, the seven part openers provide a brief, highly analytical summary of the book's seven-era periodization of the global past.

NEW
"State of the World" Part Closers

Each of the seven parts now ends with a "State of the World" essay, which reassesses the global themes that emerged in the preceding chapters. Each "State of the World" essay is accompanied by a global map and timeline, which offer students a big-picture snapshot of the world that is both textual and visual.

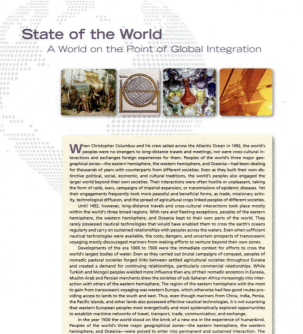

State of the World
A World on the Point of Global Integration

When Christopher Columbus and his crew sailed across the Atlantic Ocean in 1492, the world's peoples were no strangers to long-distance travels and meetings, nor were cross-cultural interactions and exchanges foreign experiences for them. Peoples of the world's three major geographical zones—the eastern hemisphere, the western hemisphere, and Oceania—had been dealing for thousands of years with counterparts from different societies. Even as they built their own distinctive political, social, economic, and cultural traditions, the world's peoples also engaged in the larger world beyond their own societies. Their interactions were often hostile or unpleasant, taking the form of raids, wars, campaigns of imperial expansion, or transmissions of epidemic diseases. Yet their engagements frequently took more peaceful and beneficial forms, as trade, missionary activity, technological diffusion, and the spread of agricultural crops linked peoples of different societies.

Until 1492, however, long-distance travels and cross-cultural interactions took place mostly within the world's three broad regions. With rare and fleeting exceptions, peoples of the eastern hemisphere, the western hemisphere, and Oceania kept to their own parts of the world. They rarely possessed nautical technologies that would have enabled them to cross the earth's oceans regularly and carry on sustained relationships with peoples across the waters. Even when sufficient nautical technologies were available, the costs, dangers, and uncertain prospects of transoceanic voyaging mostly discouraged mariners from making efforts to venture beyond their own zones.

Developments of the era 1000 to 1500 were the immediate context for efforts to cross the world's largest bodies of water. Even as they carried out brutal campaigns of conquest, peoples of nomadic pastoral societies forged links between settled agricultural societies throughout Eurasia and created a demand for continuing relationships, particularly commercial relationships. While Turkish and Mongol peoples wielded more influence than any of their nomadic ancestors in Eurasia, Muslim Arab and Persian merchants drew the societies of sub-Saharan Africa increasingly into interaction with others of the eastern hemisphere. The region of the eastern hemisphere with the most to gain from transoceanic voyaging was western Europe, which otherwise had few good routes providing access to lands to the south and east. Thus, even though mariners from China, India, Persia, the Pacific islands, and other lands also possessed effective nautical technologies, it is not surprising that western European peoples most energetically and most systematically explored opportunities to establish maritime networks of travel, transport, trade, communication, and exchange.

In the year 1500 the world stood on the brink of a new era in the experience of humankind. Peoples of the world's three major geographical zones—the eastern hemisphere, the western hemisphere, and Oceania—were poised to enter into permanent and sustained interaction. The results of their engagements were profitable or beneficial for some peoples but difficult or disastrous for others. It is impossible to comprehend them except in context of the acceleration of cross-cultural interaction in the era 1000 to 1500.

460

1000 C.E.	1100 C.E.	1200 C.E.	1300 C.E.	1400 C.E.	1500 C.E.

Turkish empires & their neighbors, 1000–1500 C.E.; Seljuq Turks, Abbasid & Byzantine empires, Sultanates of Dehli and Rum — SOUTHWEST ASIA & EURASIA

ASIA

Mongol empires, late 12th century C.E.–mid-14th century C.E.; Khanate of Chaghatai (central Asia); Khanate of the Golden Horde (Russia); Khanate of the Great Khan (China); Ikhanate of Persia — Tamerlane empire, mid-14th century C.E.–1405 C.E.

Kingdom of Ghana (11th–13th century); Swahili cities (11th–15th century); Mali empire (13th–15th century); Kingdom of Great Zimbabwe, 13th century C.E.–mid-15th century C.E.; Songhay empire (late 15th–late 16th century) — AFRICA

Medieval European regional states, 1000–1300 C.E.: Holy Roman empire, France, England, Castile, Italian states, Hungary, Byzantine empire & other states — MEDIEVAL EUROPE

Toltec empire at its height, 950–1150 C.E. — THE AMERICAS — Aztec empire, ca. mid-14th century–1520 C.E.; Inca Empire, 1471–1532 C.E.

Aboriginal societies of Australia & the Maori of New Zealand: from 1st century B.C.E.–18th-century European settlements

OCEANIA

Pacific Island (Samoa, Tonga, Society Islands) population growth (11th century C.E.) leads to emergence of Pacific Island chiefly states (13th century C.E.)

a visual program that deepens the understanding of world history

Maps Program

The entire map program has been redesigned to make topographical features clearer and boundaries more distinct. Regional maps include new globe locator icons that place individual regions in global context.

MAP 9.1
The Mauryan and Gupta empires, 321 B.C.E.–550 C.E. The Mauryan and Gupta dynasties both originated in the kingdom of Magadha.

Why was this region so important in ancient India? What advantages did it offer for purposes of trade and communication with other regions?

● New global maps display geographical information using a "view-from-space" perspective, depicting larger regions in broader and clearer context.

● Clear presentation of topographical features strengthens students' understanding of the geographical contexts of world history.

● Insets provide additional detail for especially important areas.

MAP 20.1
The Toltec and Aztec empires, 950–1520 C.E. The Aztec empire stretched from the Gulf of Mexico to the Pacific Ocean.

How were Aztec rulers able to control these diverse territories?

● Distinct colors make for clear and precise geographical representations.

● Regional maps include new globe locator icons to help students understand world regions in larger geographical context.

● Captions include highlighted salient points of the maps, followed by critical-thinking questions that prompt students to link the book's narrative to geographic information presented in the maps.

Integrated Illustrations Program

Images that personalize the past by depicting everyday individuals at work and play are well integrated with the larger narrative, enhancing and supporting the themes of traditions and encounters.

A watercolor painting from sixteenth-century Iran depicts a caravan of pilgrims traveling to Mecca while making the hajj. In what ways did the hajj facilitate social and business relationships?

● Critical-thinking questions enable students to analyze illustrations in the historical and cultural contexts discussed in the text.

a brief note on usage

This book qualifies dates as B.C.E. ("Before the Common Era") or C.E. ("Common Era"). In practice, B.C.E. refers to the same epoch as B.C. ("Before Christ"), and C.E. refers to the same epoch as A.D. (*Anno Domini,* a Latin term meaning "in the year of the Lord"). As historical study becomes a global, multicultural enterprise, however, scholars increasingly prefer terminology that does not apply the standards of one society to all the others. Thus reference in this book to B.C.E. and C.E. reflects emerging scholarly convention concerning the qualification of historical dates.

Measurements of length and distance appear here according to the metric system, followed by their English-system equivalents in parentheses.

The book transliterates Chinese names and terms into English according to the *pinyin* system, which has largely displaced the more cumbersome Wade-Giles system. Transliteration of names and terms from other languages follows contemporary scholarly conventions.

supplements

PRIMARY SOURCE INVESTIGATOR

McGraw-Hill's Primary Source Investigator is available online at www.mhhe.com/psi and gives students and instructors access to more than 650 primary and secondary sources, including documents, images, maps, and videos.

ONLINE LEARNING CENTER

The book's Online Learning Center located at http://onlinelearning.mhhe.com includes a computerized test bank, PowerPoint slides, and an instructor's manual to aid the instructor. On the student side of the OLC are self-testing quizzes.

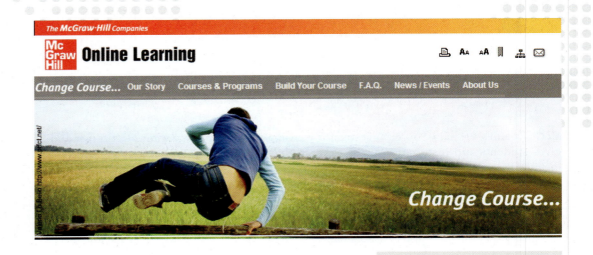

Welcome To Online Learning

Always at the forefront of learning innovation, McGraw-Hill Online Learning offers a complete range of online solutions, including the most comprehensive, engaging, thought-provoking online courses available in the market. Get ready to change course...

➤ See Our Story
➤ Examine our rigorous course development process

Featured Course

Introduction to Criminal Justice

 This course examines the past, present, and future of the American criminal justice

ADDITIONAL RESOURCES FOR STUDENTS

- Two "After the Fact Interactive" units are available for use with *Traditions & Encounters*: "After the Fact Interactive: Tracing the Silk Roads" for Volume I (ISBN 0-07-281843-3) and "After the Fact Interactive: Envisioning the Atlantic World" for Volume II (ISBN 0-07-281844-1). These rich, visually appealing modules on CD-ROM allow students to be apprentice historians, examining a variety of multimedia primary source material and constructing arguments based on their research.

- Titles in the Exploration in World History Series: This McGraw-Hill series conveys the results of recent research in world history in a form wholly accessible to beginning students. It also provides a pedagogical alternative to, or supplement for, the large and inclusive core textbooks. Each volume in the series focuses briefly on a particular theme, set in a global and comparative context. Each book in this series is "open-ended," raising questions and drawing students into the larger issues which animate world history.

- Rainer Buschmann, *Oceans in World History,* ISBN 0-07-301903-8

- Carl J. Guarneri, *America in the World: United States History in Global Context,* ISBN 0-07-254115-6

- Donald Johnson & Jean Elliot Johnson, *Universal Religions in World History: Buddhism, Christianity, and Islam,* ISBN 0-07-295428-0

- Xinru Liu & Lynda Shaffer, *Connections Across Eurasia: Transportation, Communication, and Cultural Exchange on the Silk Roads,* ISBN 0-07-284351-9

- Lauren Ristvet, *In the Beginning: World History from Human Evolution to First Civilizations,* ISBN 0-07-284803-0

- Robert Strayer, *Communist Experiment: Revolution, Socialism, and Global Conflict in the Twentieth Century,* ISBN 0-07-249744-0

- Catherine Clay, Christine Senecal & Chandrika Paul, *Envisioning Women in World History: 1500–Present, Volume 2,* ISBN 0-07-351322-9

- Pamela McVay, *Envisioning Women in World History: 1500–Present, Volume 2,* ISBN 0-07-353465-X

about the authors

Jerry H. Bentley is professor of history at the University of Hawai`i and editor of the *Journal of World History*. He has written extensively on the cultural history of early modern Europe and on cross-cultural interactions in world history. His research on the religious, moral, and political writings of the Renaissance led to the publication of *Humanists and Holy Writ: New Testament Scholarship in the Renaissance* (1983) and *Politics and Culture in Renaissance Naples* (1987). His more recent research has concentrated on global history and particularly on processes of cross-cultural interaction. His book *Old World Encounters: Cross-Cultural Contacts and Exchanges in Pre-Modern Times* (1993) studies processes of cultural exchange and religious conversion before modern times, and his pamphlet *Shapes of World History in Twentieth-Century Scholarship* (1996) discusses the historiography of world history. His current interests include processes of cross-cultural interaction and cultural exchange in modern times.

Herbert F. Ziegler is an associate professor of history at the University of Hawai`i. He has taught world history since 1980 and currently serves as director of the world history program at the University of Hawai`i. He also serves as book review editor of the *Journal of World History*. His interest in twentieth-century European social and political history led to the publication of *Nazi Germany's New Aristocracy* (1990). He is at present working on a study that explores from a global point of view the demographic trends of the past ten thousand years, along with their concomitant technological, economic, and social developments. His other current research project focuses on the application of complexity theory to a comparative study of societies and their internal dynamics.

acknowledgments

Many individuals have contributed to this book, and the authors take pleasure in recording deep thanks for all the comments, criticism, advice, and suggestions that helped to improve the work. The editorial team at McGraw-Hill did an outstanding job of keeping the authors focused on the project. Special thanks go to Chris Freitag, Lisa Pinto, Matthew Busbridge, Mika De Roo, Arthur Pomponio, Carey Eisner, Stacy Best Ruel, Elena Mackawgy, Jaclyn Mautone, Sarah Remington, Robin Mouat, Jeanne Schreiber, and Brian J. Pecko, who provided crucial support by helping the authors work through difficult issues and solve the innumerable problems of content, style, and organization that arise in any project to produce a history of the world. Many colleagues at the University of Hawai`i and elsewhere aided and advised the authors on matters of organization and composition. Finally, we would like to express our appreciation for the advice of the following individuals, who read and commented on the fifth edition, as well as previous editions of *Traditions & Encounters*.

Manuscript Reviewers

Heather J. Abdelnur
Blackburn College

Henry Abramson
Florida Atlantic University

Wayne Ackerson
Salisbury University

Roger Adelson
Arizona State University

Sanjam Ahluwalia
Northern Arizona University

William Alexander
Norfolk State University

Alfred Andrea
University of Vermont

Ed Anson
University of Arkansas at Little Rock

Henry Antkiewicz
East Tennessee State University

Maria Arbelaez
University of Nebraska at Omaha

Peter Arnade
University of California, San Marcos

Karl Bahm
University of Wisconsin, Superior

Vaughan Baker
University of Louisiana at Lafayette

Gene Barnett
Calhoun Community College

Beth Allison Barr
Baylor University

Ian Barrow
Middlebury College

Dixee Bartholomew-Feis
Buena Vista University

Mike Balyo
Chemeketa Community College

Guy Beckwith
Auburn University

Lynda Bell
University of California, Riverside

Norman Bennett
Boston University

Houri Berberian
California State University, Long Beach

Robert Blackey
California State University, San Bernardino

David Blaylock
Eastern Kentucky University

Wayne Bodle
Indiana University of Pennsylvania

Beau Bowers
Central Piedmont Community College

Connie Brand
Meridian Community College

Michael Brescia
State University of New York, Fredonia

Brian T. Brownson
Murray State University

Samuel Brunk
University of Texas, El Paso

Deborah Buffton
University of Wisconsin, La Crosse

Maureen Burgess
Colorado State University

Rainer Buschmann
Hawai`i Pacific University

Sharon L. Bush
LeMoyne-Owen College

Antonio Calabria
University of Texas, San Antonio

Lewis Call
*California Polytechnic State University,
  San Luis Obispo*

Thomas Callahan, Jr.
Rider University

Alice-Catherine Carls
University of Tennessee at Martin

Kay Carr
Southern Illinois University

James Carroll
Iona College

Carol Carter
University of Central Arkansas

Tom Carty
Springfield College

Bruce Castleman
San Diego State University

Douglas Catterall
Cameron University

Douglas Chambers
*University of Southern Mississippi,
  Hattiesburg*

Choi Chatterjee
California State University, Los Angeles

Orazio Ciccarelli
University of Southern Mississippi

Andrew Clark
University of North Carolina at Wilmington

Hugh R. Clark
Ursinus College

Harold Cline
Middle Georgia College

Tim Coates
College of Charleston

Joan Coffey
Sam Houston State University

Daniel Connerton
North Adams State

Keith Cox
California State University

Bruce Cruikshank
Hastings College

Graciella Cruz-Tara
Florida Atlantic University

Lynn Curtright
Tallahassee Community College

Richard Cusimano
University of Louisiana at Lafayette

Ken Czech
St. Cloud State University

Francis K. Danquah
Southern University

Touraj Daryaee
California State University, Fullerton

Jon Davidann
Hawai`i Pacific University

Allen Davidson
Georgia Southern University

Denise Z. Davidson
Georgia State University

Brian Davies
University of Texas, San Antonio

John Davis
Radford University

Thomas Davis
Virginia Military Institute

Elisa Denlinger
University of Wisconsin, La Crosse

Stewart Dippel
University of the Ozarks

Kevin Dougherty
University of Southern Mississippi

Ross Doughty
Ursinus College

Cathi Dunkle
Mid-Michigan Community College

Ross Dunn
San Diego State University

Peter Dykema
Arkansas Tech University

Lane Earns
University of Wisconsin, Oshkosh

Christopher Ehret
University of California, Los Angeles

Laura Endicott
Southwestern Oklahoma State

Nancy Erickson
Erskine College

James Evans
Southeastern Community College

David Fahey
Miami University

Edward Farmer
University of Minnesota

James David Farthing
Oklahoma Baptist University

Lanny Fields
*California State University,
  San Bernardino*

Allan Fisher
Michigan State University

Robert Frankle
University of Memphis

Bonnie Frederick
Washington State University

Karl Friday
University of Georgia

Amy Froide
University of Tennessee, Chattanooga

James Fuller
University of Indianapolis

Jessie Ruth Gaston
California State University, Sacramento

Kurt Gingrich
Radford University

Robert Gomez
San Antonio College

Paul Goodwin
University of Connecticut, Storrs

Matthew Gordon
Miami University of Ohio

Steve Gosch
University of Wisconsin, Eau Claire

Andrew Goss
University of New Orleans

Joseph Gowaskie
Rider University

Sherry Sanders Gray
Mid-South Community College

Brian Gurian
Harrisburg Area Community College

John Haag
University of Georgia

Dr. John Haas
Cerritos College

Raymond J. Haberski, Jr.
Marian College

Jeffrey Hamilton
Baylor University

Michael Hamm
Centre College

Travis Hanes III
University of North Carolina—Wilmington

Eric J. Hanne
Florida Atlantic University

Preston Hardy, Jr.
University of Tennessee, Martin

Stephen Harmon
Pittsburg State University

Alice K. Harris
University of California, Davis

Russell Hart
Hawai`i Pacific University

John Hayden
Southwestern Oklahoma State

Randolph Head
University of California, Riverside

Mary Hedberg
Saginaw Valley State University

Gerald Herman
Northeastern University

David Hertzel
Southwestern Oklahoma State

Udo Heyn
California State University, Los Angeles

Kathryn Hodgkinson
The Hockaday School

Caroline Hoefferle
Wingate University

Peter Hoffenberg
University of Hawai`i, Manoa

Blair Holmes
Brigham Young University

Mary Hovanec
Cuyahoga Community College

Scott Howlett
Saddleback Community College

Kailai Huang
Massachusetts College of Liberal Arts

J. Sanders Huguenin
University of Science and Arts of Oklahoma

Richard Hume
Washington State University

Carol Sue Humphrey
Oklahoma Baptist University

Alfred Hunt
State University of New York

Rebecca C. Huskey
Georgia State University

Raymond Hylton
J. Sergeant Reynolds Community College

W. Scott Jessee
Appalachian State University

Phyllis Jestice
University of Southern Mississippi, Hattiesburg

Eric F. Johnson
Kutztown University of Pennsylvania

Cheryl Johnson-Odim
Loyola University

Kimberley Jones-de Oliveira
Long Island University

Jonathan Judaken
University of Memphis

Theodore Kallman
Delta College

Alan Karras
University of California, Berkeley

Thomas Kay
Wheaton College

Charles Keller
Pittsburgh State University

David L. Kenley
Elizabethtown College

Winston Kinsey
Appalachian State University

Cengiz Kirli
Purdue University

Mark Klobas
Scottsdale Community College

Paul Knoll
University of Southern California

Keith Knuuti
University of Hawai`i, Hilo

Kenneth Koons
Virginia Military Institute

Cheryl Koos
California State University, Los Angeles

Cynthia Kosso
Northern Arizona University

Zoltan Kramer
Central Washington University

James Krokar
DePaul University

Glenn Lamar
University of Louisiana at Lafayette

Lisa Lane
Miracosta College

George Lankevich
Bronx Community College

Dennis Laumann
University of Memphis

Donald Layton
Indiana State University

Loyd Lee
SUNY-New Paltz

Jess LeVine
Brookdale Community College

Keith Lewinstein
Bridgewater State University

Richard Lewis
St. Cloud State University

Yi Li
Tacoma Community College

Tony Litherland
Oklahoma Baptist University

Paul Lococo, Jr.
Leeward Community College

James Long
Colorado State University

David Longfellow
Baylor University

Christine E. Lovasz-Kaiser
University of Southern Indiana

Ben Lowe
Florida Atlantic University

Jared Ludlow
Brigham Young University, Hawai`i

Herbert Luft
Pepperdine Univeristy

Lu Lui
University of Tennessee—Knoxville

Paul Madden
Hardin-Simmons University

Moira Maguire
University of Arkansas, Little Rock

Farid Mahdavi
San Diego State University

Dorothea A. L. Martin
Appalachian State University

Tracey Martin
Benedictine University

Ken Mason
Santa Monica College

Robert Mathews
Northshore Community College

Laura E. Mayhall
The Catholic University of America

William Maynard
Arkansas State University

Robert McCormick
University of South Carolina—Spartanburg

Jeff McEwen
Chattanooga State Technical College

University of Hawai`i, Hilo

Carolyn Neel
Arkansas Tech University

Stuart Smith III
Germanna Community College

part 3

THE POSTCLASSICAL ERA, 500 TO 1000 C.E.

The postclassical era was a period of major readjustment for societies throughout the eastern hemisphere. The early centuries C.E. brought turbulence and instability to classical societies in China, India, southwest Asia, and the Mediterranean basin. Most of the classical empires collapsed under the strain of internal power struggles, external invasions, or a combination of the two. During the postclassical era the settled societies of the eastern hemisphere underwent political, social, economic, and cultural change that would shape their experiences over the long term. Indeed, the influence of the postclassical era continues to the present day.

The first task that settled societies faced in the postclassical era was the need to restore political and social order. They went about that task in very different ways. In the eastern Mediterranean the eastern half of the Roman empire survived as the Byzantine empire—the only empire that outlasted the difficulties of the late classical era—but underwent political and social reorganization in order to deal with external pressures. In southwest Asia, Arab conquerors inspired by the recently founded Islamic faith overcame the Sasanid empire of Persia. In China the Sui and Tang dynasties restored centralized imperial authority after almost four centuries of rule by competing regional kingdoms and nomadic conquerors. In India, in contrast, centralized imperial rule did not return: authority devolved instead to a series of regional kingdoms, some of them quite large. In western Europe centralized imperial rule returned only for a brief moment during the eighth and ninth centuries under the Carolingian empire. Economic difficulties and new rounds of invasions, however, brought down the empire and encouraged devolution of authority to local rulers: the result was the development of a decentralized political order in western Europe. In different ways, then, all the settled societies of the eastern hemisphere embarked on a quest for political and social order during the centuries after the collapse of the classical empires.

The reestablishment of political and social order enabled postclassical societies to revive networks of long-distance trade and participate more actively in processes of cross-cultural communication and exchange. As a result, the postclassical era was a time of rapid economic growth in most of the eastern hemisphere. The volume of long-distance trade increased dramatically, and manufacturers began to produce goods explicitly for export rather than local consumption. Meanwhile, increased trade facilitated biological and technological as well as commercial exchanges: agricultural crops migrated far beyond the lands of their origin, and improved techniques of irrigation and cultivation spread through much of Eurasia. New crops and improved agricultural techniques led to enlarged harvests and enriched diets particularly in China, India, and southwest Asia.

As agricultural production increased, so did human population. Growing numbers of people devoted their efforts to trade and manufacturing rather than cultivation. China, India, and the eastern Mediterranean region were especially prominent sites for the production of textiles, ceramics, and metal goods. Increased trade and manufacturing activity encouraged a remarkable round of technological invention and innovation. The magnetic compass, printing technologies, and gunpowder, for example, first appeared in postclassical China and then diffused to other lands. These inventions and others of the era have profoundly influenced the course of human history since their first appearance.

The postclassical era was also crucially important for the formation and development of cultural and religious traditions. Islam first appeared during the postclassical era, and it soon became the cultural and religious foundation of an expansive empire stretching from north Africa to northern India. Buddhism expanded beyond the Indian subcontinent and central Asia, attracting converts in China, Korea, Japan, and southeast Asia. Christianity was the official religion of the Byzantine empire, where the Eastern Orthodox church emerged and gave shape to a distinctive form of Christianity. Orthodox missionaries also spread their faith to formerly pagan lands throughout much of eastern Europe and Russia. Farther west, Christianity spread from the Mediterranean basin to western and northern Europe, where papal leadership guided the emergence of the Roman Catholic church. For a millennium and more, Roman Catholic Christianity served as the foundation for cultural unity in the politically disunited world of western and northern Europe. Meanwhile, quite apart from the expansion of religious traditions, the postclassical era witnessed the spread of literacy and formal education throughout much of the eastern hemisphere.

The empires and regional states of the postclassical era disappeared long ago, but the social, economic, and cultural legacies of the age are noticeable even today. Long-distance trade surged in postclassical times and helped to structure economic and social development throughout much of the eastern hemisphere. Even more notable, perhaps, religious and cultural traditions continue to flourish in lands where they first attracted converts in postclassical times. In some ways, then, the postclassical age survives even in the modern world.

The Expansive Realm of Islam

chapter 13

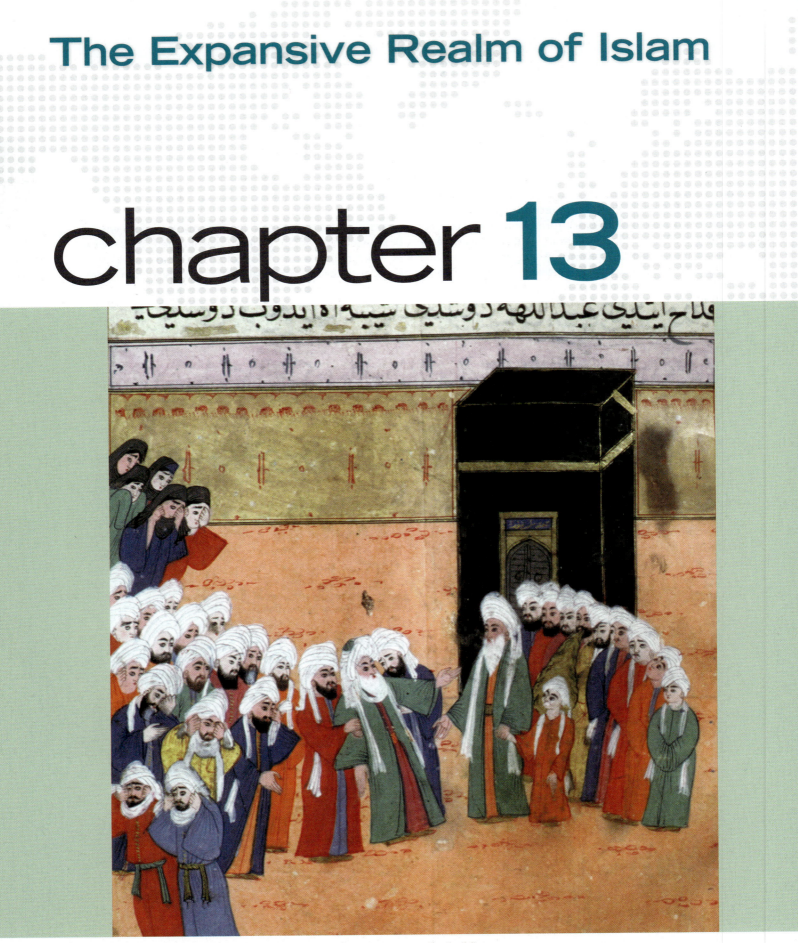

A sixteenth-century Turkish manuscript depicts pilgrims praying at Mecca in the mosque surrounding the Ka'ba.

EYEWITNESS:
Season of the Mecca Pilgrimage

In 632 C.E. the prophet Muhammad visited his native city of Mecca from his home in exile at Medina, and in doing so he set an example that devout Muslims have sought to emulate ever since. Today the *hajj*—the holy pilgrimage to Mecca—draws Muslims by the hundreds of thousands from all parts of the world to Saudi Arabia. Each year Muslims travel to Mecca by land, sea, and air to make the pilgrimage and visit the holy sites of Islam.

In centuries past the numbers of pilgrims were smaller, but their observance of the hajj was no less conscientious. By the ninth century, pilgrimage had become so popular that Muslim rulers went to some lengths to meet the needs of travelers passing through their lands. With the approach of the pilgrimage season—the last month of the Islamic lunar calendar—crowds gathered at major trading centers such as Baghdad, Damascus, and Cairo. There they lived in tent cities, surviving on food and water provided by government officials, until they could join caravans bound for Mecca. Muslim rulers invested considerable sums in the maintenance of roads, wells, cisterns, and lodgings that accommodated pilgrims—as well as castles and police forces that protected travelers—on their journeys to Mecca and back.

The hajj was not only solemn observance but also an occasion for joy and celebration. Muslim rulers and wealthy pilgrims often made lavish gifts to caravan companions and others they met en route to Mecca. During her famous hajj of 976–977, for example, the Mesopotamian princess Jamila bint Nasir al-Dawla provided food and fresh green vegetables for her fellow pilgrims and furnished five hundred camels for handicapped travelers. She also purchased freedom for five hundred slaves and distributed fifty thousand fine robes among the common people of Mecca.

Most pilgrims did not have the resources to match Jamila's generosity, but for common travelers, too, the hajj became a special occasion. Merchants and craftsmen made acquaintances and arranged business deals with pilgrims from other lands. Students and scholars exchanged ideas during their weeks of traveling together. For all pilgrims, participation in ritual activities lent new meaning and significance to their faith.

259

Yet Xuanzang persisted and arrived in India in 630. He lived there for more than twelve years, visiting the holy sites of Buddhism and devoting himself to the study of languages and Buddhist doctrine, especially at Nalanda, the center of advanced Buddhist education in India. He also amassed a huge collection of relics and images as well as 657 books, all of which he packed into 527 crates and transported back to China to advance the understanding of Buddhism in his native land.

By the time of his return in 645, Xuanzang had logged more than 16,000 kilometers (10,000 miles) on the road. News of the holy monk's efforts had reached the imperial court, and even though Xuanzang had violated the ban on travel, he received a hero's welcome and an audience with the emperor. Until his death in 664, Xuanzang spent his remaining years translating Buddhist treatises into Chinese and clarifying their doctrines. His efforts helped to popularize Buddhism throughout China.

Xuanzang undertook his journey at a propitious time. For more than 350 years after the fall of the Han dynasty, war, invasion, conquest, and foreign rule disrupted Chinese society. Toward the end of the sixth century, however, centralized imperial rule returned to China. The Sui and Tang dynasties restored order and presided over an era of rapid economic growth in China. Agricultural yields rose dramatically, and technological innovations boosted the production of manufactured goods. China ranked with the Abbasid and Byzantine empires as a political and economic anchor of the postclassical world.

For China the postclassical era was an age of intense interaction with other peoples. Chinese merchants participated in trade networks that linked most regions of the eastern hemisphere. Buddhism spread beyond its homeland of India, attracted a large popular following in China, and even influenced the thought of Confucian scholars. A resurgent China made its influence felt throughout east Asia: diplomats and armed forces introduced Chinese ways into Korea and Vietnam, and rulers of the Japanese islands looked to China for guidance in matters of political organization. Korea, Vietnam, and Japan retained their distinctiveness, but all three lands drew deep inspiration from China and participated in a larger east Asian society centered on China.

THE RESTORATION OF CENTRALIZED IMPERIAL RULE IN CHINA

During the centuries following the Han dynasty, several regional kingdoms made bids to assert their authority over all of China, but none possessed the resources to dominate its rivals over the long term. In the late sixth century, however, Yang Jian, an ambitious ruler in northern China, embarked on a series of military campaigns that brought all of China once again under centralized imperial rule. Yang Jian's Sui dynasty survived less than thirty years, but the tradition of centralized rule outlived his house. The Tang dynasty replaced the Sui, and the Song succeeded the Tang. The Tang and Song dynasties organized Chinese society so efficiently that China became a center of exceptional agricultural and industrial production. Indeed, much of the eastern hemisphere felt the effects of the powerful Chinese economy of the Tang and Song dynasties.

The Sui Dynasty

Establishment of the Dynasty Like Qin Shihuangdi some eight hundred years earlier, Yang Jian imposed tight political discipline on his state and then extended his rule to the rest of China. Yang Jian began his rise to power when a Turkish ruler appointed him duke of Sui in northern China. In 580 Yang Jian's patron died, leaving a seven-year-old son as his heir. Yang Jian installed the boy as ruler but forced his abdication one year later, claiming the throne and the Mandate of Heaven for himself. During the next decade Yang Jian sent military expeditions into central Asia and southern China. By 589 the house of Sui ruled all of China.

Like the rulers of the Qin dynasty, the emperors of the Sui dynasty (589–618 C.E.) placed enormous demands on their subjects in the course of building a strong, centralized government. The Sui emperors ordered the construction of palaces and granaries, carried out extensive repairs on defensive walls, dispatched military forces to central Asia and Korea, levied high taxes, and demanded compulsory labor services.

The Grand Canal The most elaborate project undertaken during the Sui dynasty was the construction of the Grand Canal, which was one of the world's largest waterworks projects before modern times. The second emperor, Sui Yangdi (reigned 604–618 C.E.), completed work on the canal to facilitate trade between northern and southern China, particularly to make the abundant supplies of rice and other food crops from the Yangzi River valley available to residents of northern regions. The only practical and economical way to transport food crops in large quantities was by water. But since Chinese rivers generally flow from west to east, only an artificial waterway could support a large volume of trade between north and south.

The Grand Canal was really a series of artificial waterways that ultimately reached from Hangzhou in the south to

MAP 14.1

The Sui and Tang dynasties, 589–907 C.E.
Compare the size of the Sui and Tang empires.

Why was the Tang dynasty able to extend its authority over such vast distances? Discuss the significance of the Grand Canal in linking the various regions of China.

the imperial capital of Chang'an in the west to a terminus near modern Beijing in the north. Sui Yangdi used canals dug as early as the Zhou dynasty, but he linked them into a network that served much of China. When completed, the Grand Canal extended almost 2,000 kilometers (1,240 miles) and reportedly was forty paces wide, with roads running parallel to the waterway on either side.

Though expensive to construct, Sui Yangdi's investment in the Grand Canal paid dividends for more than a thousand years. It integrated the economies of northern and southern China, thereby establishing an economic foundation for political and cultural unity. Until the arrival of railroads in the twentieth century, the Grand Canal served as the principal conduit for internal trade. Indeed, the canal continues to function even today, although mechanical transport has diminished its significance as a trade route.

Sui Yangdi's construction projects served China well over a long term, but their dependence on high taxes and forced labor generated hostility toward his rule. The Grand Canal alone required the services of conscripted laborers by the millions. Military reverses in Korea prompted discontented subjects to revolt against Sui rule. During the late 610s, rebellions broke out in northern China when Sui Yangdi sought additional resources for his Korean campaign. In 618 a disgruntled minister assassinated the emperor and brought the dynasty to an end.

The Tang Dynasty

Soon after Sui Yangdi's death, a rebel leader seized Chang'an and proclaimed himself emperor of a new dynasty that he named Tang after his hereditary title. The dynasty survived for almost three hundred years (618–907 C.E.), and Tang rulers organized China into a powerful, productive, and prosperous society.

Tang Taizong Much of the Tang's success was due to the energy, ability, and policies of the dynasty's second emperor, **Tang Taizong** (reigned 627–649 C.E.). Taizong was both ambitious and ruthless: in making his way to the imperial throne, he murdered two of his brothers and pushed his father aside. Once on the throne, however, he displayed a high sense of duty and strove conscientiously to provide an effective, stable government. He built a splendid capital at Chang'an, and he saw himself as a Confucian ruler who heeded the interests of his subjects. Contemporaries reported that banditry ended during his reign, that the price of rice remained low, and that taxes levied on peasants amounted to only one-fortieth of the annual harvest—a 2.5 percent tax rate—although required rent payments and compulsory labor services meant that the effective rate of taxation was somewhat higher. These reports suggest that China enjoyed an era of unusual stability and prosperity during the reign of Tang Taizong.

Tang Taizong (TAHNG TEYE-zohng)

Barges make their way through a portion of the Grand Canal near the city of Wuxi in southern China. Built during the Sui dynasty, the waterways of the Grand Canal fostered the economic integration of northern and southern China.

Three policies in particular help to explain the success of the early Tang dynasty: maintenance of a well-articulated transportation and communications network, distribution of land according to the principles of the equal-field system, and reliance on a bureaucracy based on merit. All three policies originated in the Sui dynasty, but Tang rulers applied them more systematically and effectively than their predecessors had.

Transportation and Communications
Apart from the Grand Canal, which served as the principal route for long-distance transportation within China, Tang rulers maintained an extensive communications network based on roads, horses, and sometimes human runners. Along the main routes, Tang officials maintained inns, postal stations, and stables, which provided rest and refreshment for travelers, couriers, and their mounts. Using couriers traveling by horse, the Tang court could communicate with the most distant cities in the empire in about eight days. Even human runners provided impressively speedy services: relay teams of some 9,600 runners supplied the Tang court at Chang'an with seafood delivered fresh from Ningbo, more than 1,000 kilometers (620 miles) away.

The Equal-Field System
The equal-field system governed the allocation of agricultural land. Its purpose was to ensure an equitable distribution of land and to avoid the concentration of landed property that had caused social problems during the Han dynasty. The system allotted land to individuals and their families according to the land's fertility and the recipients' needs. About one-fifth of the land became the hereditary possession of the recipients, and the rest remained available for redistribution when the original recipients' needs and circumstances changed.

For about a century, administrators were able to apply the principles of the equal-field system relatively consistently. By the early eighth century, however, the system showed signs of strain. A rapidly rising population placed pressure on the land available for distribution. Meanwhile, through favors, bribery, or intimidation of administrators, influential families found ways to retain land scheduled for redistribution. Furthermore, large parcels of land fell out of the system altogether when Buddhist monasteries acquired them. Nevertheless, during the first half of the Tang dynasty, the system provided a foundation for stability and prosperity in the Chinese countryside.

Bureaucracy of Merit
The Tang dynasty also relied heavily on a bureaucracy based on merit, as reflected by performance on imperial civil service examinations. Following the example of the Han dynasty, Sui and Tang rulers recruited government officials from the ranks of candidates who had progressed through the Confucian educational system and had mastered a sophisticated curriculum concentrating on the classic works of Chinese literature and philosophy. During the early Tang dynasty, most officeholders were aristocrats. By the late Tang era, however, when educational opportunities were widely available, officeholders came largely from the ranks of common families. The Confucian educational system and the related civil service

served Chinese governments so well that, with modifications and an occasional interruption, they survived for thirteen centuries, disappearing only after the collapse of the Qing dynasty in the early twentieth century.

Military Expansion Soon after its foundation, the powerful and dynamic Tang state began to flex its military muscles. In the north, Tang forces brought Manchuria under imperial authority and forced the Silla kingdom in Korea to acknowledge the Tang emperor as overlord. To the south, Tang armies conquered the northern part of Vietnam. To the west they extended Tang authority as far as the Aral Sea and brought a portion of the high plateau of Tibet under Tang control. Territorially, the Tang empire ranks among the largest in Chinese history.

Tang Foreign Relations In an effort to fashion a stable diplomatic order, the Tang emperors revived the Han dynasty's practice of maintaining tributary relationships between China and neighboring lands. According to Chinese political theory, China was the Middle Kingdom, a powerful realm with the responsibility to bring order to subordinate lands through a system of tributary relationships. Neighboring lands and peoples would recognize Chinese emperors as their overlords. As tokens of their subordinate status, envoys from those states would regularly deliver gifts to the court of the Middle Kingdom and would perform the kowtow—a ritual prostration in which subordinates knelt before the emperor and touched their foreheads to the ground. In return, tributary states received confirmation of their authority as well as lavish gifts. Because Chinese authorities often had little real influence in these supposedly subordinate lands, there was always something of a fictional quality to the system. Nevertheless, it was extremely important throughout east Asia and central Asia because it institutionalized relations between China and neighboring lands, fostering trade and cultural exchanges as well as diplomatic contacts.

Tang Decline Under able rulers such as Taizong, the Tang dynasty flourished. During the mid-eighth century, however, casual and careless leadership brought the dynasty to a crisis from which it never fully recovered. In 755, while the emperor neglected public affairs in favor of music and his favorite concubine, one of the dynasty's foremost military commanders, An Lushan, mounted a rebellion and captured the capital at Chang'an, as well as the secondary capital at Luoyang. His revolt was short-lived: in 757 a soldier murdered An Lushan, and by 763 Tang forces had suppressed his army and recovered their capitals. But the rebellion left the dynasty in a gravely weakened state. Tang commanders were unable to defeat rebellious forces

In this wall painting from the tomb of a Tang prince, three Chinese officials (at left) receive envoys from foreign lands who pay their respects to representatives of the Middle Kingdom. The envoys probably come from the Byzantine empire, Korea, and Siberia. What features of their personal appearance and dress provide clues to the envoys' lands of origin?

sources from the past

The Poet Du Fu on Tang Dynasty Wars

The eighth century was a golden age of Chinese poetry. Among the foremost writers of the era was Du Fu (712–770 c.e.), often considered China's greatest poet. Born into a prominent Confucian family, Du Fu wrote in his early years about the beauty of the natural world. After the rebellion of An Lushan, however, he fell into poverty and experienced difficulties. Not surprisingly, poetry of his later years lamented the chaos of the late eighth century. In the following verses, Du Fu offered a bitter perspective on the wars that plagued China in the 750s and 760s.

A Song of War Chariots

The war-chariots rattle,
The war-horses whinny.
Each man of you has a bow and a quiver at his belt.
Father, mother, son, wife, stare at you going,
Till dust shall have buried the bridge beyond Chang'an.
They run with you, crying, they tug at your sleeves,
And the sound of their sorrow goes up to the clouds;
And every time a bystander asks you a question,
You can only say to him that you have to go.
. . . We remember others at fifteen sent north to guard
    the river
And at forty sent west to cultivate the camp-farms.
The mayor wound their turbans for them when they
    started out.
With their turbaned hair white now, they are still at the
    border,
At the border where the blood of men spills like the
    sea—

And still the heart of Emperor Wu is beating for war.
. . . Do you know that, east of China's mountains, in two
    hundred districts
And in thousands of villages, nothing grows but weeds,
And though strong women have bent to the ploughing,
East and west the furrows all are broken down?
. . . Men of China are able to face the stiffest battle,
But their officers drive them like chickens and dogs.
Whatever is asked of them,
Dare they complain?
For example, this winter
Held west of the gate,
Challenged for taxes,
How could they pay?
. . . We have learned that to have a son is bad luck—
It is very much better to have a daughter
Who can marry and live in the house of a neighbour,
While under the sod we bury our boys.
. . . Go to the Blue Sea, look along the shore
At all the old white bones forsaken—
New ghosts are wailing there now with the old,
Loudest in the dark sky of a stormy day.

For Further Reflection

■ Assess the effects of war in the late Tang dynasty from the viewpoints of imperial rulers and individual subjects.

Source: Cyril Birch, ed. *Anthology of Chinese Literature*, 2 vols. New York: Grove Press, 1965, pp. 1:240–41.

by themselves, so they invited a nomadic Turkish people, the **Uighurs,** to bring an army into China. In return for their services, the Uighurs demanded the right to sack Chang'an and Luoyang after the expulsion of the rebels.

The Tang imperial house never regained control of affairs after this crisis. The equal-field system deteriorated, and dwindling tax receipts failed to meet dynastic needs. Imperial armies were unable to resist the encroachments of Turkish peoples in the late eighth century. During the ninth century a series of rebellions devastated the Chinese countryside. One uprising, led by the military commander Huang Chao, embroiled much of eastern China for almost a decade from 875 to 884. Huang Chao's revolt reflected and fueled popular discontent: he routinely pillaged the wealthy

and distributed a portion of his plunder among the poor. In an effort to control the rebels, the Tang emperors granted progressively greater power and authority to regional military commanders, who gradually became the effective rulers of China. In 907 the last Tang emperor abdicated his throne, and the dynasty came to an end.

The Song Dynasty

Following the Tang collapse, warlords ruled China until the Song dynasty reimposed centralized imperial rule in the late tenth century. Though it survived for more than three centuries, the Song dynasty (960–1279 c.e.) never built a very powerful state. Song rulers mistrusted military leaders, and they placed much more emphasis on civil administration, industry, education, and the arts than on military affairs.

Uighurs (WEE-goors)

Song Taizu The first Song emperor, Song Taizu (reigned 960–976 C.E.), inaugurated this policy. Song Taizu began his career as a junior military officer serving one of the most powerful warlords in northern China. He had a reputation for honesty and effectiveness, and in 960 his troops proclaimed him emperor. During the next several years, he and his army subjected the warlords to their authority and consolidated Song control throughout China. He then persuaded his generals to retire honorably to a life of leisure so that they would not seek to displace him, and he set about organizing a centralized administration that placed military forces under tight supervision.

Song Taizu regarded all state officials, even minor functionaries in distant provinces, as servants of the imperial government. In exchange for their loyalty, Song rulers rewarded these officials handsomely. They vastly expanded the bureaucracy based on merit by creating more opportunities for individuals to seek a Confucian education and take civil service examinations. They accepted many more candidates into the bureaucracy than their Sui and Tang predecessors, and they provided generous salaries for those who qualified for government appointments. They even placed civil bureaucrats in charge of military forces.

Song Weaknesses The Song approach to administration resulted in a more centralized imperial government than earlier Chinese dynasties had enjoyed. But it caused two big problems that weakened the dynasty and eventually brought about its fall. The first problem was financial: the enormous Song bureaucracy devoured China's surplus production. As the number of bureaucrats and the size of their rewards grew, the imperial treasury came under tremendous pressure. Efforts to raise taxes aggravated the peasants, who mounted two major rebellions in the early twelfth century. By that time, however, bureaucrats dominated the Song administration to the point that it was impossible to reform the system.

The second problem was military. Scholar-bureaucrats generally had little military education and little talent for military affairs, yet they led Song armies in the field and made military decisions. It was no coincidence that nomadic peoples flourished along China's northern border throughout the Song dynasty. From the early tenth through the early twelfth century, the Khitan, a seminomadic people from Manchuria, ruled a vast empire stretching from northern Korea to Mongolia. During the first half of the Song dynasty, the Khitan demanded and received large tribute payments of silk and silver from the Song state to the south. In the early twelfth century, the nomadic Jurchen conquered the Khitan, overran northern China, captured the Song capital at Kaifeng, and proclaimed establishment of the Jin empire. Thereafter the Song dynasty moved its capital to the prosperous port city of Hangzhou and survived only in southern China, so that the latter part of the dynasty is commonly known as

MAP 14.2
The Song dynasty, 960–1279 C.E.
After the establishment of the Jin empire, the Song dynasty moved its capital from Kaifeng to Hangzhou.

What advantages did Hangzhou offer to the Song rulers?

the Southern Song. This truncated Southern Song shared a border with the Jin empire about midway between the Yellow River and the Yangzi River until 1279, when Mongol forces ended the dynasty and incorporated southern China into their empire.

THE ECONOMIC DEVELOPMENT OF TANG AND SONG CHINA

Although the Song dynasty did not develop a particularly strong military capacity, it benefited from a remarkable series of agricultural, technological, industrial, and commercial developments that transformed China into the economic powerhouse of Eurasia. This economic development originated in the Tang dynasty, but its results became most clear during the Song, which presided over a land of enormous prosperity. The economic surge of Tang and Song times had implications that went well beyond China, since it stimulated trade and production throughout much of the eastern hemisphere for more than half a millennium, from about 600 to 1300 C.E.

Agricultural Development

Fast-Ripening Rice
The foundation of economic development in Tang and Song China was a surge in agricultural production. Sui and Tang armies prepared the way for increased agricultural productivity when they imposed their control over southern China and ventured into Vietnam. In Vietnam they encountered strains of fast-ripening rice that enabled cultivators to harvest two crops per year. When introduced to the fertile fields of southern China, fast-ripening rice quickly resulted in an expanded supply of food. Like the *dar al-Islam,* Tang and Song China benefited enormously from the introduction of new food crops.

New Agricultural Techniques
Chinese cultivators also increased their productivity by adopting improved agricultural techniques. They made increased use of heavy iron plows, and they harnessed oxen (in the north) and water buffaloes (in the south) to help prepare land for cultivation. They enriched the soil with manure and composted organic matter. They also organized extensive irrigation systems. These included not only reservoirs, dikes, dams, and canals but also pumps and waterwheels, powered by both animals and humans, that moved water into irrigation systems. Artificial irrigation made it possible to extend cultivation to difficult terrain, including terraced mountainsides—a development that vastly expanded China's agricultural potential.

Population Growth
Increased agricultural production had dramatic results. One was a rapid expansion of the Chinese population. After the fall of the Han dynasty, the population of China reached a low point, about 45 million in

An illustration commissioned by the Song government shows peasants how to go about the laborious task of transplanting rice seedlings into a paddy flooded with water.

A twelfth-century painting depicts the spring festival as observed in the northern Song capital of Kaifeng. Porters, shopkeepers, peddlers, fortune-tellers, and Confucian scholars deep in conversation are all in view.

600 C.E. By 800 it had rebounded to 50 million, and two centuries later to 60 million. By 1127, when the Jurchen conquered the northern half of the Song state, the Chinese population had passed 100 million, and by 1200 it stood at about 115 million. This rapid population growth reflected both the productivity of the agricultural economy and the well-organized distribution of food through transportation networks built during Sui and Tang times.

Urbanization Increased food supplies encouraged the growth of cities. During the Tang dynasty the imperial capital of Chang'an was the world's most populous city, with perhaps as many as two million residents. During the Song dynasty, China was the most urbanized land in the world. In the late thirteenth century, Hangzhou, capital of the Southern Song dynasty, had more than one million residents. They supported hundreds of restaurants, noodle shops, taverns, teahouses, brothels, music halls, theaters, clubhouses, gardens, markets, craft shops, and specialty stores dealing in

silk, gems, porcelain, lacquerware, and other goods. Hangzhou residents, like those in most cities, observed peculiar local customs. Taverns often had several stories, for example, and patrons gravitated to higher or lower stories according to their plans: those desiring only a cup or two of wine sat at street level, whereas those planning an extended evening of revelry sought tables on the higher stories.

As a capital, Hangzhou was something of a special case among cities, but during the Tang and Song eras, scores of Chinese cities boasted populations of one hundred thousand or more. Li Bai (701–761 C.E.), who was perhaps the most popular poet of the Tang era, took the social life of these Chinese cities as one of his principal themes. Li Bai mostly wrote light, pleasing verse celebrating life, friendship, and especially wine. (Tradition holds that the drunken poet died by drowning when he fell out of a boat while attempting to embrace the moon's reflection in the water.) The annual spring festival was an occasion dear to the heart of urban residents, who flocked to the streets to shop for new products, have their fortunes told, and eat tasty snacks from food vendors.

Another result of increased food production was the emergence of a commercialized agricultural economy. Because fast-ripening rice yielded bountiful harvests, many cultivators could purchase inexpensive rice and raise vegetables and fruits for sale on the commercial market. Cultivators piece of monastic furniture, the chair quickly became popular in secular society and found a place in domestic interiors throughout the land. Buddhist monks also introduced refined sugar into China and thus influenced both diet and cuisine.

In some ways, Buddhism posed a challenge to Chinese cultural and social traditions. Buddhist theologians typically took written texts as points of departure for elaborate, speculative investigations into metaphysical themes such as the nature of the soul. Among Chinese intellectuals, however, only the Confucians placed great emphasis on written texts, and they devoted their energies mostly to practical rather than metaphysical issues. Meanwhile, Daoists had limited interest in written texts of any kind. Buddhist morality called for individuals to strive for perfection by observing an ascetic ideal, and it encouraged serious Buddhists to follow a celibate, monastic lifestyle. In contrast, Chinese morality centered on the family unit and the obligations of filial piety, and it strongly encouraged procreation so that generations of offspring would be available to venerate family ancestors. Some Chinese held that Buddhist monasteries were economically harmful, since they paid no taxes, whereas others scorned Buddhism as an inferior creed because of its foreign origins.

Buddhism and Daoism Because of those differences and concerns, Buddhist missionaries sought to tailor their message to Chinese audiences. They explained Buddhist concepts in vocabulary borrowed from Chinese cultural traditions, particularly Daoism. They translated the Indian term *dharma* (the basic Buddhist doctrine) as *dao* ("the way" in the Daoist sense of the term), and they translated the Indian term *nirvana* (personal salvation that comes after an individual soul escapes from the cycle of incarnation) as *wuwei* (the Daoist ethic of noncompetition). While encouraging the establishment of monasteries and the observance of celibacy, they also recognized the validity of family life and offered Buddhism as a religion that would benefit the extended Chinese family: one son in the monastery, they taught, would bring salvation for ten generations of his kin.

Pilgrimage to India Monks and pilgrims helped popularize Buddhism in China. The monk Xuanzang (602–664 C.E.) was only one among hundreds of Chinese pilgrims who made the dangerous and difficult journey to India to visit holy sites and learn about Buddhism in its homeland. Xuanzang and other pilgrims returned to China with copies of treatises that deepened the understanding of Buddhism, and they were able to relate the teachings of Indian Buddhist masters to Chinese disciples.

Schools of Buddhism Over the years, monks and scholars organized several distinctive schools of Buddhism that appealed to Chinese tastes and interests. Buddhists of the Chan school (also known by its Japanese name, Zen) placed little emphasis on written texts but held intuition and sudden flashes of insight in high regard. Thus Chan Buddhists made a place for Daoist values in Chinese Buddhism. Even more popular than Chan Buddhism was the Pure Land school, which held out the prospect of personal salvation for those who devoted themselves to the Buddha. The lady emperor Wu Zhao herself followed Pure Land teachings, and she enthusiastically promoted the school—especially after friendly monks circulated a treatise predicting reincarnation of the Buddha as a female ruler. Wu Zhao eventually proclaimed herself the universal ruler and protector of Buddhism, and she sponsored the construction of monasteries and stupas throughout China.

This scroll painting depicts the return of the monk Xuanzang to China. His baggage included 657 books, mostly Buddhist treatises but also a few works on grammar and logic, as well as hundreds of relics and images.

A Japanese screen painting from the fourteenth century depicts a group of monks hard at work translating the Buddhist texts that the pilgrim Xuanzang transported from India to China.

Hostility to Buddhism In spite of its popularity, Buddhism met determined resistance from Daoists and Confucians. Daoists resented the popular following that Buddhists attracted, which resulted in diminished resources available for their tradition. Confucians despised Buddhists' exaltation of celibacy, and they denounced its teachings as alien superstition. They also condemned Buddhist monasteries as wasteful, unproductive burdens on society.

Persecution During the late Tang dynasty, Daoist and Confucian critics of Buddhism found allies in the imperial court. Beginning in the 840s the Tang emperors ordered the closure of monasteries and the expulsion of Buddhists as well as Zoroastrians, Nestorian Christians, and Manichaeans. Motivated largely by a desire to seize property belonging to foreign religious establishments, the Tang rulers did

not implement their policy in a thorough way. Although it discouraged further expansion, Tang policy did not eradicate foreign faiths from China. Buddhism in particular enjoyed popular support that enabled it to survive. Indeed, it even influenced the development of the Confucian tradition during the Song dynasty.

Neo-Confucianism

The Song emperors did not persecute Buddhists, but they actively supported native Chinese cultural traditions in hopes of limiting the influence of foreign religions. They contributed particularly generously to the Confucian tradition. They sponsored the studies of Confucian scholars, for example, and subsidized the printing and dissemination of Confucian writings.

Confucians and Buddhism Yet the Confucian tradition of the Song dynasty differed from that of earlier times. The earliest Confucians had concentrated resolutely on practical issues of politics and morality, since they took the organization of a stable social order as their principal concern. Confucians of the Song dynasty studied the classic works of their tradition, but they also became familiar with the writings of Buddhists. They found much to admire in Buddhist thought. Buddhism not only offered a tradition of logical thought and argumentation but also dealt with issues, such as the

thinking about ENCOUNTERS

The Influence of a Determined Individual
After traveling to India in search of Buddhist knowledge and wisdom, the monk Xuanzang and other pilgrims helped to bring about cultural and religious change in China. To what extent can you attribute the spread of Buddhism to the efforts of individuals like Xuanzang? To what extent might general social conditions help to explain the popularity of Buddhism in China?

nature of the soul and the individual's relationship with the cosmos, not systematically explored by Confucian thinkers. Thus Confucians of the Song dynasty drew a great deal of inspiration from Buddhism. Because their thought reflected the influence of Buddhism as well as original Confucian values, it has come to be known as neo-Confucianism.

Zhu Xi The most important representative of Song neo-Confucianism was the philosopher **Zhu Xi** (1130–1200 C.E.). A prolific writer, Zhu Xi maintained a deep commitment to Confucian values emphasizing proper personal behavior and social harmony. Among his writings was an influential treatise entitled *Family Rituals* that provided detailed instructions for weddings, funerals, veneration of ancestors, and other family ceremonies. As a good Confucian, Zhu Xi considered it a matter of the highest importance that individuals play their proper roles both in their family and in the larger society.

Yet Zhu Xi became fascinated with the philosophical and speculative features of Buddhist thought. He argued in good Confucian fashion for the observance of high moral standards, and he believed that academic and philosophical investigations were important for practical affairs. But he concentrated his efforts on abstract and abstruse issues of more theoretical than practical significance. He wrote extensively on metaphysical themes such as the nature of reality. He argued in a manner reminiscent of Plato that two elements accounted for all physical being: *li,* a principle somewhat similar to Plato's Forms or Ideas that defines the essence of the being, and *qi,* its material form.

Neo-Confucian Influence Neo-Confucianism ranks as an important cultural development for two reasons. First, it illustrates the deep influence of Buddhism in Chinese society. Even though the neo-Confucians rejected Buddhist religious teachings, their writings adapted Buddhist themes and reasoning to Confucian interests and values. Second, neo-Confucianism influenced east Asian thought over a very long term. In China, neo-Confucianism enjoyed the status of an officially recognized creed from the Song dynasty until the early twentieth century, and in lands that fell within China's cultural orbit—particularly Korea, Vietnam, and Japan—neo-Confucianism shaped philosophical, political, and moral thought for half a millennium and more.

CHINESE INFLUENCE IN EAST ASIA

Like the *dar al-Islam,* Chinese society influenced the development of neighboring lands during postclassical times. Chinese armies periodically invaded Korea and Vietnam, and Chinese merchants established commercial relations with Japan as well as with Korea and Vietnam. Chinese techniques of government and administration helped shape public life in Korea, Vietnam, and Japan, and Chinese values and cultural traditions won a prominent place alongside native traditions. By no means did those lands become absorbed into China: all maintained distinctive identities and cultural traditions. Yet they also drew deep inspiration from Chinese examples and built societies that reflected their participation in a larger east Asian society revolving around China.

Korea and Vietnam

Chinese armies ventured into Korea and Vietnam on campaigns of imperial expansion as early as the Qin and Han dynasties. As the Han dynasty weakened, however, local aristocrats organized movements that ousted Chinese forces from both lands. Only during the powerful Tang dynasty did Chinese resources once again enable military authorities to mount large-scale campaigns. Although the two lands responded differently to Chinese imperial expansion, both borrowed Chinese political and cultural traditions and used them in their societies.

The Silla Dynasty During the seventh century, Tang armies conquered much of Korea before the native Silla dynasty rallied to prevent Chinese domination of the peninsula. Both Tang and Silla authorities preferred to avoid a long and costly conflict, so they agreed to a political compromise: Chinese forces withdrew from Korea, and the Silla king recognized the Tang emperor as his overlord. In theory, Korea was a vassal state in a vast Chinese empire. In practice, however, Korea was in most respects an independent kingdom, although the ruling dynasty prudently maintained cordial relations with its powerful neighbor.

Thus Korea entered into a tributary relationship with China. Envoys of the Silla kings regularly delivered gifts to Chinese emperors and performed the kowtow, but those concessions brought considerable benefits to the Koreans. In return for their recognition of Chinese supremacy, they received gifts more valuable than the tribute they delivered to China. Moreover, the tributary relationship opened the doors for Korean merchants to trade in China.

Chinese Influence in Korea Meanwhile, the tributary relationship facilitated the spread of Chinese political and cultural influences to Korea. Embassies delivering tribute to China included Korean royal officials who observed the workings of the Chinese court and bureaucracy and then organized the Korean court on similar lines. The Silla kings built a lavish new capital at their ancestral town of Kumsong (modern-day Kyongju in southeastern Korea), taking the Tang capital at Chang'an as their model. Silla rulers developed Kumsong from a small walled town with a few hundred families into a major capital with 179,000 households and nearly one million people. Their embassies to China included not only royal officials but also scholars who studied Chinese thought and literature and who took copies of Chinese writings back to Korea. Their efforts

MAP 14.3
Borderlands of postclassical China: Korea, Vietnam, and Japan.
Note the geographic relationship of Korea, Vietnam, and Japan to China.
What geographic conditions help to account for the varying degrees of Chinese influence in Korea, Vietnam, and Japan?

helped to build Korean interest in the Confucian tradition, particularly among educated aristocrats. While Korean elite classes turned to Confucius, Chinese schools of Buddhism attracted widespread popular interest. Chan Buddhism, which promised individual salvation, won the allegiance of peasants and commoners.

China and Korea differed in many respects. Most notably, perhaps, aristocrats and royal houses dominated Korean society much more than was the case in China. Although the Korean monarchy sponsored Chinese schools and a Confucian examination system, Korea never established a bureaucracy based on merit such as that of Tang and Song China. Political initiative remained firmly in the hands of the ruling classes. Nevertheless, extensive dealings with its powerful neighbor ensured that Korea reflected the influence of Chinese political and cultural traditions.

China and Vietnam Chinese relations with Vietnam were far more tense than with Korea. When Tang armies ventured into the land that Chinese called Nam Viet, they encountered spirited resistance on the part of the Viet people, who had settled in the region around the Red River. Tang forces soon won control of Viet towns and cities, and they launched efforts to absorb the Viets into Chinese society, just as their predecessors had absorbed the indigenous peoples of the Yangzi River valley. The Viets readily adopted Chinese agricultural methods and irrigation systems as well as Chi-

nese schools and administrative techniques. Like their Korean counterparts, Viet elites studied Confucian texts and took examinations based on a Chinese-style education, and Viet traders marketed their wares in China. Vietnamese authorities even entered into tributary relationships with the Chinese court. Yet the Viets resented Chinese efforts to dominate the southern land, and they mounted a series of revolts against Tang authorities. As the Tang dynasty fell during the early tenth century, the Viets won their independence and successfully resisted later Chinese efforts at imperial expansion to the south.

Like Korea, Vietnam differed from China in many ways. Many Vietnamese retained their indigenous religions in preference to Chinese cultural traditions. Women played a much more prominent role in Vietnamese society and economy than did their counterparts in China. Southeast Asian women had dominated local and regional markets for centuries, and they participated actively in business ventures closed to women in the more rigidly patriarchal society of China.

Chinese Influence in Vietnam Nevertheless, Chinese traditions found a place in the southern land. Vietnamese authorities established an administrative system and bureaucracy modeled on that of China, and Viet ruling classes prepared for their careers by pursuing a Confucian education. Furthermore, Buddhism came to Vietnam from China as well as India and won a large popular following. Thus, like Korea, Vietnam absorbed political and cultural influence from China and reflected the development of a larger east Asian society centered on China.

Early Japan

Chinese armies never invaded Japan, but Chinese traditions deeply influenced Japanese political and cultural development. The earliest inhabitants of Japan were nomadic peoples from northeast Asia who migrated to Japan about thirty-five thousand years ago. Their language, material culture, and religion derived from their parent society in northeast Asia. Later migrants, who arrived in several waves from the Korean peninsula, introduced cultivation of rice, bronze and iron metallurgy, and horses into Japan. As the population of the Japanese islands grew and built a settled agricultural society, small states dominated by aristocratic clans emerged. By the middle of the first millennium C.E., several dozen states ruled small regions.

Nara Japan The establishment of the powerful Sui and Tang dynasties in China had repercussions in Japan, where they suggested the value of centralized imperial government. One of the aristocratic clans in Japan insisted on its precedence over the others, although in fact it had never wielded effective authority outside its territory in central Japan. Inspired by the Tang example, this clan claimed imperial authority and introduced a series of reforms designed to centralize Japanese politics. The imperial house established a court modeled on that of the Tang, instituted a Chinese-style bureaucracy, implemented an equal-field system, provided official support for Confucianism and Buddhism, and in the year 710 moved to a new capital city at Nara (near modern Kyoto) that was a replica of the Tang capital at Chang'an. Never was Chinese influence more prominent in Japan than during the Nara period (710–794 C.E.).

Yet Japan did not lose its distinctive characteristics or become simply a smaller model of Chinese society. While adopting Confucian and Buddhist traditions from China, for example, the Japanese continued to observe the rites of Shinto, their indigenous religion, which revolved around the veneration of ancestors and a host of nature spirits and deities. Japanese society reflected the influence of Chinese traditions but still developed along its own lines.

The experiences of the Heian, Kamakura, and Muromachi periods clearly illustrate this point. In 794 the emperor of Japan transferred his court from Nara to a newly constructed capital at nearby Heian (modern Kyoto). During the next four centuries, Heian became the seat of a refined and sophisticated society that drew inspiration from China but also elaborated distinctively Japanese political and cultural traditions.

Heian Japan During the Heian period (794–1185 C.E.), local rulers on the island of Honshu mostly recognized the emperor as Japan's supreme political authority. Unlike their Chinese counterparts, however, Japanese emperors rarely ruled but, rather, served as ceremonial figureheads and symbols of authority. Effective power lay in the hands of the Fujiwara family, an aristocratic clan that controlled affairs from behind the throne through its influence over the imperial house and manipulation of its members.

Tang dynasty pottery figure of a Vietnamese dancer. Commercial and tributary relationships introduced southeast Asian performers to China, where sophisticated urban communities appreciated their exotic entertainment.

After the ninth century the Japanese political order almost continuously featured a split between a publicly recognized imperial authority and a separate agent of effective rule. This pattern helps to account for the remarkable longevity of the Japanese imperial house. Because emperors have not ruled, they have not been subject to deposition during times of turmoil: ruling parties and factions have come and gone, but the imperial house has survived.

The cultural development of Heian Japan also reflected both the influence of Chinese traditions and the elaboration of peculiarly Japanese ways. Most literature imitated Chinese models and indeed was written in the Chinese language. Boys and young men who received a formal education in Heian Japan learned Chinese, read the classic works of China, and wrote in the foreign tongue. Officials at court conducted business and kept records in Chinese, and literary figures wrote histories and treatises in the style popular in China. Even Japanese writing reflected Chinese influence, since scholars borrowed many Chinese characters and used them to represent Japanese words. They also adapted some Chinese characters into a Japanese syllabic script, in which symbols represent whole syllables rather than a single sound, as in an alphabetic script.

The Tale of Genji Because Japanese women rarely received a formal Chinese-style education, in Heian times aristocratic women made the most notable contributions to literature in the Japanese language. Of the many literary works that have survived from that era, none reflects Heian court life better than *The Tale of Genji*. Composed by Murasaki Shikibu, a lady-in-waiting at the Heian court who wrote in Japanese syllabic script rather than Chinese characters, this sophisticated work relates the experiences of a fictitious imperial prince named Genji. Living amid gardens and palaces, Genji and his friends devoted themselves to the cultivation of an ultra-refined lifestyle, and they became adept at mixing subtle perfumes, composing splendid verses in fine calligraphic hand, and wooing sophisticated women.

The Tale of Genji also offers a meditation on the passing of time and the sorrows that time brings to sensitive human beings. As Genji and his friends age, they reflect on past joys and relationships no longer recoverable. Their thoughts suffuse *The Tale of Genji* with a melancholy spirit that presents a subtle contrast to the elegant atmosphere of their surroundings at the Heian court. Because of her limited command of Chinese, Lady Murasaki created one of the most remarkable literary works in the Japanese language.

Samurai depart from a palace in Kyoto after capturing it, murdering the guards, seizing an enemy general there, and setting the structure ablaze. The armor and weaponry of the samurai bespeak the militarism of the Kamakura era.

Decline of Heian Japan As the charmed circle of aristocrats and courtiers led elegant lives at the imperial capital, the Japanese countryside underwent fundamental changes that brought an end to the Heian court and its refined society. The equal-field system gradually fell into disuse in Japan as it had in China, and aristocratic clans accumulated most of the islands' lands into vast estates. By the late eleventh century, two clans in particular—the Taira and the Minamoto—overshadowed the others. During the mid-twelfth century the two engaged in outright war, and in 1185 the Minamoto emerged victorious. The Minamoto did not seek to abolish imperial authority in Japan but, rather, claimed to rule the land in the name of the emperor. They installed the clan leader as *shogun*—a military governor who ruled in place of the emperor—and established the seat of their government at Kamakura, near modern Tokyo, while the imperial court remained at Kyoto. For most of the next four centuries, one branch or another of the Minamoto clan dominated political life in Japan.

Medieval Japan

Historians refer to the Kamakura and Muromachi periods as Japan's medieval period—a middle era falling between the age of Chinese influence and court domination of political life in Japan, as represented by the Nara and Heian periods, and the modern age, inaugurated by the Tokugawa dynasty in the sixteenth century, when a centralized government unified and ruled all of Japan. During this middle era, Japanese society and culture took on increasingly distinctive characteristics.

Political Decentralization In the Kamakura (1185–1333 C.E.) and Muromachi (1336–1573 C.E.) periods, Japan developed a decentralized political order in which provincial lords wielded effective power and authority in local regions where they controlled land and economic affairs. As these lords and their clans vied for power and authority in the countryside, they found little use for the Chinese-style bureaucracy that Nara and Heian rulers had instituted in Japan and still less use for the elaborate protocol and refined conduct that prevailed at the courts. In place of etiquette and courtesy, they valued military talent and discipline. The mounted warrior, the *samurai,* thus played the most distinctive role in Japanese political and military affairs.

The Samurai The samurai were professional warriors, specialists in the use of force and the arts of fighting. They served the provincial lords of Japan, who relied on the samurai both to enforce their authority in their own territories and to extend their claims to other lands. In return for those police and military services, the lords supported the samurai from the agricultural surplus and labor services of peasants working under their jurisdiction. Freed of obligations to feed, clothe, and house themselves and their families, samurai devoted themselves to hunting, riding, archery, and martial arts.

Thus, although it had taken its original inspiration from the Tang empire in China, the Japanese political order developed along lines different from those of the Middle Kingdom. Yet Japan clearly had a place in the larger east Asian society centered on China. Japan borrowed from China, among other things, Confucian values, Buddhist religion, a system of writing, and the ideal of centralized imperial rule. Though somewhat suppressed during the Kamakura and Muromachi periods, those elements of Chinese society not only survived in Japan but also decisively influenced Japanese development during later periods.

in perspective

The revival of centralized imperial rule in China had profound implications for all of east Asia and indeed for most of the eastern hemisphere. When the Sui and Tang dynasties imposed their authority throughout China, they established a powerful state that guided political affairs throughout east Asia. Tang armies extended Chinese influence to Korea, Vietnam, and central Asia. They did not invade Japan, but the impressive political organization of China prompted the islands' rulers to imitate Tang examples. Moreover, the Sui and Tang dynasties laid a strong political foundation for rapid economic development. Chinese society prospered throughout the postclassical era, partly because of technological and industrial innovation. Tang and Song prosperity touched all of China's neighbors, since it encouraged surging commerce in east Asia. Chinese silk, porcelain, and lacquerware were prized commodities among trading peoples from southeast Asia to east Africa. Chinese inventions such as paper, printing, gunpowder, and the magnetic compass found a place in societies throughout the eastern hemisphere as they diffused across the silk roads and the sea lanes. The postclassical era was an age of religious as well as commercial and technological exchanges: Nestorian Christians, Zoroastrians, Manichaeans, and Muslims all maintained communities in Tang China, and Buddhism became the most popular religious tradition in all of east Asia. During the postclassical era, Chinese social organization and economic dynamism helped to sustain interactions between the peoples of the eastern hemisphere on an unprecedented scale. ●

CHRONOLOGY	
589–618	Sui dynasty (China)
602–664	Life of Xuanzang
604–618	Reign of Sui Yangdi
618–907	Tang dynasty (China)
627–649	Reign of Tang Taizong
669–935	Silla dynasty (Korea)
710–794	Nara period (Japan)
755–757	An Lushan's rebellion
794–1185	Heian period (Japan)
875–884	Huang Chao's rebellion
960–1279	Song dynasty (China)
960–976	Reign of Song Taizu
1024	First issuance of government-sponsored paper money
1130–1200	Life of Zhu Xi
1185–1333	Kamakura period (Japan)
1336–1573	Muromachi period (Japan)

For Further Reading

Hugh R. Clark. *Community, Trade, and Networks: Southern Fujian Province from the Third to the Thirteenth Century.* Cambridge, 1991. Excellent scholarly study exploring the transformation of a region by trade and market forces.

Mark Elvin. *The Pattern of the Chinese Past.* Stanford, 1973. A brilliant analysis of Chinese history, concentrating particularly on economic, social, and technological themes.

Robert Finlay. *The Pilgrim Art: The Culture of Porcelain in World History.* Berkeley, 2010. Brilliant study outlining the Chinese invention of porcelain and the product's appeal in the larger world.

Karl Friday. *Samurai, Warfare and the State in Early Medieval Japan.* New York, 2004. A lively analysis with apt comparisons to medieval Europe.

Jacques Gernet. *Buddhism in Chinese Society: An Economic History from the Fifth to the Tenth Century.* Trans. by F. Verellen. New York, 1995. An important study emphasizing the economic and social significance of Buddhist monasteries in the Chinese countryside.

Peter D. Hershock. *Chan Buddhism.* Honolulu, 2005. An accessible introduction to Chan Buddhism focusing on four renowned masters.

Thomas P. Kasulis. *Shinto: The Way Home.* Honolulu, 2004. The best short introduction.

John Kieschnick. *The Impact of Buddhism on Chinese Material Culture.* Princeton, 2003. Fascinating scholarly study exploring the social effects of Buddhism in China.

Dieter Kuhn. *The Age of Confucian Rule: The Song Transformation of China.* Cambridge, Mass., 2009. Emphasizes social and economic developments.

Mark Edward Lewis. *China's Cosmopolitan Empire: The Tang Dynasty.* Cambridge, Mass., 2009. Perhaps the best single volume on Tang China.

Joseph Needham. *Science in Traditional China.* Cambridge, Mass., 1981. Essays on the history of Chinese science and technology.

Edward H. Schafer. *The Golden Peaches of Samarkand: A Study of T'ang Exotics.* Berkeley, 1963. Deals with relations between China and central Asian lands during the Tang dynasty.

———. *The Vermilion Bird: T'ang Images of the South.* Berkeley, 1967. Evocative study of relations between China and Vietnam during the Tang dynasty.

Tansen Sen. *Buddhism, Diplomacy, and Trade: The Realignment of Sino-Indian Relations, 600–1400.* Honolulu, 2003. A pathbreaking study exploring trade, diplomacy, and cultural exchanges between postclassical India and China.

Murasaki Shikibu. *The Tale of Genji.* 2 vols. Trans. by E. Seidensticker. New York, 1976. Fresh and readable translation of Lady Murasaki's classic work.

Pierre François Souyri. *The World Turned Upside Down: Medieval Japanese Society.* Trans. by K. Roth. New York, 2001. Reliable survey that places political developments in social and economic context.

H. Paul Varley. *Japanese Culture.* 4th ed. Honolulu, 2000. An authoritative analysis of Japanese cultural development from early times to the present.

James C. Y. Watt. *China: Dawn of a Golden Age, 200–750 A.D.* New York, 2004. Lavishly illustrated volume surveying the arts in postclassical China.

Roderick Whitfield, Susan Whitfield, and Neville Agnew. *Mogao: Art and History on the Silk Road.* Los Angeles, 2000. Excellent brief discussion of the cave temples and archaeological remains from Dunhuang.

Susan Whitfield. *Life along the Silk Road.* Berkeley, 1999. Focuses on the experiences of ten individuals who lived or traveled on the silk roads during the postclassical era.

Sally Hovey Wriggins. *The Silk Road Journey with Xuanzang.* Boulder, 2004. A fascinating and well-illustrated account of Xuanzang's journey to India and his influence on the development of Buddhism in China.

Arthur F. Wright. *Buddhism in Chinese History.* Stanford, 1959. A brief and incisive study of Buddhism in China by an eminent scholar.

Don J. Wyatt. *The Blacks of Premodern China.* Philadelphia, 2010. Pioneering study of Africans and other dark-skinned peoples in premodern China.

PART

India and the Indian Ocean Basin

chapter 15

Kabir, the blind guru, weaves cloth while discussing religious matters with disciples.

EYEWITNESS:
Buzurg Sets His Sights on the Seven Seas

Buzurg ibn Shahriyar was a tenth-century shipmaster from Siraf, a prosperous and bustling port city on the Persian Gulf coast. He probably sailed frequently to Arabia and India, and he may have ventured also to Malaya, the islands of southeast Asia, China, and east Africa. Like all sailors, he heard stories about the distant lands that mariners had visited, the different customs they observed, and the adventures that befell them during their travels. About 953 C.E. he compiled 136 such stories in his *Book of the Wonders of India*.

Buzurg's collection included a generous proportion of tall tales. He told of a giant lobster that seized a ship's anchor and dragged the vessel through the water, of mermaids and sea dragons, of creatures born from human fathers and fish mothers who lived in human society but had flippers that enabled them to swim through the water like fish, of serpents that ate cattle and elephants, of birds so large that they crushed houses, of a monkey that seduced a sailor, and of a talking lizard. Yet alongside the tall tales, many of Buzurg's stories accurately reflected the conditions of his time. One recounted the story of a king from northern India who converted to Islam and requested translations of Islamic law. Others reported on Hindu customs, shipwrecks, encounters with pirates, and slave trading.

Several of Buzurg's stories tempted readers with visions of vast wealth attainable through maritime trade. Buzurg mentioned fine diamonds from Kashmir, pearls from Ceylon, and a Jewish merchant who left Persia penniless and returned from India and China with a shipload of priceless merchandise. Despite their embellishments and exaggerations, his stories faithfully reflected the trade networks that linked the lands surrounding the Indian Ocean in the tenth century. Although Buzurg clearly thought of India as a distinct land with its own customs, he also recognized a larger world of trade and communication that extended from east Africa to southeast Asia and beyond to China.

Just as China served as the principal inspiration of a larger east Asian society in the postclassical era, India influenced the development of a larger cultural zone in south and southeast Asia. Yet China and India played different roles in their respective spheres of influence. In east Asia, China was the dominant power, even if it did not always exercise

In India as in other lands, Sufi mystics were the most effective Muslim missionaries. This eighteenth-century painting depicts the Sufi Khwaja Khidr, beloved in Muslim communities throughout northern India as one associated with springtime, fertility, and happiness. Why would Sufis emphasize nonreligious values while promoting Islam?

harmonizing Hinduism and Islam. Nevertheless, like the Sufis, bhakti teachers promoted values that helped to build bridges between India's social and cultural communities.

THE INFLUENCE OF INDIAN SOCIETY IN SOUTHEAST ASIA

Just as China stood at the center of a larger east Asian society, India served as the principal source of political and cultural traditions widely observed throughout south and southeast Asia. For a millennium and more, southeast Asian peoples adapted Indian political structures and religions to local needs and interests. Although Indian armed forces rarely ventured into the region, southeast Asian lands reflected the influence of Indian society, as merchants introduced Hinduism, Buddhism, Sanskrit writings, and Indian forms of political organization. Beginning about the twelfth century, Islam also found solid footing in southeast Asia, as

Muslim merchants, many of them Indians, established trading communities in the important port cities of the region. During the next five hundred years, Islam attracted a sizable following and became a permanent feature in much of southeast Asia.

The States of Southeast Asia

Indian Influence in Southeast Asia Indian merchants visited the islands and mainland of southeast Asia from an early date, perhaps as early as 500 B.C.E. By the early centuries C.E., they had become familiar figures throughout southeast Asia, and their presence brought opportunities for the native ruling elites of the region. In exchange for spices and exotic products such as pearls, aromatics, and animal skins, Indian merchants brought textiles, beads, gold, silver, manufactured metal goods, and objects used in political or religious rituals. Southeast Asian rulers used the profits from that trade to consolidate their political control.

Meanwhile, southeast Asian ruling elites became acquainted with Indian political and cultural traditions. Without necessarily giving up their own traditions, they borrowed Indian forms of political organization and accepted Indian religious faiths. On the model of Indian states, for example, they adopted kingship as the principal form of political authority. Regional kings in southeast Asia surrounded themselves with courts featuring administrators and rituals similar to those found in India.

Ruling elites also sponsored the introduction of Hinduism or Buddhism—sometimes both—into their courts. They embraced Indian literature such as the *Ramayana* and the *Mahabharata,* which promoted Hindu values, as well as treatises that explained Buddhist views on the world. They did not show much enthusiasm for the Indian caste system and continued to acknowledge the deities and nature spirits that southeast Asian peoples had venerated for centuries. But ruling elites readily adopted Hinduism and Buddhism, which they found attractive because the Indian faiths reinforced the principle of monarchical rule.

Funan The first state known to have reflected Indian influence in this fashion was Funan, which dominated the lower reaches of the Mekong River (including parts of modern Cambodia and Vietnam) between the first and the sixth centuries C.E. The rulers of Funan consolidated their grip on the Mekong valley and built a capital city at the port of Oc Eo. Funan grew wealthy because it dominated the Isthmus of Kra, the narrow portion of the Malay peninsula where merchants transported trade goods between China and India. (The short portage enabled them to avoid a long voyage around the Malay peninsula.) The rulers of Funan drew enormous wealth by controlling trade between China and India. They used their profits to construct an elaborate system of water storage and irrigation—so extensive that aerial photography still reveals its lines—that served a productive agricultural economy in the Mekong delta.

MAP 15.3

Early states of southeast Asia: Funan and Srivijaya, 100–1025 C.E.
Both Funan and Srivijaya relied heavily on maritime trade.

To what extent were they able to take advantage of the trading networks shown on Map 15.2?

CHINA

PACIFIC OCEAN

PHILIPPINES

Bay of Bengal

ISTHMUS OF KRA

Sulu Sea

Oc Eo

MALAY PENINSULA

Celebes Sea

Strait of Melaka

INDIAN OCEAN

SUMATRA

BORNEO

MALUKU ISLANDS

CELEBES

Palembang

JAVA

Funan
Srivijaya

As trade with India became an increasingly important part of Funan's economy, the ruling classes adopted Indian political, cultural, and religious traditions. They took the Sanskrit term *raja* ("king") for themselves and claimed divine sanction for their rule in the manner of Hindu rulers in India. They established positions for administrators and bureaucrats such as those found at Indian courts and conducted official business in Sanskrit. They introduced Indian ceremonies and rituals and worshiped Vishnu, Shiva, and other Hindu deities. They continued to honor local deities, particularly water spirits venerated widely throughout southeast Asia, but they eagerly welcomed Hinduism, which offered additional recognition and divine legitimacy for their rule. At first, Indian cultural and religious traditions were most prominent and most often observed at ruling courts. Over the longer term, however, those traditions extended well beyond ruling elites and won a secure place in southeast Asian society.

During the sixth century C.E., a bitter power struggle weakened Funan internally. Peoples from the north took advantage of that weakness, migrated to the lower Mekong valley in large numbers, and overwhelmed Funan. Chams settled in the southern portion of modern Vietnam, and Khmers dominated in the region occupied by modern Cambodia. By the late sixth century, Funan's intricate irrigation system had fallen into ruin, and Funan itself soon passed into oblivion.

Srivijaya After the fall of Funan, political leadership in southeast Asia passed to the kingdom of Srivijaya (670–1025 C.E.) based on the island of Sumatra. The kings of Srivijaya built a powerful navy and controlled commerce in southeast Asian waters. They compelled port cities in southeast Asia to recognize their authority, and they financed their navy and bureaucracy from taxes levied on ships passing through the region. They maintained an all-sea trade route between China and India, eliminating the need for the portage of trade goods across the Isthmus of Kra. As the volume of shipping increased in the postclassical era, the Srivijaya kingdom prospered until the expansive Chola kingdom of southern India eclipsed it in the eleventh century.

With the decline of Srivijaya, the kingdoms of Angkor (889–1431 C.E.), Singosari (1222–1292 C.E.), and Majapahit (1293–1520 C.E.) dominated affairs in southeast Asia. Many differences characterized these states. Funan had its base of operations in the Mekong valley, Srivijaya at Palembang in southern Sumatra, Angkor in Cambodia, and Singosari and Majapahit on the island of Java. Funan and Angkor were land-based states that derived most of their wealth from productive agricultural economies, whereas Srivijaya, Singosari, and Majapahit were island-based states that prospered because

The Two Worlds of Christendom

chapter 16

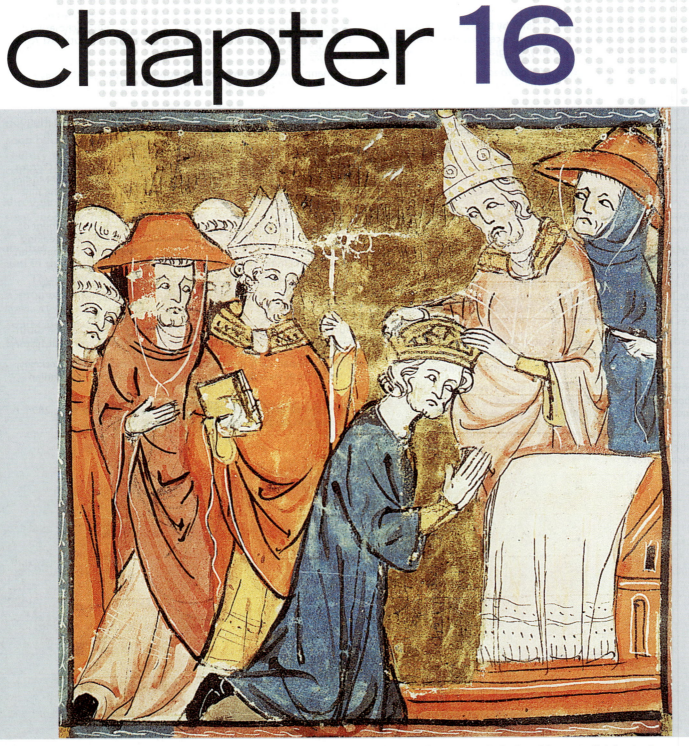

Pope Leo III crowns Charlemagne emperor in a manuscript illustration. The coronation symbolized the firm alliance between the Franks and the western Christian church.

EYEWITNESS:
Emperor Charlemagne and His Elephant

In the year 802 C.E., an unusual traveler arrived at Aachen (in modern Germany), capital of the western European empire ruled by Charlemagne. The traveler was a rare albino elephant, a diplomatic gift from the Abbasid caliph Harun al-Rashid to Charlemagne. The elephant—whom Harun named Abu al-Abbas, in honor of the Abbasid dynasty's founder—was born in India and went to Baghdad with his trainer in about 798. From Baghdad the animal accompanied an embassy overland through Syria and Egypt to a port on the Tunisian coast, then sailed across the Mediterranean to Portovenere (near Genoa in northern Italy), and finally trekked across the Alps and overland to Charlemagne's court. Abu al-Abbas must have shivered through the cold, damp winters of Europe. Yet he enjoyed swimming in the Rhine River, and until his death in 810, he amazed and delighted all who beheld him.

Charlemagne was not a friend of Islam. At the battle of Tours (732 C.E.), his grandfather, Charles Martel, had defeated a Muslim army that ventured into Frankish territory after Muslim forces had conquered most of the Iberian peninsula. Charlemagne himself fought Muslims in an unsuccessful effort to restore Christian rule in northern Spain. One of the battles from his campaign provided the raw material for a popular poetic work called the *Song of Roland*. Nevertheless, in spite of his personal religious preferences, Charlemagne found it both necessary and convenient to have diplomatic dealings with Harun al-Rashid.

Charlemagne dispatched at least three embassies to Baghdad and received three in return. The embassies dealt with several issues: the safety of Christian pilgrims and merchants traveling in Abbasid-controlled Syria and Palestine, Charlemagne's relations with Muslim neighbors, and policy toward the Byzantine empire, which stood between western Europe and the Abbasid caliphate. Charlemagne's realm was weak and poor compared with the Abbasid empire, but for about half a century, it seemed that Charlemagne and his successors might be able to reestablish a centralized imperial state in western Europe. His dealings with Harun al-Rashid—and the unusual odyssey of the elephant Abu al-Abbas—reflected a general recognition that Charlemagne had the potential to establish a western European empire similar to the Byzantine and Abbasid realms.

Historians refer to the period from about 500 to 1500 C.E. as the medieval period of European history—the "middle ages" falling between the classical era and modern times. During the early medieval period, from about 500 to 1000 C.E., European peoples recovered from the many problems that plagued the later Roman empire—epidemic disease, declining population, economic contraction, political turmoil, social unrest, and invasions by Germanic peoples. In doing so, they laid the foundations of European Christendom—a region that never experienced political unity but that adopted Christianity as the dominant source of cultural authority.

The two very different halves of medieval Christendom were the Byzantine empire in the eastern half of the Mediterranean basin and the Germanic states that succeeded the western Roman empire after its collapse in the fifth century C.E. The Byzantine empire was in fact a direct continuation of the Roman empire in the east. It did not extend its authority to the entire Mediterranean basin, but it inherited the most prosperous and productive regions of the classical Roman empire. Even after Muslim conquerors seized the wealthy provinces of Egypt and Syria in the seventh century, the Byzantine empire remained a political and economic powerhouse of the postclassical world. As a centralized imperial state like the Abbasid empire in southwest Asia or the Tang and Song dynasties in China, the Byzantine empire dominated the eastern Mediterranean and Black Sea regions. As an urbanized center of manufacturing, the Byzantine empire was also a highly productive society that both supported and benefited from trade throughout the eastern hemisphere.

Meanwhile, lands to the west of the Byzantine empire fell under the sway of invading peoples who dismantled the western part of the Roman empire and established a series of Germanic successor states. Charlemagne made heroic efforts to unify the western half of Christendom and establish a western counterpart to the Byzantine empire, but internal tensions and new rounds of invasions brought an early end to his own imperial creation. Thus, during the era 500 to 1000 C.E., western Christendom resembled postclassical India, where a restoration of imperial unity also turned out to be a fleeting experience, more than the Abbasid, Tang, Song, and Byzantine realms. When Charlemagne's empire dissolved, western European peoples fashioned alternatives to imperial rule by creating new decentralized forms of government that vested public authority mostly in local or regional rulers. At the same time, they also began a process of economic recovery by dramatically boosting agricultural production.

Both the Byzantine empire and the European states to the west inherited Christianity from the Roman empire, and rulers in both regions promoted Christianity as a cultural and moral foundation for their rule. After the eighth century C.E., however, political and religious tensions increasingly complicated relations between the two halves of the former Roman empire. Byzantine rulers bristled at the claims to empire made by Charlemagne and other western Christian rulers, and theologians in the two regions developed differing views on proper religious doctrine and practice. By the mid-eleventh century, the Byzantine and Roman churches had publicly and formally condemned each other. Byzantine missionaries promoted their brand of Christianity in Russia and other Slavic lands, while western Christians following the leadership of the popes in Rome spread their own views from the British Isles to Scandinavia and eastern Europe. Just as Abbasid leaders helped consolidate Islam as the principal cultural influence in the Muslim world, Byzantine and western Christians expanded the religious and moral authority of Christianity throughout Europe. In doing so, they created two worlds of Christendom.

THE QUEST FOR POLITICAL ORDER

The eastern half of the Roman empire suffered from invasions by Germanic peoples, but it did not collapse. The political challenge for rulers in this region—direct successors of the Roman emperors—was to restore order following the invasions. In the sixth century Byzantine rulers even tried to reestablish Roman authority throughout the Mediterranean basin. Their efforts fell short of that goal, and they soon lost considerable territories to expansive Muslim forces, but they nevertheless presided over a powerful society in the eastern Mediterranean region.

Political challenges were greater in lands to the west. Germanic invaders mostly passed through the eastern Roman empire, but they mostly settled down in western regions. Throughout Roman Europe and north Africa, Germanic invaders disrupted Roman authority, deposed Roman officials, and imposed new states of their own making. After two centuries of fighting, it looked as though one group of Germanic invaders, the Franks, might reestablish imperial authority in much of Roman Europe. If they had succeeded, they might have played a role similar to that of the Sui and Tang dynasties in China by reviving centralized imperial rule after a hiatus of several centuries. By the late ninth century, however, the Frankish empire had fallen victim to internal power struggles and a fresh series of devastating invasions. Political authority in western Europe then devolved to local and regional jurisdictions, whose leaders fashioned a decentralized political order.

The Early Byzantine Empire

The Byzantine empire takes its name from Byzantion—latinized as Byzantium—a modest market town and fishing village that occupied a site of enormous strategic significance. Situated on a defensible peninsula and blessed with a magnificent natural harbor known as the Golden Horn, Byzantion had the potential to control the Bosporus, the strait of water leading from the Black Sea to the Sea of Marmara and beyond to the Dardanelles, the Aegean Sea, and the Mediterranean. Apart from its maritime significance, Byzantion offered convenient access to the rich lands of Anatolia, southwestern Asia, and southeastern Europe. Sea lanes linked the city to ports throughout the Mediterranean basin.

The City of Constantine Recognizing its strategic value, the Roman emperor Constantine designated Byzantion the site of a new imperial capital, which he named Constantinople ("city of Constantine"). He built the new capital partly because the eastern Mediterranean was the wealthiest and most productive region of the Roman empire and partly because relocation enabled him to maintain close watch over both the Sasanid empire in Persia and the Germanic peoples who lived along the lower stretches of the Danube River. The imperial government moved to Constantinople after 330 C.E., and the new capital rapidly reached metropolitan dimensions. Constantine filled the city with libraries, museums, and artistic treasures, and he constructed magnificent marble palaces, churches, baths, and public buildings—all in an effort to create a new Rome fit for the ruler of a mighty empire. The city kept the name Constantinople until it fell to the Ottoman Turks (1453 C.E.), who renamed it Istanbul. By convention, however, historians refer to the realm

---

MAP 16.1

Successor states to the Roman empire, ca. 600 C.E.
Compare this map with Map 11.2 showing the Roman empire at its height.

How did the territories of the Byzantine empire differ from those of the classical Roman empire?

Justinian wears imperial purple robes in this mosaic, from the church of San Vitale in Ravenna, which depicts him in the company of ecclesiastical, military, and court officials.

governed from Constantinople between the fifth and fifteenth centuries C.E. as the Byzantine empire, or simply Byzantium, in honor of the original settlement.

Caesaropapism Constantine and his successors hedged their rule with the aura of divinity and awesome splendor. As a Christian, Constantine could not claim the divine status that some of the earlier Roman emperors had appropriated for themselves. As the first Christian emperor, however, he claimed divine favor and sanction for his rule. He intervened in theological disputes and used his political position to support the views he considered orthodox while condemning those he deemed heretical. He initiated the policy of "caesaropapism," whereby the emperor not only ruled as secular lord but also played an active and prominent role in ecclesiastical affairs.

Following Constantine's example, Byzantine emperors presented themselves as exalted, absolute rulers. Even dress and court etiquette testified to their lofty status. The em-

perors wore bejeweled crowns and dressed in magnificent silk robes dyed a dark, rich purple—a color reserved for imperial use and strictly forbidden to those not associated with the ruling house. High officials presented themselves to the emperor as slaves. When approaching the imperial majesty, they prostrated themselves three times and then ceremoniously kissed the imperial hands and feet before raising matters of business. By the tenth century engineers had contrived a series of mechanical devices that worked dazzling effects and impressed foreign envoys at the Byzantine court: imitation birds sang as ambassadors approached the emperor while mechanical lions roared and swished their tails. During an audience the imperial throne itself sometimes moved up and down to emphasize the awesome splendor of the emperor.

Justinian and Theodora The most important of the early Byzantine emperors was Justinian (reigned 527–565 C.E.), an energetic worker known to his subjects as "the sleepless emperor," who ruled with the aid of his ambitious wife, Theodora. The couple came from obscure origins: Justinian was born into a Macedonian peasant family, and Theodora, the daughter of a bear keeper in the circus, worked

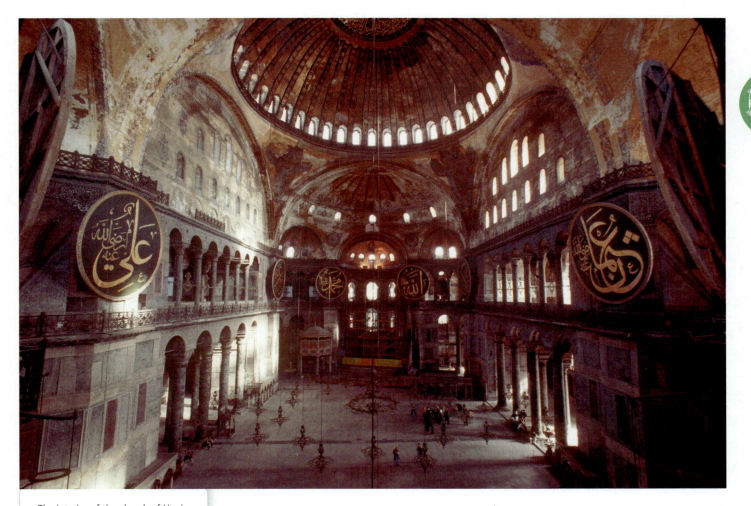

The interior of the church of Hagia Sophia ("Holy Wisdom"), built by Justinian and transformed into a mosque in the fifteenth century. The dome rises almost 60 meters (197 feet) above the floor, and its windows allow abundant light to enter the massive structure.

as a striptease artist before meeting the future emperor. Yet both Justinian and Theodora were smart, strong-willed, and disciplined. Thanks to those qualities, Justinian received an education, found a position in the imperial bureaucracy, and mastered the intricacies of Byzantine finance. Theodora proved to be a sagacious advisor and a determined supporter of her emperor husband.

Like Constantine, Justinian lavished resources on the imperial capital. His most notable construction project was the church of Hagia Sophia ("holy wisdom"), a magnificent domed structure—later turned into a mosque by Ottoman conquerors—that ranks as one of the world's most important examples of Christian architecture. Visitors marveled at the church's enormous dome, which they likened to the heavens encircling the earth, and at the gold, silver, gems, and thousands of lamps that decorated and illuminated Hagia Sophia.

Justinian's Code Justinian's most significant political contribution was his codification of Roman law. The origins of Roman law went back to the times of the kings of Rome, and even though earlier scholars worked to codify the law, it had become a confusing mass of sometimes conflicting injunctions. Justinian ordered a systematic review of Roman law and issued the *Corpus iuris civilis* (*Body of the Civil Law*), which immediately won recognition as the definitive codification of Roman law. Updated by later emperors, Justinian's code has influenced civil law codes in most of Europe, in Japan, and in the state of Louisiana in the United States.

Byzantine Conquests Justinian's most ambitious venture was his effort to reconquer the western Roman empire from Germanic peoples and reestablish Roman authority throughout the Mediterranean basin. Between 533 and 565, Byzantine forces gained control over Italy, Sicily, much of northwestern Africa, and southern Spain. Yet Byzantium did not possess the resources to sustain a long-term occupation and consolidate those conquests. Shortly after Justinian's death, Byzantine forces abandoned Rome, leaving the city of Ravenna on Italy's Adriatic coast as the headquarters of Byzantine authority in the western Mediterranean. As a result, Ravenna possesses magnificent examples of Byzantine art and architecture, but Justinian's dream of reconstituting the old Roman empire soon faded into oblivion.

Muslim Conquests and Byzantine Revival

Justinian's efforts showed that the classical Roman empire was beyond recovery. While the emperor devoted his efforts to the western Mediterranean, the Sasanids threatened Byzantium from the east and Slavic peoples approached from the north. Later Byzantine emperors had no choice but to redeploy their resources to meet other threats.

Muslim Conquests After the seventh century C.E., the expansion of Islam (discussed in chapter 13) posed even more serious challenges to Byzantium. Shortly after Muhammad's death, Arab warriors conquered the Sasanid empire in Persia and overran large portions of the Byzantine empire as well. By the mid-seventh century, Byzantine Syria, Palestine, Egypt, and north Africa had fallen under Muslim rule. Muslim forces later subjected Constantinople itself to two prolonged sieges (in 674–678 and again in 717–718). Byzantium resisted this northward thrust of Islam partly because of advanced military technology. Byzantine forces used a weapon known as "Greek fire"—a nasty incendiary weapon compounded of sulphur, lime, and petroleum—which they launched at both the fleets and the ground forces of the invaders. Greek fire burned even when floating on water and thus created a hazard when deployed around wooden ships. On land it caused panic among enemy forces, since it was extremely difficult to extinguish and often burned troops to death. As a result of this defensive effort, the Byzantine empire retained its hold on Anatolia, Greece, and the Balkan region.

The *Theme* System Though diminished by Muslim conquests, the Byzantine empire was more manageable after the eighth century than was the far-flung realm of Justinian. Byzantine rulers responded to the threat of Islam with political and social adjustments that strengthened their reduced empire. Their most important innovation was the reorganization of Byzantine society under the *theme* system. They placed an imperial province called a *theme* under the authority of a general, who assumed responsibility for both its military defense and its civil administration. Generals received their appointments from the emperor, who closely monitored their activities to prevent decentralization of power and authority. Generals recruited armies from the ranks of free peasants, who received allotments of land for their military service.

Armies raised under the *theme* system were effective fighting forces, and they enabled Byzantium to expand its influence between the ninth and the twelfth centuries. During the tenth century Byzantine forces reconquered Syria and pushed their authority west into the Balkan region. By the mid-eleventh century, the Byzantine empire encompassed lands from Syria and Armenia in the east to southern Italy in the west, from the Danube River in the north to the islands of Cyprus and Crete in the south. Once again, Byzantium dominated the eastern Mediterranean region.

The Rise of the Franks

In the year 476 C.E., the Germanic general Odoacer deposed the last of the western Roman emperors. He did not claim the imperial title for himself, however, nor did he appoint anyone else as a replacement. The emperor's post simply remained vacant. Roman administrators and armies continued to function, temporarily, but urban populations declined as continuing invasions and power struggles disrupted trade and manufacturing. Deprived of legitimacy and resources

A manuscript illustration depicts Byzantine naval forces turning Greek fire on their Arab enemies.

supplied from Rome and other major cities, imperial institutions progressively weakened.

Germanic Kingdoms Gradually, a series of Germanic kingdoms emerged as successor states to the Roman empire. Visigoths, Ostrogoths, Lombards, Franks, and other Germanic peoples occupied imperial provinces, displacing Roman authorities and institutions. As they built successor states, Germanic peoples absorbed a great deal of Roman influence. Many of them converted to Christianity, for example, and others adapted Roman law to the needs of their own societies.

The Franks Most successful and most influential of the Germanic peoples were the Franks. By the early sixth century, the Franks had conquered most of Roman Gaul and emerged as the preeminent military and political power in western Europe. They also gained popular support when they abandoned their inherited polytheistic religion and converted to Christianity—a move that brought them the allegiance of the Christian population of the former Roman empire as well as support from the pope and the western Christian church.

In the eighth century the aristocratic clan of the Carolingians dramatically extended Frankish power. The Carolingian dynasty takes its name from its founder, Charles (*Carolus* in Latin)—known as Charles Martel ("Charles the Hammer") because of his military prowess. In 732 at the battle of Tours (in central France), he turned back a Muslim army that had ventured north from recently conquered Spain. His victory helped persuade Muslim rulers of Spain that it was not worthwhile for them to seek further conquests in western Europe.

Charlemagne The Frankish realm reached its high point under Charles Martel's grandson Charlemagne ("Charles the Great"), who reigned from 768 to 814. Like King Harsha in India, Charlemagne temporarily reestablished centralized imperial rule in a society disrupted by invasion and contests for power between ambitious local rulers. Like Harsha again, Charlemagne possessed enormous energy, and the building of the Carolingian empire was in large measure his personal accomplishment. Although barely literate, Charlemagne was quite intelligent. He spoke Latin, understood some Greek, and regularly conversed with learned men. He maintained diplomatic relations with the Byzantine empire and the Abbasid caliphate. The gift of the albino elephant Abu al-Abbas symbolized relations between the Carolingian and Abbasid empires, and until its death in 810, the animal accompanied Charlemagne on many of his travels.

When Charlemagne inherited the Frankish throne, his realm included most of modern France as well as the lands that now form Belgium, the Netherlands, and southwestern Germany. By the time of his death in 814, Charlemagne had extended his authority to northeastern Spain, Bavaria, and

A bronze statue depicts Charlemagne riding a horse and carrying an orb symbolizing his imperial authority.

Italy as far south as Rome. He campaigned for thirty-two years to impose his rule on the Saxons of northern Germany and to repress their rebellions. Beyond the Carolingian empire proper, rulers in eastern Europe and southern Italy paid tribute to Charlemagne as imperial overlord.

Charlemagne's Administration Charlemagne built a court and capital at Aachen (in modern Germany), but like Harsha in India, he spent most of his reign on horseback, traveling throughout his realm to maintain authority. Constant travel was necessary because Charlemagne did not have the financial resources to maintain an elaborate bureaucracy or an administrative apparatus that could enforce his policies. Instead, he relied on aristocratic deputies, known

MAP 16.2

The Carolingian empire, 814 C.E.
Notice the location of Charlemagne's capital at Aachen and also the extent of his empire.

What geographic challenges did he face in his efforts to hold his empire together?

as counts, who held political, military, and legal authority in local jurisdictions. In an effort to keep the counts under control, Charlemagne instituted a group of imperial officials called the *missi dominici* ("envoys of the lord ruler"), who traveled annually to all jurisdictions and reviewed the accounts of local authorities.

Thus Charlemagne built the Frankish kingdom into an empire on the basis of military expeditions, and he began to outfit it with some centralized institutions. Yet he hesitated to call himself emperor because an imperial claim would constitute a direct challenge to the authority of the Byzantine emperors, who regarded themselves as the only legitimate successors of the Roman emperors.

Charlemagne as Emperor Only in the year 800 did Charlemagne accept the title of emperor. While campaigning in Italy, Charlemagne attended religious services conducted by Pope Leo III on Christmas Day. During the

services, the pope proclaimed Charlemagne emperor and placed an imperial crown on his head. It is not certain, but it is possible that Charlemagne did not know of the pope's plan and that Leo surprised him with an impromptu coronation. Charlemagne had no desire for strained relations with the Byzantine emperors, who deeply resented his imperial title as a pretentious affront to their own dignity. In any case, Charlemagne had already built an imperial state, and his coronation constituted public recognition of his accomplishments.

The Age of the Vikings

If Charlemagne's empire had endured, Carolingian rulers might well have built a bureaucracy, used the *missi dominici* to enhance the authority of the central government, and reestablished imperial rule in western Europe. As it happened, however, internal disunity and external invasions brought the Carolingian empire to an early end.

The Oseberg ship, pictured here, is the best-preserved Viking vessel from the early middle ages. Built about 800 C.E., it served as a royal tomb until its discovery in 1903. A ship this size would accommodate about forty men.

Louis the Pious Charlemagne's only surviving son, Louis the Pious (reigned 814–840), succeeded his father and held the empire together. Lacking Charlemagne's strong will and military skills, however, Louis lost control of local authorities, who increasingly pursued their own interests. Moreover, Louis's three sons disputed the inheritance of the empire and waged bitter wars against one another. In 843 they divided the empire into three roughly equal portions and ruled as three kings. Thus, less than a century after its creation, the Carolingian empire dissolved.

Danish Vikings prepare to invade England in this manuscript illustration produced at an English monastery about 1130. The geographic range of Viking activity extended from England, France, northern Germany, and Russia to territories throughout the Mediterranean basin.

Invasions Even if internal divisions had not dismembered the Carolingian empire, external pressures might well have brought it down. Beginning in the late eighth century, three groups of invaders pillaged the Frankish realm in search of wealth stored in towns and monasteries. From the south came Muslims, who raided towns, villages, churches, and monasteries in Mediterranean Europe. Muslim invaders also conquered the island of Sicily and seized territories in southern Italy and southern France. From the east came the **Magyars,** descendants of nomadic peoples who had settled in Hungary. Expert horsemen, the Magyars raided settlements in Germany, Italy, and southern France. From the north came the Vikings, most feared of all the invaders, who began mounting raids in northern France even during Charlemagne's lifetime.

The Viking invasions were part of a much larger process of expansion by the Nordic peoples of Scandinavia. One cause of Norse expansion was probably population growth fueled by increased agricultural production in Scandinavia. The main cause, however, was the quest for wealth through trading and raiding in European lands to the south of Scandinavia. Norse expansion depended on a remarkable set of shipbuilding techniques and seafaring skills that Scandinavian mariners developed during the seventh and eighth centuries. They built rugged, shallow-draft boats outfitted both with sails, which enabled them to travel through the open ocean, and with oars, which enabled them to navigate rivers.

Vikings Many Norse seafarers were merchants seeking commercial opportunities or migrants seeking lands to settle and cultivate. Some, however, turned their maritime skills more toward raiding and plundering than trading or raising crops. These were the Vikings. The term *Viking* originally

Magyars (MAH-jahrs)

MAP 16.3

The dissolution of the Carolingian empire (843 C.E.) and the invasions of early medieval Europe in the ninth and tenth centuries.

The various invaders of early medieval Europe took many routes and attacked both coastal and interior regions.

What were the political and economic effects of the invasions?

Kingdom of Charles the Bald	→ Vikings
Kingdom of Louis the German	→ Magyars
Kingdom of Lothar I	→ Muslims

referred to a group that raided the British Isles from their home at Vik in southern Norway. Over time, however, the term came to refer more generally to Norse mariners who mounted invasions and plundered settlements from Russia and eastern Europe to Mediterranean lands. With their shallow-draft boats, the Vikings were able to make their way up the many rivers offering access to interior regions of Europe. Vikings coordinated their ships' movements and timed their attacks to take advantage of the tides. Fleets of Viking boats with ferocious dragon heads mounted on their prows could sail up a river, surprise a village or a monastery far from the sea, and spill out crews of warriors who conducted lightning raids on unprepared victims.

The first Viking invaders began to attack unprotected monasteries in the 790s. Learning from experience, Viking forces mounted increasingly daring raids. In 844 C.E., more than 150 Viking ships sailed up the Garonne River in southern France, plundering settlements along the way. Sometimes Viking fleets attacked sizable cities: in 845, some 800 vessels appeared without warning before the city of Hamburg in northern Germany; in 885, a Viking force consisting of at least 700 ships sailed up the Seine River and besieged Paris; and in 994, an armada of about 100 ships sprinted up the Thames River and raided London. Some Vikings bypassed relatively close targets and ventured into the Mediterranean, where they

plundered sites in the Balearic Islands, Sicily, and southern Italy. By following the Russian rivers to the Black Sea, other Vikings made their way to Constantinople, which they raided at least three times during the ninth and tenth centuries.

Devolution of Political Authority The Carolingians had no navy, no means to protect vulnerable sites, and no way to predict the movements of Viking raiders. Defense against the Magyars and the Muslims as well as the Vikings rested principally with local forces that could respond rapidly to invasions. Because imperial authorities were unable to defend their territories, the Carolingian empire became the chief casualty of the invasions. After the ninth century, political and military initiative in western Europe increasingly devolved to regional and local authorities.

The devolution of political authority took different forms in different lands. In England and Germany, regional kingdoms emerged and successfully defended territories more compact than the sprawling Carolingian empire. In France, the counts and other Carolingian subordinates usurped royal rights and prerogatives for themselves. The Vikings themselves established settlements in northern France and southern Italy, where they carved out small, independent states. Following a century of internal conflict and external invasion, the emergence of regional kingdoms and local authorities made it increasingly unlikely that imperial rule would return to western Europe. Like postclassical India but unlike postclassical societies in China, southwest Asia, and the eastern Mediterranean region, western Europe became a society of competing regional states. By putting an end to the ninth-century invasions and establishing a stable political order, these states laid a foundation for social, economic, and cultural development in later centuries.

ECONOMY AND SOCIETY IN EARLY MEDIEVAL EUROPE

Economic and social development in the two big provinces of Christendom mirrored their different political fortunes in the postclassical era. Byzantium was an economic powerhouse in the eastern Mediterranean region. The Byzantine countryside produced abundant agricultural surpluses, which supported large urban populations and fueled the work of manufacturers. Byzantine merchants participated in long-distance commercial networks that linked lands throughout the eastern hemisphere. Western Christendom, by contrast, experienced both a decline of agricultural production and a weakening of cities as repeated invasions disrupted economic and social as well as political affairs. By the tenth century, however, a measure of political stability served as a foundation for economic recovery, and western European peoples began to participate more actively in the larger trading world of the eastern hemisphere.

The Two Economies of Early Medieval Europe

The Byzantine Peasantry Byzantium was strongest when its large class of free peasants flourished. After adoption of the *theme* system in the eighth century, soldiers received allotments of land when they mustered out of the army. This arrangement supported a large and prosperous class of free peasants, who cultivated their land intensively in hopes of improving their families' fortunes. The free peasantry entered an era of gradual decline after the eleventh century as wealthy cultivators managed to accumulate large estates. For as long as it flourished, however, the free peasantry provided agricultural surpluses that served as the foundation for general prosperity in the Byzantine empire.

Manufacturing Agricultural surpluses supported manufacturing in Byzantium's cities, especially Constantinople, which was already a manufacturing megalopolis in classical times. The city was home to throngs of artisans and crafts workers, not to mention thousands of imperial officials and bureaucrats. Byzantine crafts workers enjoyed a reputation especially for their glassware, linen and woolen textiles, gems, jewelry, and fine work in gold and silver.

Silk In the sixth century, crafts workers added high-quality silk textiles to the list of products manufactured in the Byzan-

Peasants—probably sharecroppers—receive seeds and tend to vineyards in this painting from a Byzantine manuscript. What does this illustration suggest about the relationship between the two landowners or overseers (left, in the top register) and the five laborers?

tine empire. The Byzantine historian Procopius reported that two Christian monks from Persia traveled to China, where they observed the techniques of silk production, which at that time were unknown outside China. According to Procopius, the monks hollowed out their walking staffs and filled them with silkworm eggs, which they smuggled out of China, through their native land of Persia, and into the Byzantine empire. It is likely that Procopius simplified a more complex story by focusing attention on the monks, who by themselves could hardly have introduced a full-blown silk industry to Byzantium. The production of fine, Chinese-style silks required more than a few silkworm eggs. It called also for the mastery of sophisticated technologies and elaborate procedures that probably reached Byzantium by several routes.

In any case, silk textiles soon made major contributions to the Byzantine economy. By the late sixth century, Byzantine silks matched the quality of Chinese textiles, and Byzantium had become the principal supplier of the fashionable fabric to lands in the Mediterranean basin. The silk industry was so important to the Byzantine economy that the government closely supervised every step in its production and sale. Regulations allowed individuals to participate in only one activity—such as weaving, dyeing, or sales—to prevent the creation of a monopoly by a few wealthy or powerful entrepreneurs.

Byzantine Trade The Byzantine economy also benefited from trade. Sitting astride routes going east and west as well as north and south, Constantinople served as the main clearinghouse for trade in the western part of Eurasia. The merchants of Constantinople maintained commercial links with manufacturers and merchants in central Asia, Russia, Scandinavia, northern Europe, and the lands of the Black Sea and the Mediterranean basin. Even after the early Islamic conquests, Byzantine merchants traded regularly with their Muslim counterparts in Persia, Syria, Palestine, and Egypt except during periods of outright war between Byzantium and Muslim states. Indeed, Byzantium was so dominant in trade that the Byzantine gold coin, the *bezant,* served as the standard currency of the Mediterranean basin for more than half a millennium, from the sixth through the twelfth century.

Byzantium drew enormous wealth simply by controlling trade and levying customs duties on merchandise that passed through its lands. Moreover, Byzantium served as the western anchor of the Eurasian trading network that revived the silk roads of classical times. Silk and porcelain came to Constantinople from China, spices from India and southeast Asia. Carpets arrived from Persia and woolen textiles from western Europe, while timber, furs, honey, amber, and slaves came from Russia and Scandinavia. Byzantine subjects consumed some commodities from distant lands, but they redistributed most products, often after adding to their value by further processing—by fashioning jewelry out of gems imported from India, for example, or by dyeing raw woolen cloth imported from western Europe.

As Byzantium prospered, western Europe struggled to find its economic footing in an era of intermittent invasion and political turmoil, which disrupted both agricultural production and large-scale manufacturing. While dealing with political and military challenges, though, western Europeans also adopted a series of innovations that yielded increased agricultural production.

Heavy Plows One innovation involved a new kind of heavy plow that gradually replaced the light Mediterranean plows that had made their way north at the time of the Roman empire. In light, well-drained Mediterranean soils, cultivators used small wooden plows that broke the surface of the soil, created a furrow, and uprooted weeds. This type of plow made little headway in the heavy, moist soils of the north. After the eighth century a more serviceable plow came into use: a heavy tool equipped with iron tips and a mouldboard that turned the soil so as to aerate it thoroughly and break up the root networks of weeds. The heavy plow was a more expensive piece of equipment than the light Mediterranean plow, and it required cultivators to harness more energy to pull it through damp northern soils. Once hitched to oxen or draft horses, however, the heavy plow contributed to greater agricultural production.

As the heavy plow spread throughout western Europe, cultivators took several additional steps that increased agricultural production. They cleared new lands for cultivation and built ponds for fish. They constructed water mills, which enabled them to take advantage of a ready and renewable source of inanimate energy, thus freeing human and animal energy for other work. They employed a special horse collar, which allowed them to rely less on slow-moving oxen and more on speedier horses to pull their heavy plows. They increased cultivation of beans and other legumes, which enriched diets throughout western Chris-

In this twelfth-century manuscript illustration, a peasant guides a heavy, wheeled plow while his wife prods the oxen that pull the plow.

tendom. Thus western Europeans made numerous small adaptations that created a foundation for rural prosperity after 1000 C.E.

Trade in Western Christendom

By no means did trade disappear from western Europe. Local markets and fairs offered opportunities for small-scale exchange, and itinerant peddlers shopped their wares from one settlement to another. Maritime trade flourished in the Mediterranean despite Muslim conquests in the region. Christian merchants from Italy and Spain regularly traded across religious boundary lines with Muslims of Sicily, Spain, and north Africa, who linked Europe indirectly with a larger world of communication and exchange.

Norse Merchant-Mariners

Maritime trade flourished also in the North Sea and the Baltic Sea. Most active among the early medieval merchants in the northern seas were Norse seafarers, kinsmen of the Vikings. Norse traders followed the same routes as Viking raiders, and many individual mariners no doubt turned from commerce to plunder and back again as opportunities arose. Norse merchants called at ports from Russia to Ireland, carrying cargoes of fish and furs from Scandinavia, honey from Poland, wheat from England, wine from France, beer from the Low Countries, and swords from Germany. By traveling down the Russian rivers to the Black Sea, they were able to trade actively in both the Byzantine and the Abbasid empires. Thus, like Mediterranean merchants, but by different routes, Norse mariners linked western Europe with the world of Islam. Indeed, the Carolingian empire depended heavily on this connection: Norse merchants took Scandinavian products to the Abbasid empire and exchanged them for silver, which they traded at Carolingian ports for wine, jugs, glassware, and other products. The silver transported from the Abbasid empire by Norse merchants was a principal source of bullion used for minting coins in early medieval Europe and hence a crucially important element of the western European economy. Thus, even if western European merchants were not as numerous or prominent as their Byzantine counterparts, they nevertheless participated in the trading networks of the larger eastern hemisphere.

Social Development in the Two Worlds of Christendom

Byzantium: An Urban Society

The Byzantine empire was rich in large, prosperous, cosmopolitan cities, including Alexandria, Antioch, and Damascus, to mention only a few. Indeed, until the Muslim conquests of the late seventh and eighth centuries, Byzantium was probably the world's most urbanized society, and residents of its cities enjoyed the benefits and observed urban traditions inherited from the classical Mediterranean world. Yet Constantinople had no rival among Byzantine cities. Subjects of the Byzantine empire referred to it simply as "the City." The heart of the City was the imperial palace, which employed twenty thousand workers as palace staff. Peacocks strutted through gardens filled with sculptures and fountains. Most famous of them was a gold fountain that spouted wine for imperial guests.

City Life

Aristocrats maintained enormous palaces that included courtyards, reception halls, libraries, chapels, and quarters for members of the extended family as well as servants and slaves. In the fifth century Constantinople boasted 4,388 mansions, as well as 14 imperial and princely palaces. Women lived in separate apartments and did not receive male visitors from outside the household. Nor did they participate in banquets and parties, especially when wine flowed freely or when the affairs were likely to become so festive that they could compromise a woman's reputation. In Constantinople as well as other cities, upper-class women generally wore veils, like their Mediterranean ancestors from centuries past, to discourage the attention of men outside their own families.

Dwellings of less privileged classes were not so splendid. Artisans and crafts workers commonly lived in rooms above their shops, while clerks and government officials occupied multistory apartment buildings. Workers and the poor lived in rickety tenements where they shared kitchens and sanitary facilities with their neighbors.

Attractions of Constantinople

Even for the poor, though, the City had its attractions. As the heir of Rome, Constantinople was a city of baths, which were sites of relaxation and exercise as well as hygienic bathing. Taverns and restaurants offered settings for social gatherings—checkers, chess, and dice games were especially popular activities at taverns—and theaters provided entertainment in the form of song, dance, and striptease. Mass entertainment took place in the Hippodrome, a large stadium adjacent to the imperial palace, where Byzantine subjects watched chariot races, athletic matches, contests

thinking about ENCOUNTERS

Northern Connections

During the postclassical era, Norse mariners found their way to most regions of Europe as well as the Abbasid empire and even ventured across the Atlantic Ocean to Greenland and North America. In what specific ways did Norse merchants and travelers create links between Europe and the larger world? What were the effects of those connections for Byzantine and western European peoples?

A manuscript illustration depicts one Byzantine woman weaving cloth (left) while another spins thread (right). Both women veil their hair for modesty. Women workers were prominent in Byzantine textile production.

between wild animals, and circuses featuring acts by clowns, jugglers, acrobats, and dwarfs.

Western Europe: A Rural Society

Cities to the west had once offered similar pleasures, but they largely disappeared in the wake of Germanic invasions and the collapse of the western Roman empire in the late fifth century. The agricultural surplus of western Europe was sufficient to sustain local political elites but not substantial enough to support large, urban populations of artisans, crafts workers, merchants, and professionals. Towns survived, but they served more as economic hubs of surrounding regions than as vibrant centers integrating the economic activities of distant lands.

The Question of Feudalism

How did the peoples of western Christendom reorganize their society after the collapse of the western Roman empire? Historians once used the term *feudalism* to characterize the political and social order of medieval Europe. They spoke routinely of a "feudal system" involving a neat hierarchy of lords and vassals, who collectively took charge of political and military affairs on the basis of personal relationships. Lords supposedly provided grants of land to their retainers in exchange for loyalty and military service. Over the years, scholarship has thoroughly undermined that view of medieval society, and historians have largely abandoned the concept of feudalism as a model that grossly oversimplifies a complex society. It is more accurate to view early medieval Europe as a society in which local political and military elites worked in various ad hoc ways to organize their territories and maintain social order. The arrangements they adopted had deep implica-

tions for the lives of political and military elites themselves and also for their relationships with commoners.

In the absence of an effective central authority such as an emperor, local notables or lords mobilized small private armies composed of armed retainers. Some of these lords were descendants of Carolingian or other ruling houses, and others were ambitious strongmen—essentially local warlords. Both the lords and their retainers were warriors with horses, weapons, and military expertise. Lords sometimes rewarded their retainers with grants of land or some other valuable, such as the right to income generated by a mill, the right to receive rents or payments from a village, or even a payment of money. In other cases, lords supported their retainers by maintaining them in their own households, where they provided equipment and training in military affairs. After the year 1000, lords increasingly hired their retainers, paying them for services on the basis of need. By one mechanism or another, lords and retainers constituted themselves as privileged political and military elites who dominated local regions.

Peasants

Lords and retainers supported themselves and their families principally on the basis of the surplus agricultural production that they commandeered from a subject peasantry. Political and military elites obliged local peasants to provide labor services and payments of rents in kind, such as a portion of the harvest, a chicken, or a dozen eggs. Male peasants typically worked three days a week for their lords while also providing additional labor services during planting and harvesting season. Women peasants churned butter, made cheese, brewed beer, spun thread, wove cloth, or sewed clothes for their lords as well as for their own families. Some peasants also kept sheep or

sources from the past

The Wealth and Commerce of Constantinople

The Spanish rabbi Benjamin of Tudela traveled throughout Europe, north Africa, and southwest Asia between 1165 and 1173 C.E. He may have ventured as far as India, and he mentioned both India and China in his travel account. His main purpose was to record the conditions of Jewish communities, but he also described the many lands and about three hundred cities that he visited. His travels took place during an era of political decline for the Byzantine empire, yet he still found Constantinople a flourishing and prosperous city.

The circumference of the city of Constantinople is eighteen miles; half of it is surrounded by the sea, and half by land, and it is situated upon two arms of the sea, one coming from the sea of Russia [the Black Sea], and one from the sea of Sepharad [the Mediterranean].

All sorts of merchants come here from the land of Babylon, from the land of Shinar [Mesopotamia], from Persia, Media [western Iran], and all the sovereignty of the land of Egypt, from the land of Canaan [Palestine], and the empire of Russia, from Hungary, Patzinakia [Ukraine], Khazaria [southern Russia], and the land of Lombardy [northern Italy] and Sepharad [Spain].

Constantinople is a busy city, and merchants come to it from every country by sea or land, and there is none like it in the world except Baghdad, the great city of Islam. In Constantinople is the church of Hagia Sophia, and the seat of the pope of the Greeks, since Greeks do not obey the pope of Rome. There are also as many churches as there are days of the year. . . . And in this church [Hagia Sophia] there are pillars of gold and silver, and lamps of silver and gold more than a man can count.

Close to the walls of the palace is also a place of amusement belonging to the emperor, which is called the Hippodrome, and every year on the anniversary of the birth of Jesus the emperor gives a great entertainment there. And in that place men from all the races of the world come before the emperor and empress with jugglery and without jugglery, and they introduce lions, leopards, bears, and wild asses, and they engage them in combat with one another; and the same thing is done with birds. No entertainment like this is to be found in any other land. . . .

From every part of the Byzantine empire tribute is brought here every year, and they fill strongholds with garments of silk, purple, and gold. Like unto these storehouses and this wealth there is nothing in the whole world to be found. It is said that the tribute of the city amounts every year to 20,000 gold pieces, derived both from the rents of shops and markets and from the tribute of merchants who enter by sea or land.

The Greek inhabitants are very rich in gold and precious stones, and they go clothed in garments of silk and gold embroidery, and they ride horses and look like princes. Indeed, the land is very rich in all cloth stuffs and in bread, meat, and wine.

Wealth like that of Constantinople is not to be found in the whole world. Here also are men learned in all the books of the Greeks, and they eat and drink, every man under his vine and his fig-tree.

For Further Reflection

■ How is it possible to account for the prosperity that Benjamin of Tudela found in Constantinople?

Source: Benjamin of Tudela. *The Itinerary of Benjamin of Tudela.* Trans. by M. N. Adler. London: H. Frowde, 1907. (Translation slightly modified.)

cattle, and their obligations to lords included products from their herds. Because lords provided peasants with land to cultivate and often with tools and animals as well, peasants had little opportunity to move to different lands. Indeed, they were commonly able to do so only with permission from their lords. They even had to pay fees for the right to marry a peasant who worked for a different lord.

Population   During the fifth and sixth centuries, epidemic disease and political turmoil took a demographic toll in both Byzantium and western Europe. From a high point of about thirty-six million at the time of the Roman empire in 200 C.E., population fell to about twenty-six million in the year 600—nineteen million in Byzantium and seven million in western Europe. Population fluctuated dramatically over the next two centuries, as Byzantium lost territories to Muslims and western Europeans suffered repeated invasion. After the eighth century, however, both Byzantium and western Europe entered an era of demographic recovery. Political stability created a foundation for a more productive agricultural economy just as new food crops made their way from the Muslim world to Byzantium and Mediterranean Europe. Hard durum wheat, rice, spinach, artichokes, eggplant, lemons, limes, oranges, and melons brought increased calories and

sourcesfromthepast

Life on an Early Medieval Manor

Some useful insights into the lives and experiences of common people come from a decree known as the "Capitulary de Villis" issued by the emperor Charlemagne in 807 C.E. as a guide for stewards of Carolingian estates. The decree envisions a community with sophisticated agricultural and craft skills. Probably few estates observed all provisions of Charlemagne's decree, but the capitulary nonetheless communicates clearly how lords hoped to control their manors and profit from their production.

Each steward shall make an annual statement of all our income: an account of our lands cultivated by the oxen which our ploughmen drive and of our lands which the tenants of farms ought to plough; an account of the pigs, of the rents, of the obligations and fines; of the game taken in our forests without our permission; . . . of the mills, of the forest, of the fields, of the bridges, and ships; of the free men and the hundreds who are under obligations to our treasury; of markets, vineyards, and those who owe wine to us; of the hay, firewood, torches, planks, and other kinds of lumber; of the waste lands; of the fruits of the trees, of the nut trees, larger and smaller; of the grafted trees of all kinds; of the gardens; of the turnips; of the fish ponds; of the hides, skins, and horns; of the honey, wax; of the fat, tallow and soap; of the mulberry wine, cooked wine, mead, vinegar, beer, wine new and old; of the new grain and the old; of the hens and eggs; of the geese; the number of fishermen, [metal] smiths, sword-makers, and shoemakers; . . . of the forges and mines, that is iron and other mines; of the lead mines; . . . of the colts and fillies; they shall make all these known to us, set forth separately and in order, at Christmas, in order that we may know what and how much of each thing we have. . . .

[Stewards] must provide the greatest care, that whatever is prepared or made with the hands, that is, lard, smoked meat, salt meat, partially salted meat, wine, vinegar, mulberry wine, cooked wine . . . mustard, cheese, butter, malt, beer, mead, honey, wax, flour, all should be prepared and made with the greatest cleanliness. . . .

[Stewards should ensure] that in each of our estates, the chambers [living quarters] shall be provided with counterpanes, cushions, pillows, bed clothes, coverings for the tables and benches; vessels of brass, lead, iron and wood; andirons, chains, pot-hooks, adzes, axes, augers, cutlasses and all other kinds of tools, so that it shall never be necessary to go elsewhere for them, or to borrow them. And the weapons, which are carried against the enemy, shall be well cared for, so as to keep them in good condition; and when they are brought back they shall be placed in the chamber.

For our women's work they are to give at the proper time, as has been ordered, the materials, that is the linen, wool, woad, vermillion, madder, wool-combs, teasels, soap, grease, vessels and the other objects which are necessary.

Of the food products other than meat, two-thirds shall be sent each year for our own use, that is of the vegetables, fish, cheese, honey, mustard, vinegar, millet, panic [a grain similar to millet], dried and green herbs, radishes, and in addition of the wax, soap and other small products; and they shall tell us how much is left by a statement, as we have said above; and they shall not neglect this as in the past; because from those two-thirds, we wish to know how much remains.

Each steward shall have in his district good workmen, namely, blacksmiths, goldsmiths, silversmiths, shoemakers, [wood] turners, carpenters, sword-makers, fishermen, foilers [fine metalworkers], soap-makers, men who know how to make beer, cider, berry, and all other kinds of beverages, bakers to make pastry for our table, net-makers who know how to make nets for hunting, fishing and fowling, and the others who are too numerous to be designated.

For Further Reflection

■ On the basis of the "Capitulary de Villis," how would you characterize the conditions of material life in the Carolingian countryside?

Source: *Translations and Reprints from the Original Sources of European History,* vol. 2. Philadelphia: University of Pennsylvania Press, 1900. (Translation slightly modified.)

dietetic variety that supported increasing populations. By the year 800 the two provinces of Christendom had a combined population of about twenty-nine million, which rose to about thirty-two million in 900 and thirty-six million in 1000—the level of the Roman empire's population some eight centuries earlier. Thus by the year 1000, both Byzantium and western Europe had built productive agricultural economies that sustained sizable and increasing populations.

THE EVOLUTION OF CHRISTIAN SOCIETIES IN BYZANTIUM AND WESTERN EUROPE

As heirs of the Roman empire, Byzantium and western Europe were both Christian societies. As in the cases of political, social, and economic affairs, though, the two big realms of Christendom created distinctive and ultimately competing forms of their common religious inheritance. In both Byzantium and western Europe, Christianity served as the principal source of religious, moral, and cultural authority. Both lands supported ecclesiastical hierarchies with networks of monasteries. Both societies also worked to extend the reach of Christianity by sending missionaries to seek converts in northerly territories from Russia and Slavic lands to Scandinavia and the British Isles. By the year 1000 the twin heirs of Roman Christianity had laid the foundations for a large Christian cultural zone in the western part of the Eurasian continent that paralleled the Buddhist and Islamic cultural zones farther east. Yet even as they were promoting Christianity in their own societies and beyond, church authorities in Byzantium and western Europe fell into deep disagreement on matters of doctrine, ritual, and church authority. By the mid-eleventh century, their differences had become so great that church leaders formally denounced one another and established two rival communities: the Eastern Orthodox church in Byzantium and the Roman Catholic church in western Europe.

Popes and Patriarchs

Christianity had a more hierarchical organizational structure than any other major religious tradition. There was no pope of Buddhism, no patriarch in the Islamic world. Christianity, however, inherited a strong organizational structure from the time of the late Roman empire. In the early middle ages, the two most important Christian authorities were the bishop of Rome, known as the pope, and the patriarch of Constantinople.

The Papacy When the western Roman empire collapsed, the papacy survived and claimed continuing spiritual authority over all the lands formerly embraced by the Roman empire. At first the popes cooperated closely with the Byzantine emperors, who seemed to be the natural heirs of the emperors of Rome. Beginning in the late sixth century, however, the popes acted more independently and devoted their efforts to strengthening the western Christian church based at Rome and clearly distinguishing it from the eastern Christian church based at Constantinople.

Pope Gregory I The individual most responsible for charting an independent course for the Roman church was Pope Gregory I (590–604 C.E.), also known as Gregory the Great. As pope, Gregory faced an array of challenges. During the late sixth century, the Germanic Lombards campaigned in Italy, menacing Rome and the church in the process. Gregory mobilized local resources and organized the defense of Rome, thus saving both the city and the church. He also faced difficulties within the church, since bishops frequently acted as though they were supreme ecclesiastical authorities within their own dioceses. To regain the initiative, Gregory reasserted claims to papal primacy—the notion that the bishop of Rome was the ultimate authority for all the Christian church. Gregory also made

contributions as a theologian. He emphasized the sacrament of penance, which required individuals to confess their sins to their priests and atone for them by penitential acts—a practice that enhanced the influence of the Roman church in the lives of individuals.

The Patriarchs The patriarchs of Constantinople were powerful officials, but they did not enjoy the independence of their brethren to the west. Following the tradition of caesaropapism inaugurated by the emperor Constantine in the fourth century, Byzantine emperors treated the church as a department of state. They appointed the patriarchs, and they instructed patriarchs, bishops, and priests to deliver sermons that supported imperial policy and encouraged obedience to imperial authorities. This caesaropapism was a source of tension between imperial and ecclesiastical authorities, and it also had the potential to provoke popular dissent when imperial views clashed with those of the larger society.

Iconoclasm The most divisive ecclesiastical policy implemented by Byzantine emperors was iconoclasm, inaugurated by Emperor Leo III (reigned 717–741 C.E.). Byzantium had a long tradition of producing icons—paintings of Jesus, saints, and other religious figures—many of which were splendid works of art. Most theologians took these icons as visual stimulations that inspired reverence for holy personages. Leo, however, became convinced that the veneration of images was sinful, tantamount to the worship of idols. In 726 C.E., he embarked on a policy of iconoclasm (which literally means "breaking of icons"), destroying religious images and prohibiting their use in churches. The policy immediately sparked protests and even riots throughout the empire, because icons were extremely popular among the laity. Debates about iconoclasm raged for more than a century. Only in 843 did Leo's followers abandon the policy of iconoclasm.

Monks and Missionaries

Consumed with matters of theology, ritual, and church politics, popes and patriarchs rarely dealt directly with the lay population of their churches. For personal religious instruction and inspiration, lay Christians looked less to the church hierarchy than to local monasteries.

Asceticism Christian monasticism grew out of the efforts of devout individuals to lead especially holy lives. Early Christian ascetics in Egypt, Mesopotamia, and Persia adopted extreme regimes of self-denial in order to focus all their attention on religious matters. Some lived alone as hermits. Others formed communes where they devoted themselves to the pursuit of holiness rather than worldly success. Many dedicated themselves to celibacy, fasting, and prayer.

Drawn by their reputation for piety, disciples gathered around these ascetics and established communities of men and women determined to follow their example. These communities became the earliest monasteries. During the early

This illustration from a psalter prepared about 900 C.E. depicts an iconoclast whitewashing an image of Jesus painted on a wall.

days of monasticism, each community developed its own rules, procedures, and priorities. The result was wild inconsistency: some monasteries imposed harsh and austere regimes of self-denial, and others offered little or no guidance.

St. Basil and St. Benedict

Monasteries became much more influential when reformers provided them with discipline and a sense of purpose. The two most important reformers were the patriarch St. Basil of Caesarea (329–379 C.E.) in Byzantium and St. Benedict of Nursia (480–547 C.E.) in Italy. Both men prepared regulations for monasteries that provided for mild but not debilitating asceticism combined with meditation and work on behalf of the church. In both Basilian and Benedictine monasteries, individuals gave up their personal possessions and lived communal, celibate lives under the direction of the abbots who supervised the communities. Poverty, chastity, and obedience became the prime virtues for Basilian and Benedictine monks. At certain hours monks came together for religious services and prayers, dividing the remainder of the day into periods for study, reflection, and labor.

St. Scholastica

Monasteries throughout Byzantium adopted the Basilian rule for their own use, while their counterparts in western Europe largely followed the rule of St. Benedict. Through the influence of St. Benedict's sister, the nun St. Scholastica (482–543 C.E.), an adaptation of the Benedictine rule soon provided guidance for the religious life of women living in convents.

Monasticism and Society

Like Buddhist monasteries in Asian lands and charitable religious foundations in Muslim lands, Christian monasteries provided a variety of social services that enabled them to build close relations with local communities. Monks and nuns offered spiritual counsel to local laity, and they organized relief efforts by supplying food and medical attention at times of natural or other calamities. Monasteries and convents served both as orphanages and as inns for travelers. Sometimes they also provided rudimentary educational services for local communities.

Because of the various roles they played in the larger society, monasteries were particularly effective agents in the spread of Christianity. While providing social services, monks also zealously preached Christianity and tended to the spiritual needs of rural populations. For many people, a local neighboring monastery was the only source of instruc-

A fourteenth-century manuscript illustration shows St. Benedict with his crosier, the staff carried by abbots to symbolize their position (above), and meeting with two monks beside a fishpond at their monastery (below). What does the fishpond suggest about the economic significance of monasteries?

tion in Christian doctrine, and a local monastic church offered the only practical opportunity for them to take part in religious services. Through patience and persistence over decades and centuries, monks and nuns helped to instill Christian values in countless generations of European peasants.

Missionaries Some monks went beyond the bounds of their own society and sought to spread Christianity in the larger world. Indeed, one of the remarkable developments of the early middle ages was the creation of a large Christian cultural zone in the western part of the Eurasian continent.

Christianity was already well established in the Mediterranean region, but pagan Germanic and Slavic peoples occupied the more northerly parts of Europe. In the late sixth century, Pope Gregory I sent missionaries to England and targeted the pagan Germanic kings who ruled various parts of the island, hoping that their conversion would induce their subjects to adopt Christianity. This tactic largely succeeded: by the early seventh century Christianity enjoyed a stable foothold, and by 800 England was securely within the fold of the Roman church. The Franks and Charlemagne later sponsored efforts to extend Christianity to northern Germany and Scandinavia. They met spirited resistance from Germanic peoples, who had no desire to abandon their inherited gods or pagan beliefs, but by the year 1000 Christianity had won a sizable and growing following.

Meanwhile, Byzantine authorities sent missionaries to Balkan and Slavic lands. The most famous of the missionaries to the Slavs were Saints Cyril and Methodius, two brothers from Thessaloniki in Greece. During the mid-ninth century, Cyril and Methodius conducted missions in Bulgaria and Moravia (which included much of the modern Czech, Slovakian, and Hungarian territories). There they devised an alphabet, known as the Cyrillic alphabet, for the previously illiterate Slavic peoples. Though adapted from written Greek, the Cyrillic alphabet represented the sounds of Slavic languages more precisely than did the Greek, and it remained in use in much of eastern Europe until supplanted by the Roman alphabet in the twentieth century. In Russia and most other parts of the former Soviet Union, the Cyrillic alphabet survives to the present day.

North of Bulgaria another Slavic people began to organize large states: the Russians. About 989, at the urging of Byzantine missionaries, Prince Vladimir of Kiev converted to Christianity and ordered his subjects to follow his example. Vladimir was no paragon of virtue: he lauded drunkenness and reportedly maintained a harem of eight hundred girls. After his conversion, however, Byzantine influences flowed rapidly into Russia. Cyrillic writing, literacy, and Christian missions all spread quickly throughout Russia. Byzantine teachers traveled north to establish schools, and Byzantine priests conducted services for Russian converts. Thus Kiev served as a conduit for the spread of Byzantine cultural and religious influence in Russia.

Two Churches

Although they professed the same basic Christian doctrine, the churches of Constantinople and Rome experienced increasing friction after the sixth century. Tensions mirrored political strains, such as deep resentment in Byzantium after Charlemagne accepted the title of emperor from the pope in Rome. Yet church authorities in Constantinople and Rome also harbored different views on religious and theological issues. The iconoclastic movement of the eighth and ninth centuries was one focus of difference. Western theologians regarded religious images as perfectly appropriate aids to devotion and resented Byzantine claims to the contrary, whereas the iconoclasts took offense at the efforts of their Roman counterparts to have images restored in Byzantium.

Monasteries were the principal centers of literacy in western Europe during the early middle ages. In this manuscript illustration, one monk copies a manuscript, another makes geometric calculations, a third cuts parchment, two work on the building, and one more rings the bells that call monks and members of the surrounding community to religious services.

Religious Rivalry Over time the Christian churches based in Constantinople and Rome disagreed on many other points. Some ritual and doctrinal differences concerned forms of worship and the precise wording of theological teachings—relatively minor issues that in and of themselves need not have caused deep division in the larger Christian community. Byzantine theologians objected, for example, to

thinking about TRADITIONS

Competing Christianities
The Byzantine empire and western Europe inherited the same Christianity from the late Roman empire. How did Christianity develop along distinct lines in the two regions? What influences contributed to the development of such different understandings of Christianity?

the fact that western priests shaved their beards and used unleavened rather than leavened bread when saying Mass. Other differences concerned more substantive theological matters, such as the precise relationship between God, Jesus, and the Holy Spirit—all regarded as manifestations of God by most Christian theologians of the day.

Schism Alongside ritual and doctrinal differences, the Byzantine patriarchs and the Roman popes disputed their respective rights and powers. Patriarchs argued for the autonomy of all major Christian jurisdictions, including that of Constantinople, whereas popes asserted the primacy of Rome as the sole seat of authority for all Christendom. Ultimately, relations became so strained that the eastern and western churches went separate ways. In 1054 the patriarch and pope mutually excommunicated each other, each refusing to recognize the other's church as properly Christian. Despite efforts at reconciliation, the schism between eastern and western churches persists to the present day. In light of the schism, historians refer to the eastern Christian church after 1054 as the Eastern Orthodox church and its western counterpart as the Roman Catholic church.

in perspective

After the collapse of the western Roman empire, the two worlds of Christendom followed very different historical paths. Byzantium inherited a thriving economy, a set of governing institutions, an imperial bureaucracy, an established church, and a rich cultural tradition from classical Mediterranean society and the Roman empire. Even after the loss of territories to Muslim conquerors, Byzantium remained a powerful and productive society in the eastern Mediterranean region. By contrast, western Europe experienced turmoil in the face of repeated invasion, which thoroughly disrupted social and economic as well as political affairs. Only after the ninth century did western Europeans gradually manage to achieve political stability and lay the foundations for a more predictable and prosperous society. For all their differences, though, the two worlds of Christendom both advanced the construction of a large Christian cultural zone that paralleled the lands of Islamic and Buddhist influence to the east. This Christian cultural zone harbored different and competing versions of a common religion—like the Islamic cultural zone with both Sunni and Shia advocates or the Buddhist cultural zone with Mahayana as well as Theravada adherents—but Byzantium and western Europe both relied on religion as a foundation for cultural unity and made Christianity the most important source of cultural and moral authority throughout Europe. ●

CHRONOLOGY

313–337	Reign of Constantine
329–379	Life of St. Basil of Caesarea
476	Fall of the western Roman empire
480–547	Life of St. Benedict of Nursia
482–543	Life of St. Scholastica
527–565	Reign of Justinian
590–604	Reign of Pope Gregory I
717–741	Reign of Leo III
726–843	Iconoclastic controversy
732	Battle of Tours
751–843	Carolingian kingdom
768–814	Reign of Charlemagne
800	Coronation of Charlemagne as emperor
9th century	Missions of St. Cyril and St. Methodius to the Slavs
989	Conversion of Prince Vladimir of Kiev to Christianity
1054	Schism between Eastern Orthodox and Roman Catholic churches

For Further Reading

Marc Bloch. *Feudal Society.* 2 vols. Trans. by L. A. Manyon. Chicago, 1961. A classic interpretation concentrating on social and economic history.

Peter Brown. *The Rise of Western Christendom: Triumph and Diversity, A.D. 200–1000.* 2nd ed. Oxford, 2003. A landmark analysis of early Christian history.

Einhard and Notker the Stammerer. *Two Lives of Charlemagne.* Trans. by Lewis Thorpe. New York, 1969. Translations of two early biographies of Charlemagne.

Patrick J. Geary. *Before France and Germany: The Creation and Transformation of the Merovingian World.* 2nd ed. New York, 1997. Insightful study of Germanic societies in early medieval Europe.

Judith Herrin. *Byzantium: The Surprising Life of a Medieval Empire.* Princeton, 2009. A judicious survey of Byzantine history.

Richard Hodges and David Whitehouse. *Mohammed, Charlemagne, and the Origins of Europe: Archaeology and the Pirenne Thesis.* Ithaca, 1983. Views early medieval Europe in hemispheric context.

Michael McCormick. *Origins of the European Economy: Communications and Commerce, A.D. 300–900.* Cambridge, Mass., 2001. A comprehensive analysis that emphasizes the participation of early medieval Europe in a larger Mediterranean economy.

Procopius. *History of the Wars, Secret History, and Buildings.* Trans. by A. Cameron. New York, 1967. Translations of writings by the most important historian in the time of Justinian.

Susan Reynolds. *Fiefs and Vassals: The Medieval Evidence Reinterpreted.* Oxford, 1994. A densely written but important book offering a powerful scholarly critique of the concept of feudalism.

Mark Whittow. *The Making of Byzantium, 600–1025.* Berkeley, 1996. Emphasizes relations between Byzantium and neighboring societies.

State of the World
Revived Networks and New Cultural Zones

The establishment of classical societies was a remarkable feat of political and social organization. For about a millennium, a series of large, centralized imperial states dominated the temperate and subtropical zones of Eurasia and north Africa—by far the most densely populated part of the world at the time. The classical societies were fertile incubators of cultural and religious traditions, and they drove trade, missionary activity, and cross-cultural interaction throughout much of the eastern hemisphere.

When the classical societies declined and (mostly) collapsed, it was by no means certain that a network of interaction embracing much of the eastern hemisphere would survive. The reorganization of states and societies might well have taken place on a local or regional basis. Similarly, social and economic activity might have integrated compact territories rather than large empires. Cultural and religious leaders might have focused on the needs and interests of their own societies rather than dispatching missionaries to seek converts in distant lands. Indeed, Chinese, Indian, and western European societies reorganized themselves, at least temporarily, on smaller scales than in classical times.

Over the longer term, however, large-scale political and social organization returned to the eastern hemisphere, and by the year 1000 it served as a framework for even more intense and more widespread cross-cultural interaction than in earlier times. Three societies were particularly important for this development: the Byzantine empire in the eastern Mediterranean region, the Abbasid empire in southwestern Asia, and the revived Chinese empire under the Tang and Song dynasties. Those three societies generated so much economic production and so much demand for foreign products that they fueled hemispheric trade for half a millennium. They contributed to revival of the overland silk roads linking the most densely populated parts of Eurasia from the Mediterranean region through Muslim lands and India to China. Moreover, they sponsored the creation of an elaborate maritime network of sea lanes linking lands in all parts of the Indian Ocean basin.

The reconstitution of large-scale societies and extensive trading networks had dramatic cultural implications. During the half-millennium from 500 to 1000 C.E., advocates of Buddhism, Christianity, and Islam introduced writing and formal education to regions that had never seen them before. The three religious traditions themselves emerged as the dominant sources of cultural and moral inspiration in vast cultural zones embracing most of Eurasia and north Africa. Indeed, Islam began to influence cultural and religious life in sub-Saharan Africa as well. By the year 1000 the postclassical societies had spread their cultural traditions far more extensively than their classical predecessors, and they had laid the foundations for the long-term influence of Buddhism, Christianity, and Islam throughout most of the eastern hemisphere.

Kingdom of the
Angles and Saxons

Kingdom of the Franks

Kingdom of the Visigoths

Umayyad dynasty
Abbasid dynasty

Silla dynasty

Nara period
Heian period
Kamakura period
Muromachi period

Sui dynasty
Tang dynasty
Song dynasty

Sasanid empire
Byzantine empire

Harsha's kingdom
Chola kingdom
Sultanate of Delhi
Vijayanagar kingdom

Funan kingdom
Srivijaya kingdom
Angkor kingdom

Singosari kingdom
Majapahit kingdom

500 C.E.	600 C.E.	700 C.E.	800 C.E.	900 C.E.	1000 C.E.	1100 C.E.	1200 C.E.	1300 C.E.	1400 C.E.	1500 C.E.	1600 C.E.

EAST ASIA

China: Sui dynasty, 589–618 C.E.
China: Tang dynasty, 618–907 C.E.
Korea: Silla dynasty, 669–935 C.E.

China: Song dynasty, 960–1279 C.E.

Japan: Nara period, 710–794 C.E.; Heian period, 794–1185 C.E.; Kamakura period, 1185–1333 C.E.;
Muromachi period, 1336–1573 C.E.

India: Harsha's kingdom, 606–648 C.E.; Chola kingdom, 850–1267 C.E.; Sultanate of Delhi, 1206–1526 C.E.;
Vijayanagar kingdom, ca. 1350–1565 C.E.

Funan kingdom, ca. 100 C.E.–ca. 599 C.E.; Srivijaya kingdom, 670–1025 C.E.;
Angkor kingdom, 889–1431 C.E.; Singosari kingdom, 1222–1292 C.E.; Majapahit kingdom, 1293–1520 C.E.

SOUTHEAST ASIA

Sasanid empire, 224–641 C.E.; Byzantine empire, 5th–15th century C.E.

**EUROPE &
SOUTHWEST ASIA**

Kingdoms of the Visigoths (ca. 470–early 8th century), Franks (late 5th century–
early 8th century), and Angles and Saxons (5th century–mid-11th century)

AFRICA

Southwest Asia & northern Africa: Umayyad dynasty, 661–750 C.E.; Abbasid dynasty, 750–1258 C.E.

part4

THE ACCELERATION OF CROSS-CULTURAL INTERACTION, 1000 TO 1500 C.E.

The half millennium from 1000 to 1500 C.E. differed markedly from earlier eras. During classical and post-classical times, large, regional societies situated in China, India, southwest Asia, and the Mediterranean basin dominated the eastern hemisphere. Peoples of these lands built extensive networks of trade and communication that spanned the eastern hemisphere and influenced the development of all its societies. From 1000 to 1500 C.E., however, nomadic Turkish and Mongol peoples overran settled societies and established vast transregional empires from China to eastern Europe.

Nomadic peoples toppled several postclassical states, most notably the Song empire in China and the Abbasid realm in southwest Asia. By building empires that transcended the boundaries of postclassical states, however, nomadic Turks and Mongols laid a political foundation for sharply increased trade and communication between peoples of different societies and cultural regions. Indeed, their empires prompted the peoples of the eastern hemisphere to forge closer links than ever before in history. By the mid-fourteenth century, merchants, diplomats, and missionaries traveled frequently between lands as far removed as Italy and China.

Increased trade in the Indian Ocean basin also promoted more intense cross-cultural communications. Maritime trade built on the political stability, economic expansion, and demographic growth of the postclassical era. By the fourteenth century, mariners called at ports throughout the Indian Ocean basin from southeast Asia to India, Ceylon, Arabia, and east Africa, while sea lanes through the South China Sea offered access to ports in the islands of southeast Asia, China, Japan, and Korea. Commercial goods traveled over the Indian Ocean in larger quantities than ever before. From the eleventh century forward, cargoes increasingly consisted of bulky commodities such as timber, coral, steel, building materials, grains, dates, and other foodstuffs. This trade in bulk goods indicated a movement toward economic integration as societies of the Indian Ocean basin concentrated increasingly on cultivating crops or producing goods for export while importing foods or goods that they could not produce very well themselves.

Demographic growth, increased agricultural production, and economic expansion helped to underwrite rapid political development in sub-Saharan Africa and western Europe. Powerful regional states and centralized empires emerged in west Africa and central Africa while a series of wealthy city-states dominated the east African coast. In western Europe the decentralized states of the early middle ages evolved into more tightly centralized regional states. Rulers in several of these states were able to organize networks of military retainers and political supporters who strengthened the claims of central authorities against local challengers. Increasing volumes of trade favored this movement toward centralization in sub-Saharan Africa and western Europe, since taxes levied on trade helped to finance the professional bureaucrats and armed forces that centralized states required.

Although they did not participate in the demographic and economic expansion of the eastern hemisphere, the indigenous peoples of the Americas and Oceania also built larger and more centralized societies from 1000 to 1500 C.E. Centralized empires appeared in Mesoamerica and Andean South America while agricultural societies emerged in several regions of North America. Even in the absence of large domesticated animals, trade networks linked peoples as far distant as Mexico and the Great Lakes region. Pacific island societies also moved toward tighter political organization. Because they lived on small land bases distributed irregularly throughout a vast ocean, Pacific islanders had no realistic possibility of building large imperial states. Within their own agricultural and fishing societies, however, they established tightly centralized kingdoms that organized public affairs and sponsored distinctive cultural traditions.

During the fourteenth and fifteenth centuries C.E., much of the eastern hemisphere experienced difficulties not only because of warfare arising from the conquests of nomadic peoples but also because of epidemic bubonic plague and global climatic changes that brought cooler temperatures. In building their transregional empires, nomadic peoples sometimes devastated the lands that they conquered, throwing societies and economies into turmoil. While facilitating trade and travel, nomadic empires also made it possible for diseases to spread rapidly over long distances, and during the fourteenth century, epidemic bubonic plague became a hemispheric phenomenon. Meanwhile, cooler weather resulted in lower agricultural yields in many lands, and in some far northern lands, it made agriculture impractical. Together with military destruction and pandemic plague, reduced agricultural production led to political, social, and economic problems throughout much of the eastern hemisphere.

Nevertheless, by the mid-fifteenth century, peoples from China to western Europe were recovering from those difficulties and rebuilding prosperous societies. In their own quest for prosperity, western European peoples unwittingly laid the foundations of a new era in world history. While searching for sea routes to Asian markets, European mariners happened upon the continents of North and South America. They soon ventured into the Pacific Ocean, where they found their way to Australia and the Pacific islands. Their voyages brought the world's various peoples for the first time into permanent and sustained communication with one another, and their interactions triggered a series of consequences that profoundly influenced modern world history. The European voyages that gave rise to this interdependent and interconnected world took place precisely because of the movement toward increasing interaction in the eastern hemisphere during the centuries following 1000 C.E. The period from 1000 to 1500 C.E. set the stage for the modern era of world history.

Nomadic Empires and Eurasian Integration

chapter 17

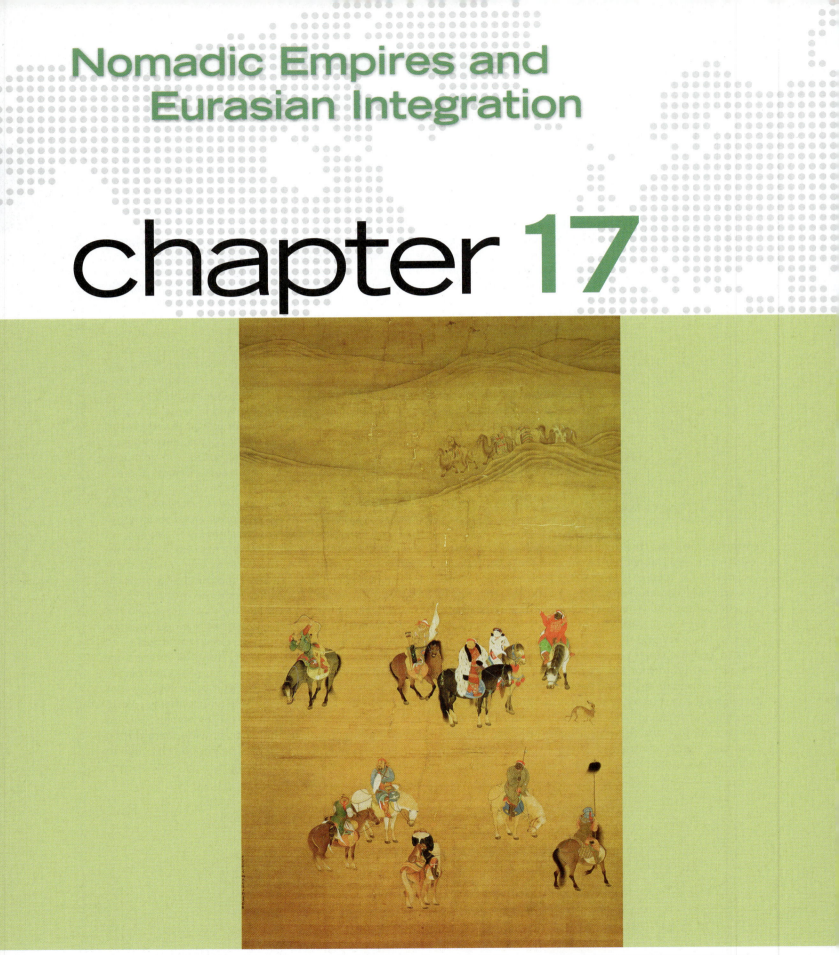

An elegant painting on silk by the thirteenth-century painter Liu Guandao depicts the Mongol emperor Khubilai Khan (center, in Chinese silks under Mongolian furs) with a hunting party bearing Mongolian bows, arrows, and satchels.

EYEWITNESS:
The Goldsmith of the Mongolian Steppe

Guillaume Boucher was a goldsmith who lived during the early and middle decades of the thirteenth century. At some point, perhaps during the 1230s, he left his native Paris and went to Budapest, which was then a part of the kingdom of Hungary. There he was captured by Mongol warriors campaigning in Hungary. The Mongols noticed and appreciated Boucher's talents, and when they left Hungary in 1242, they took him along with other skilled captives to their central Asian homeland.

For at least the next fifteen years, Boucher lived at the Mongol capital at Karakorum. Though technically a slave, he enjoyed some prestige. He supervised fifty assistants in a workshop that produced decorative objects of gold and silver for the Mongol court. His most ingenious creation was a spectacular silver fountain in the form of a tree. Four pipes, concealed by the tree's trunk, carried wines and other intoxicating drinks to the top of the tree and then dispensed them into silver bowls from which courtiers and guests filled their cups. Apart from his famous fountain, Boucher also produced statues in gold and silver, built carriages, designed buildings, and even sewed ritual garments for Roman Catholic priests who conducted services for Christians living at Karakorum and sought converts in the Mongol empire.

Boucher was by no means the only European living at the Mongol court. His wife was a woman of French ancestry whom Boucher had met and married in Hungary. The Flemish missionary William of Rubruck visited Karakorum in 1254, and during his sojourn there he encountered a Frenchwoman named Paquette who was an attendant to a Mongol princess, an artisan from Russia (Paquette's husband), an unnamed nephew of a French bishop, a Greek soldier, and an Englishman named Basil. Other European visitors to the Mongol court found Germans, Slavs, and Hungarians as well as Chinese, Koreans, Turks, Persians, and Armenians, among others. Many thirteenth-century roads led to Karakorum.

Nomadic peoples had made their influence felt throughout much of Eurasia as early as classical times. The Xiongnu confederation dominated central Asia and posed a formidable threat to the Han dynasty in China from the third to the first century B.C.E. During the second

MAP 18.1

Kingdoms, empires, and city-states of sub-Saharan Africa, 800–1500 C.E.

After the emergence of Islam, trans-Saharan overland routes linked sub-Saharan west Africa with the Mediterranean region, and maritime trade routes linked sub-Saharan east Africa to the Indian Ocean basin.

What role did trade play in the emergence of cities and states in sub-Saharan Africa?

of stone and more than a dozen mosques. Koumbi-Saleh's wealth also supported a large number of *qadis* and Muslim scholars. From taxes levied on trade passing through Ghana, the kings financed a large army—al-Bakri reported that they could field two hundred thousand warriors—that protected the sources of gold, maintained order in the kingdom, kept allied and tributary states in line, and defended Ghana against nomadic incursions from the Sahara.

Islam in West Africa By about the tenth century, the kings of Ghana had converted to Islam. Their conversion led to improved relations with Muslim merchants from north Africa as well as Muslim nomads from the desert who

transported trade goods across the Sahara. It also brought them recognition and support from Muslim states in north Africa. The kings of Ghana made no attempt to impose Islam forcibly on their society—unlike the neighboring kings of Takrur, who zealously campaigned for the conversion of their entire kingdom—nor did they accept Islam exclusively even for their own purposes. Instead, they continued to observe traditional religious customs: al-Bakri mentioned, for example, that native religious specialists practiced magic and kept idols in the woods surrounding the royal palace at Koumbi-Saleh. Even in the absence of efforts to impose Islam on Ghana, however, the faith attracted converts, particularly among those engaged in trade with Muslim merchants from the north.

As the kingdom expanded to the north, it became vulnerable to attacks by nomadic peoples from the Sahara who sought to seize some of the kingdom's wealth. During the early thirteenth century, raids from the desert weakened the kingdom, and it soon collapsed. Several successor states took over portions of Ghana's territory, but political leadership in west Africa fell to the powerful Mali empire, which emerged just as the kingdom of Ghana dissolved.

Sundiata The lion prince Sundiata (reigned 1230–1255) built the Mali empire during the first half of the thirteenth century after his return from exile. While away from home, he made astute alliances with local rulers, gained a reputation for courage in battle, and assembled a large army dominated by cavalry. By about 1235 he had consolidated his hold on the Mali empire, which expanded to include Ghana as well as other neighboring kingdoms in the regions surrounding the Senegal and Niger rivers. The empire included most of the modern state of Mali and extended also to lands now known as Mauritania, Senegal, Gambia, Guinea-Bissau, Guinea, and Sierra Leone.

This west African terra-cotta sculpture from the thirteenth or fourteenth century depicts a helmeted and armored warrior astride a horse with elaborate harness and head protection.

The Mali Empire and Trade

Mali benefited from trans-Saharan trade on an even larger scale than Ghana did. From the thirteenth until the late fifteenth century, Mali controlled and taxed almost all trade passing through west Africa. Enormous caravans with as many as twenty-five thousand camels linked Mali to north Africa. The capital city of Niani attracted merchants seeking to enter the gold trade, and market cities on the caravan routes such as Timbuktu, Gao, and Jenne became prosperous centers featuring buildings of brick and stone. Like the later kings of Ghana, the rulers of Mali honored Islam and provided protection, lodging, and comforts for Muslim merchants from the north. Although they did not force Islam on their realm, they encouraged its spread on a voluntary basis.

Mansa Musa The significance of trade and Islam for west Africa became clearest during the reign of Sundiata's grand-nephew Mansa Musa, who ruled Mali from 1312 to 1337, during the high point of the empire. Mansa Musa observed Islamic tradition by making his pilgrimage to Mecca in 1324–1325. His party formed a gargantuan caravan that included thousands of soldiers,

Mansa Musa enjoyed a widespread reputation as the wealthiest king in the world. On this map, prepared in 1375 by a cartographer from the Mediterranean island of Majorca, Mansa Musa holds a gold nugget about the size of a grapefruit. What does this illustration reveal about the image of west Africa in the Mediterranean world?

The Increasing Influence of Europe

chapter 19

Cloth merchants cut and sew woolen fabrics in a town market while customers shop.

PART

EYEWITNESS:
From Venice to China and Back

In 1260 C.E. two brothers, Niccolò and Maffeo Polo, traveled from their native Venice to Constantinople. The Polo brothers were jewel merchants, and while in Constantinople, they decided to pursue opportunities farther east. They went first to Soldaia (modern Sudak), near Caffa on the Black Sea, and then to the trading cities of Sarai and Bulghar on the Volga River. At that point they might have returned home except that a war broke out behind them and prevented them from retracing their steps, so they joined a caravan and continued east. They spent three years in the great central Asian trading city of Bokhara, where they received an invitation to join a diplomatic embassy going to the court of Khubilai Khan. They readily agreed and traveled by caravan to the Mongol court, where the great khan received them and inquired about their land, rulers, and religion.

Khubilai was especially interested in learning more about Roman Catholic Christianity, most likely because he ruled a multicultural empire and wished to maintain harmony among the cultural and religious groups inhabiting his realm. Thus he asked the Polo brothers to return to Europe and request the pope to send learned theologians who could serve as authoritative sources of information on Christian doctrine. They accepted the mission and returned to Italy in 1269 as envoys of the great khan.

The Polo brothers were not able to satisfy the great khan's desire for expertise in Christian doctrine. The pope designated two missionaries to accompany the Polos, and the party set out in 1271, together with Niccolò's seventeen-year-old son, Marco Polo. Soon, however, the missionaries became alarmed at fighting along the route, and they decided to abandon the embassy and return to Europe. Thus only the Polos completed the journey, arriving at the Mongol court of Shangdu in 1274. Although they presented Khubilai with presents and letters from the pope rather than the requested missionaries, the great khan received them warmly and welcomed them to his court. In fact, they remained in China in the service of the great khan for the next seventeen years. Their mission gave rise to Marco Polo's celebrated account of his travels, and it signaled the reintegration of Europe into the political and economic affairs of the larger eastern hemisphere.

During the early middle ages, western Europe was a violent and disorderly land. The collapse of the western Roman empire and invasions by migratory peoples wrecked European society and economy. The Carolingian empire provided order only for a short time before a new series of invasions brought it down. As a result of the turmoil and disarray that plagued Europe during the half millennium from 500 to 1000 C.E., western Europeans played little role in the development of a hemispheric economy during the era dominated by the Tang, Song, Abbasid, and Byzantine empires.

During the early middle ages, however, Europeans laid the foundations of a more dynamic society. Regional states became the basis for a stable political order. New tools and technologies led to increased agricultural production and economic growth. The missionary efforts of the western Christian church brought cultural and religious unity to most of Europe. During the "high middle ages" of European history—the period from about 1000 to 1300 C.E.—European peoples built a vibrant and powerful society on the political, economic, and cultural foundations laid during the early middle ages.

Although the idea of empire continued to fascinate political thinkers and leaders, empire builders of the high middle ages did not manage to bring all of Europe under their control. Instead, local rulers organized powerful regional states. Increased agricultural production fueled rapid population growth. Economic expansion led to increased long-distance trade, enriched cities, and supported the establishment of new towns. Cultural and religious affairs also reflected the dynamism of the high middle ages, as European philosophers and theologians reconsidered traditional doctrines in light of fresh knowledge.

Political organization, demographic increase, and economic growth pushed Europeans once again into the larger world. European merchants began to participate directly in the commercial economy of the eastern hemisphere, sometimes traveling as far as China in search of luxury goods. Ambitious military and political leaders expanded the boundaries of Christendom by seizing Muslim-held territories in Spain and the Mediterranean islands. European forces even mounted a series of military crusades that sought to bring Islamic lands of the eastern Mediterranean basin under Christian control. They ultimately failed, but the crusades clearly demonstrated that Europeans were beginning to play a much larger role in the world than they had for the previous half millennium.

THE REGIONAL STATES OF MEDIEVAL EUROPE

Long after its disappearance the Roman empire inspired European philosophers, theologians, and rulers, who dreamed of a centralized political structure embracing all of Christian Europe. The Byzantine empire survived as the dominant power in the eastern Mediterranean region, where it flourished through the early eleventh century. By 1100 C.E., however, Byzantium experienced domestic social and economic difficulties as well as foreign pressure from both east and west. Even as Byzantium influenced the emergence of new states in Russia and eastern Europe, the empire itself gradually declined and in 1453 fell to Muslim Turkish invaders. As Byzantium weakened, western Europe underwent an impressive round of state building. Beginning in the late tenth century, German princes formed the so-called Holy Roman Empire, which they viewed as a Christian revival of the earlier Roman empire. Meanwhile, independent monarchies emerged in France and England, and other authorities ruled in the various regions of Italy and Spain. Thus medieval Europe was a political mosaic of independent and competing regional states.

The Late Byzantine Empire

Social and Economic Problems For about three centuries, the *theme* system (discussed in chapter 16) served the Byzantine empire well by supporting both a powerful army and a prosperous independent peasantry. About the eleventh century, however, wealthy landowners increasingly undermined the *theme* system by acquiring the properties of independent peasants and accumulating them into large estates. That development transformed formerly free peasants into a class of dependent agricultural laborers while reducing incentives for individuals to serve in Byzantine military forces. It also led to diminished tax receipts for the central government.

Challenges from the West As domestic problems mounted, Byzantium also faced fresh foreign challenges. From the west came representatives of a dynamic western Europe, where rapid economic development supported a round of military and political expansion. During the early eleventh century, Norman adventurers—descendants of Vikings who had settled on the Norman peninsula in northern France—carved out a regional state in southern Italy and expelled the last Byzantine authorities there. During

MAP 19.1

The regional states of medieval Europe, 1000–1300 C.E.
Note the large number of states and the different kinds of states that claimed sovereignty in medieval Europe.

How did the invasions of the ninth and tenth centuries (depicted on Map 16.3) influence the political development of medieval Europe?

the twelfth and thirteenth centuries, the Normans and other western European peoples mounted a series of crusades—vast military campaigns intended to recapture Jerusalem and other sites holy to Christians from Muslim rule—and took the opportunity to plunder the Byzantine empire. Venetian merchants even managed to hijack the fourth crusade (1202–1204 C.E.) from its original mission in the eastern Mediterranean and target Constantinople instead. Venetians had become prominent in the commercial life of the eastern Mediterranean, and they viewed the fourth crusade as an opportunity to strengthen their position against Byzantine competition. In 1204 the crusaders conquered Constantinople and subjected it to a devastating sack. Byzantine forces recaptured the city in 1261, but the humiliating destruction of the imperial capital dealt the empire a blow from which it never completely recovered.

Challenges from the East As Europeans advanced from the west, nomadic Turkish peoples invaded from the east. Most important among them were the Muslim Saljuqs, who beginning in the eleventh century sent waves of invaders into Anatolia, the agricultural heartland of the Byzantine empire. Given the military and financial problems of Byzantium, the Saljuqs found Anatolia ripe for plunder. In 1071 they handed the Byzantine army a demoralizing defeat at the battle of Manzikert. Byzantine forces then turned on each other in civil war, allowing the Saljuqs almost free rein in Anatolia. By the late twelfth century, the Saljuqs had seized much of Anatolia, while crusaders from western Europe held most of the remainder.

The loss of Anatolia sealed the fate of the Byzantine empire. A territorially truncated Byzantium survived until the mid-fifteenth century, but it enjoyed little autonomy and faced a series of challenges from Italian merchants, western European adventurers, and Turkish invaders. In 1453, following

During the sack of Constantinople in 1204, crusading forces seized and carted away Byzantine treasures of all sorts—including the great bronze horses that now stand over the entrance to St. Mark's basilica in Venice.

a long era of decline, the Byzantine empire came to an end when Ottoman Turks captured Constantinople and absorbed Byzantium's last remaining territories into their expanding realm.

The Holy Roman Empire

Otto I As the Carolingian empire faded during the ninth century, counts, dukes, and other local authorities took responsibility for providing order in their own regions. Gradually, some of them extended their influence beyond their own jurisdictions and built larger states. Otto of Saxony was particularly aggressive. By the mid-tenth century, he had established himself as king in northern Germany. He cam-

paigned east of the Elbe River in lands populated by Slavic peoples (in what is now eastern Germany, western Poland, and the Czech Republic), and twice he ventured into Italy to quell political disturbances, protect the church, and seek opportunities in the south. In appreciation for his aid to the church, Pope John XII proclaimed Otto emperor in 962 C.E. Thus was born the Holy Roman Empire.

The imperial title had considerable cachet, and on several occasions energetic emperors almost transformed the Holy Roman Empire into a hegemonic state that might have reintroduced imperial unity to Europe. Conflict with the papacy, however, prevented the emperors from building a strong and dynamic state. Although the popes crowned the medieval emperors, their relations were usually tense, since both popes and emperors made large claims to authority in Christian Europe. Relations became especially strained when emperors sought to influence the selection of church officials, which the popes regarded as their own prerogative, or when emperors sought to extend their authority into Italy, where the popes had long provided political leadership.

Investiture Contest

Neither the popes nor the emperors were strong enough to dominate the other, but the popes were able to prevent the emperors from building a powerful imperial state that would threaten the papacy as Europe's principal spiritual authority. The capacity of the papacy to weaken the empire became apparent during the Investiture Contest, a controversy over the appointment of church officials in the late eleventh and early twelfth centuries. From the earliest days of the Holy Roman Empire, imperial authorities had named important church officials to their positions, since the higher clergy provided political as well as religious services. In an effort to regain control of the clergy and ensure that church officials met appropriate spiritual criteria, Pope Gregory VII (1073–1085 C.E.) ordered an end to the practice of lay investiture—the selection and installation of church officials by lay rulers such as the emperors. When Emperor Henry IV (1056–1106 C.E.) challenged the pope's policy, Gregory excommunicated him and released his subjects from their duty to obey him. The German princes then took the opportunity to rebel against the emperor. Henry eventually regained control of the empire but only after beseeching Gregory's mercy while standing barefoot in the snow. Because of the pope's intervention in imperial affairs, however, the German princes won concessions that enhanced their independence and diminished the emperor's authority.

Frederick Barbarossa

Popes and emperors clashed over their conflicting interests in Italy as well as over the appointment of church officials. Among the most vigorous of the medieval emperors was Frederick I, known as Frederick Barbarossa—"the red beard"—a vigorous and gallant man who reigned from 1152 to 1190 C.E. Working from his ancestral lands in southern Germany, Barbarossa sought to absorb the wealthy and increasingly urban region of Lombardy in northern Italy. Integration of Lombardy with his German holdings might have provided Barbarossa with the resources to control the German princes, build a powerful state, and dominate much of Europe. That prospect did not appeal to the popes, who marshaled support from other European states on behalf of the Italian cities. By the end of Barbarossa's reign, the papal coalition had forced the emperor to relinquish his rights in Lombardy. Once again, papal policies forestalled the transformation of the Holy Roman Empire into a powerful state.

Voltaire, the eighteenth-century French writer, once quipped that the Holy Roman Empire was "neither holy, nor Roman, nor an empire." Indeed, the Holy Roman Empire was an empire principally in name. In reality, it was a

King Louis IX (reigned 1226–1270), also known as St. Louis, helped to consolidate the Capetian hold on the French monarchy. In this fourteenth-century manuscript illustration, he hears the petitions of humble subjects (right), while hanged criminals (left) serve as a reminder of felony's results.

The Bayeux tapestry, a magnificent mural of woven linen about 70 meters (230 feet) long, depicts the Norman invasion and conquest of England in 1066. In this section Norman warriors sail across the English Channel and disembark in southern England.

regional state ruling Germany, though it also wielded influence intermittently in eastern Europe and Italy. In no sense, however, did the Holy Roman Empire restore imperial unity to western Europe.

Regional Monarchies in France and England

In the absence of an effective imperial power, regional states emerged throughout medieval Europe. In France and England, princes established regional monarchies on the basis of relationships between lords and their retainers.

Capetian France The French monarchy grew slowly from humble beginnings. When the last of the Carolingians died, in 987 C.E., the lords of France elected a minor noble named Hugh Capet to serve as king. Capet held only a small territory around Paris, and he was in no position to challenge his retainers, some of whom were far more powerful than the king himself. During the next three centuries, however, his descendants, known as the Capetian kings, gradually added to their resources and expanded their political influence. Relying on relationships between lords and retainers, they absorbed the territories of retainers who died without heirs and established the right to administer justice throughout the realm. By the early fourteenth century, the Capetian kings had gradually centralized power and authority in France.

The Normans The English monarchy developed quite differently. Its founders were the Normans. Though nom-

inally subject to Carolingian and later to Capetian rulers, the dukes of Normandy in fact pursued their own interests with little regard for their lords. Within Normandy the dukes built a tightly centralized state in which all authority stemmed from the dukes themselves. The dukes also retained title to all land in Normandy, and in an effort to forestall conflicts of interest they strictly limited the right of their retainers to grant land to others. By the late tenth century, Norman lords had built a series of castles from which disciplined armies dominated their territories, and in the eleventh century they emerged as prominent political and military leaders throughout Europe and beyond to much of the Mediterranean basin as well.

Norman England In 1066 Duke William of Normandy invaded England, then ruled by descendants of the Angles, the Saxons, and other Germanic peoples who had migrated there during the fifth and sixth centuries. Following a speedy military victory, the duke, now known as William the Conqueror, introduced Norman principles of government and land tenure to England. While retaining many institutions of their Anglo-Saxon predecessors, the Norman kings of England ruled over a much more tightly centralized realm than did the Capetian kings of France.

Both the Capetians and the Normans faced challenges from retainers seeking to pursue independent policies or enlarge their powers at the expense of the monarchs. Both dynasties also faced external challenges: indeed, they often battled each other, since the Normans periodically sought to expand their possessions in France. On the basis of relationships between lords and retainers, however, both the Capetians and the Normans managed to organize regional monarchies that maintained order and provided reasonably good government.

Regional States in Italy and Iberia

Church Influence in Italy

Regional states emerged also in other lands of medieval Europe, though not on such a large scale as the monarchies of France and England. In Italy, for example, no single regime controlled the entire peninsula. Rather, a series of ecclesiastical states, city-states, and principalities competed for power and position. In central Italy the popes had provided political leadership since the Carolingian era. Indeed, although the papacy was a spiritual rather than a political post, the popes ruled a good-sized territory in central Italy known as the Papal State. In northern Italy, too, the church influenced political affairs, since bishops of the major cities took much of the initiative in organizing public life in their regions. During the high middle ages, however, as the cities grew wealthy from trade and manufacturing, lay classes challenged the bishops and eventually displaced them as ruling authorities.

Italian States

By about the twelfth century, a series of prosperous city-states—including Florence, Bologna, Genoa, Milan, and Venice—dominated not only their own urban districts but also the surrounding hinterlands. Meanwhile, in southern Italy, Norman adventurers—cousins of those who conquered Anglo-Saxon England—invaded territories still claimed by the Byzantine empire and various Muslim states. Norman adventurers first intervened in Italian affairs in the year 999, when a group of Norman pilgrims aided the people of Salerno as they fought off an attack by Muslim raiders. Other Normans later aided the city of Bari in its struggle for independence from Byzantine authority (1017–1018). When they learned that opportunities might be available for ambitious adventurers in an unstable region, Norman mercenar-

ies soon made their way to southern Italy in large numbers. With papal approval and support, they overcame Byzantine and Muslim authorities, brought southern Italy into the orbit of Roman Catholic Christianity, and laid the foundations for the emergence of the powerful kingdom of Naples.

Christian and Muslim States in Iberia

As in Italy, a series of regional states competed for power in the Iberian peninsula. From the eighth to the eleventh century, a series of Muslim states ruled most of the peninsula. Only in northern Spain did small Christian states hold sway, mostly in mountainous regions. Beginning in the mid-eleventh century, though, Christian adventurers from those states began to attack Muslim territories and enlarge their own domains. As in southern Italy, political and military instability attracted the attention of Norman adventurers, many of whom traveled to Spain and joined the armies of the Christian kingdoms as soldiers of fortune. By the late thirteenth century, the Christian kingdoms of Castile, Aragon, and Portugal controlled most of the Iberian peninsula, leaving only the small kingdom of Granada in Muslim hands.

With its Byzantine empire, Holy Roman Empire, regional monarchies, ecclesiastical principalities, city-states, and new states founded on conquest, medieval Europe might seem to present a chaotic and confusing political spectacle, particularly when compared with a land such as China, reunified by centralized imperial rule. Moreover, European rulers rarely

The Italian city-state of Florence grew rapidly during the high middle ages. This portrait of the city concentrates on the space enclosed by walls completed in the early fourteenth century.

FIORENZA

sought to maintain the current state of affairs but, rather, campaigned constantly to enlarge their holdings at the expense of their neighbors. As a result, the political history of medieval Europe was a complicated affair. Yet the regional states of the high middle ages effectively tended to public affairs in limited regions. In doing so, they fashioned alternatives to a centralized empire as a form of political organization.

ECONOMIC GROWTH AND SOCIAL DEVELOPMENT

As regional states provided increasingly effective political organization, medieval Europe experienced dramatic economic growth and social development. The economic revival closely resembled the processes that in an earlier era had strengthened China, India, and the Islamic world. Increased agricultural production, urbanization, manufacturing, and trade transformed Europe into a powerful society and drew it once again into commercial relationships with distant lands.

Growth of the Agricultural Economy

As in China, India, and the Islamic world during the early postclassical era, a dramatic increase in agricultural yields was the foundation of economic growth and social development in medieval Europe. Several developments help to account for this increased agricultural production: the opening of new lands to cultivation, improved agricultural techniques, the use of new tools and technologies, and the introduction of new crops.

Expansion of Arable Land Beginning in the late tenth century, as local lords pacified their territories and put an end to invasions, Europe began to experience population pressure. In response serfs and monks cleared forests, drained swamps, and increased the amount of land devoted to agriculture. At first, some lords opposed those efforts, since they reduced the amount of land available for game preserves, where nobles enjoyed hunting wild animals. Gradually, however, the lords realized that expanding agricultural production would yield higher taxes and increase their own wealth. By the early twelfth century, lords were encouraging the expansion of cultivation, and the process gathered momentum.

Improved Agricultural Techniques Meanwhile, reliance on improved methods of cultivation and better agricultural technology led to significantly higher productivity. During the high middle ages, European cultivators refined and improved their techniques in the interests of larger yields. They experimented with new crops and with different cycles of crop rotation to ensure the most abundant harvests possible without compromising the fertility of the soil. They increased cultivation especially of beans, which

not only provided dietary protein but also enriched the land because of their property of fixing nitrogen in the soils where they grow. They kept more domestic animals, which not only served as beasts of burden and sources of food but also enriched fields with their droppings. They dug ponds in which they raised fish, which provided yet another dietary supplement. By the thirteenth century, observation and experimentation with new crops and new techniques had vastly increased understanding of agricultural affairs. News of those discoveries circulated widely throughout Europe in books and treatises on household economics and agricultural methods. Written in vernacular languages for lay readers, these works helped to publicize innovations, which in turn led to increased agricultural productivity.

New Tools and Technologies During the high middle ages, European peoples expanded their use of water mills and heavy plows, which had appeared during the early middle ages, and also introduced new tools and tech-

"By the early 12th century, lords were encouraging the expansion of cultivation, and the process gathered momentum."

nologies. Two simple items in particular—the horseshoe and the horse collar—made it possible to increase sharply the amount of land that cultivators could work. Horseshoes helped to prevent softened and split hooves on horses that tramped through moist European soils. Horse collars placed the burden of a heavy load on an animal's chest and shoulders rather than its neck and enabled horses to pull heavy plows without choking. Thus Europeans could hitch their plows to horses rather than to slower oxen and bring more land under the plow.

New Crops Expansion of land under cultivation, improved methods of cultivation, and the use of new tools and technologies combined to increase both the quantity and the quality of food supplies. During the early middle ages, the European diet consisted almost entirely of grains and grain products such as gruel and bread. During the centuries from 1000 to 1300, meat, dairy products, fish, vegetables, and legumes such as beans and peas became much more prominent in the European diet, though without displacing grains as staple foods. Spain, Italy, and other Mediterranean lands benefited also from widespread cultivation of crops that had earlier been disseminated through the Islamic world: hard durum wheat, rice, spinach, artichokes, eggplant, lemons, limes, oranges, and melons all became prominent items in Mediterranean diets during the high middle ages.

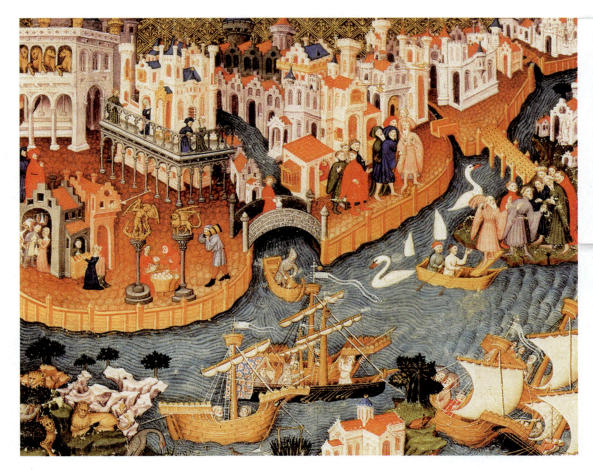

Venice, home of Marco Polo and a legion of merchants, drew enormous prosperity from trade. Street vendors, shopkeepers, and merchant ships figure prominently in this illustration from a fourteenth-century manuscript. How did its geographic location help Venice become a center of Mediterranean trade?

PART 4

Population Growth

As in other lands, increased agricultural productivity supported rapid population growth in medieval Europe. In 800 C.E., during the Carolingian era, European population stood at about twenty-nine million. By 1000, when regional states had ended invasions and restored order, it had edged up to thirty-six million. During the next few centuries, as the agricultural economy expanded, population surged. By 1100 it had reached forty-four million; by 1200 it had risen to fifty-eight million, an increase of more than 30 percent within one century; and by 1300 it had grown an additional 36 percent, to seventy-nine million. During the fourteenth century, epidemic plague severely reduced populations and disrupted economies in Europe as well as Asia and north Africa—a development discussed in chapter 21. Between 1000 and 1300, however, rapid demographic growth helped stimulate a vigorous revival of towns and trade in medieval Europe.

The Revival of Towns and Trade

Urbanization

With abundant supplies of food, European society was able to support large numbers of urban residents—artisans, crafts workers, merchants, and professionals. Attracted by urban opportunities, peasants and serfs from the countryside flocked to established cities and founded new towns at strategically located sites. Cities founded during Roman times, such as Paris, London, and Toledo, became thriving centers of government and business, and new urban centers emerged from Venice in northern Italy to Bergen on the west coast of Norway. Northern Italy and Flanders (the northwestern part of modern Belgium) experienced especially strong urbanization. For the first time since the fall of the western Roman empire, cities began to play a major role in European economic and social development.

Textile Production

The growth of towns and cities brought about increasing specialization of labor, which in turn resulted in a dramatic expansion of manufacturing and trade. Manufacturing concentrated especially on the production of wool textiles. The cities of Italy and Flanders in particular became lively centers for the spinning, weaving, and dyeing of wool. Trade in wool products helped to fuel economic development throughout Europe. By the twelfth century the counts of Champagne in northern France sponsored fairs that operated almost year-round and that served as vast marketplaces where merchants from all parts of Europe compared and exchanged goods.

As trade expanded, Italian merchants established colonies in the major ports and commercial centers of the Mediterranean and the Black Sea. By the thirteenth century, Venetian and Genoese merchants maintained large communities in Constantinople, Alexandria, Cairo, Damascus, and the Black Sea ports of Tana, Caffa, and Trebizond. Caffa was the first destination of the Venetian brothers Niccolò and Maffeo Polo when they embarked on their commercial venture of 1260. Those trading posts enabled them to deal with Muslim merchants engaged in the Indian Ocean and overland trade with India, southeast Asia, and China. By the mid-thirteenth century the Polos and a few other Italian merchants were beginning to venture beyond the eastern Mediterranean region to central Asia, India, and China in search of commercial opportunities.

The Hanseatic League

Although medieval trade was most active in the Mediterranean basin, a lively commerce grew up also in the northern seas. The Baltic Sea and the North Sea were sites of a particularly well-developed trade network known as the Hanseatic League, or more simply as the Hansa—an association of trading cities stretching from Novgorod to London and embracing all the significant commercial centers of Poland, northern Germany, and Scandinavia. The Hansa dominated trade in grain, fish, furs, timber, and pitch from northern Europe. The fairs of Champagne and the Rhine, the Danube, and other major European rivers linked the Hansa trade network with that of the Mediterranean.

Improved Business Techniques

As in postclassical China and the Islamic world, a rapidly increasing volume of trade encouraged the development of credit, banking, and new forms of business organization in Europe. Bankers issued letters of credit to merchants traveling to distant markets, thus freeing them from the risk and inconvenience of carrying cash or bullion. Having arrived at their destinations, merchants exchanged their letters of credit for merchandise or cash in the local currency. In the absence of credit and banking, it would have been impossible for merchants to trade on a large scale.

Meanwhile, merchants devised new ways of spreading and pooling the risks of commercial investments. They entered into partnerships with other merchants, and they limited the liability of partners to the extent of their individual investments. The limitation on individual liability encouraged the formation of commercial partnerships, thus further stimulating the European economy.

Social Change

The Three Estates

Medieval social commentators frequently held that European society embraced three estates or classes: "those who pray, those who fight, and those who work." Those who prayed were clergy of the Roman Catholic church. From lowly parish priests to bishops, cardinals,

Genoese bankers change money and check the accounts of their clients in this fourteenth-century manuscript illustration.

Mediterranean Trade

The revival of urban society was most pronounced in Italy, which was geographically well situated to participate in the trade networks of the Mediterranean basin. During the tenth century the cities of Amalfi and Venice served as ports for merchants engaged in trade with Byzantine and Muslim partners in the eastern Mediterranean. During the next century the commercial networks of the Mediterranean widened to embrace Genoa, Pisa, Naples, and other Italian cities. Italian merchants exchanged salt, olive oil, wine, wool fabrics, leather products, and glass for luxury goods such as gems, spices, silk, and other goods from India, southeast Asia, and China that Muslim merchants brought to eastern Mediterranean markets.

sources from the past

Francesco Balducci Pegolotti on Trade between Europe and China

Francesco Balducci Pegolotti was an employee of a Florentine banking company. He traveled as far as London and Cyprus on bank business. Although he probably did not travel to Asia, Pegolotti learned about conditions that long-distance traders faced from many merchants who ventured far from home. About 1340 Pegolotti compiled their reports into a book of information and advice for merchants traveling to China from the port of Tana (modern Rostov) on the Sea of Azov.

In the first place, you must let your beard grow long and not shave. And at Tana you should furnish yourself with a dragoman [guide and interpreter]. And you must not try to save money in the matter of dragomen by taking a bad one instead of a good one. For the additional wages of the good one will not cost you so much as you will save by having him. And besides the dragoman it will be well to take at least two good men servants who are acquainted with the [Turkish] Cumanian tongue. . . .

The road you travel from Tana to Cathay [China] is perfectly safe, whether by day or by night, according to what the merchants say who have used it. Only if the merchant, in going or coming, should die upon the road, everything belonging to him will become the perquisite of the lord of the country in which he dies, and the officers of the lord will take possession of all. And in like manner if he die in Cathay. But if his brother be with him, or an intimate friend and comrade calling himself his brother, then to him they will surrender the property of the deceased, and so it will be rescued. . . .

Cathay is a province which contains a multitude of cities and towns. Among others there is one in particular, that is to say the capital city, to which is great resort of merchants, and in which there is a vast amount of trade; and this city is called Khanbaliq. And the said city hath a circuit of one hundred miles, and is all full of people and houses and of dwellers in the said city.

You may calculate that a merchant with a dragoman and two men servants and with goods to the value of twenty-five thousand golden florins should spend on his way to Cathay from sixty to eighty ingots of silver, and not more if he manages well; and for all the road back again from Cathay to Tana, including the expenses of living and the pay of servants, and all other charges, the cost will be about five ingots per head of pack animals, or something less. And you may reckon the ingot to be worth five golden florins. . . .

Anyone from Genoa or Venice wishing to go to the places above named and to make the journey to Cathay should carry linens with him, and if he visits Urgench [in modern Uzbekistan] he will dispose of these well. In Urgench he should purchase ingots of silver, and with these he should proceed without making any further investment, unless it be some bales of the very finest stuffs which go in small bulk, and cost no more for carriage than coarser stuffs would do.

Whatever silver the merchants may carry with them as far as Cathay the lord of Cathay will take from them and put into his treasury. And to merchants who thus bring silver they give that paper money of theirs in exchange. This is of yellow paper, stamped with the seal of the lord aforesaid. And this money is called balishi; and with this money you can readily buy silk and all other merchandise that you have a desire to buy. And all the people of the country are bound to receive it. And yet you shall not pay a higher price for your goods because your money is of paper. And of the said paper money there are three kinds, one being worth more than another, according to the value which has been established for each by that lord.

For Further Reflection

■ On the basis of Pegolotti's report, how could you characterize the various commercial, financial, and economic risks faced by European merchants traveling to China and trading there?

Source: Henry Yule and Henri Cordier, eds. *Cathay and the Way Thither,* 2nd ed., 4 vols. London: Hakluyt Society, 1913–16, 3:151–55. (Translation slightly modified.)

and popes, the clergy constituted a spiritual estate owing its loyalty to the church rather than secular rulers. The fighters came from the ranks of nobles. They inherited their positions in society and received an education that concentrated on equestrian skills and military arts. Finally, there were those who worked—the vast majority of the population—who mostly cultivated land as peasants dependent for protection on their lords, those who fought.

The formula dividing society neatly into three classes captures some important truths about medieval Europe. It clearly reflects a society marked by political, social, and economic inequality: although they did not necessarily lead lives of luxury, those who prayed and those who fought enjoyed rights and honors denied to those who worked. Though bound by secular law, for example, clerics were members of an international spiritual society before they

Women were prominent in the markets of medieval Europe and sometimes worked as bankers or tailors, as in this manuscript illustration.

and cities offered fresh opportunities for women as well as for men. In the patriarchal society of medieval Europe, few routes to public authority were open to women, but in the larger towns and cities women worked alongside men as butchers, brewers, bakers, candle makers, fishmongers, shoemakers, gemsmiths, innkeepers, launderers, money changers, merchants, and occasionally physicians and pharmacists. Women dominated some occupations, particularly those involving textiles and decorative arts, such as sewing, spinning, weaving, and the making of hats, wigs, and fur garments.

Most guilds admitted women into their ranks, and some guilds had exclusively female memberships. In thirteenth-century Paris, for example, there were approximately one hundred guilds. Six of them admitted only women, but eighty others included women as well as men among their members. The increasing prominence of women in European society illustrates the significance of towns and cities as agents of social change in medieval Europe.

EUROPEAN CHRISTIANITY DURING THE HIGH MIDDLE AGES

Throughout the middle ages, Christianity guided European thought on religious, moral, and ethical matters—Eastern Orthodox Christianity in the Byzantine empire and Roman Catholic Christianity in western Europe. Representatives of the Orthodox and Roman Catholic churches administered

the rituals associated with birth, marriage, and death. Most of the art, literature, and music of the high middle ages drew inspiration from Christian doctrines and stories. Just as mosques and minarets defined the skylines of Muslim cities, the spires of churches and cathedrals dominated the landscape of medieval Europe, testifying visually to the importance of religion and the pervasive presence of the Eastern Orthodox and Roman Catholic churches.

Schools, Universities, and Scholastic Theology

During the early middle ages, European society was not stable and wealthy enough to support institutions of advanced education. Monasteries sometimes maintained schools that provided a rudimentary education, and political leaders occasionally supported scholars who lived at their courts, but very few schools offered formal education beyond an elementary level. In the absence of a widely observed curriculum or course of study, early medieval scholars drew their inspiration from the Bible and from major spokesmen of the early Christian church such as St. Augustine of Hippo.

Cathedral Schools During the high middle ages, economic development sharply increased the wealth of Europe and made more resources available for education. Meanwhile, an increasingly complex society created a demand for educated individuals who could deal with complicated political, legal, and theological issues. Beginning in the early eleventh century, bishops and archbishops in France and northern Italy organized schools in their cathedrals and invited well-known scholars to serve as master teachers. Schools in the cathedrals of Paris, Chartres, and Bologna in particular attracted students from all parts of Europe.

By the twelfth century the cathedral schools had established formal curricula based on writings in Latin, the official language of the Roman Catholic church. Instruction concentrated on the liberal arts, especially literature and philosophy. Students read the Bible and the writings of the church fathers, such as St. Augustine, St. Jerome, and St. Ambrose, as well as classical Latin literature and the few works of Plato and Aristotle that were available in Latin translation. Some cathedral schools also offered advanced instruction in law, medicine, and theology.

Universities About the mid-twelfth century, students and teachers organized academic guilds and persuaded political authorities to grant charters guaranteeing their rights. Student guilds demanded fair treatment for students from townspeople, who sometimes charged excessive rates for room and board, and called on their teachers to provide rigorous, high-quality instruction. Faculty guilds sought to vest teachers with the right to bestow academic degrees, which served as licenses to teach in other cities, and to control the curriculum in their institutions. These guilds had the effect of

transforming cathedral schools into universities. The first universities were those of Bologna, Paris, and Salerno—noted for instruction in law, theology, and medicine, respectively—but by the late thirteenth century, universities had appeared also in Rome, Naples, Seville, Salamanca, Oxford, Cambridge, and other cities throughout Europe.

The Influence of Aristotle

The evolution of the university coincided with the rediscovery of the works of Aristotle. Western European scholars of the early middle ages knew only a few of Aristotle's minor works that were available in Latin translation. Byzantine scholars knew Aristotle in the original Greek, but they rarely

A manuscript illustration depicts a professor, at top left, lecturing in a medieval German university. About half the students listen and take notes diligently, while the others catch up on their sleep or chat with friends.

had any dealings with their Roman Catholic counterparts. During the high middle ages, as commerce and communication increased between Byzantine Orthodox and Roman Catholic Christians, western Europeans learned about Aristotle's thought and obtained Latin translations from Byzantine philosophers. Western European scholars learned about Aristotle also through Muslim philosophers who appreciated the power of his thought and had most of his works translated into Arabic. Christian and Jewish scholars in Sicily and Spain became aware of those Arabic translations, which they retranslated into Latin. Although the resulting works had their flaws—since they filtered Aristotle's original Greek through both Arabic and Latin—they made Aristotle's thought accessible to Western European scholars.

Scholasticism: St. Thomas Aquinas

During the thirteenth century, understanding of Aristotle's thought and Latin translations of his works spread throughout Europe, and they profoundly influenced almost all branches of thought. The most notable result was the emergence of scholastic theology, which sought to synthesize the beliefs and values of Christianity with the logical rigor of Greek philosophy. The most famous of the scholastic theologians was St. Thomas Aquinas (1225–1274), who spent most of his career teaching at the University of Paris. While holding fervently to his Christian convictions, St. Thomas believed that Aristotle had understood and explained the workings of the world better than any other thinker of any era. St. Thomas saw no contradiction between Aristotle and Christian revelation but, rather, viewed them as complementary authorities: Aristotle provided the most powerful analysis of the world according to human reason and Christianity explained the

world and human life as the results of a divine plan. By combining Aristotle's rational power with the teachings of Christianity, St. Thomas expected to formulate the most truthful and persuasive system of thought possible.

In St. Thomas's view, for example, belief in the existence of God did not depend exclusively on an individual's faith. By drawing on Aristotle, St. Thomas believed, it was possible to prove rationally that God exists. Aristotle himself never recognized a personal deity such as the Jewish and Christian God, but he argued that a conscious agent had set the world in motion. St. Thomas borrowed Aristotle's arguments and identified the conscious agent with the Jewish and Christian God, who outlined his plan for the world in the Hebrew scriptures and the Christian New Testament. Thus, as expressed in the thought of St. Thomas Aquinas, scholastic theology represented the harmonization of Aristotle with Christianity and the synthesis of reason and faith. Like the neo-Confucianism of Zhu Xi or the Islamic philosophy of Ibn Rushd, scholastic theology reinterpreted inherited beliefs in light of the most advanced knowledge of the time.

Popular Religion

St. Thomas and the other scholastic theologians addressed a sophisticated, intellectual elite, not the common people of medieval Europe. The popular masses neither knew nor cared much about Aristotle. For their purposes, Christianity was important primarily as a set of beliefs and rituals that gave meaning to individual lives and that bound them together into coherent communities. Thus formal doctrine and theology did not appeal to popular audiences as much as the ceremonies and observances that involved individuals in the life of a larger community—and that also brought benefits in the form of supernatural aid or protection for an individual's crops or family.

Sacraments

Popular piety generally entailed observance of the sacraments and devotion to the saints recognized by the Roman Catholic church. Sacraments are holy rituals that bring spiritual blessings on the observants. The church recognized seven sacraments, including baptism, matrimony, penance, and the Eucharist. Most important was the Eucharist, during which priests offered a ritual meal commemorating Jesus' last meal with his disciples before his trial and execution by Roman authorities. In addition to preparing individuals for salvation and symbolizing their membership in a holy community, the Eucharist had mundane uses: popular beliefs held that the sacrament would protect individuals from sudden death and advance their worldly interests.

Devotion to Saints

Popular religion also took the form of devotion to the saints. According to church teachings, saints were human beings who had led such exemplary lives that God held them in special esteem. As a result, they enjoyed special influence with heavenly authorities and were able to intervene on behalf of individuals living in the world. Medieval Europeans constantly prayed for saints to look after their spiritual interests and to ensure their admission to heaven. Often, they also invoked the aid of saints who had reputations for helping living people as well as souls of the dead. Tradition held that certain saints could cure diseases, relieve toothaches, and guide sailors through storms to a port.

The Virgin Mary

During the high middle ages, the most popular saint was always the Virgin Mary, mother of Jesus, who personified the Christian ideal of womanhood, love, and sympathy, and who reportedly lavished aid on her devotees. According to a widely circulated story, the Virgin once even spared a criminal from hanging when he called upon her name. During the twelfth and thirteenth centuries, Europeans dedicated hundreds of churches and cathedrals to the Virgin, among them the splendid cathedral of Notre Dame ("Our Lady") of Paris.

Saints' Relics

Medieval Europeans went to great lengths to express their adoration of the Virgin and other saints through veneration of their relics and physical remains, widely believed to retain the powers associated with those holy individuals. Churches assembled vast collections of relics, such as clothes, locks of hair, teeth, and bones of famous saints. Especially esteemed were relics associated with Jesus or the Virgin, such as the crown of thorns that Jesus reportedly wore during his crucifixion or drops of the Virgin's milk miraculously preserved in a vial. The practice of assembling relics clearly opened the door to fraud, but medieval Europeans avidly continued to admire and venerate saints' relics.

Pilgrimage

Some collections of relics became famous well beyond their own regions. Like Muslims making the hajj, pilgrims trekked long distances to honor the saints the relics represented. Throughout the high middle ages, streams of pilgrims visited two European cities in particular—Rome in Italy and Compostela in Spain—and some ventured even farther to Jerusalem and the holy land of Christian origins. Rome was the spiritual center of western Christian society: apart from the popes and the central administration of the Roman Catholic church, the relics of St. Peter and St. Paul, the two most prominent apostles of early Christianity, rested in the churches of Rome. Compostela stood on the very periphery of Christian society, in a remote corner of northwestern Spain. Yet the relics of St. James preserved in the cathedral of Santiago de Compostela exercised a powerful attraction for the pious, who made Compostela the second-most popular pilgrimage destination of medieval Europe. Some devoted pilgrims also visited Jerusalem and the sites associated with the origins of Christianity: spiritual as well as commercial interests called Europeans into the larger world.

The Virgin Mary was a popular subject for devout medieval artists. Here a fourteenth-century stained glass window from the Notre Dame Cathedral in Evreux, France, represents the Virgin holding the infant Jesus in the company of an admirer.

The making of pilgrimages became so common during the high middle ages that a travel industry emerged to serve the needs of pilgrims. Inns dotted the routes leading to popular churches and shrines, and guides shepherded groups of pilgrims to religious sites and explained their significance. There were even guidebooks that pointed out the major attractions along pilgrims' routes and warned them of difficult terrain and unscrupulous scoundrels who took advantage of visitors.

Reform Movements and Popular Heresies

Although veneration of the saints and the making of pilgrimages indicated a deep reservoir of piety, popular religion also reflected the social and economic development of medieval Europe. Particularly in western Europe, as wealth increased, several groups of particularly devout individuals feared that European society was becoming excessively materialistic. Even the Roman Catholic church seemed tainted by materialism. Benedictine monasteries, in which monks originally observed the virtues of poverty, chastity, and obedience, had in many cases become comfortable retreats where privileged individuals led leisurely lives. Meanwhile, the central administration of the Roman church expanded dramatically as lawyers and bureaucrats ran the church's affairs and sought ways to swell its treasury.

Dominicans and Franciscans The devout responded to this state of affairs in several ways. Working within the Roman church, some individuals organized movements designed to champion spiritual over materialistic values. Most prominent of them were St. Dominic (1170–1221) and St. Francis (1182–1226). During the thirteenth century St. Dominic and St. Francis founded orders of mendicants (beggars), known as the Dominican and Franciscan friars, who would have no personal possessions and would have to beg for their food and other needs from audiences to whom they preached. Mendicants were especially active in towns and cities, where they addressed throngs of recently arrived migrants whose numbers were so large that existing urban churches and clergy could not serve them well. The Dominicans and the Franciscans also worked zealously to combat heterodox movements and to persuade heretics to return to the Roman Catholic church.

Popular Heresy Whereas the Dominicans and the Franciscans worked within the church, others rejected the Roman Catholic church altogether and organized alternative religious movements. During the twelfth and thirteenth centuries in particular, several popular movements protested the increasing materialism of European society. The Waldensians, who were most active in southern France and northern Italy, despised the Roman Catholic clergy as

St. Francis of Assisi was the son of a wealthy merchant in central Italy, but he abandoned the comforts that he inherited and pledged himself to a life of poverty and preaching. Stories represented in this fresco from the basilica of St. Francis at Assisi report that he preached to the birds and encouraged them to sing in praise of God.

thinking about TRADITIONS

Prosperity and Its Problems

For three centuries following the year 1000, western Europe enjoyed a general rise in productivity and prosperity. This was an era of bustling towns, expanding trade, the establishment of universities, and the construction of massive cathedrals. Did prosperity bring problems in its wake? Why did Dominicans, Franciscans, and popular heretics criticize medieval European society? To what extent did they offer realistic solutions for the problems they identified?

sources from the past

Thomas of Celano on St. Francis of Assisi

Thomas of Celano was an early disciple of St. Francis. He joined the Franciscan Order about 1215, and in 1228, at the request of Pope Gregory IX, he composed a biography of St. Francis. His account emphasizes the transformation of St. Francis from a spoiled rich brat to a man of deep spirituality who made special efforts to help the poor.

In the city of Assisi, which lies at the edge of the Spoleto valley, there was a man by the name of Francis, who from his earliest years was brought up by his parents proud of spirit, in accordance with the vanity of the world; and imitating their wretched life and habits for a long time, he became even more vain and proud. . . .

These are the wretched circumstances among which the man whom we venerate today as a saint, for he truly is a saint, lived in his youth; and almost up to the twenty-fifth year of his age, he squandered and wasted his time miserably. Indeed, he outdid all his contemporaries in vanities and he came to be a promoter of evil and was more abundantly zealous for all kinds of foolishness. He was the admiration of all and strove to outdo the rest in the pomp of vainglory, in jokes, in strange doings, in idle and useless talk, in songs, in soft and flowing garments, for he was very rich, not however avaricious but prodigal, not a hoarder of money but a squanderer of his possession, a cautious business man but a very unreliable steward. On the other hand, he was a very kindly person, easy and affable, even making himself foolish because of it; for because of these qualities many ran after him, doers of evil and promoters of crime. . . .

[After his conversion] his greatest concern was to be free from everything of this world, lest the serenity of his mind be disturbed even for an hour by the taint of anything that was mere dust. He made himself insensible to all external noise, and bridling his external senses with all his strength and repressing the movements of his nature, he occupied himself with God alone. . . . He therefore frequently chose solitary places so that he could direct his mind completely to God; yet he was not slothful about entering into the affairs of his neighbors, when he saw the time was opportune, and

he willingly took care of things pertaining to their salvation. For his safest haven was prayer; not prayer of a single moment, or idle or presumptuous prayer, but prayer of long duration, full of devotion, serene in humility. If he began late, he would scarcely finish before morning. Walking, sitting, eating, or drinking, he was always intent upon prayer. . . .

The father of the poor, the poor Francis, conforming himself to the poor in all things, was grieved when he saw some one poorer than himself, not because he longed for vainglory, but only from a feeling of compassion. And, though he was content with a tunic that was quite poor and rough, he very frequently longed to divide it with some poor person. But that this very rich poor man, drawn on by a great feeling of affection, might be able to help the poor in some way, he would ask the rich of this world, when the weather was cold, to give him a mantle or some furs. And when, out of devotion, they willingly did what the most blessed father asked of them, he would say to them: "I will accept this from you with the understanding that you do not expect ever to have it back again." And when he met the first poor man, he would clothe him with what he had received with joy and gladness. He bore it very ill if he saw a poor person reproached or if he heard a curse hurled upon any creature by anyone. . . .

For, he was accustomed to say: "Who curses a poor man does an injury to Christ, whose noble image he wears, the image of him who made himself poor for us in this world." Frequently, therefore, when he found the poor burdened down with wood or other things, he offered his own shoulders to help them, though his shoulders were very weak.

For Further Reflection

■ In what ways did St. Francis's life experiences—his dissolute youth and his later concern for the poor—reflect the social and economic conditions of medieval Europe?

Source: Marion A. Habig, ed. *St. Francis of Assisi's Writings and Early Biographies: English Omnibus Sources for the Life of St. Francis.* Chicago: Franciscan Herald Press, 1972, pp. 229–31, 288–92.

---

immoral and corrupt, and they advocated modest and simple lives. They asserted the right of the laity to preach and administer sacraments—functions that the church reserved exclusively for priests—and they did not hesitate to criticize the church on the basis of biblical teachings. Although church authorities declared them heretical, the Waldensians continued to attract enthusiastic participants: a few Waldensians survive even today.

Bogomils and Cathars Some popular heresies flourished in both the Byzantine empire and western Europe. As long-distance trade networks linked Mediterranean lands, alternative religious ideas spread readily throughout the region. Reviving the dualistic views of the ancient Manichaeans, the Bogomils of Bulgaria and Byzantium viewed the world as a site of unrelenting, cosmic struggle between the forces of good and evil. In a quest for purity and spiritual perfection, they despised the material world and adopted an ascetic regime, renouncing wealth, marriage, and material pleasures. Their movement grew rapidly in the late tenth century, and in the eleventh century the Cathars (sometimes called Albigensians) were promoting similar views in southern France and northern Italy. Bogomils and Cathars rejected official churches, which they considered hopelessly corrupt, along with their priests and sacraments.

Both in Byzantium and in western Europe, established authorities took a dim view of these popular movements, which they regarded as threats to cultural stability. Beginning in the late eleventh century, government and church officials teamed up and mounted ruthless campaigns to destroy the Bogomils and the Cathars. By the fourteenth century, Bogomils and Cathars survived in a few remote regions, but their influence was decidedly on the wane.

THE MEDIEVAL EXPANSION OF EUROPE

During the high middle ages, the relationship between western European peoples and their neighbors underwent dramatic change. Powerful states, economic expansion, and demographic growth all strengthened European society, and church officials encouraged the colonization of pagan and Muslim lands as a way to extend the influence of Roman Catholic Christianity. Beginning about the mid-eleventh century, Europeans embarked on expansive ventures on several fronts: Atlantic, Baltic, and Mediterranean. Scandinavian seafarers ventured into the Atlantic Ocean, establishing colonies in Iceland, Greenland, and even for a short time North America. In the Baltic region, Europeans conquered and introduced

MAP 19.3

The medieval expansion of Europe, 1000–1250 C.E.
Compare Map 19.3 with Map 16.3. How can you explain the differences between these two maps?

What does Map 19.3 suggest about the military and organizational capabilities of medieval Europe?

Christianity to Prussia, Livonia, Lithuania, and Finland. In the Mediterranean basin, Europeans recaptured Spain and the Mediterranean islands that Muslims had conquered between the eighth and the tenth centuries. Finally, knights from all over Europe mounted enormous campaigns designed to seize the holy land of Palestine from Muslims and place it under Christian authority. As military ventures, the crusades achieved limited success, since they brought the holy land into Christian hands only temporarily. Nevertheless, the crusades signaled clearly that Europeans were beginning to play a much larger role in the affairs of the eastern hemisphere than they had during the early middle ages.

Atlantic and Baltic Colonization

Vinland
When regional states began to emerge and protect western Europe from Viking raids during the ninth and tenth centuries, Scandinavian seafarers turned their attention to the islands of the North Atlantic Ocean. They occupied Iceland beginning in the late ninth century, and at the end of the tenth century a party led by Eric the Red discovered Greenland and established a small colony there. About 1000 c.e. his son Leif Ericsson led another exploratory party south and west of Greenland, arriving eventually at modern Newfoundland in Canada. There the party found plentiful supplies of fish and timber. Because of the wild grapes growing in the region, Leif called it Vinland. During the years following Leif's voyage, Greenlanders made several efforts to establish permanent colonies in Vinland.

Since the 1960s, archaeologists in northern Newfoundland have uncovered Scandinavian tools and building foundations dating to the early eleventh century. From this evidence and the stories of maritime ventures preserved in Scandinavian sagas, it is clear that the Greenlanders founded a colony in Newfoundland and maintained it for several decades. Ultimately, they left Vinland—or died there—since they did not have the resources to sustain a settlement over the stormy seas of the North Atlantic Ocean. Nonetheless, the establishment of even a short-lived colony indicated a growing capacity of Europeans to venture into the larger world.

Christianity in Scandinavia
While Scandinavians explored the North Atlantic, the Roman Catholic church drew Scandinavia itself into the community of Christian Europe. The kings of Denmark and Norway converted to Christianity in the tenth century. Conversion of their subjects came gradually and with considerable resistance, since most held tightly to their inherited traditions. Yet royal support for the Roman Catholic church ensured that Christianity would have a place in Danish and Norwegian societies. In 999 or 1000 the Norwegian colony in Iceland also formally adopted Christianity. Between the twelfth and the fourteenth centuries, Sweden and Finland followed their neighbors into the Christian faith.

Crusading Orders and Baltic Expansion
In the Baltic lands of Prussia, Livonia, and Lithuania, Christian authority arrived in the wake of military conquest. During the era of crusades, zealous Christians formed a series of hybrid, military-religious orders. The most prominent were the Templars, Hospitallers, and Teutonic Knights, who not only took religious vows but also pledged to devote their lives and efforts to the struggle against Muslims and pagans. The Teutonic Knights were most active in the Baltic region, where they waged military campaigns against the pagan Slavic peoples during the twelfth and thirteenth centuries. Aided by German missionaries, the Knights founded churches and monasteries in the territories they subdued. By the late thirteenth century, the Roman Catholic church had established its presence throughout the Baltic region, which progressively became absorbed into the larger society of Christian Europe.

The Reconquest of Sicily and Spain

The boundaries of Christian Europe also expanded in the Mediterranean basin. There, Europeans came into conflict with Muslims, whose ancestors had conquered the major Mediterranean islands and most of the Iberian peninsula between the eighth and the tenth centuries. As their society became stronger, Europeans undertook to reconquer those territories and reintegrate them into Christian society.

The Reconquest of Sicily
Most important of the islands was Sicily, which Muslims had conquered in the ninth century. During the eleventh century, Norman warriors returned Sicily to Christian hands. The Norman adventurer Robert Guiscard carved out a state for himself in southern Italy while his brother Roger undertook the conquest of Sicily. By 1090, after almost twenty years of conflict, Roger had established his authority throughout the island. Missionaries and clergy soon appeared and reintroduced Roman Catholic Christianity to Sicily. Islam did not disappear immediately: Muslims continued to practice their faith privately, and Muslim scholars in Sicily introduced their Christian counterparts to the Arabic translations of Aristotle that inspired the scholastic philosophers. Over the longer term, however, as Muslims either left Sicily or converted to Christianity, Islam gradually disappeared from the island.

The *Reconquista* of Spain
The reconquest of Spain—known as the **reconquista**—took a much longer time than did the recapture of Sicily. Following the Muslim invasion and conquest of the early eighth century, the caliphate of Córdoba ruled almost all of the Iberian peninsula. A small Christian state survived in Catalonia in the far northeast, and the kingdom of León resisted Muslim advances in the far northwest. The process of *reconquista* began in the 1060s from those Christian toeholds. By 1085 Christian forces had pushed as far south as Toledo, and by 1150 they had recaptured Lisbon and established their authority over half of the peninsula.

reconquista (ray-kohn-KEE-stah)

Their successes lured reinforcements from France and England, and in the first half of the thirteenth century a new round of campaigns brought most of Iberia as well as the Balearic Islands into Christian hands. Only the kingdom of Granada in the far south of the peninsula remained Muslim. It survived as an outpost of Islam until 1492, when Christian forces mounted a campaign that conquered Granada and completed the *reconquista*.

The political, economic, and demographic strength of Christian Europe helps to explain the reconquests of Sicily and Spain as military ventures. Especially in the case of Spain, however, it is clear that religious concerns also helped to drive the *reconquista*. The popes and other leading clergy of the Roman Catholic church regarded Islam as an affront to Christianity, and they enthusiastically encouraged campaigns against the Muslims. When reconquered territories fell into Christian hands, church officials immediately established bishoprics and asserted Christian authority. They also organized campaigns to convert local populations. Dominican friars were especially active in Spain. They appealed to learned audiences by explaining Christianity in the terms of scholastic theology and arguments derived from Aristotle, whom Muslim intellectuals held in high esteem. When addressing popular audiences, they simply outlined the basic teachings of Christianity and urged their listeners to convert. With the establishment of Christian rule, the Roman Catholic church began to displace Islam in conquered Spain.

The Crusades

The term *crusade* refers to a holy war. It derives from the Latin word *crux,* meaning "cross," the device on which Roman authorities had executed Jesus. When a pope declared a crusade, warriors would "take up the cross" as a symbol of their faith, sew strips of cloth in the form of a cross on the backs of their garments, and venture forth to fight on behalf of Christianity. The wars that Christians fought against pagans in the Baltic and Muslims in the Mediterranean were crusades in this sense of the term, as was the campaign waged by Roman Catholic Christians against Cathar heretics in southern France. In popular usage, though, *crusades* generally refers to the huge expeditions that Roman Catholic Christians mounted in an effort to recapture Palestine, the land of Christian origins, and the holy city of Jerusalem from Muslim authorities.

The crusades involved brutal conflict and atrocities from all sides. In this twelfth-century manuscript illustration, crusaders lob severed enemy heads at Muslims defending a fortress.

Urban II Pope Urban II launched the crusades in 1095. Speaking at the Council of Clermont (in central France), Urban warned church leaders that Muslim Turks were threatening the eastern borders of Christendom. Indeed, the pope had recently received an urgent appeal from the Byzantine emperor, who requested military forces from western Europe to reinforce his own armies as Turkish invaders advanced toward Constantinople. Urban urged European princes to stabilize Christendom's borders and then go further to recapture Jerusalem and restore Christian rule to the holy land. He added emphasis to his appeal with the assertion that "Deus vult"—"God wills it!"

The First Crusade Shortly after Pope Urban announced the crusade, French and Norman nobles began to organize a military expedition to the holy land. In late 1096 the crusading armies began the long trek to Palestine. In 1097 and 1098 they captured Edessa, Antioch, and other strategic sites. In 1099 Jerusalem fell to the crusaders, who then proceeded to extend their conquests and carve conquered territories into Christian states.

Although the crusaders did not realize it, hindsight shows that their quick victories came largely because of division and disarray in the ranks of their Muslim foes. The crusaders' successes, however, encouraged Turks, Egyptians, and other Muslims to settle their differences, at least temporarily, in the interests of expelling European Christians from the eastern Mediterranean. By the mid-twelfth century, the crusader communities had come under tremendous pressure. The crusader state of Edessa fell to Turks in 1144, and the Muslim leader Salah al-Din, known to Europeans as Saladin, recaptured Jerusalem in 1187. Crusaders maintained several of their enclaves for another century, but Saladin's victories sealed the fate of Christian forces in the eastern Mediterranean.

Later Crusades Europeans did not immediately concede Palestine to the Muslims. By the mid-thirteenth century, they had launched five major crusades, but none of the later ventures succeeded in reestablishing a Christian presence in Palestine. The fourth crusade (1202–1204) was a particularly demoralizing affair, as crusaders ravaged Constantinople, the seat of Eastern Orthodox Christianity. Nevertheless, even though the later crusades failed in their principal objective, the crusading idea inspired European dreams of conquest in the eastern Mediterranean until the late sixteenth century.

Consequences of the Crusades

As holy wars intended to reestablish Roman Catholic Christianity in the eastern Mediterranean basin, the crusades were wars of military and political expansion. Yet in the long run, the crusades were much more important for their social, economic, commercial, and cultural consequences. Even as European armies built crusader states in Palestine and

A fourteenth-century manuscript illustration depicts Muslims burning captured crusaders at the stake.

Syria, European scholars and missionaries dealt with Muslim philosophers and theologians, and European merchants traded eagerly with their Muslim counterparts. The result was a large-scale exchange of ideas, technologies, and trade goods that profoundly influenced European development. Through their sojourns in Palestine and their regular dealings with Muslims throughout the Mediterranean basin, European Christians became acquainted with the works of Aristotle, Islamic science and astronomy, "Arabic" numerals (which Muslims had borrowed from India), and techniques of paper production (which Muslims had learned from China). They also learned to appreciate new food and agricultural products such as spices, granulated sugar, coffee, and dates as well as trade goods such as silk products, cotton textiles, carpets, and tapestries.

In the early days of the crusades, Europeans had little to exchange for those products other than rough wool textiles, furs, and timber. During the crusading era, however, demand for the new commodities increased throughout western Europe as large numbers of people developed a taste for goods previously available only to wealthy elites. Seeking to meet the rising demand for luxury goods, Italian

merchants developed new products and marketed them in commercial centers and port cities such as Constantinople, Alexandria, Cairo, Damascus, Tana, Caffa, and Trebizond. Thus Niccolò, Maffeo, and Marco Polo traded in gems and jewelry, and other merchants marketed fine woolen textiles or glassware. By the thirteenth century, large numbers of Italian merchants had begun to travel well beyond Egypt, Palestine, and Syria to avoid Muslim intermediaries and to deal directly with the producers of silks and spices in India, China, and southeast Asia. Thus, although the crusades largely failed as military ventures, they encouraged the reintegration of western Europe into the larger economy of the eastern hemisphere.

inperspective

From 1000 to 1300, Europe underwent thorough political and economic reorganization. Building on foundations laid during the early middle ages, political leaders founded a series of independent regional states. Despite the establishment of the Holy Roman Empire, they did not revive central imperial authority in western Europe. Regional states maintained good order and fostered rapid economic growth. Agricultural improvements brought increased food supplies, which encouraged urbanization, manufacturing, and trade. By the thirteenth century, European peoples traded actively throughout the Mediterranean, Baltic, and North Sea regions, and a few plucky merchants even ventured as far away as China in search of commercial opportunities. In the high middle ages, as in the early middle ages, Christianity was the cultural foundation of European society. The church prospered during the high middle ages, and advanced educational institutions such as cathedral schools and universities reinforced the influence of Christianity throughout Europe. Christianity even played a role in European political and military expansion, since church officials encouraged crusaders to conquer pagan and Muslim peoples in Baltic and Mediterranean lands. Thus between 1000 and 1300, western European peoples strengthened their own society and began in various ways to interact regularly with their counterparts in other regions of the eastern hemisphere. ●

thinking about ENCOUNTERS

The Historical Significance of the Crusades
Military campaigns commonly bring about death and destruction, and the crusades were no exception to the rule. Yet the crusades also prompted important cultural and intellectual exchanges. Taking into account their constructive as well as destructive consequences, how would you characterize the general historical significance of the crusades?

CHRONOLOGY

962	Coronation of Otto I as Holy Roman emperor
1056–1106	Reign of Emperor Henry IV
1066	Norman invasion of England
1073–1085	Reign of Pope Gregory VII
1096–1099	First crusade
1122–1204	Life of Eleanor of Aquitaine
1152–1190	Reign of Emperor Frederick Barbarossa
1170–1221	Life of St. Dominic
1182–1226	Life of St. Francis
1187	Recapture of Jerusalem by Saladin
1202–1204	Fourth crusade
1225–1274	Life of St. Thomas Aquinas
1271–1295	Marco Polo's trip to China
1453	Fall of Constantinople to Ottoman Turks

For Further Reading

Thomas Asbridge. *The Crusades.* New York, 2010. A breezy narrative history of the early crusades.

Robert Bartlett. *The Making of Europe: Conquest, Colonization, and Cultural Change, 950–1350.* Princeton, 1993. A well-documented examination of European expansion from a cultural point of view.

Marc Bloch. *Feudal Society.* 2 vols. Trans. by L. A. Manyon. Chicago, 1961. A classic interpretation concentrating on social and economic history that has decisively influenced the way historians think about medieval Europe.

Rosalind Brooke and Christopher Brooke. *Popular Religion in the Middle Ages: Western Europe, 1000–1300.* London, 1984. Well-illustrated essays on the faith of the masses.

Jean Gimpel. *The Medieval Machine: The Industrial Revolution of the Middle Ages.* New York, 1976. Explores the role of science and technology in the economy and society of medieval Europe.

David Herlihy. *Opera Muliebria: Women and Work in Medieval Europe.* New York, 1990. Examines women's roles both in their own households and in the larger society of medieval Europe.

Hubert Houben. *Roger II of Sicily: A Ruler between East and West.* Cambridge, 2002. Brief and clear account of Roger's reign with emphasis on the cultural exchanges that took place between Christians and Muslims in Norman Sicily.

Benjamin Z. Kedar. *Crusade and Mission: European Approaches toward the Muslims.* Princeton, 1984. Insightful scholarly analysis of European policies toward Muslims during the crusading era.

Robert S. Lopez. *The Commercial Revolution of the Middle Ages, 950–1350.* Englewood Cliffs, N.J., 1971. A succinct account of economic development during the high middle ages.

Hans Eberhard Mayer. *The Crusades.* 2nd ed. Oxford, 1988. Perhaps the best short history of the crusades.

Alex Metcalfe. *Muslims and Christians in Norman Sicily: Arabic Speakers and the End of Islam.* London, 2003. Scholarly study exploring the social, cultural, and linguistic dimensions of Sicilian history as the island made the transition from Muslim to Christian rule.

J. R. S. Phillips. *The Medieval Expansion of Europe.* Oxford, 1988. Excellent survey of European ventures in the larger world during the high and late middle ages.

Daniel Power, ed. *The Central Middle Ages.* Oxford, 2006. Seven leading scholars discuss aspects of medieval European history.

Susan Reynolds. *Fiefs and Vassals: The Medieval Evidence Reinterpreted.* Oxford, 1994. A powerful scholarly critique of the concept of feudalism.

Shulamith Shahar. *The Fourth Estate: A History of Women in the Middle Ages.* Trans. by C. Galai. London, 1983. Well-documented study of women and their status in medieval society.

Christopher Tyerman. *God's War: A New History of the Crusades.* Cambridge, Mass., 2006. A comprehensive review of crusades throughout Europe and the larger Mediterranean basin.

Elisabeth van Houts, ed. *The Normans in Europe.* Manchester, 2000. Presents English translations of sources illuminating Norman roles in medieval Europe.

Lynn White Jr. *Medieval Technology and Social Change.* Oxford, 1962. Pioneering study of technological diffusion and the role of technology in European economy and society.

Worlds Apart: The Americas and Oceania

chapter20

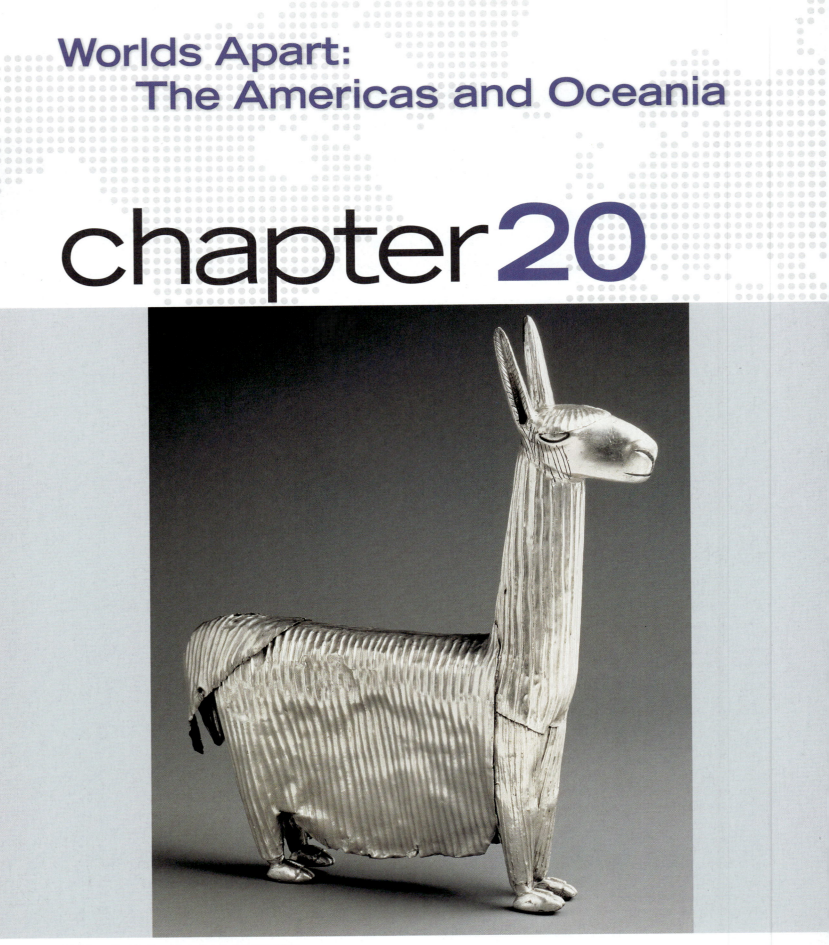

A handsome llama fashioned from silver sheet from Inca Peru.

EYEWITNESS:
First Impressions of the Aztec Capital

In November 1519 a small Spanish army entered **Tenochtitlan,** capital city of the Aztec empire. The Spanish forces came in search of gold, and they had heard many reports about the wealth of the Aztec empire. Yet none of those reports prepared them adequately for what they saw.

Years after the conquest of the Aztec empire, Bernal Díaz del Castillo, a soldier in the Spanish army, described Tenochtitlan at its high point. The city itself sat in the water of Lake Texcoco, connected to the surrounding land by three broad causeways, and as in Venice, canals allowed canoes to navigate to all parts of the city. The imperial palace included many large rooms and apartments. Its armory, well stocked with swords, lances, knives, bows, arrows, slings, armor, and shields, attracted Bernal Díaz's professional attention. The aviary of Tenochtitlan included eagles, hawks, parrots, and smaller birds in its collection, while jaguars, mountain lions, wolves, foxes, and rattlesnakes were noteworthy residents of the zoo.

To Bernal Díaz the two most impressive sights were the markets and the temples of Tenochtitlan. The markets astonished him because of their size, the variety of goods they offered, and the order that prevailed there. In the principal market at Tlatelolco, a district of Tenochtitlan, Bernal Díaz found gold and silver jewelry, gems, feathers, embroidery, slaves, cotton, cacao, animal skins, maize, beans, vegetables, fruits, poultry, meat, fish, salt, paper, and tools. It would take more than two days, he said, to walk around the market and investigate all the goods offered for sale. His well-traveled companions-in-arms compared the market of Tlatelolco favorably to those of Rome and Constantinople.

The temples also struck Bernal Díaz, though in a different way. Aztec temples were the principal sites of rituals involving human sacrifice. Bernal Díaz described his ascent to the top of the main pyramidal temple in Tenochtitlan, where fresh blood lay pooled around the stone that served as a sacrificial altar. He described priests with hair entangled and matted with blood. Interior rooms of the temple were so encrusted with blood, Bernal

Tenochtitlan (teh-NOCH-tee-tlahn)

Díaz reported, that their walls and floors had turned black, and the stench overcame even professional Spanish soldiers. Some of the interior rooms held the dismembered limbs of sacrificial victims, and others were resting places for thousands of human skulls and bones.

The contrast between Tenochtitlan's markets and its temples challenged Bernal Díaz and his fellow soldiers. In the markets they witnessed peaceful and orderly exchange of the kind that took place all over the world. In the temples, however, they saw signs of human sacrifice on a scale rarely matched, if ever, anywhere in the world. Yet by the cultural standards of the Aztec empire, there was no difficulty reconciling the commercial activity of the marketplaces with the human sacrifice of the temples. Both had a place in the maintenance of the world: trade enabled a complex society to function, while sacrificial rituals pleased the gods and persuaded them to keep the world going.

Although the peoples of Africa, Asia, and Europe interacted regularly before modern times, the indigenous peoples of the Americas had only sporadic dealings with their contemporaries across the oceans. Scandinavian seafarers established a short-lived colony in Newfoundland, and occasional ships from Europe and west Africa may have made their way to the western hemisphere. Before 1492, however, interaction between peoples of the eastern and western hemispheres was fleeting and random rather than a sustained and regular affair. During the period from 1000 to 1500 C.E., however, the peoples of North and South America, like their counterparts in the eastern hemisphere, organized large empires with distinctive cultural and religious traditions, and they created elaborate trade networks touching most regions of the American continents.

The indigenous peoples of Australia and the Pacific islands had irregular and sporadic dealings with peoples outside Oceania. Asian trade networks extended to the Philippines, the islands of Indonesia, and New Guinea. They even touched a few regions of northern Australia and the Mariana Islands, including Guam, but they did not extend to the more distant island societies of the Pacific Ocean. Pacific islanders themselves often sailed over the open ocean, creating and sustaining links between the societies of various island groups. They also had some dealings with the inhabitants of Asian and American lands bordering the Pacific Ocean. Like their counterparts in the western hemisphere, however, the indigenous peoples of Australia and the Pacific islands built self-sufficient societies that tended to their own needs. Even though they had extremely limited amounts of land and other natural resources to work with, by the thirteenth century C.E. they had established well-organized agricultural societies and chiefly states throughout the Pacific islands.

STATES AND EMPIRES IN MESOAMERICA AND NORTH AMERICA

Mesoamerica entered an era of war and conquest in the eighth century C.E. Great stores of wealth had accumulated in Teotihuacan, the largest early city in Mesoamerica. When Teotihuacan declined, it became a target for less-prosperous but well-organized forces from the countryside and northern Mexico. Attacks on Teotihuacan opened a long era of militarization and empire building in Mesoamerica that lasted until Spanish forces conquered the region in the sixteenth century. Most prominent of the peoples contesting for power in Mesoamerica were the Mexica, the architects of the Aztec empire.

The Toltecs and the Mexica

During the ninth and early tenth centuries, after the collapse of Teotihuacan, several regional states dominated portions of the high central valley of Mexico, the area surrounding Mexico City where agricultural societies had flourished since the late centuries B.C.E. Although these successor states and their societies shared the religious and cultural traditions of Teotihuacan, they fought relentlessly among themselves. Their capital cities all stood on well-defended hill sites, and warriors figured prominently in their works of art.

Toltecs With the emergence of the Toltecs and later the Mexica, much of central Mexico again came under unified rule. The Toltecs began to migrate into the area about the eighth century. They came from the arid land of northwestern Mexico, and they settled mostly at Tula, about 50 kilometers (31 miles) northwest of modern Mexico City. Though situated in a corner of the valley of Mexico that possesses thin soil and receives little rainfall, the Toltecs tapped the waters of the nearby River Tula to irrigate crops of maize, beans, peppers, tomatoes, chiles, and cotton. At its high point, from about 950 to 1150 C.E., Tula supported an urban population that might have reached sixty thousand people. Another sixty thousand lived in the surrounding region.

The Toltecs maintained a large and powerful army that campaigned periodically throughout central Mexico. They built a compact regional empire and maintained fortresses far to the northwest to protect their state from invasion by nomadic peoples. From the mid-tenth through the mid-twelfth century, they exacted tribute from subject peoples and transformed their capital into a wealthy city. Residents lived in spacious houses made of stone, adobe, or mud and sometimes covered their packed-earth floors with plaster.

Tula   The city of Tula became an important center of weaving, pottery, and obsidian work, and residents imported large quantities of jade, turquoise, animal skins, exotic bird feathers, and other luxury goods from elsewhere in Mesoamerica. The Toltecs maintained close relations with societies on the Gulf coast as well as with the Maya of Yucatan. Indeed, Tula shared numerous architectural designs and art motifs with the Maya city of Chichén Itzá some 1,500 kilometers (932 miles) to the east.

Beginning about 1125 C.E. the Toltec empire faced serious difficulties as conflicts between the different ethnic groups living at Tula led to civil strife. By the mid-twelfth century, large numbers of migrants—mostly nomadic peoples from northwestern Mexico—had entered Tula and settled in the surrounding area. By 1175 the combination of civil conflict and nomadic incursion had destroyed the Toltec state. Archaeological evidence suggests that fire destroyed much of Tula about the same time. Large numbers

of people continued to inhabit the region around Tula, but by the end of the twelfth century the Toltecs no longer dominated Mesoamerica.

The Mexica   Among the migrants drawn to central Mexico from northwestern regions was a people who called themselves the Mexica, often referred to as Aztecs because they dominated the alliance that built the Aztec empire in the fifteenth century. (The term *Aztec* derives from *Aztlán,* "the place of the seven legendary caves," which the Mexica remembered as the home of their ancestors.) The Mexica arrived in central Mexico about the middle of the thirteenth century. They had a reputation for making trouble by kidnapping women from nearby communities and seizing land already cultivated by others. On several occasions their neighbors became tired of their disorderly behavior and forced them to move. For a century they migrated around central Mexico, jostling and fighting with other peoples and sometimes surviving only by eating fly eggs and snakes.

Tenochtitlan   About 1345 the Mexica settled on an island in a marshy region of Lake Texcoco and founded the city that would become their capital—Tenochtitlan, on top of which Spanish conquerors later built Mexico City. Though inconvenient at first, the site offered several advantages. The lake harbored plentiful supplies of fish, frogs, and waterfowl.

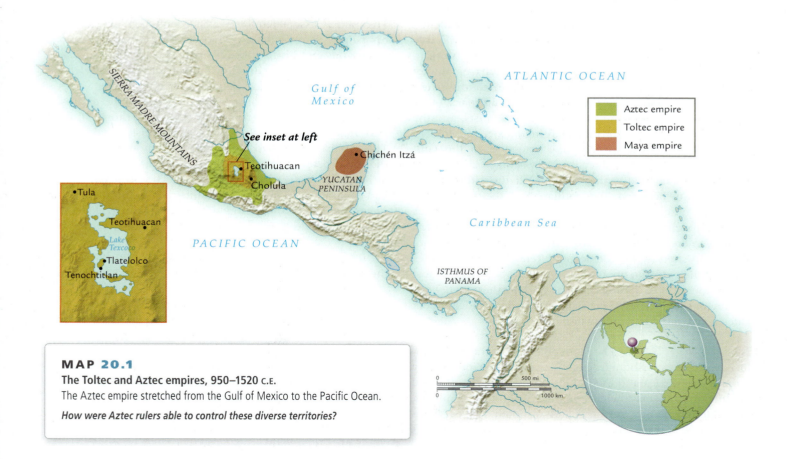

MAP 20.1

The Toltec and Aztec empires, 950–1520 C.E.

The Aztec empire stretched from the Gulf of Mexico to the Pacific Ocean.

How were Aztec rulers able to control these diverse territories?

Moreover, the lake enabled the Mexica to develop the *chinampa* system of agriculture. The Mexica dredged a rich and fertile muck from the lake's bottom and built it up into small plots of land known as *chinampas*. During the dry season, cultivators tapped water from canals leading from the lake to their plots, and in the temperate climate they grew crops of maize, beans, squashes, tomatoes, peppers, and chiles year-round. *Chinampas* were so fertile and productive that cultivators were sometimes able to harvest seven crops per year from their gardens. Finally, the lake served as a natural defense: waters protected Tenochtitlan on all sides, and Mexica warriors patrolled the three causeways that eventually linked their capital to the surrounding mainland.

Although the lakes of central Mexico have largely disappeared, a few *chinampas* survive, such as this one in Xochimilco, near modern Mexico City.

The Aztec Empire

By the early fifteenth century, the Mexica were powerful enough to overcome their immediate neighbors and demand tribute from their new subjects. During the middle decades of the century, prodded by the military elite that ruled Tenochtitlan, the Mexica launched ambitious campaigns of imperial expansion. Under the rule of "the Obsidian Serpent" Itzcóatl (1428–1440) and Motecuzoma I (1440–1469), also known as Moctezuma or Montezuma, they advanced first against Oaxaca in southwestern Mexico. After conquering the city and slaying many of its inhabitants, they populated Oaxaca with colonists, and the city became a bulwark for the emerging Mexica empire.

The Mexica next turned their attention to the Gulf coast, whose tropical products made welcome tribute items in Tenochtitlan. Finally, they conquered the cities of the high plateaus between Tenochtitlan and the Gulf coast. About the mid-fifteenth century, the Mexica joined forces with two neighboring cities, Texcoco and Tlacopan (modern Tacuba), to create a triple alliance that guided the Aztec empire. Dominated by the Mexica and Tenochtitlan, the allies imposed their rule on about twelve million people and most of Mesoamerica, excluding only the arid northern and western regions and a few small pockets where independent states resisted the expanding empire.

Tribute and Trade

The main objective of the triple alliance was to exact tribute from subject peoples. From nearby peoples the Mexica and their allies received food crops and manufactured items such as textiles, rabbit-fur blankets, embroidered clothes, jewelry, and obsidian knives. Tribute obligations were sometimes very oppressive for subject peoples. The annual tribute owed by the state of Tochtepec on the Gulf coast, for example, included 9,600 cloaks, 1,600 women's garments, 200 loads of cacao, and 16,000 rubber balls, among other items. Ruling elites entrusted some of these tribute items to officially recognized merchants, who took them to distant lands and exchanged them for local products. These included luxury items such as translucent jade, emeralds, tortoise shells, jaguar skins, parrot feathers, seashells, and game animals. The tropical lowlands also supplied vanilla beans and cacao—the source of cocoa and chocolate—from which Mexica elites prepared tasty beverages.

Unlike imperial states in the eastern hemisphere, the Aztec empire had no elaborate bureaucracy or administration. The Mexica and their allies simply conquered their subjects and assessed tribute, leaving local governance and the collection of tribute in the hands of the conquered peoples. The allies did not even maintain military garrisons throughout their empire. Nor did they keep a permanent, standing army. They simply assembled forces as needed when they launched campaigns of expansion or mounted punitive expeditions against insubordinate subjects. Nevertheless, the Mexica in particular had a reputation for military prowess, and fear of reprisal kept most subject peoples in line.

At the high point of the Aztec empire in the early sixteenth century, tribute from 489 subject territories flowed into Tenochtitlan, which was an enormously wealthy city. The Mexica capital had a population of about two hundred thousand people, and three hundred thousand others lived in nearby towns and suburban areas. The principal market had separate sections for merchants dealing in gold, silver, slaves, henequen and cotton cloth, shoes, animal skins, turkeys, dogs, wild game, maize, beans, peppers, cacao, and fruits.

The Spanish soldier Bernal Díaz del Castillo marveled at the sight before him when he first laid eyes on Tenochtitlan:

> And when we saw so many cities and villages built in the water and other great towns on dry land and that straight and level causeway going towards Mexico [Tenochtitlan], we were amazed . . . on account of the great towers and [temples] and buildings rising from the water, and all built of masonry. And some of our soldiers even asked whether the things that we saw were not a dream? It is not to be wondered at that I here write it

down in this manner, for there is so much to think over that I do not know how to describe it, seeing things as we did that had never been heard of or seen before, not even dreamed about.

Mexica Society

More information survives about the Mexica and their subjects than about any other people of the pre-Columbian Americas. A few Mexica books survived the Spanish conquest of the Aztec empire, and they offer direct testimony about the Mexica way of life. Moreover, a great deal of information survives from lengthy interviews conducted by Spanish missionaries with priests, elders, and other leaders of the Mexica during the mid-sixteenth century. Their reports fill many thick volumes and shed considerable light on Mexica society.

Social Structure Mexica society was rigidly hierarchical, with public honors and rewards going mostly to the military elite. The Mexica looked upon all males as potential warriors, and individuals of common birth could distinguish themselves on the battlefield and thereby improve their social standing. For the most part, however, the military elite came from the Mexica aristocracy. Men of noble birth received the most careful instruction and intense training in military affairs, and they enjoyed the best opportunities to display their talents on the battlefield.

Warriors The Mexica showered wealth and honors on the military elite. Accomplished warriors received extensive land grants as well as tribute from commoners for their support. The most successful warriors formed a council whose members selected the ruler, discussed public issues, and filled government positions. They ate the best foods—turkey, pheasant, duck, deer, boar, and rabbit—and they consumed most of the luxury items such as vanilla and cacao that came into Mexica society by way of trade or tribute. Even dress reflected social status in Mexica society. Sumptuary laws required commoners to wear coarse, burlaplike garments made of henequen but permitted aristocrats to drape themselves in cotton. Warriors enjoyed the right to don brightly colored capes and adorn themselves with lip plugs and eagle feathers after they captured enemies on the battlefield and brought them back to Tenochtitlan.

Mexica Women Women played almost no role in the political affairs of a society so dominated by military values, but they wielded influence within their families and enjoyed high honor as mothers of warriors. Mexica women did not inherit property or hold official positions, and the law subjected them to the strict authority of their fathers and their husbands. Women were prominent in the marketplaces, as well as in crafts involving embroidery and needlework. Yet Mexica society prodded them toward motherhood and homemaking.

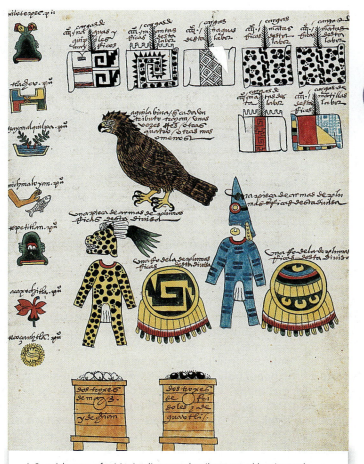

A Spanish copy of a Mexica list records tribute owed by six northwestern towns to the ruler Motecuzoma II. Each two years the towns delivered, among other items, women's skirts and blouses, men's shirts, warriors' armor and shields, an eagle, and various quantities of maize, beans, and other foods.

With the exception of a few who dedicated themselves to the service of a temple, all Mexica women married. Mexica values taught that their principal function was to bear children, especially males who might become distinguished warriors, and society recognized the bearing of children as equal to a warrior's capture of enemy in battle. Indeed, women who died in childbirth won the same fame as warriors who died valiantly on the battlefield. Even among the elite classes, Mexica women had the responsibilities of raising young children and preparing food for their families.

Priests In addition to the military aristocracy, a priestly class also ranked among the Mexica elite. Priests received a special education in calendrical and ritual lore, and they presided over religious ceremonies that the Mexica viewed as crucial to the continuation of the world. Priests read omens and explained the forces that drove the world, thereby

sources from the past

Mexica Expectations of Boys and Girls

Bernardino de Sahagún was a Franciscan missionary who worked to convert the native peoples of Mesoamerica to Christianity in the mid-sixteenth century. He interviewed Mexica elders and assembled a vast amount of information about their society before the arrival of Europeans. His records include the speeches made by midwives as they delivered infants to aristocratic families. The speeches indicate clearly the roles men and women were expected to play in Mexica society.

[To a newborn boy the midwife said:] "Heed, hearken: thy home is not here, for thou art an eagle, thou art an ocelot; thou art a roseate spoonbill, thou art a troupial. Thou art the serpent, the bird of the lord of the near, of the nigh. Here is only the place of thy nest. Thou hast only been hatched here; thou hast only come, arrived. Thou art only come forth on earth here. Here dost thou bud, blossom, germinate. Here thou becomest the chip, the fragment [of thy mother]. Here are only the cradle, thy cradle blanket, the resting place of thy head: only thy place of arrival. Thou belongest out there; out there thou hast been consecrated. Thou hast been sent into warfare. War is thy desert, thy task. Thou shalt give drink, nourishment, food to the sun, the lord of the earth. Thy real home, thy property, thy lot is the home of the sun there in the heavens. . . . Perhaps thou wilt receive the gift, perhaps thou wilt merit death [in battle] by the obsidian knife, the flowered death by the obsidian knife. . . ."

And if it were a female, the midwife said to her when she cut her umbilical cord: "My beloved maiden, my beloved noblewoman, thou has endured fatigue! Our lord, the lord of the near, of the nigh, hath sent thee. Thou hast come to arrive at a place of weariness, a place of anguish, a place of fatigue where there is cold, there is wind. . . . Thou wilt be in the heart of the home, thou wilt go nowhere, thou wilt nowhere become a wanderer, thou becomest the banked fire, the hearth stones. Here our lord planteth thee, burieth thee. And thou wilt become fatigued, thou wilt become tired; thou art to provide water, to grind maize, to drudge; thou art to sweat by the ashes, by the hearth."

Then the midwife buried the umbilical cord of the noblewoman by the hearth. It was said that by this she signified that the little woman would nowhere wander. Her dwelling place was only within the house; her home was only within the house; it was not necessary for her to go anywhere. And it meant that her very duty was drink, food. She was to prepare drink, to prepare food, to grind, to spin, to weave.

For Further Reflection

■ How did gender roles and expectations of Mexica society compare with those of other settled, agricultural societies, such as China, India, the Islamic world, sub-Saharan Africa, and Europe?

Source: Bernardino de Sahagún. *Florentine Codex: General History of the Things of New Spain,* 13 vols. Trans. by Charles E. Dibble and Arthur J. O. Anderson. Salt Lake City: University of Utah Press, 1950–82, 7:171–73 (book 6, chapter 31).

wielding considerable influence as advisors to Mexica rulers. On a few occasions, priests even became supreme rulers of the Aztec empire: the ill-fated Motecuzoma II (reigned 1502–1520), ruler of the Aztec empire when Spanish invaders appeared in 1519, was a priest of the most popular Mexica cult.

Cultivators and Slaves The bulk of the Mexica population consisted of commoners who lived in hamlets cultivating *chinampas* and fields allocated to their families by community groups known as *calpulli.* Originally, *calpulli* were clans or groups of families claiming descent from common ancestors. With the passage of time, ancestry became less important to the nature of the *calpulli* than the fact that groups of families lived together in communities, organized their own affairs, and allocated community property to individual families. Apart from cultivating plots assigned by their *calpulli,* Mexica commoners worked on lands awarded to aristocrats or prominent warriors and contributed labor services to public works projects involving the construction of palaces, temples, roads, and irrigation systems. Cultivators delivered periodic tribute payments to state agents, who distributed a portion of what they collected to the elite classes and stored the remainder in state granaries and warehouses. In addition to these cultivators of common birth, Mexica society included a large number of slaves, who usually worked as domestic servants. Most slaves were not foreigners, but Mexica. Families sometimes sold younger members into servitude out of financial distress, and other Mexica were forced into slavery because of criminal behavior.

Artisans and Merchants Skilled artisans, particularly those who worked with gold, silver, cotton textiles, tropical bird feathers, and other items destined for consumption by the elite, enjoyed considerable prestige in Mexica society. Merchants specializing in long-distance trade occupied an important but somewhat more tenuous position in Mexica society. Merchants supplied the exotic products such as gems, animal skins, and tropical bird feathers consumed by the elites and provided political and military intelligence about the lands they visited. Yet they often fell under suspicion as greedy profiteers, and aristocratic warriors frequently extorted wealth and goods from merchants who lacked powerful patrons or protectors.

Mexica Religion

When they migrated to central Mexico, the Mexica already spoke the Nahuatl language, which had been the prevalent tongue in the region since the time of the Toltecs. The Mexica soon adopted other cultural and religious traditions, some of which dated from the time of the Olmecs, shared by all the peoples of Mesoamerica. Most Mesoamerican peoples played a ball game in formal courts, for example, and maintained a complicated calendar based on a solar year of 365 days and a ritual year of 260 days. The Mexica enthusiastically adopted the ball game, and they kept a sophisticated calendar, although it was not as elaborate as the Maya calendar.

Mexica Gods The Mexica also absorbed the religious beliefs common to Mesoamerica. Two of their principal gods—Tezcatlipoca, "the Smoking Mirror," and Quetzalcóatl, "the Feathered Serpent"—had figured in Mesoamerican pantheons at least since the time of Teotihuacan, although different peoples knew them by various names. Tezcatlipoca was a powerful figure, the giver and taker of life and the patron deity of warriors, whereas Quetzalcóatl had a reputation

A Mexica manuscript known as the Codex Borgia depicts Quetzalcóatl (left) as the lord of life and Tezcatlipoca (right) as the god of death.

for supporting arts, crafts, and agriculture.

Ritual Bloodletting Like their predecessors, the Mexica believed that their gods had set the world in motion through acts of individual sacrifice. By letting their blood flow, the gods had given the earth the moisture it needed to bear maize and other crops. To propitiate the gods and ensure the continuation of the world, the Mexica honored their deities through sacrificial bloodletting. Mexica priests regularly performed acts of self-sacrifice, piercing their earlobes or penises with cactus spines in honor of the primeval acts of their gods. The religious beliefs and bloodletting rituals clearly reflected the desire of the Mexica to keep their agricultural society going.

Huitzilopochtli Mexica priests also presided over the sacrificial killing of human victims. From the time of the Olmecs, and possibly even earlier, Mesoamerican peoples had regarded the ritual sacrifice of human beings as essential to the world's survival. The Mexica, however, placed much more emphasis on human sacrifice than their predecessors had. To a large extent the Mexica enthusiasm for human sacrifice followed from their devotion to the god Huitzilopochtli. Mexica warriors took Huitzilopochtli as their patron deity in the early years of the fourteenth century as they subjected neighboring peoples to their rule. Military success persuaded them that Huitzilopochtli especially favored the Mexica, and as military successes mounted, the priests of Huitzilopochtli's cult demanded sacrificial victims to keep the war god appeased.

Some of the victims were Mexica criminals, but others came as tribute from neighboring peoples or from the ranks of warriors captured on the battlefield during the many conflicts between the Mexica and their neighbors. In all cases, the Mexica viewed human sacrifice not as a gruesome form of entertainment but, rather, as a ritual essential to the world's survival. They believed that the blood of sacrificial victims sustained the sun and secured a continuing supply of moisture for the earth, thus ensuring that human communities would be able to cultivate their crops and perpetuate their societies.

thinking about TRADITIONS

The Mexica and Mesoamerican Bloodletting Rituals
The Mexica practiced bloodletting rituals much like those observed in Maya, Teotihuacan, Toltec, and other earlier Mesoamerican societies. Yet the Mexica shed human blood much more copiously than their predecessors. Why might the Mexica have emphasized this particular cultural tradition so much more strongly than earlier Mesoamerican peoples?

In this manuscript illustration an aide stretches a victim over a sacrificial altar while a priest opens his chest, removes the still-beating heart, and offers it to Huitzilopochtli. At the bottom of the structure, attendants remove the body of an earlier victim.

Peoples and Societies of the North

Beyond Mexico the peoples of North America developed a rich variety of political, social, and cultural traditions. Many North American peoples depended on hunting, fishing, and collecting edible plants. In the arctic and subarctic regions, for example, diets included sea mammals such as whale, seal, and walrus supplemented by land mammals such as moose and caribou. Peoples in coastal regions consumed fish, but in interior regions (the North American plains, for example), they hunted large animals such as bison and deer. Throughout the continent nuts, berries, roots, and grasses such as wild rice supplemented the meat provided by hunters and fishers. Like their counterparts elsewhere, hunting, fishing, and foraging peoples of North America built societies on a relatively small scale, since food resources in the wild would not support dense populations.

Pueblo and Navajo Societies In several regions of North America, agricultural economies enabled peoples to maintain settled societies with large populations. In what is now the American southwest, for example, Pueblo and Navajo peoples tapped river waters to irrigate crops of maize, which constituted as much as 80 percent of their diets. They also cultivated beans, squashes, and sunflowers, and they supplemented their crops with wild plants and small game such as rabbit. The hot and dry environment periodically brought drought and famine. Nevertheless, by about 700 C.E. the Pueblo and the Navajo began to construct permanent stone and adobe buildings. Archaeologists have discovered about 125 sites where agricultural peoples built such communities.

Iroquois Peoples Large-scale agricultural societies emerged also in the woodlands east of the Mississippi River. Woodlands peoples began to cultivate maize and beans during the early centuries C.E., and after about 800 these cultivated foods made up the bulk of their diets. They lived in settled communities, and they often surrounded their larger settlements with wooden palisades, which served as defensive walls. By 1000, for example, the Owasco people had established a distinct society in what is now upstate New York, and by about 1400 the five **Iroquois** nations (Mohawk, Oneida, Onondaga, Cayuga, and Seneca) had emerged from Owasco society. Women were in charge of Iroquois villages and longhouses, in which several related families lived together, and supervised cultivation of fields surrounding their settlements. Men took responsibility for affairs beyond the village—hunting, fishing, and war.

Iroquois (EAR-uh-kwoi)

Mound-Building Peoples The most impressive structures of the woodlands were the enormous earthen mounds that dotted the countryside throughout the eastern half of North America. Woodlands peoples used those mounds sometimes as stages for ceremonies and rituals, often as platforms for dwellings, and occasionally as burial sites. Modern agriculture, road building, and real estate development have destroyed most of the mounds, but several surviving examples demonstrate that they sometimes reached gigantic proportions.

Cahokia The largest surviving structure is a mound at Cahokia near East St. Louis, Illinois. More than 30 meters (100 feet) high, 300 meters (1,000 feet) long, and 200 meters (650 feet) wide, it was the third-largest structure in the western hemisphere before the arrival of Europeans. Only the temple of the sun in Teotihuacan and the temple of Quetzalcóatl in Cholula were larger. When the Cahokia society was at its height, from approximately 900 to 1250 C.E., more than one hundred smaller mounds stood within a few kilometers of the highest and most massive mound. Scholars have estimated that during the twelfth century, fifteen thousand to thirty-eight thousand people lived in the vicinity of the Cahokia mounds.

Trade Because peoples north of Mexico had no writing, information about their societies comes almost exclusively from archaeological discoveries. Burial sites reveal that mound-building peoples recognized various social classes, since they bestowed grave goods of differing quality and quantities on their departed kin. Archaeologists have shown, too, that trade linked widely separated regions and peoples of North America. An elaborate network of rivers—notably the Mississippi, Missouri, Ohio, and Tennessee rivers, along with their many tributaries—facilitated travel and trade by canoe in the eastern half of North America. Throughout the eastern woodlands, archaeologists have turned up stones with sharp cutting edges from the Rocky Mountains, copper from the Great Lakes region, seashells from Florida, minerals from the upper reaches of the Mississippi River, and mica from the southern Appalachian mountains. Indeed, the community at Cahokia probably owed its size and prominence to its location at the hub of North American trade networks. Situated near the confluence of the Mississippi, Missouri, and Ohio rivers, Cahokia was most likely the center of trade and communication networks linking the eastern woodlands of North America with the lower Mississippi valley and lands bordering the Gulf of Mexico.

STATES AND EMPIRES IN SOUTH AMERICA

South American peoples had no script and no tradition of writing before the arrival of Spanish invaders in the early sixteenth century. As a result, the experiences of early South American societies are much more difficult to recover than those of Mesoamerica, where writing had been in use since the fifth century B.C.E. Yet, from archaeological evidence and

Originally constructed about 1000 C.E., the Great Serpent Mound sits atop a ridge in modern Ohio. The serpent's coiled tail is visible at the left, while its open mouth holds an egg on the right. What uses might a ridgetop mound like this have served?

MAP 20.2

The Inca empire, 1471–1532 C.E.

The Incas built the largest empire in the pre-Columbian Americas.

How were they able to maintain control over their extensive realm?

information recorded by Spanish conquerors, it is possible to reconstruct much of the historical experience of Andean South America, which had been the site of complex societies since the first millennium B.C.E. As in Mesoamerica, cities and secular government in South America began to overshadow ceremonial centers and priestly regimes during the centuries from 1000 to 1500 C.E. Toward the end of the period, like the Mexica in Mesoamerica, the Incas built a powerful state, extended their authority over a vast region, and established the largest empire South America had ever seen.

The Coming of the Incas

After the disappearance of the Chavín and Moche societies, a series of autonomous regional states organized public affairs

in Andean South America. The states frequently clashed, but rarely did one of them gain a long-term advantage over the others. For the most part they controlled areas either in the mountainous highlands or in the valleys and coastal plains.

Chucuito After the twelfth century, for example, the kingdom of Chucuito dominated the highlands region around Lake Titicaca, which straddles the border between modern Peru and Bolivia at about 4,000 meters (13,000 feet) of elevation. Chucuito depended on the cultivation of potatoes and the herding of llamas and alpacas—camel-like beasts that were the only large domesticated animals anywhere in the Americas before the sixteenth century. In elaborately terraced fields built with stone retaining walls, cultivators harvested potatoes of many colors, sizes, and tastes. Like maize in Mesoamerica, potatoes served as the staple of the highlanders' diet, which revolved around a potato-based stew enlivened by maize, tomatoes, green vegetables, peppers, chiles, and meat from llamas, alpacas, or tender, domesticated guinea pigs.

Apart from meat, llamas and alpacas provided the highlanders with wool, hides, and dung, widely used as fuel in a land with few trees. In exchange for potatoes and woolen textiles, the highlanders obtained maize and coca leaves from societies in lower valleys. They used maize to enhance their diet and to brew a beerlike beverage, and they chewed the coca leaves, which worked as a mild stimulant and enhanced stamina in the thin air of the high Andes. (When processed, coca leaves yield a much more powerful stimulant with addictive properties—cocaine.)

Chimu In the lowlands the powerful kingdom of Chimu (sometimes referred to as Chimor) emerged in the tenth century and expanded to dominate some 900 kilometers (560 miles) of the Peruvian coast for about a century before the arrival of the Incas in the mid-fifteenth century. Chimu governed a large and thriving society. Irrigation networks tapped the rivers and streams flowing from the Andes mountains, watered fields in the lowlands, and helped to generate abundant yields of maize and sweet potatoes. Judging from goods excavated at grave sites, Chimu society enjoyed considerable wealth and recognized clear distinctions between social classes.

Chimu's capital city, Chanchan, whose ruins lie close to the modern city of Trujillo, had a population that exceeded fifty thousand and may have approached one hundred thousand. Chanchan featured massive brick buildings, which indicated a capacity for mobilizing large numbers of people and resources for public purposes. The city's geography reflected a well-defined social order: each block belonged to an individual clan that supervised the affairs of its members and coordinated their efforts with those of other clans.

For several centuries, regional states such as Chucuito and Chimu maintained order in Andean South America. Yet, within a period of about thirty years, these and other regional states fell under the domination of the dynamic and expansive society of the Incas. The word *Inca* originally was the title of the rulers of a small kingdom in the valley of Cuzco, but in modern usage the term refers more broadly to those who spoke the Incas' Quechua language, or even to all subjects of the Inca empire.

The Inca Empire

After a long period of migration in the highlands, the Incas settled in the region around Lake Titicaca about the mid-thirteenth century. At first, they lived as one among many peoples inhabiting the region. About 1438, however, the Inca ruler Pachacuti (reigned 1438–1471) launched a series of military campaigns that vastly expanded the In-

The different colors of quipu threads designated the different items recorded: population, animals, textiles, weapons, and perhaps even rulers and notable events of their reigns. People needed an advanced education to record and "read" information by quipu.

cas' authority. Pachacuti ("Earthshaker") was a fierce warrior. According to Inca legends, he fought so furiously in one early battle that he inspired the stones in the field to stand up and combat his enemies. The campaigns of the Earthshaker were long and brutal. Pachacuti first extended Inca control over the southern and northern highlands and then turned his forces on the coastal kingdom of Chimu. Though well defended, Chimu had to submit to the Incas when Pachacuti gained control of the waters that supplied Chimu's irrigation system.

By the late fifteenth century, the Incas had built a huge empire stretching more than 4,000 kilometers (2,500 miles) from modern Quito to Santiago. It embraced almost all of modern Peru, most of Ecuador, much of Bolivia, and parts of Chile and Argentina as well. Only the tropical rain forests of the Amazon and other river valleys set a limit to Inca expansion to the east, and the Pacific Ocean defined its western boundary. With a population of about 11.5 million, the Inca empire easily ranked as the largest state ever built in South America.

The Incas ruled as a military and administrative elite. They led armies composed mostly of conquered peoples, and they staffed the bureaucracy that managed the empire's political affairs. But the Incas were not numerous enough to overwhelm their subjects. They routinely sought to encourage obedience among subject peoples by taking hostages from their ruling classes and forcing them to live at the Inca capital. When conquered peoples became restive or uncooperative, the Incas sent loyal subjects as colonists, provided them with choice land and economic benefits, and established them in garrisons to maintain order. When con-

quered peoples rebelled, Inca armies forced them to leave their homes and resettle in distant parts of the empire.

Inca Administration

The vast Inca realm presented a serious administrative challenge to its rulers. The Inca administrative system was the invention of Pachacuti himself—the same Earthshaker who conquered the territories that made up the Inca empire. Toward the end of his reign, about 1463, Pachacuti entrusted military affairs to his son and settled in the highland village of Cuzco, where he designed a system of government to consolidate his conquests. He implemented taxes to support Inca rulers and administrators, and he organized a system of state-owned storehouses to stock agricultural surpluses and craft products such as textiles. He also began construction on an extensive network of roads that enabled Inca military forces and administrators to travel quickly to all parts of the empire.

Quipu

In the absence of any script or system of writing, Inca bureaucrats and administrators relied on a mnemonic aid known as *quipu* to keep track of their responsibilities. Quipu consisted of an array of small cords of various colors and lengths, all suspended from one large, thick cord. Experts tied a series of knots in the small cords, which sometimes numbered a hundred or more, to help them remember certain kinds of information. Most quipu recorded statistical information having to do with population, state property, taxes, and labor services that communities owed to the central government. Occasionally, though, quipu also helped experts to remember historical information having to do with the establishment of the Inca empire, the Inca rulers, and their deeds. Although much more unwieldy and less flexible than writing, quipu enabled Inca bureaucrats to keep track of information well enough to run an orderly empire.

Cuzco

Cuzco served as the administrative, religious, and ceremonial center of the Inca empire. When Pachacuti retired there, Cuzco was a modest village, but the conqueror soon transformed it into a magnificent capital that Incas considered "the navel of the universe." At the center was a huge plaza filled with glistening white sand transported from Pacific beaches to the high Andean city. Surrounding

quipu (KEE-poo)

the plaza were handsome buildings constructed of red stone cut so precisely by expert masons that no mortar was necessary to hold them together. The most important buildings sported gold facings, which threw off dazzling reflections when rays of the Andean sun fell on them.

Since Cuzco was primarily a capital and a ceremonial center, the city's permanent population was sizable but not enormous—perhaps forty thousand—but some two hundred thousand Inca subjects lived in the immediate vicinity. Apart from high-ranking imperial administrators, the most prominent permanent residents of Cuzco proper included the Inca rulers and high nobility, the high priests of the various religious cults, and the hostages of conquered peoples who lived with their families under the watchful eyes of Inca guardians.

Inca Roads A magnificent and extensive road system enabled the central government at Cuzco to communicate with all parts of the far-flung Inca empire and to dispatch large military forces rapidly to distant trouble spots. Two roads linked the Inca realm from north to south—one passing through the mountains, the other running along the coast. Scholars have estimated the combined length of those trunk routes at 16,000 kilometers (almost 10,000 miles). The combined length of the entire network of all Inca roads, including lesser thoroughfares as well as the major trunk routes, may have amounted to 40,000 kilometers (almost 25,000 miles).

Inca roads were among the best ever constructed before modern times. During the early sixteenth century, Spanish conquerors marveled at the roads—paved with stone, shaded by trees, and wide enough to accommodate eight horsemen riding abreast. A corps of official runners carried messages along the roads so that news and information could travel between Cuzco and the most distant parts of the empire within a few days. When the Inca rulers desired a meal of fresh fish, they dispatched runners from Cuzco to the coast, more than 320 kilometers (200 miles) away, and had their catch within two days. Like roads in empires in other parts of the world, the Incas' roads favored their efforts at centralization. Their roads even facilitated the spread of the Quechua language and their religious cult focusing on the sun, both of which became established throughout their empire.

Inca Society and Religion

Trade Despite those splendid roads, Inca society did not generate large

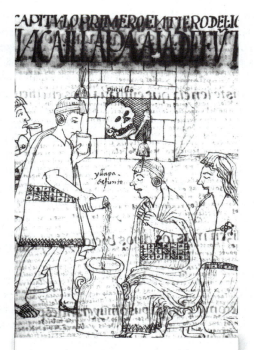

Descendants prepare a ritual meal for a mummified Inca ruler (depicted in the background).

classes of merchants and skilled artisans. On the local level the Incas and their subjects bartered surplus agricultural production and handcrafted goods among themselves. Long-distance trade, however, fell under the supervision of the central government. Administrators organized exchanges of agricultural products, textiles, pottery, jewelry, and craft goods, but the Inca state did not permit individuals to become independent merchants. In the absence of a market economy, there was no opportunity for a large class of professional, skilled artisans to emerge. Many individuals produced pottery, textiles, and tools for local consumption, and a few produced especially fine goods for the ruling, priestly, and aristocratic classes. But skilled crafts workers were much less prominent among the Incas than among the Mexica and the peoples of the eastern hemisphere.

Ruling Elites The main classes in Inca society were the rulers, the aristocrats, the priests, and the peasant cultivators of common birth. The Incas considered their chief ruler a deity descended from the sun. In theory, this god-king owned all land, livestock, and property in the Inca realm, which he governed as an absolute and infallible ruler. Inca rulers retained their prestige even after death. Their descendants mummified the royal remains and regarded departed kings as intermediaries with the gods. Succeeding rulers often deliberated state policy in the presence of royal mummies so as to benefit from their counsel. Indeed, on the occasion of certain festivals, rulers brought out the mummified remains of their ancestors, dressed them in fine clothes, adorned them with gold and silver jewelry, honored them, and presented them with offerings of food and drink to maintain cordial relations with former rulers. Meanwhile, by way of tending to the needs of their living subjects, the Inca god-kings supervised a class of bureaucrats, mostly aristocrats, who allocated plots of land for commoners to cultivate on behalf of the state.

Aristocrats and Priests Like the ruling elites, Inca aristocrats and priests led privileged lives. Aristocrats consumed fine foods and dressed in embroidered clothes provided by common subjects. Aristocrats also had the right to wear large ear spools that distended their lobes so much that Spanish conquerors referred to them as "big ears." Priests often came from royal and aristocratic families. They led celibate and ascetic lives, but they deeply influenced Inca society because of their education and their responsibility for overseeing religious rituals. The major temples supported hundreds of priests, along with attendants and virgin women devoted to divine service who prepared ceremonial meals and wove fine ritual garments for the priestly staff.

Peasants   The cultivators were mostly peasants of common birth who lived in communities known as *ayllu,* similar to the Mexicas' *calpulli,* which were the basic units of rural society. Ranging in size from small villages to larger towns, *ayllus* consisted of several families who lived together, sharing land, tools, animals, crops, and work. Peasants supported themselves by working on lands allocated to individual families by their *ayllu.* Instead of paying taxes or tribute, peasants also worked on state lands administered by aristocrats. Much of the production from these state lands went to support the ruling, aristocratic, and priestly classes. The rest went into state storehouses for public relief in times of famine and for the support of widows, orphans, and others unable to cultivate land for themselves. Apart from agricultural work, peasants also owed compulsory labor services to the Inca state. Men provided the heavy labor required for the construction, maintenance, and repair of roads, buildings, and irrigation systems. Women delivered tribute in the form of textiles, pottery, and jewelry. With the aid of quipu, Inca bureaucrats kept track of the labor service and tribute owed by local communities.

Inca Gods: Inti and Viracocha   Members of the Inca ruling class venerated the sun as a god and as their major deity, whom they called Inti. They also recognized the moon, stars, planets, rain, and other natural forces as divine. Some Incas, including the energetic ruler Pachacuti, also showed special favor to the god Viracocha, creator of the world, humankind, and all else in the universe. The cult of the sun, however, outshone all the others. In Cuzco alone some four thousand priests, attendants, and virgin devotees served Inti, whose temple attracted pilgrims from all parts of the Inca empire. The first Spanish visitors to Cuzco reported that it took four hundred paces for them to walk around the temple complex, and they expressed amazement at its lavish decoration, including a golden sculpture of the sun encrusted with gems. Particularly astonishing to the visitors was an imitation garden in which grains of gold represented a field, which was planted with stalks of maize

Fulfilling her tribute duty to the Inca state, an Inca woman weaves woolen fabric on a loom attached to a tree.

fabricated from gold and surrounded by twenty golden llamas with their attendants, also sculpted in gold. Priests of Inti and those serving other cults honored their deities with sacrifices, which in Inca society usually took the form of agricultural produce or animals such as llamas and guinea pigs rather than humans.

Moral Thought   In addition to sacrifices and ritual ceremonies, Inca religion had a strong moral dimension. The Incas taught a concept of sin as a violation of the established social or natural order, and they believed in a life beyond death, during which individuals would receive rewards or punishments based on the quality of their earthly lives. Sin, they believed, would bring divine disaster both for individuals and for their larger communities. The Incas also observed rituals of confession and penance by which priests absolved individuals of their sins and returned them to the good graces of the gods.

THE SOCIETIES OF OCEANIA

Inhabitants of Oceania did not interact with peoples of different societies as frequently or systematically as did their counterparts in the eastern hemisphere, but they built and maintained flourishing societies of their own. The aboriginal peoples of Australia ventured over vast stretches of their continent and created networks of trade and exchange between hunting and gathering societies. Only in the far north, however, did they deal with peoples beyond Australia as they traded sporadically with merchants from New Guinea and the islands of southeast Asia. Meanwhile, throughout the Pacific Ocean, islanders built complex agricultural societies. By the time European mariners sailed into the Pacific Ocean in the sixteenth century, the larger island groups had sizable populations, hierarchical social orders, and hereditary chiefly rulers. In the central and western Pacific, mariners sailed regularly between island groups and established elaborate trade networks. Islanders living toward the eastern and western edges of the Pacific Ocean also had occasional dealings with American and Asian peoples, sometimes with significant consequences for the Pacific island societies.

The Nomadic Foragers of Australia

After the aboriginal peoples of Australia learned how to exploit the resources of the continent's varied regions, they led

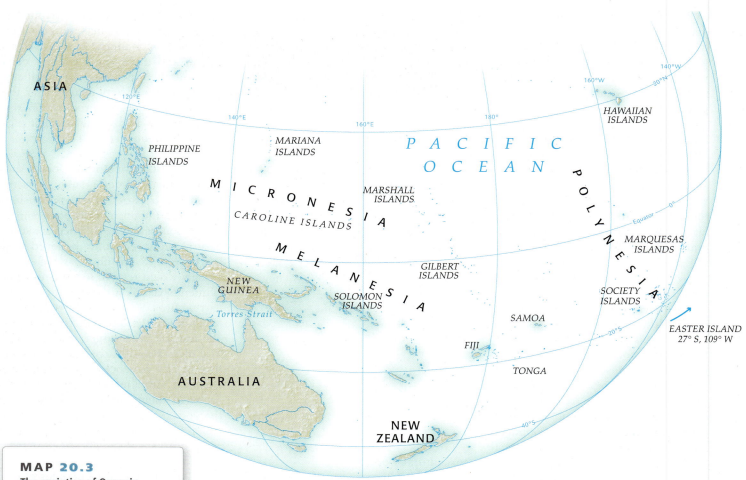

ASIA

PHILIPPINE
ISLANDS

MARIANA
ISLANDS

*PACIFIC
OCEAN*

HAWAIIAN
ISLANDS

M I C R O N E S I A

MARSHALL
ISLANDS

CAROLINE ISLANDS

P O L Y N E S I A

M E L A N E S I A

GILBERT
ISLANDS

MARQUESAS
ISLANDS

NEW
GUINEA

SOLOMON
ISLANDS

SOCIETY
ISLANDS

Torres Strait

SAMOA

EASTER ISLAND
27° S, 109° W

FIJI

AUSTRALIA

TONGA

NEW
ZEALAND

MAP 20.3

The societies of Oceania.
Islands are much more numerous and much closer together in
the western Pacific than in the
eastern Pacific.

*In what ways did proximity to or
distance from other islands influence the development of Pacific
island societies?*

lives that in some ways
changed little over the
centuries. Unlike their
neighbors to the north,
they did not turn to agriculture. The inhabitants
of New Guinea began to
herd swine and cultivate
root crops about 5000
B.C.E., and the inhabi-
tants of islands in the Torres Strait (which separates Australia from New Guinea) took up gardening soon thereafter.
Although aboriginal peoples of northern Australia must
have known about foods cultivated in neighboring lands,
they maintained nomadic, foraging societies until European
peoples migrated to Australia in large numbers during the
nineteenth and twentieth centuries.

Trade As a result of their mobile and nomadic way of life,
aboriginal Australians frequently met and interacted with
peoples of neighboring societies. Because Australia is a
continent of enormous climatic and ecological diversity, dif-

ferent peoples enjoyed access to food and other resources
unknown to others they encountered during their seasonal
migrations. Even though as nomads they did not accumulate large quantities of material goods, groups regularly exchanged surplus food and small items when they met.

That sort of small-scale exchange eventually enabled
trade goods to spread throughout most of Australia. Individuals did not travel along all the trade routes. Instead, trade
goods passed from one aboriginal community to another
until they came to rest in regions often distant from their
origins. Pearly oyster shells were among the most popular
trade items. Archaeologists have turned up many of these
shells fashioned into jewelry more than 1,600 kilometers
(1,000 miles) from the waters where the oysters bred. From
interior regions came stone axe heads, spears, boomerangs,
furs, skins, and fibers.

Aboriginal peoples occasionally traded foodstuffs, but
with the exception of some root vegetables, those items
were generally too perishable for exchange. Peoples on
the north coast also engaged in a limited amount of trade
with mariners from New Guinea and the islands of southeast Asia. Australian spears and highly prized pearly shells

went north in exchange for exotic items such as the striking flowers of the bird-of-paradise plant, stone clubs, decorative trinkets—and occasionally iron axes, much coveted by aboriginal peoples who had no tradition of metallurgy.

Cultural and Religious Traditions In spite of seasonal migrations, frequent encounters with peoples from other aboriginal societies, and trade over long distances, the cultural traditions of Australian peoples mostly did not diffuse much beyond the regions inhabited by individual societies. Aboriginal peoples paid close attention to the prominent geographic features of the lands around them. Rocks, mountains, forests, mineral deposits, and bodies of water were crucial for their survival, and they related stories and myths about those and other geographic features. Often, they conducted religious observances designed to ensure continuing supplies of animals, plant life, and water. Given the intense concern of aboriginal peoples with their immediate environments, their cultural and religious traditions focused on local matters and did not appeal to peoples from other regions.

The Development of Pacific Island Societies

By the early centuries C.E., human migrants had established agricultural societies in almost all the island groups of the Pacific Ocean. About the middle of the first millennium C.E., they ventured to the large islands of New Zealand—the last large, habitable region of the earth to receive members of the human species. After 1000 C.E., Polynesians inhabiting the larger Pacific islands grew especially numerous, and their surging population prompted remarkable social and political development.

Trade between Island Groups In the central and western regions of the Pacific, where several clusters of islands are relatively close to one another, mariners linked island societies. Regional trade networks facilitated exchanges of useful goods such as axes and pottery, exotic items such as shells and decorative ornaments, and sometimes even foodstuffs such as yams. Regional trade within individual island groups served social and political as well as economic functions, since it helped ruling elites establish and maintain harmonious relations with one another. In some cases, trade crossed longer distances and linked different island groups. Inhabitants of the Tonga, Samoa, and Fiji islands traded mats and canoes, for example, and also intermarried, thus creating political and social relationships.

Long-Distance Voyaging Elsewhere in Polynesia, vast stretches of deep blue water made it much more complicated to travel between different island groups and societies. As a result, regular trade networks did not emerge in the eastern Pacific Ocean. Nevertheless, mariners undertook lengthy voyages on an intermittent basis, sometimes with momentous results. After the original settlement of Easter Island about 300 C.E., for example, Polynesian mariners probably ventured to the western coast of South America,

A painting from 1825 shows several fishponds in active use near Honolulu in Hawai`i. How did ponds like these enable Hawaiians to catch more fish?

thinking about ENCOUNTERS

Maritime Encounters and Their Effects

Polynesian peoples inhabited tiny islands scattered throughout a vast ocean, and they necessarily relied on local resources to meet most of their needs. Yet they also sailed thousands of kilometers over open oceans to establish cultural contacts and trading relationships with inhabitants of other islands. What were the most important results of the encounters between residents of distant islands?

where they learned about the cultivation of sweet potatoes. Between about 400 and 700 C.E., mariners spread sweet potatoes throughout Polynesia and beyond to New Caledonia and Vanuatu. The new crop quickly became a prominent source of food in all the islands it reached. Sweet potatoes were especially important for the **Maori** population of New Zealand because the staple crops of the tropical Pacific did not flourish in the temperate climes of New Zealand. Thus long-distance voyages were responsible for the dissemination of sweet potatoes to remote islands situated thousands of kilometers from the nearest inhabited lands.

Another case of long-distance voyaging prompted social changes in the Hawaiian Islands. For centuries after the voyages that brought the original settlers to the islands in the early centuries C.E., there was little travel or communication between Hawai`i and other Polynesian societies. During the twelfth and thirteenth centuries, however, a series of two-way voyages linked Hawai`i with Tahiti and the Marquesas Islands. Memories of those voyages survive in oral traditions that relate the introduction into Hawai`i of new chiefly and priestly lines from Tahiti. Evidence for the voyages comes also from Hawaiian adoption of fishhook styles from Tahiti and words from the Tahitian language.

Population Growth

While undertaking regular or intermittent voyages over long distances, islanders throughout the Pacific Ocean also built productive agricultural and fishing societies. They cultivated taro, yams, sweet potatoes, bananas, breadfruit, and coconuts, and they kept domesticated chickens, pigs, and dogs. They also fed on abundant supplies of fish, which they caught by spear, net, and hook. After about the fourteenth century, as their population increased, the inhabitants of Hawai`i built ingenious fishponds that allowed small fry to swim from the ocean through narrow gates into rock-enclosed spaces but prevented larger fish from escaping. Fishponds enabled Hawaiians to harvest large quantities of mature fish with relative ease and thus contributed to the islanders' food supplies. The establishment of agricultural and fishing societies led to rapid

population growth in all the larger Pacific island groups—Samoa, Tonga, the Society Islands (including Tahiti), and Hawai`i. In Hawai`i, the most heavily populated of the Polynesian island groups, the human population may have exceeded five hundred thousand when European mariners arrived in the late eighteenth century.

Dense populations sometimes led to environmental degradation and social strife on small islands with limited resources. Easter Island in particular was the site of dramatic problems arising from overpopulation. Polynesian migrants originally settled Easter Island in the early centuries C.E., and during the era from about 1100 to 1500, their descendants numbered about ten thousand. This population placed tremendous pressure on the island's resources and also competed fiercely among themselves for those resources. By 1500, having divided into hostile camps, islanders fought one another ferociously, engaging in brutal massacres of their enemies and the desecration of their bodies. As their society disintegrated, they sometimes resorted to cannibalism for lack of sufficient food.

Nan Madol

In other lands, dense populations promoted social organization on a scale never before seen in Oceania. On Pohnpei in the Caroline Islands, for example, the Sandeleur dynasty built a powerful state and organized construction of a massive stone palace and administrative center at Nan Madol. Built mostly during the period from 1200 to 1600, the complex included ninety-three artificial islets protected by seawalls and breakwaters on three sides.

Development of Social Classes

Indeed, beginning about the thirteenth century, expanding populations prompted residents of many Pacific islands to develop

A massive wall constructed of basalt rock protects a burial site at Nan Madol in Pohnpei.

Maori (MAU-ree)

sources from the past

Mo`ikeha's Migration from Tahiti to Hawai`i

A group of Polynesian oral traditions preserve memories of numerous two-way voyages between Tahiti and Hawai`i in the twelfth and thirteenth centuries. One of them has to do with Mo`ikeha, a high chief who left Tahiti because of domestic difficulties and migrated to Hawai`i, where he founded a new chiefly line. The legend recounts several voyages between Tahiti and Hawai`i. The following excerpts deal with Mo`ikeha's establishment as a chief in Hawai`i and the later arrival of his Tahitian son La`amaikahiki, who is credited with the introduction of Tahitian religious and cultural traditions to Hawai`i.

It was dark by the time they arrived [at the Hawaiian island of Kaua`i], so they did not land, instead, mooring their canoe offshore. Early the next morning the people saw this double-hulled canoe floating offshore with the kapu sticks of a chief aboard. The canoe was brought ashore and the travellers got off. Meanwhile the locals were gathering in a crowd to go surf-riding. . . . Among them were the two daughters of the ali`i nui [chief] of Kaua`i, Ho`oipoikamalanai and Hinauu.

Mo`ikeha and his companions saw the crowd and followed along to take part in the morning exercise. Mo`ikeha was a handsome man with dark reddish hair and a tall, commanding figure.

When Ho`oipoikamalanai and her sister saw Mo`ikeha, they immediately fell in love with him, and they decided to take him for their husband. Mo`ikeha in the meantime was also struck with the beauty and grace of the two sisters, and he, too, fell in love with them and decided to take one of them to be his wife. After enjoying the surf for a time, Ho`oipoikamalanai and her sister returned home and told their father about the new arrival and said: "We wish to take that young chief as a husband for one of us." The father approved.

Orders were issued that Mo`ikeha be brought to the house of the two ali`i women. Mo`ikeha and his company were sent for and brought in the presence of the king [the ali`i nui of Kaua`i]. The love of these young people being mutual, Ho`oipoikamalanai and Hinauu took Mo`ikeha to be their husband. Mo`ikeha became ali`i nui of Kaua`i after the death of his father-in-law. . . .

Mo`ikeha worked to make his two wives and five children happy, giving his undivided attention to the bringing up of his boys. He thought no more of Lu`ukia [his lover in Tahiti], but after a while, he began to feel a yearning desire to see his son La`amaikahiki, his child by his first wife Kapo. So he called his five sons together and said to them: "I'm thinking of sending one of you boys to bring your elder brother to Hawai`i." . . .

[After Mo`ikeha's son Kila sailed to Tahiti and found his elder half-brother] La`amaikahiki immediately prepared to accompany his brother to Hawai`i, as Mo`ikeha wished. La`amaikahiki took his priests and his god Lonoika`ouali`i, and set sail for Hawai`i with the men who had come with Kila. When they were approaching Kaua`i, La`amaikahiki began beating his drum. Mo`ikeha heard his drum and ordered everything, the land as well as the house, to be made ready for the reception of the chief La`amaikahiki. Upon the arrival of La`amaikahiki and Kila, the high priest of Kaua`i, Poloahilani, took La`amaikahiki and his god Lonoila`ouali`i ("Lono at the Chiefly Supremacy") to the heiau [temple]. It is said that La`amaikahiki was the first person to bring a god (akua) to Hawai`i. . . .

[After returning to Tahiti, then sailing again to Hawai`i, La`amaikahiki] set sail again, going up the Kona coast [of Hawai`i Island]. . . . It was on this visit that La`amaikahiki introduced hula dancing, accompanied by the drum, to Hawai`i. . . .

La`amaikahiki stayed a long time on Kaua`i teaching the people the art of dancing. From Kaua`i La`amaikahiki visited all the other islands of this group and thus the drum dance (hula ka`eke) spread to the other islands.

For Further Reflection

■ How would you characterize the political, social, and cultural significance of two-way voyaging between Tahiti and Hawai`i?

Source: Teuira Henry and others. *Voyaging Chiefs of Havai`i.* Ed. by Dennis Kawaharada. Honolulu: Kalamaku Press, 1995, pp. 138–39, 144–46.

increasingly complex social and political structures. Especially on the larger islands, workers became more specialized: some concentrated on cultivating certain crops, and others devoted their efforts to fishing, producing axes, or constructing large, seagoing canoes. Distinct classes emerged as aristocratic and ruling elites decided the course of public affairs in their societies and extracted surplus agricultural production from those of common birth. The islands of Tonga, Tahiti, and Hawai`i had especially stratified societies with sharp distinctions between various classes of high chiefs, lesser chiefs, and commoners. Hawaiian society also recognized distinct classes of priests and skilled artisans, such as adze makers and canoe builders, ranking between the chiefly and common classes.

The Formation of Chiefly States
In addition to distinct social classes, island societies generated strong political leadership. Ruling chiefs generally oversaw public affairs in portions of an island, sometimes in an entire island, and occasionally in several islands situated close to one another. In Tonga and Hawai`i, high chiefs frequently launched campaigns to bring additional islands under their control and create large centralized states. Rarely, however, were these militant chiefs able to overcome geographic and logistic difficulties and realize their expansionist ambitions before the nineteenth century.

Nevertheless, high chiefs guided the affairs of complex societies throughout Polynesia. They allocated lands to families, mobilized labor for construction projects, and organized men into military forces. They commanded enormous respect within their societies. In Hawai`i, for example, the classes of high chiefs known as *ali`i nui* intermarried, ate the best fish and other foods that were *kapu* ("taboo") to commoners, and had the right to wear magnificent cloaks adorned with thousands of bright red and yellow bird feathers. Indeed, a *kapu* forbade commoners to approach or even cast a shadow on the *ali`i nui*.

Polynesian Religion
High chiefs worked closely with priests, who served as intermediaries between human communities and the gods. Gods of war and agriculture were common throughout the Pacific islands, but individual islands and island groups recognized deities particular to their own regions and interests. The most distinctive architecture of early Pacific societies was the ceremonial precinct and temple structure known as *marae* (or *heiau* in Hawaiian). *Marae* often had several terraced floors with a rock or coral wall designating the boundaries of the sacred space. In Tonga and Samoa, temples made of timber and thatched roofs served as places of worship, sacrifice, and communication between priests and the gods, whereas in eastern Polynesia religious ceremonies took place on platforms in open-air courtyards. The largest of those structures, the *marae* Mahaiatea on Tahiti, took the form of a step pyramid about 15 meters (49 feet) high with a base measuring 81 by 22 meters (266 by 72 feet).

Pacific island societies did not enjoy access to the range of technologies developed by continental peoples until the sixteenth and later centuries. Yet Pacific islanders cleverly exploited their environments, established productive agricultural economies, built elaborate, well-organized societies, and reached out when possible to engage in trade with their neighbors. Their achievements testify anew to the human impulses toward densely populated communities and interaction with other societies.

in perspective

The original inhabitants of the Americas and Oceania lived in societies that were considerably smaller than those of the eastern hemisphere. They did not possess the metallurgical technologies that enabled their counterparts to exploit the natural environment, nor did they possess the transportation technologies based on wheeled vehicles and domesticated animals that facilitated trade and communication among peoples of the eastern hemisphere. Nevertheless, long before they entered into sustained interaction with European and other peoples, they built complex societies and developed sophisticated cultural and religious traditions. Indigenous peoples established foraging, fishing, and agricultural societies throughout the Americas, and they fashioned tools from wood, stone, and bone that enabled them to produce enough food to support sizable communities. In Mesoamerica and Andean South America, they also built imperial states that organized public affairs on a large scale. The cultural and religious traditions of these imperial societies reflected their concern for agricultural production and the maintenance of complex social structures.

The original inhabitants of Australia and the Pacific islands built societies on a smaller scale than did the peoples of the Americas, but they too devised effective means of exploiting the natural environment and organizing flourishing communities. Australia was a continent of foraging nomadic peoples, whereas the Pacific islands supported densely populated agricultural societies. Although they had limited communication with peoples of the Americas or the eastern hemisphere, the peoples of Oceania traded and interacted regularly with their neighbors, and inhabitants of the Pacific islands sometimes undertook lengthy voyages to trade with distant island groups. ●

CHRONOLOGY

AMERICAS

950–1150	High point of the Toltec empire
1175	Collapse of the Toltec empire
1250	Inca settlement near Cuzco
1345	Foundation of Tenochtitlan by the Mexica
1400	Emergence of the five Iroquois nations
1428–1440	Reign of the Aztec ruler Itzcóatl
1438–1471	Reign of the Inca ruler Pachacuti
1440–1469	Reign of the Aztec ruler Motecuzoma I
1502–1520	Reign of the Aztec ruler Motecuzoma II
1519	Arrival of Spanish conquerors in Mexico

OCEANIA

11th century	Beginning of population growth in Pacific islands
12th century	Beginning of two-way voyages between Hawai`i and Tahiti and the Marquesas islands
13th century	Emergence of distinct social classes and chiefly states
14th century	Construction of fishponds in Hawai`i

PART 4

For Further Reading

Peter Bellwood. *The Polynesians: Prehistory of an Island People.* Rev. ed. London, 1987. Well-illustrated popular account emphasizing the origins and early development of Polynesian societies.

Geoffrey Blainey. *Triumph of the Nomads: A History of Aboriginal Australia.* Melbourne, 1975. A sympathetic account of Australia before European arrival, well informed by archaeological discoveries.

Inga Clendinnen. *Aztecs: An Interpretation.* Cambridge, 1991. A brilliant re-creation of the Mexica world, concentrating on cultural and social themes.

George A. Collier, Renato I. Rosaldo, and John D. Wirth, eds. *The Inca and Aztec States, 1400–1800: Anthropology and History.* New York, 1982. Seventeen well-focused essays represent approaches that scholars have taken to the Inca and Aztec empires.

Nigel Davies. *The Ancient Kingdoms of Mexico.* Harmondsworth, 1983. Reliable popular account.

Hans Dietrich Disselhoff. *Daily Life in Ancient Peru.* Trans. by A. Jaffa. New York, 1967. A well-illustrated volume concentrating on social history that places Inca society in larger historical context.

Ben Finney. *Voyage of Rediscovery: A Cultural Odyssey through Polynesia.* Berkeley, 1994. Fascinating account of efforts to understand ancient Polynesian techniques of seafaring and migrations.

Ross Hassig. *Aztec Warfare: Imperial Expansion and Political Control.* Norman, Okla., 1988. A solid scholarly study of Mexica military affairs and their role in the building of the Aztec empire.

John Hyslop. *The Inka Road System.* New York, 1984. A careful archaeological study.

Patrick V. Kirch. *The Evolution of the Polynesian Chiefdoms.* Cambridge, 1984. Examines the development of Polynesian societies in light of archaeological discoveries.

———. *On the Road of the Winds: An Archaeological History of the Pacific Islands before European Contact.* Berkeley, 2000. A valuable synthesis of recent scholarship by the foremost contemporary archaeologist of the Pacific islands.

Miguel León-Portilla. *The Aztec Image of Self and Society: An Introduction to Nahua Culture.* Salt Lake City, 1992. An excellent guide to Mexica social and cultural history.

David Lewis. *We, the Navigators: The Ancient Art of Landfinding in the Pacific.* Honolulu, 1973. Fascinating reconstruction of traditional methods of noninstrumental navigation used by Pacific Islanders.

Charles C. Mann. *1491: New Revelations of the Americas before Columbus.* New York, 2006. Summarizes a great deal of archaeological research on the pre-Columbian Americas.

Michael E. Moseley. *The Incas and Their Ancestors: The Archaeology of Peru.* Rev. ed. London, 2001. A comprehensive survey of Andean history through the era of the Incas.

Lynda Norene Shaffer. *Native Americans before 1492: The Mound-building Centers of the Eastern Woodlands.* Armonk, N.Y., 1992. Places the mound-building societies in historical context.

Reaching Out: Expanding Horizons of Cross-Cultural Interaction

chapter 21

A giraffe from east Africa sent as a present to China in 1414 and painted by a Chinese artist at the Ming zoo.

PART 4

EYEWITNESS:
On the Road with Ibn Battuta

One of the great world travelers of all time was the Moroccan legal scholar Ibn Battuta. Born in 1304 at Tangier, Ibn Battuta followed family tradition and studied Islamic law. In 1325 he left Morocco, perhaps for the first time, to make a pilgrimage to Mecca. He traveled by caravan across north Africa and through Egypt, Palestine, and Syria, arriving at Mecca in 1326. After completing his hajj, Ibn Battuta did not head for home but spent a year visiting Mesopotamia and Persia, then traveled by ship through the Red Sea and down the east African coast as far south as Kilwa. By 1330 he had returned to Mecca, but he did not stay there long. When he learned that the sultan of Delhi offered handsome rewards to foreign legal scholars, he set off for India. Instead of traveling there directly by sailing across the Arabian Sea, however, he followed a long and circuitous land route that took him through Egypt, Syria, Anatolia, Constantinople, the Black Sea, and the great trading cities of central Asia, Bokhara and Samarkand. Only in 1333 did he arrive in Delhi, from the north.

For the next eight years, Ibn Battuta remained in India, serving mostly as a *qadi* (judge) in the government of Muhammad ibn Tughluq, the sultan of Delhi. In 1341 Muhammad appointed him to head an enormous embassy to China, but a violent storm destroyed the party's ships as they prepared to depart Calicut for the sea voyage to China. All personal goods and diplomatic presents sank with the ships, and many of the passengers drowned. (Ibn Battuta survived because he was on shore attending Friday prayers at the mosque when the storm struck.) For the next several years, Ibn Battuta made his way around southern India, Ceylon, and the Maldive Islands, where he served as a *qadi* for the recently founded Islamic sultanate, before continuing to China on his own about 1345. He visited the bustling southern Chinese port cities of Quanzhou and Guangzhou, where he found large communities of Muslim merchants, before returning to Morocco in 1349 by way of southern India, the Persian Gulf, Syria, Egypt, and Mecca.

Still, Ibn Battuta's travels were not complete. In 1350 he made a short trip to the kingdom of Granada in southern Spain, and in 1353 he joined a camel caravan across the Sahara desert to visit the Mali empire, returning to Morocco in 1355. During his travels Ibn Battuta visited the equivalent of forty-four modern countries and logged more than 117,000 kilometers (73,000 miles). His account of his adventures stands with Marco Polo's book among the classic works of travel literature.

Between 1000 and 1500 C.E., the peoples of the eastern hemisphere traveled, traded, communicated, and interacted more regularly and intensively than ever before. The large empires of the Mongols and other nomadic peoples provided a political foundation for this cross-cultural interaction. When they conquered and pacified vast regions, nomadic peoples provided safe roads for merchants, diplomats, missionaries, and other travelers. Quite apart from the nomadic empires, improvements in maritime technology led to increased traffic in the sea lanes of the Indian Ocean and the South China Sea. As a result, long-distance travel became much more common than in earlier eras, and individual travelers such as Ibn Battuta and Marco Polo sometimes ventured throughout much of the eastern hemisphere.

Merchants and travelers exchanged more than trade goods. They diffused technologies and spread religious faiths. They also exchanged diseases and facilitated the spread of pathogens that caused widespread and deadly epidemics. During the middle decades of the fourteenth century, bubonic plague traveled the trade routes from western China to central Asia, southwest Asia, north Africa, and Europe. During its initial, furious onslaught, bubonic plague ravaged societies wherever it struck, and it continued to cause epidemics for three centuries and more.

Gradually, however, societies recovered from the plague. By the early fifteenth century, Chinese and western European peoples in particular had restabilized their societies and begun to renew cross-cultural contacts. In Europe, that effort had profound consequences for modern world history. As they sought entry to the markets of Asia, European mariners not only established direct connections with African and Asian peoples but also sailed to the western hemisphere and the Pacific Ocean. Their voyages brought the peoples of the eastern hemisphere, the western hemisphere, and Oceania into permanent and sustained interaction. Thus cross-cultural interactions of the period 1000 to 1500 pointed toward global interdependence, a principal characteristic of modern world history.

LONG-DISTANCE TRADE AND TRAVEL

Travelers embarked on long-distance journeys for a variety of reasons. Nomadic peoples ranged widely in the course of migrations and campaigns of conquest. East European and African slaves traveled involuntarily to the Mediterranean basin, southwest Asia, India, and sometimes even southern China. Buddhist, Christian, and Muslim pilgrims undertook extraordinary journeys to visit holy shrines. Three of the more important motives for long-distance travel between 1000 and 1500 C.E. were trade, diplomacy, and missionary activity. The cross-cultural interactions that resulted helped spread technological innovations throughout the eastern hemisphere.

Patterns of Long-Distance Trade

Merchants engaged in long-distance trade relied on two principal networks of trade routes. Luxury goods of high value relative to their weight, such as silk textiles and precious stones, often traveled overland on the silk roads used since classical times. Bulkier commodities, such as steel, stone, coral, and building materials, traveled the sea lanes of the Indian Ocean, since it would have been unprofitable to transport them overland. The silk roads linked all of the Eurasian landmass, and trans-Saharan caravan routes drew west Africa into the larger economy of the eastern hemisphere. The sea lanes of the Indian Ocean served ports in southeast Asia, India, Arabia, and east Africa while also offering access via the South China Sea to ports in China, Japan, Korea, and the spice-bearing islands of southeast Asia. Thus, in combination, land and sea routes touched almost every corner of the eastern hemisphere.

Trading Cities As the volume of trade increased, the major trading cities and ports grew rapidly, attracting buyers, sellers, brokers, and bankers from parts near and far. Khanbaliq (modern Beijing), Hangzhou, Quanzhou, Melaka, Cambay, Samarkand, Hormuz, Baghdad, Caffa, Cairo, Alexandria, Kilwa, Constantinople, Venice, Timbuktu, and many other cities had large quarters occupied by communities of foreign merchants. When a trading or port city enjoyed a strategic location, maintained good order, and resisted the temptation to levy excessive customs fees, it had the potential to become a major emporium serving long-distance trade networks. A case in point is Melaka (in modern Malaysia). Founded in the 1390s, within a few decades Melaka became the principal clearinghouse of trade in the eastern Indian Ocean. The city's authorities policed the strategic Strait of Melaka and maintained a safe market that welcomed all merchants and levied reasonable fees on goods exchanged there. By the end of the fifteenth century, Melaka had a

The massive walls of this caravanserai in Cairo protected travelers and their goods, while food, drink, and lodging were available inside for merchants as well as their animals.

population of some fifty thousand people, and in the early sixteenth century the Portuguese merchant Tomé Pires reported that more than eighty languages could be heard in the city's streets.

During the early and middle decades of the thirteenth century, the Mongols' campaigns caused economic disruption throughout much of Eurasia—particularly in China and southwest Asia, where Mongol forces toppled the Song and Abbasid dynasties. Mongol conquests inaugurated a long period of economic decline in southwest Asia where the conquerors destroyed cities and allowed irrigation systems to fall into disrepair. As the Mongols consolidated their hold on conquered lands, however, they laid the political foundation for a surge in long-distance trade along the silk roads. Merchants traveling the silk roads faced less risk of banditry or political turbulence than in previous times. Meanwhile, strong economies in China, India, and western Europe fueled demand for foreign commodities. Many merchants traveled the whole distance from Europe to China in pursuit of profit.

Marco Polo The best-known long-distance traveler of Mongol times was the Venetian Marco Polo (1253–1324). Marco's father, Niccolò, and uncle Maffeo were among the first European merchants to visit China. Between 1260 and

1269 they traveled and traded throughout Mongol lands, and they met Khubilai Khan as he was consolidating his hold on China. When they returned to China in 1271, seventeen-year-old Marco Polo accompanied them. The great khan took a special liking to Marco, who was a marvelous conversationalist and storyteller. Khubilai allowed Marco to pursue his mercantile interests in China and also sent him on numerous diplomatic missions, partly because Marco regaled him with stories about the distant parts of his realm. After seventeen years in China, the Polos decided to return to Venice, and Khubilai granted them permission to leave. They went back on the sea route by way of Sumatra, Ceylon, India, and Arabia, arriving in Venice in 1295.

A historical accident has preserved the story of Marco Polo's travels. After his return from China, Marco was captured and made a prisoner of war during a conflict between his native Venice and its commercial rival, Genoa. While imprisoned, Marco related tales of his travels to his fellow prisoners. One of them was a writer of romances, and he compiled the stories into a large volume that circulated rapidly throughout Europe.

In spite of occasional exaggerations and tall tales, Marco's stories deeply influenced European readers. Marco always mentioned the textiles, spices, gems, and other goods

MAP 21.1

Travels of Marco Polo and Ibn Battuta.
Between them, Marco Polo and Ibn Battuta traveled across much of the Eurasian landmass, as well as parts of Africa and southeast Asia.

Compare the routes taken by Marco Polo and Ibn Battuta during their travels. How did the two men choose where to travel? What conditions made it possible for them to travel so far from their homes?

Mongol empires

Marco Polo's travels

Ibn Battuta's travels

he observed during his travels, and European merchants took note, eager to participate in the lucrative trade networks of Eurasia. The Polos were among the first Europeans to visit China, but they were not the last. In their wake came hundreds of others, mostly Italians. In most cases, their stories do not survive, but their travels helped to increase European participation in the larger economy of the eastern hemisphere.

Political and Diplomatic Travel

Marco Polo came from a family of merchants, and merchants were among the most avid readers of his stories. Marco himself most likely collaborated closely with Italian merchants during his years in China. Yet his experiences also throw light on long-distance travel undertaken for political and diplomatic purposes. Khubilai Khan and the other Mongol rulers of China did not entirely trust their Chinese subjects and regularly appointed foreigners to administrative posts. In his account of his travels, Marco reported that Khubilai appointed him governor of the large trading city of Yangzhou. There is no independent evidence to confirm that claim, but Marco may well have filled some sort of administrative position. In addition, he represented Khubilai Khan's interests on diplomatic missions. To support himself in China, then, Marco supplemented his mercantile ventures with various official duties assigned to him by his patron, the great khan.

Mongol-Christian Diplomacy   The emergence of elaborate trading networks and the establishment of vast imperial states created great demand for political and diplomatic representation during the centuries after 1000 C.E. The thirteenth century was a time of especially active diplomacy involving parties as distant as the Mongols and western Europeans, both of whom considered a military alliance against their common Muslim foes. As European Christians sought to revive the crusading movement and recapture Jerusalem from Muslim forces, the Mongols were attacking the Abbasid empire from the east. During the 1240s and 1250s, Pope Innocent IV dispatched a series of envoys who invited the Mongol khans to convert to Christianity and join Europeans in an alliance against the Muslims. The khans declined the invitation, proposing in reply that the pope and European Christians submit to Mongol rule or face destruction.

Rabban Sauma   Although the early round of Mongol-European diplomacy offered little promise of cooperation, the Mongols later initiated another effort. In 1287 the Mongol ilkhan of Persia planned to invade the Muslim-held lands of southwest Asia, capture Jerusalem, and crush Islam as a political force in the region. In hopes of attracting support for the project, he dispatched Rabban Sauma, a Nestorian Christian priest born in the Mongol capital of Khanbaliq but of Turkish ancestry, as an envoy to the pope and European political leaders.

An illustration from a fourteenth-century French manuscript depicts Marco Polo picking pepper with local workers in southern India.

Rabban Sauma met with the kings of France and England, the pope, and other high officials of the Roman Catholic church. He enjoyed a fine reception, but he did not succeed in attracting European support for the ilkhan. Only a few years later, in 1295, Ghazan, the new ilkhan of Persia, converted to Islam, thus precluding any further possibility of an alliance between the Mongols of Persia and European Christians. Nevertheless, the flurry of diplomatic activity illustrates the complexity of political affairs in the eastern hemisphere and the need for diplomatic consultation over long distances.

The expansion of Islamic influence in the eastern hemisphere encouraged a different kind of politically motivated travel. Legal scholars and judges played a crucial role in Islamic societies, since the *sharia* prescribed religious observances and social relationships based on the Quran. Conversions to Islam and the establishment of Islamic states in India, southeast Asia, and sub-Saharan Africa created a demand for Muslims educated in Islamic law. After about the eleventh century, educated Muslims from southwest Asia and north Africa regularly traveled to recently converted lands to help instill Islamic values.

Ibn Battuta Best known of the Muslim travelers was Ibn Battuta (1304–1369). Islamic rulers governed most of the lands Ibn Battuta visited—including India, the Maldive Islands, the Swahili city-states of east Africa, and the Mali empire—but very few Muslims educated in the law were available in those lands. With his legal credentials Ibn Battuta had little difficulty finding government positions. As *qadi* and advisor to the sultan of Delhi, he supervised the affairs of a wealthy mosque and heard cases at law, which he strictly enforced according to Islamic standards of justice. On one occasion Ibn Buttuta sentenced a man to receive eighty lashes because he had drunk wine eight years earlier.

After leaving northern India, Ibn Battuta obtained a post as *qadi* in the Maldive Islands. There he heard cases at law and worked zealously to promote proper observance of Islam. He ordered lashings for men who did not attend Friday prayers, and he once sentenced a thief to lose his right hand in accordance with punishment prescribed by the *sharia*. He also attempted, unsuccessfully, to persuade island women to meet the standards of modesty observed in other Islamic lands by covering their breasts. In both east

sources from the past

Ibn Battuta on Customs in the Mali Empire

Long-distance travelers often encountered unfamiliar customs in foreign societies. The Moroccan traveler Ibn Battuta approved heartily when staying with hosts who honored the values of his own Muslim society, but he had little tolerance for those who did not. Here he describes what he witnessed at the sultan's court in the Mali empire.

The Blacks are the most respectful of people to their king and abase themselves most before him. They swear by him, saying *Mansa Sulaiman ki* [the law of Mansa Sulaiman, the Mali sultan]. If he summons one of them at his session in the cupola . . . the man summoned removes his robe and puts on a shabby one, takes off his turban, puts on a dirty skull-cap and goes in with his robe and his trousers lifted half way to his knees. He comes forward humbly and abjectly, and strikes the ground hard with his elbows. He stands as if he were prostrating himself in prayer, and hears what the Sultan says like this. If one of them speaks to the Sultan and he answers him, he takes his robe off his back, and throws dust on his head and back like someone making his ablutions with water. I was astonished that they did not blind themselves.

When the Sultan makes a speech in his audience those present take off their turbans from their heads and listen in silence. Sometimes one of them stands before him, recounts what he has done for his service, and says: "On such and such a day I did such and such, and I killed so and so on such and such a day." Those who know vouch for the truth of that and he does it in this way. One of them draws the string of his bow, then lets it go as he would do if he were shooting. If the Sultan says to him: "You are right" or thanks him, he takes off his robe and pours dust on himself. That is good manners among them. . . .

Among their good practices are their avoidance of injustice; there is no people more averse to it, and their Sultan does not allow anyone to practice it in any measure; [other good practices include] the universal security in their coun-

try, for neither the traveller nor the resident there has to fear thieves or bandits . . . their punctiliousness in praying, their perseverance in joining the congregation, and in compelling their children to do so; if a man does not come early to the mosque he will not find a place to pray because of the dense crowd; it is customary for each man to send his servant with his prayer-mat to spread it out in a place reserved for him until he goes to the mosque himself. . . . They dress in clean white clothes on Fridays; if one of them has only a threadbare shirt he washes it and cleans it and wears it for prayer on Friday. They pay great attention to memorizing the Holy Qur'an. . . .

Among their bad practices are that the women servants, slave-girls and young daughters appear naked before people, exposing their genitals. I used to see many like this in [the fasting month of] Ramadan, for it is customary for the *fararis* [commanders] to break the fast in the Sultan's palace, where their food is brought to them by twenty or more slave-girls, who are naked. Women who come before the Sultan are naked and unveiled, and so are his daughters. On the night of the twenty-seventh of Ramadan I have seen about a hundred naked slave-girls come out of his palace with food; with them were two daughters of the Sultan with full breasts and they too had no veil. They put dust and ashes on their heads as a matter of good manners. [Another bad practice:] Many of them eat carrion, dogs and donkeys.

For Further Reflection

■ Discuss the various ways in which Islamic influences and established local customs came together in the Mali empire.

Source: H. A. R. Gibb, trans. *The Travels of Ibn Battuta,* A.D. *1325–1354,* 4 vols. London: Hakluyt Society, 1958–94, 4:960, 965–66.

and west Africa, Ibn Battuta consulted with Muslim rulers and offered advice about government, women's dress, and proper relationships between the sexes. Like many legal scholars whose stories went unrecorded, Ibn Battuta provided guidance in the ways of Islam in societies recently converted to the faith.

Missionary Campaigns

Sufi Missionaries Islamic values spread not only through the efforts of legal scholars but also through the missionary activities of Sufi mystics. As in the early days of Islam, Sufis in

the period from 1000 to 1500 ventured to recently conquered or converted lands and sought to win a popular following for the faith in India, southeast Asia, and sub-Saharan Africa. Sufis did not insist on a strict, doctrinally correct understanding of Islam but, rather, emphasized piety and devotion to Allah. They even tolerated continuing reverence of traditional deities, whom the Sufis treated as manifestations of Allah and his powers. By taking a flexible approach to their missions, the Sufis spread Islamic values without facing the resistance that unyielding and doctrinaire campaigns would likely have provoked.

Christian Missionaries Meanwhile, Roman Catholic missionaries also traveled long distances, in the interests of spreading Christianity. Missionaries accompanied the crusaders and other forces to all the lands where Europeans extended their influence after the year 1000. In lands where European conquerors maintained a long-term presence—such as the Baltic lands, the Balkan region, Sicily, and Spain—missionaries attracted converts in large numbers, and Roman Catholic Christianity became securely established. In the eastern Mediterranean region, however, where crusaders were unable to hold their conquests permanently, Christianity remained a minority faith.

The most ambitious missions sought to convert Mongols and Chinese to Roman Catholic Christianity. Until the arrival of European merchants and diplomats in the thirteenth century, probably no Roman Catholic Christian had ever ventured as far east as China, although Nestorian Christians from central Asia had maintained communities there since the seventh century. As more Europeans traveled to China, their expatriate communities created a demand for Roman Catholic services. Many of the Roman Catholic priests who traveled to China probably intended to serve the needs of those communities, but some of them also sought to attract converts.

John of Montecorvino Most active of the Roman Catholic missionaries in China was John of Montecorvino, an Italian Franciscan who went to China in 1291, became the first archbishop of Khanbaliq in 1307, and died there in 1328. While serving the community of Roman Catholic expatriates in China, John worked energetically to establish Christianity in the host society. He translated the New Testament and the book of Psalms into Turkish, a language commonly used at the Mongol court, and he built several churches in China. He took in young boys from Mongol and Chinese families, baptized them, and taught them Latin and Roman Catholic rituals. He claimed to have baptized six thousand individuals by 1305, and he invited the great khan himself to convert to Christianity. Although popular and widely respected among Europeans, Chinese, and Mongols alike, John attracted few Asian peoples to Christianity.

Roman Catholic authorities in Europe dispatched many other priests and missionaries to China during the early fourteenth century, but like John of Montecorvino, they won few converts. Missions successfully established Christian communities in Scan-

dinavia, eastern Europe, Spain, and the Mediterranean islands that European armies recaptured from Muslims during the centuries after 1000 C.E., but east Asia was too distant for the resources available to the Roman Catholic church. Moreover, east Asian peoples already possessed sophisticated religious and cultural traditions, so Christianity had little appeal. Nevertheless, Christian missions to China continued until the mid-fourteenth century, when the collapse of the Mongols' Yuan dynasty and the eruption of epidemic disease temporarily disrupted long-distance travel across Eurasia.

Long-Distance Travel and Cross-Cultural Exchanges

Cultural Exchanges Long-distance travel of all kinds, whether for commercial, political, diplomatic, or missionary purposes, encouraged cultural exchanges between peoples of different societies. Songs, stories, religious ideas, philosophical views, and scientific knowledge all passed readily among travelers who ventured into the larger world during the era from 1000 to 1500 C.E. The troubadours of western Europe, for example, drew on the poetry, music, and love songs of Muslim performers when developing the literature of courtly love. Similarly, European scientists avidly consulted their Muslim and Jewish counterparts in Sicily and Spain to learn about their understanding of the natural world.

Large numbers of travelers also facilitated agricultural and technological diffusion during the period from 1000 to 1500. Indeed, technological diffusion sometimes facilitated long-distance travel. The magnetic compass, for example, invented in China during the Tang or the Song dynasty, spread throughout the Indian Ocean basin during the eleventh century, and by the mid-twelfth century European mariners used compasses in the Mediterranean and the Atlantic Ocean. Diffusion of the compass was a boon to maritime trade, since it allowed mariners to sail over long stretches of deep water with confidence in their ability to find their destinations and return home safely.

Caterina Vilioni, daughter of the Venetian merchant Domenico Vilioni, died in the Chinese trading city of Yangzhou in 1342. Her tombstone, which shows she was part of the Roman Catholic community in Yangzhou, came to light during a construction project in 1951.

Spread of Crops Long-distance journeys enabled Muslim travelers to introduce new food and commercial crops to sub-Saharan Africa. Food crops included citrus fruits and Asian strains of rice, which enriched diets in west Africa after the eleventh century. Muslims also introduced cotton to west Africa, and by 1100, cotton fab-

sources fromthe past

John of Montecorvino on His Mission in China

The Franciscan John of Montecorvino (1247–1328) served as a Roman Catholic missionary in Armenia, Persia, and India before going to China in 1291. There he served as priest to expatriate European Christians, and he sought to attract converts to Christianity from the Mongol and Chinese communities. In a letter of 8 January 1305 asking for support from his fellow Franciscans in Italy, John outlined some of his activities during the previous thirteen years.

[After spending thirteen months in India] I proceeded on my further journey and made my way to China, the realm of the emperor of the Mongols who is called the great khan. To him I presented the letter of our lord the pope and invited him to adopt the Catholic faith of our Lord Jesus Christ, but he had grown too old in idolatry. However, he bestows many kindnesses upon the Christians, and these two years past I have gotten along well with him. . . .

I have built a church in the city of Khanbaliq, in which the king has his chief residence. This I completed six years ago; and I have built a bell tower to it and put three bells in it. I have baptized there, as well as I can estimate, up to this time some 6,000 persons. . . . And I am often still engaged in baptizing.

Also I have gradually bought one hundred and fifty boys, the children of pagan parents and of ages varying from seven to eleven, who had never learned any religion. These boys I have baptized, and I have taught them Greek and Latin after our manner. Also I have written out Psalters for them, with thirty hymnals and breviaries [prayer books]. By help of these, eleven of the boys already know our service and form a choir and take their weekly turn of duty as

they do in convents, whether I am there or not. Many of the boys are also employed in writing out Psalters and other suitable things. His Majesty the Emperor moreover delights much to hear them chanting. I have the bells rung at all the canonical hours, and with my congregation of babes and sucklings I perform divine service, and the chanting we do by ear because I have no service book with the notes. . . .

Indeed if I had but two or three comrades to aid me, it is possible that the emperor khan himself would have been baptized by this time! I ask then for such brethren to come, if any are willing to come, such I mean as will make it their great business to lead exemplary lives. . . .

I have myself grown old and grey, more with toil and trouble than with years, for I am not more than fifty-eight. I have got a competent knowledge of the language and script which is most generally used by the Tartars. And I have already translated into that language and script the New Testament and the Psalter and have caused them to be written out in the fairest penmanship they have, and so by writing, reading, and preaching, I bear open and public testimony to the law of Christ.

For Further Reflection

■ To what extent did John of Montecorvino's missionary work reflect conditions different from those that motivated St. Francis of Assisi to found a mendicant order?

Source: Henry Yule and Henri Cordier, eds. *Cathay and the Way Thither*, 4 vols. London: Hakluyt Society, 1913–16, 3:45–50. (Translation slightly modified.)

---

rics had become popular with the ruling elites and wealthy merchants of the west African kingdoms. Cotton grew well in the savannas, and by 1500 it was the principal textile produced in sub-Saharan Africa.

Sugarcane Muslims were also instrumental in the continuing diffusion of sugarcane. Muslim merchants and other travelers had begun large-scale cultivation of sugarcane in southwest Asia and north Africa during the Abbasid caliphate. They experimented with the plant in west Africa but had limited success because of adverse environmental conditions.

After the twelfth century, however, Muslims facilitated the westward spread of sugarcane by acquainting European crusaders with crystallized sugar refined from cane. Up to that time Europeans had little access to refined sugar, and they relied on honey and fruits as sweeteners. They imme-

diately appreciated the convenience of refined sugar. Italian entrepreneurs began to organize sugarcane plantations on Mediterranean islands such as Sicily, Cyprus, Crete, and Rhodes. Rapidly increasing demand for refined sugar encouraged investors to seek suitable locations throughout the Mediterranean basin. The cultivation of sugarcane had deep social and economic implications. Besides influencing local economic development in lands where it spread, it touched distant societies. Like their Muslim predecessors, European sugar producers often staffed their plantations with slave laborers, and the growth of plantations fueled an increasing demand for Muslim war captives and black Africans who could supply labor services.

Gunpowder Technologies Although Muslim merchants and travelers were especially prominent agents of

An illustration from a manuscript of 1282 depicts a Christian (left) playing chess with a Muslim (right). Chess was one of many cultural elements that passed from Muslim to Christian societies during the crusading era.

diffusion, Mongols also contributed to the process, notably by helping to spread gunpowder technologies west from China. Mongol invaders learned about gunpowder from Chinese military engineers in the early thirteenth century and soon incorporated gunpowder-based weapons into their arsenal: as early as 1214 Chinggis Khan's armies included an artillery unit. During the 1250s, as they campaigned in Persia and southwest Asia, the Mongols used catapults and trebuchets to lob gunpowder bombs into cities under siege. Muslim armies soon developed similar weapons in response.

By the mid-thirteenth century, gunpowder had reached Europe—possibly by way of Mongol-ruled Russia—and Eu-

ropeans had begun to experiment with gunpowder-fueled rockets. By the early fourteenth century, armies from China to Europe possessed primitive cannons. Although not especially accurate, the weapons were powerful enough to blow holes in the defensive walls of cities under siege. Thus, with the assistance of Mongol warriors, gunpowder technology rapidly spread from its homeland in China across the entire Eurasian landmass.

Agricultural and technological diffusions of the era 1000 to 1500 were by no means unique processes in world history. For millennia, agricultural crops and technological skills had spread widely whenever peoples of different socie-

English forces besiege a French citadel during the Hundred Years' War (1337–1453). Note that the besiegers on the left side of this manuscript illustration employ cannons and smaller firearms that launch gunpowder bombs.

ties interacted with one another. Because of the particularly intense interactions of the period from 1000 to 1500, however, agricultural and technological diffusion profoundly influenced the lives of peoples throughout the eastern hemisphere. The spread of food crops enriched diets and supported increasing populations, and the spread of industrial crops such as cotton promoted economic development. The diffusion of the magnetic compass enabled mariners to sail the seas more safely and effectively, and the spread of gunpowder technology changed forever the nature of war.

CRISIS AND RECOVERY

As Eurasian peoples traveled over long distances, they not only exchanged trade goods, agricultural crops, and technological expertise but also unwittingly helped disease patho-

gens to spread. When diseases broke out among previously unexposed populations, they often caused deadly epidemics that severely disrupted whole societies. During the fourteenth century, bubonic plague erupted in epidemics that ravaged societies throughout most of Asia, Europe, and north Africa. Epidemic plague struck intermittently until the seventeenth century, but by the fifteenth century Chinese and European societies had begun to recover from its effects and wield their influence in the larger world.

Bubonic Plague

The Little Ice Age   About 1300 C.E. a process of global climatic change caused temperatures to decline significantly and abruptly throughout much of the world. For more than five hundred years, the earth experienced a "little ice age," when temperatures were much cooler than in the era from

A painting of 1503 graphically communicates the horror felt by medieval Europeans when bubonic plague struck their communities. Here death takes away a cartload of victims while others die beside the road.

infects rodents such as rats, squirrels, and prairie dogs, and fleas transmit the pathogen from one rodent to another. If rodent populations decline, fleas seek other hosts and sometimes spread the disease to human victims. In the early fourteenth century, Mongol military campaigns helped spread plague from Yunnan to China's interior: an epidemic in 1331 reportedly killed 90 percent of the population in Hebei province in northeastern China, near modern Beijing. During the 1350s epidemics broke out in widely scattered regions of China, and contemporaries reported that plague carried away two-thirds of the population in some afflicted areas.

Spread of Plague

During the 1340s Mongols, merchants, and other travelers spread the disease along trade routes to points west of China. It thrived in the oases and trading cities of central Asia, where domestic animals and rodents provided abundant breeding grounds for fleas and the plague bacillus. By 1346 it had reached the Black Sea ports of Caffa and Tana. In 1347, Italian merchants fled plague-infected Black Sea ports and unwittingly spread the disease throughout the Mediterranean basin. By 1348, following the trade routes, plague had sparked epidemics in most of western Europe.

Wherever it appeared, bubonic plague struck with frightful effects. Victims developed inflamed lymph nodes, particularly in the neck, armpit, and groin areas, and most died within a few days after the onset of symptoms. Internal hemorrhaging often discolored the inflammations known as buboes—which gave rise to the term *bubonic*—and because of the black or purple swellings, Europeans referred to the plague as the "Black Death." Bubonic plague typically killed 60 to 70 percent of its human victims and had the potential to ravage a society within a few months. In some small villages and towns, disease wiped out the entire population. A spate of new births generally followed outbreaks of plague as societies tried to replenish their numbers, but plague also returned and claimed new victims. In Europe plague erupted intermittently from the 1340s until the late seventeenth century.

Some parts of the eastern hemisphere did not suffer directly from plague epidemics. The long, cold winters of Scandinavia discouraged the proliferation of plague-bearing

1000 to 1300 C.E. With markedly cooler temperatures and shorter growing seasons, agricultural production declined in many lands, leading to famine and sometimes even starvation. In some northerly lands, agriculture ceased to be a practical possibility: after the onset of the little ice age, Norse settlers abandoned the colonies they had occupied in Greenland since the tenth century.

Origins of Epidemic Bubonic Plague

As they struggled to cope with the cooling climate, peoples in much of the eastern hemisphere suddenly encountered a new challenge in the form of devastating epidemic disease. Bubonic plague spread from the Yunnan region of southwestern China, where it probably had been endemic for centuries. The plague bacillus

thinking about ENCOUNTERS

Long-Distance Travel and Cross-Cultural Exchanges

With the aid of long-distance travelers, many cultural traditions, technologies, and biological species spread widely through the eastern hemisphere: Islam, Christianity, gunpowder, the compass, sugarcane, bubonic plague, and others as well. Taking both a short-term and a long-term view, which do you consider the most important effects of long-distance travel in the era 1200 to 1500?

rodents and fleas, so the northernmost parts of Europe escaped the plague's worst effects. For reasons unknown, India also seems to have avoided serious difficulties. In fact, the Indian population grew from 91 million in the year 1300 to 97 million a century later and 105 million in 1500. Epidemics also largely bypassed sub-Saharan Africa, even though plague had long been endemic in the Great Lakes region of east Africa.

Population Decline In lands hard hit by plague, however, it took a century and more to begin recovery from the demographic consequences of epidemic disease. In 1300 China's population, already reduced by conflicts with the Mongols since the early thirteenth century, stood at eighty-five million. In 1400, after about seventy years of epidemic plague, Chinese numbers amounted to only seventy-five million. A century later demographic recovery was under way, and China's population rebounded to one hundred million.

European society also reeled from the effects of bubonic plague. From seventy-nine million in 1300, Europe's population dropped by almost 25 percent to sixty million in 1400. As in China, demographic recovery in Europe was under way in 1500 when the European population climbed to eighty-one million. Islamic societies in southwest Asia, Egypt, and north Africa also suffered devastating population losses, and demographic recovery took much longer there than in China and Europe. In Egypt human population probably did not reach preplague levels until the nineteenth century.

Social and Economic Effects Because of the heavy demographic toll that it levied, bubonic plague disrupted societies and economies throughout Eurasia and north Africa. Epidemics killed the young, the weak, and the old in especially high numbers, but they spared no group. Peasants and laborers, artisans and crafts workers, merchants and bankers, priests and nuns, rulers and bureaucrats all fell before the plague's onslaught. The disease caused severe labor shortages, which in turn generated social unrest.

In western Europe, for example, urban workers demanded higher wages, and many left their homes in search of better conditions. Political authorities responded by freezing wages and forbidding workers to leave their homes. For their part, peasants in the countryside also sought to improve their circumstances by moving to regions where landlords offered better terms. Landlords responded to that challenge by restricting the freedom of peasants to move and by reimposing labor requirements: in effect, the lords

sought to reinstate conditions of serfdom that they had allowed to lapse before the arrival of plague. As a result of sharply conflicting interests, disgruntled workers and peasants mounted a series of rebellions that rocked both the towns and the countryside of western Europe. Authorities eventually extinguished the revolts but only after considerable social disruption and loss of life.

By the seventeenth century the plague had lost much of its ferocity. Epidemics occurred more sporadically, and they did not seriously diminish human populations. Since the 1940s, antibiotic drugs have brought the disease largely under control among human populations, although it survives in rodent communities throughout much of the world.

Recovery in China: The Ming Dynasty

By the mid-fourteenth century, the Mongols' Yuan dynasty was experiencing very difficult times. Financial mismanagement led to serious economic difficulties, and political conflicts led to assassinations and factional fighting among the Mongols. In 1368, with bubonic plague raging, the Yuan dynasty collapsed, and the Mongols departed China en masse and returned to the steppes, leaving China in a state of both demographic and political turmoil. An increasing birthrate soon helped to replenish human numbers. Political recovery accompanied the demographic rebound.

Hongwu When the Yuan dynasty fell, the governance of China returned to Chinese hands. The new emperor came from a family so poor that he spent much of his youth as a beggar. Orphaned, he entered a Buddhist monastery to assure himself of food, clothing, and shelter. Because of his size and strength, he came to the notice of military commanders, and he made his way through the ranks to lead the rebellious forces that toppled the Yuan dynasty. In 1368 he became Emperor Hongwu, and he proclaimed the establishment of the Ming ("brilliant") dynasty, which lasted until 1644.

Ming Centralization Hongwu immediately set about eliminating all traces of Mongol rule and establishing a government on the model of traditional Chinese dynasties. Like the founders of several earlier Chinese dynasties, Hongwu had little interest in scholarly matters, but he reestablished the Confucian educational and civil service systems to ensure a supply of talented officials and bureaucrats. At the same time, he moved to centralize authority more tightly than ever before in Chinese history. In 1380, when he suspected his chief minister of involvement in a treasonous plot, Hongwu executed the minister and his bureaucratic allies

Ming artisans won worldwide fame for their blue-and-white porcelain, which inspired the founders of the Delft porcelain factory in the Netherlands. This covered jar dates from the early fifteenth century.

and also abolished the minister's position altogether. From that time forward the Ming emperors ruled directly, without the aid of chief ministers, and they closely supervised imperial affairs.

Mandarins and Eunuchs

The Ming emperors insisted on absolute obedience to the policies and initiatives of the central government. They relied heavily on the mandarins, a special class of powerful officials sent out as emissaries of the central government to ensure that local officials implemented imperial policy. The Ming emperors also turned to eunuchs for governmental services. Earlier Chinese emperors, as well as rulers of other lands, had long relied on eunuchs, since they could not generate families and build power bases that might challenge ruling houses. In keeping with their centralizing policy, however, the Ming emperors employed eunuchs much more extensively than any of their predecessors, in the expectation that servants whose fortunes depended exclusively on the emperors' favor would work especially diligently to advance the emperors' interests.

The employment of mandarins and eunuchs enhanced the authority of the central government. The tightly centralized administration instituted by the early Ming emperors lasted more than five hundred years. Although the dynasty fell in 1644 to Manchu invaders, who founded the Qing dynasty, the Manchus retained the administrative framework of the Ming state, which largely survived until the collapse of the Qing dynasty in 1911.

Economic Recovery

While building a centralized administration, the Ming emperors also worked toward economic recovery from nomadic rule and epidemic disease. The new rulers conscripted laborers to rebuild irrigation systems that had fallen into disrepair during the previous century, and agricultural production surged as a result. At the same time, they promoted the manufacture of porcelain, lacquerware, and fine silk and cotton textiles. Ming rulers did not actively promote trade with other lands, but private Chinese merchants eagerly sought commercial opportunities and conducted a thriving business marketing Chinese products in ports and trading cities from Japan to the islands of southeast Asia. Meanwhile, domestic trade surged within China, reflecting increasing productivity and prosperity.

Cultural Revival

In addition to political and economic recovery, the Ming dynasty sponsored a kind of cultural revival in China. Emperor Hongwu tried to eradicate all signs of the recent nomadic occupation by discouraging the use of Mongol names and the wearing of Mongol dress. Ming emperors actively promoted Chinese cultural traditions, particularly the Confucian and neo-Confucian schools. Hongwu's successor, **Yongle,** organized the preparation of a vast encyclopedia that compiled all significant works of Chinese history, philosophy, and literature. This *Yongle Encyclopedia* ran to almost twenty-three thousand manuscript rolls, each equivalent to a medium-size book. The government originally planned to issue a printed edition of the encyclopedia but abandoned the project because of its enormous expense. Nevertheless, the *Yongle Encyclopedia* was a remarkable anthology, and it signaled the Ming rulers' interest in supporting native Chinese cultural traditions.

Recovery in Europe: State Building

Demographic recovery strengthened states in Europe as it did in China. In Europe, however, political authority rested with a series of regional states rather than a centralized empire. By the late fifteenth century, states in Italy, Spain, France, England, and Russia had devised techniques of government that vastly enhanced their power.

During the later middle ages (1300–1500), internal problems as well as bubonic plague complicated European political affairs. The Holy Roman Empire survived in name, but after the mid-thirteenth century effective authority lay with the German princes and the Italian city-states rather than the emperor. In Spain descendants of Muslim conquerors held the kingdom of Granada in the southern portion of the Iberian peninsula. The kings of France and England sparred constantly over lands claimed by both. Their hostilities eventually resulted in the Hundred Years' War (1337–1453), a protracted series of intermittent campaigns in which the warring factions sought control of lands in France. Russia had even more difficult problems. In the late 1230s Mongol armies conquered the flourishing commercial center of Kiev, and descendants of Chinggis Khan extracted tribute from Russia for almost 250 years thereafter. In the fifteenth century, however, the Mongol states fell into disorder, giving rise to a vast power vacuum in Russia.

Taxes and Armies

By the late fifteenth century, however, regional states in western Europe had greatly strengthened their societies, and some had also laid the foundations for the emergence of powerful monarchies. The state-building efforts of the later middle ages involved two especially important elements. The first was the development of fresh sources of finance, usually through new taxes levied directly on citizens and subjects, which supplemented the income that rulers received from their subordinates. The second was the maintenance of large standing armies, often composed of mercenary forces and equipped with gunpowder weapons, supported by state funds.

Italian States

The state-building process began in Italy, where profits from industrial production and trade enriched the major cities. The principal Italian states—the city-states of Milan, Venice, and Florence, the papal state based in Rome, and the kingdom of Naples—needed large numbers of officials to administer their complex affairs. They also needed ready access to military forces that could protect

Yongle (YAWNG-leh)

The Florentine painter Masaccio was a pioneer of Renaissance art. His fresco *Tribute Money*, produced about 1427, relies on the technique of linear perspective to depict figures in realistic relationship to one another and their surroundings. How does linear perspective lend a sense of depth to this scene?

their interests. Beginning as early as the thirteenth century, the Italian city-states financed those needs by levying direct taxes and issuing long-term bonds that they repaid from treasury receipts. With fresh sources of finance, the principal Italian states strengthened their authority within their own boundaries and between them controlled public affairs in most of the Italian peninsula.

France and England During the fourteenth and fifteenth centuries, Italian administrative methods made their way beyond the Alps. Partly because of the enormous expenses they incurred during the Hundred Years' War, the kings of France and England began to levy direct taxes and assemble powerful armies. The French kings taxed sales, hearths, and salt; their English counterparts instituted annual taxes on hearths, individuals, and plow teams. Rulers in both lands asserted the authority of the central government over the nobility. The English kings did not establish a standing army, but they were able to raise powerful forces when rebellion threatened public order. In France, however, King Louis XI (reigned 1461–1483) maintained a permanent army of about fifteen thousand troops, many of them professional mercenary soldiers equipped with firearms. Because the high expense of maintaining such forces was beyond the means of the nobility, Louis and his successors enjoyed a decisive edge over ambitious subordinates seeking to challenge royal authority or build local power bases.

Spain The process of state building was most dramatic in Spain, where the marriage in 1469 of Fernando of Aragon and Isabel of Castile united the two wealthiest and most important Iberian realms. Receipts from the sales tax, the primary source of royal income, supported a powerful standing army. Under Fernando and Isabel, popularly known as the Catholic Kings, Christian forces completed the *reconquista* by conquering the kingdom of Granada and absorbing it into their state. The Catholic Kings also projected their authority beyond Iberia. When a French army threatened the kingdom of Naples in 1494, they seized southern Italy, and by 1559 Spanish forces had established their hegemony throughout most of the Italian peninsula. Fernando and Isabel also sought to make a place for Spain in the markets of Asia by sponsoring Christopher Columbus's quest for a western route to China.

Russia State building took place in Russia as well as in western Europe. After the fourteenth century, as Mongol power waned, Russian princes sought to expand their territories. Most successful of them were the grand princes of Moscow. As early as the mid-fourteenth century, the princes began the process of "gathering the Russian land" by acquiring territories surrounding their strategically located commercial town of Moscow on the Volga River. In 1480 Grand Prince Ivan III (reigned 1462–1505), later known as Ivan the Great, stopped paying tribute to the Mongol khan. By refusing to acknowledge the khan's supremacy, Ivan in effect declared

thinking about ENCOUNTERS

Trading-Post Empires

Trading-post empires provided the most prominent spaces for cross-cultural interactions between Europeans, Africans, and Asians. Trading posts also limited European intrusion into Africa and Asia, especially in contrast to the settlement empires of the Americas. What characterized the relations between, for example, the Portuguese and the inhabitants of the Indian Ocean basin? Why were Europeans confined to such posts?

neither the Philippines nor Indonesia had a powerful state when Europeans arrived there in the sixteenth century. Nor did imperial authorities in China or India lay claim to the island regions. Heavily armed ships enabled Europeans to bring considerable force to bear and to establish imperial regimes that favored the interests of European merchants.

Conquest of the Philippines

Spanish forces approached the Philippines in 1565 under the command of Miguel López de Legazpi, who named the islands after King Philip II of Spain. Legazpi overcame local authorities in Cebu and Manila in almost bloodless contests. Because the Philippines had no central government, there was no organized resistance to the intrusion. Spanish forces faced a series of small, disunited chiefdoms, most of which soon fell before Spanish ships and guns. By 1575 Spanish forces controlled the coastal regions of the central and northern islands, and during the seventeenth century they extended their authority to most parts of the archipelago. The main region outside their control was the southern island of Mindanao, where a large Muslim community stoutly resisted Spanish expansion.

Manila

Spanish policy in the Philippines revolved around trade and Christianity. Manila soon emerged as a bustling, multicultural port city—an entrepôt for trade particularly in silk—and it quickly became the hub of Spanish commercial activity in Asia. Chinese merchants were especially prominent in Manila. They occupied a specially designated commercial district of the city, and they accounted for about one-quarter of Manila's forty-two thousand residents in the mid-seventeenth century. They supplied the silk goods that Spanish traders shipped to Mexico in the so-called Manila galleons. Their commercial success brought suspicion on their community, and resentful Spanish and Filipino residents massacred Chinese merchants by the thousands in at least six major eruptions of violence in 1603, 1639, 1662, 1686, 1762, and 1819. Nevertheless, Spanish authorities continued to rely heavily on the wealth that Chinese merchants brought to Manila.

Apart from promoting trade, Spanish authorities in the Philippines also sought to spread Roman Catholicism throughout the archipelago. Spanish rulers and missionaries pressured prominent Filipinos to convert to Christianity in hopes of persuading others to follow their example. They opened schools to teach the fundamentals of Christian doctrine, along with basic literacy, in densely populated regions throughout the islands. The missionaries encountered stiff resistance in highland regions, where Spanish authority was not as strong as on the coasts, and resistance drew support from opponents of Spanish domination as well as from resentment of the newly arrived faith. Over the long term, however, Filipinos turned increasingly to Christianity, and by the nineteenth century the Philippines had become one of the most fervent Roman Catholic lands in the world.

Conquest of Java

Dutch mariners, who imposed their rule on the islands of Indonesia, did not worry about seeking converts to Christianity, but concentrated instead on the trade in spices, particularly cloves, nutmeg, and mace. The architect of Dutch policy was Jan Pieterszoon Coen, who in 1619 founded Batavia on the island of Java to serve as an entrepôt for the VOC. Batavia occupied a strategic site near the Sunda Strait, and its market attracted both Chinese and Malay vessels. Coen's plan was to establish a VOC monopoly over spice production and trade, thus enabling Dutch merchants to reap enormous profits in European markets. Coen brought his naval power to bear on the small Indonesian islands and forced them to deliver spices only to VOC merchants. On larger islands such as Java, he took advantage of tensions between local princes and authorities and extracted concessions from many in return for providing them with aid against the others. By the late seventeenth century, the VOC controlled all the ports of Java as well as most of the important spice-bearing islands throughout the Indonesian archipelago.

Dutch numbers were too few for them to rule directly over their whole southeast Asian empire. They made alliances with local authorities to maintain order in most regions, reserving for direct Dutch rule only Batavia and the most important spice-bearing islands such as clove-producing Amboina and the Banda Islands. They sought less to rule than to control the production of spices. The Dutch did not embark on campaigns of conquest for purposes of adding to their holdings, but they uprooted spice-bearing plants on islands they did not control and mercilessly attacked peoples who sold their spices to merchants not associated with the VOC. Monopoly profits from the spice trade not only enriched the VOC but also made the Netherlands the most prosperous land in Europe throughout most of the seventeenth century.

Workers are harvesting mace, a spice derived from nutmeg trees that are indigenous to the Banda Islands of Indonesia. Until the nineteenth century, these islands were the world's only source of this valuable spice.

Foundations of the Russian Empire in Asia

While western European peoples were building maritime empires, Russians were laying the foundations for a vast land empire that embraced most of northern Eurasia. This round of expansion began in the mid-sixteenth century, as Russian forces took over several Mongol khanates in central Asia. These acquisitions resulted in Russian control over the Volga River and offered opportunities for trade with the Ottoman empire, Iran, and even India through the Caspian Sea. Because of its strategic location on the Volga delta where the river flows into the Caspian Sea, the city of Astrakhan became a bustling commercial center, home to a community

A woodcut illustration depicts indigenous peoples of Siberia delivering fur tribute to Russian merchants in a walled, riverside fort.

of several hundred foreign merchants from as far away as northern India. During the seventeenth and eighteenth centuries, some of the Indian merchants regularly made their way up the Volga River to trade in Moscow and the Russian interior, while others devised plans (which they never realized) to extend their activities to the Baltic Sea and take their business to western Europe. In the eighteenth century, Russian forces extended their presence in the Caspian Sea region by absorbing much of the Caucasus, a vibrant multiethnic region embracing the modern-day states of Georgia, Armenia, and Azerbaijan.

Encounters in Siberia

Far more extensive were Russian acquisitions in northeastern Eurasia. The frozen tundras and dense forests of Siberia posed formidable challenges, but explorers and merchants made their way into the region in a quest for fur. Throughout the early modern era, fur was a lucrative commodity that lured Russians eastward, just as North American fur attracted the interest of English, French, and Dutch merchants. Russian expansion in northeastern

Eurasia began in 1581 when the wealthy Stroganov family hired a freebooting adventurer named Yermak to capture the khanate of Sibir in the Ural Mountains. In the following decades, Russian explorers pushed into the interior regions of Siberia by way of the region's great rivers. By 1639 they had made their way across the Eurasian landmass and reached the Pacific Ocean.

Native Peoples of Siberia

Siberia was home to about twenty-six major ethnic groups that lived by hunting, trapping, fishing, or herding reindeer. These indigenous peoples varied widely in language and religion, and they responded in different ways to the arrival of Russian adventurers who sought to exact tribute from them by coercing them to supply pelts on a regular basis. Some groups readily accepted iron tools, woven cloth, flour, tea, and liquor for the skins of fur-bearing animals such as otter, lynx, marten, arctic fox, and especially the sleek sable. Others resented the ever-increasing demands for tribute and resisted Russian encroachment on their lands. Russian forces then resorted to punishing raids and hostage taking to induce Siberian peoples to deliver furs. The Yakut people of the Lena and Aldan River valleys in central Siberia mounted a revolt against Russian oppression in 1642 and experienced a brutal retribution that continued for forty years, forcing many Yakut out of their settlements and reducing their population by an estimated 70 percent. Quite apart from military violence, the peoples of Siberia also reeled from epidemic diseases that reduced many populations by more than half.

As violence and disease sharply diminished the delivery of furs, the Russian government recognized that its interests lay in protection of the "small peoples," as state officials called the indigenous inhabitants of Siberia. Government-sponsored missionaries sought to convert Siberian peoples to Orthodox Christianity and bring them into Russian society, but they had little success. Few Siberians expressed an interest in Christianity, and those few came mostly from the ranks of criminals, abandoned hostages, slaves, and others who had little status in their own societies. Furthermore, once indigenous peoples converted to Christianity, they were exempt from obligations to provide fur tributes, so the Russian government demonstrated less zeal in its religious mission than did the Spanish monarchs, who made the spread of Roman Catholic Christianity a prime goal of imperial expansion. Although they managed to attract a few Siberian converts, Orthodox missionaries mostly served the needs of Russian merchants, adventurers, and explorers in Siberia. For their part, the indigenous peoples of Siberia continued to practice their inherited religions guided by native shamans.

The Russian Occupation of Siberia

The settlers who established a Russian presence in Siberia included social misfits, convicted criminals, and even prisoners of war. Despite the region's harsh terrain, Russian migrants gradually filtered into Siberia and thoroughly altered its demographic complexion. Small agricultural settlements grew up near many trading posts, particularly in the fertile Amur River valley. Siberian landowners offered working conditions that were much lighter than those of Russia proper, so disgruntled peasants sometimes fled to settlements east of the Ural Mountains. Over time, Siberian trading posts with their garrisons developed into Russian towns with Russian-speaking populations attending Russian Orthodox churches. By 1763 some 420,000 Russians lived in Siberia, nearly double the number of indigenous inhabitants. In the nineteenth century, large numbers of additional migrants moved east to mine Siberian gold, silver, copper, and iron, and the Russian state was well on the way toward consolidating its control over the region.

Commercial Rivalries and the Seven Years' War

Exploration and imperial expansion led to conflicts not only between Europeans and Asians but also among Europeans themselves. Mariners competed vigorously for trade in Asia and the Americas, and their efforts to establish markets—and sometimes monopolies as well—led frequently to clashes with their counterparts from different lands.

Competition and Conflict

Indeed, throughout the seventeenth and early eighteenth centuries, commercial and political rivalries led to running wars between ships flying different flags. Dutch vessels were most numerous in the Indian Ocean, and they enabled the VOC to dominate the spice trade. Dutch forces expelled most Portuguese merchants from southeast Asia and prevented English mariners from establishing secure footholds there. By the early eighteenth century, trade in Indian cotton and tea from Ceylon had begun to overshadow the spice trade, and English and French merchants working from trading posts in India became the dominant carriers in the Indian Ocean. Fierce competition again generated violence: in 1746 French forces seized the English trading post at Madras, one of the three principal centers of British operations in India.

Commercial competition led to conflict also in the Caribbean and the Americas. English pirates and privateers preyed on Spanish shipping from Mexico, often seizing vessels carrying cargoes of silver. English and French forces constantly skirmished and fought over sugar islands in the Caribbean while also contesting territorial claims in North America. Almost all conflicts between European states in the eighteenth century spilled over into the Caribbean and the Americas.

The Seven Years' War

Commercial rivalries combined with political differences and came to a head in the Seven Years' War (1756–1763). The Seven Years' War was a global conflict in that it took place in several distinct geographic theaters—Europe, India, the Caribbean, and North America—and involved Asian and indigenous American peoples as well as Europeans. Sometimes called "the great war for empire," the Seven Years' War had deep implications for global affairs, since it laid the foundation for 150 years of British imperial hegemony in the world.

In Europe the war pitted Britain and Prussia against France, Austria, and Russia. In India, British and French forces each allied with local rulers and engaged in a contest for hegemony in the Indian Ocean. In the Caribbean, Spanish forces joined with the French in an effort to limit British expansion in the western hemisphere. In North America—where the Seven Years' War merged with a conflict already under way known as the French and Indian War (1754–1763)—British and French armies made separate alliances with indigenous peoples in an effort to outmaneuver each other.

British Hegemony

British forces fought little in Europe, where their Prussian allies held off massive armies seeking to surround and crush the expansive Prussian state. Elsewhere, however, British armies and navies handily overcame their enemies. They ousted French merchants from

MAP 22.5

Russian expansion, 1462–1795.
Observe how vast the empire became after it added the territory of Siberia.

How did Russians exert their control over such a huge and unforgiving territory?

PART 5

Fort Ross
1812

ALASKA

Bering
Strait

135°W

180°

75°N

150°W

165°W

60°N

Bering 1741

KAMCHATKA PENINSULA

Sea of
Okhotsk

45°N

165°E

150°E

30°N

*HAWAIIAN
ISLANDS*

PACIFIC OCEAN

Duchy of Muscovy in 1462	Russian expansion to 1795
Russian expansion to 1584	→ Bering's exploration of 1741
Russian expansion to 1689	→ Russian voyages to the Hawaiian Islands and California
Russian expansion to 1762	

India and took control of French colonies in Canada, although they allowed French authorities to retain most of their Caribbean possessions. They allowed Spanish forces to retain Cuba but took Florida from the Spanish empire. By no means did these victories make Britain master of the world, or even of Europe: both in Europe and in the larger world, powerful states challenged British ambitions. Yet victory in the Seven Years' War placed Britain in a position to dominate world trade for the foreseeable future, and "the great war for empire" paved the way for the establishment of the British empire in the nineteenth century. The war also suggested how close together earlier global exchanges had brought the peoples of the world.

ECOLOGICAL EXCHANGES

European explorers and those who followed them established links between all lands and peoples of the world. Interaction between peoples in turn resulted in an unprecedented volume of exchange across the boundary lines of societies and cultural regions. Some of that exchange involved biological species: plants, food crops, animals, human populations, and disease pathogens all spread to regions they had not previously visited. These biological exchanges had differing and dramatic effects on human populations, destroying some of them through epidemic diseases while enlarging others through increased food supplies and richer diets. Commercial exchange also flourished in the wake of the voyages of exploration as European merchants traveled to ports throughout the world in search of trade. By the late sixteenth century, they had built fortified trading posts at strategic sites in the Indian, Atlantic, and Pacific Ocean basins. By the mid-eighteenth century, they had established global networks of trade and communication.

The Columbian Exchange

Processes of biological exchange were prominent features of world history well before modern times. The early expansion of Islam had facilitated the diffusion of plants and food crops throughout much of the eastern hemisphere during the period from about 700 to 1100 C.E., and transplanted species helped spark demographic and economic growth in all the lands where they took root. During the fourteenth century the spread of bubonic plague caused drastic demographic losses when epidemic disease struck Eurasian and north African lands.

Biological Exchanges
Yet the "Columbian exchange"—the global diffusion of plants, food crops, animals, human populations, and disease pathogens that took place after voyages of exploration by Christopher Columbus and other European mariners—had consequences much more profound than did earlier rounds of biological exchange. Unlike the earlier processes, the Columbian exchange involved lands with radically different flora, fauna, and diseases. For thousands of years the various species of the eastern hemisphere, the western hemisphere, and Oceania had evolved along separate lines. By creating links between these biological zones, the European voyages of exploration set off a round of biological exchange that permanently altered the world's human geography and natural environment.

Beginning in the early sixteenth century, infectious and contagious diseases brought sharp demographic losses to indigenous peoples of the Americas and the Pacific islands. The worst scourge was smallpox, but measles, diphtheria, whooping cough, and influenza also took heavy tolls. Before the voyages of exploration, none of these maladies had reached the western hemisphere or Oceania, and the peoples of those regions consequently had no inherited or acquired immunities to those pathogens. In the eastern hemisphere, these diseases had mostly become endemic: they claimed a certain number of victims from the ranks of infants and small children, but survivors gained immunity to the diseases through exposure at an early age. In some areas of Europe, for example, smallpox was responsible for 10 to 15 percent of deaths, but most victims were age ten or younger. Although its effects were tragic for individual families and communities, smallpox did not pose a threat to European society as a whole because it did not carry away adults, who were mostly responsible for economic production and social organization.

Epidemic Diseases and Population Decline
When infectious and contagious diseases traveled to previously unexposed populations, however, they touched off ferocious epidemics that sometimes destroyed entire societies. Beginning in 1519, epidemic smallpox ravaged the Az-

Smallpox victims in the Aztec empire. The disease killed most of those it infected and left disfiguring scars on survivors.

tec empire, often in combination with other diseases, and within a century the indigenous population of Mexico had declined by as much as 90 percent, from about 17 million to 1.3 million. By that time Spanish conquerors had imposed their rule on Mexico, and the political, social, and cultural traditions of the indigenous peoples had either disappeared or fallen under Spanish domination.

Imported diseases took their worst tolls in densely populated areas such as the Aztec and Inca empires, but they did not spare other regions. Smallpox and other diseases were so easily transmissible that they raced to remote areas of North and South America and sparked epidemics even before the first European explorers arrived in those regions. By the 1530s smallpox may have spread as far from Mexico as the Great Lakes in the north and the pampas of Argentina in the south.

When introduced to the Pacific islands, infectious and contagious diseases struck vulnerable populations with the same horrifying effects as in the Americas, albeit on a smaller scale. All told, disease epidemics sparked by the Columbian exchange probably caused the worst demographic calamity in all of world history. Between 1500 and 1800, upwards of 100 million people may have died of diseases imported into the Americas and the Pacific islands.

Food Crops and Animals

Over the long term, however, the Columbian exchange increased rather than diminished human population because of the global spread of food crops and animals that it sponsored. In the long term, a better-nourished world was an important contributing factor in the growth of the world's population, which began in the eighteenth century and has continued to the present. Out of Eurasia to the western hemisphere traveled wheat, rice, sugar, bananas, apples, cherries, peaches, peas, and citrus fruits. Wheat in particular grew well on the plains of North America and on the pampas of Argentina, regions either too dry or too cold for the cultivation of indigenous maize (corn). Africa contributed yams, okra, collard greens, and coffee. Dairy and meat-yielding animals—horses, cattle, pigs, sheep, goats, and chickens—went from Europe to the Americas, where they sharply increased supplies of food and animal energy.

American Crops

Food crops native to the Americas also played prominent roles in the Columbian exchange. American crops that took root in Africa, Asia, and Europe include maize, potatoes, beans, tomatoes, peppers, peanuts, manioc, papayas, guavas, avocados, pineapples, and cacao, to name only the most important. (A less nutritious transplant was tobacco.) Residents of the eastern hemisphere only gradually developed a taste for American crops, but by the eighteenth century maize and potatoes had contributed to a sharply increased number of calories in Eurasian diets. Maize became especially important in China because it grew in eco-niches unsuitable for rice and millet produc-

tion. With the exception of Bengal (India), Asian lands proved less welcoming to the potato. It did eventually conquer most of northern Europe, from Ireland to Russia, because of its impressive nutritional qualities. American bean varieties added protein, and tomatoes and peppers provided vitamins and zesty flavors in lands from western Europe to China. Peanuts and manioc flourished in tropical southeast Asian and west African soils that otherwise would not produce large yields or support large populations. The Americas also supplied medicinal plants. Derived from the bark of the Peruvian cinchona tree, bitter-tasting quinine was the first effective treatment for malaria and proved vital to Europeans trying to survive mosquito-ridden tropics.

Population Growth

The Columbian exchange of plants and animals fueled a surge in world population. In 1500, as Eurasian peoples were recovering from epidemic bubonic plague, world population stood at about 425 million. By 1600 it had increased more than 25 percent to 545 million. Human numbers increased less rapidly during the next century,

Tabacum latifolium.

Tobacco was long used for religious and spiritual purposes in the Americas. After their arrival in the Americas, Europeans quickly popularized tobacco as a trade item and as a recreational drug to be smoked, snuffed, or chewed.

thinking about TRADITIONS

Local Foodways

For millennia, humans had generally relied on locally tended crops and foraged foods for their sustenance. How did the Columbian exchange alter those traditional foodways? What new crops and animals traveled between the eastern and western hemispheres—and what were the consequences?

reaching 610 million in 1700. But thereafter they increased at a faster rate than ever before in world history. By 1750 human population stood at 720 million, and by 1800 it had surged to 900 million, having grown by almost 50 percent during the previous century. Much of the rise was due to the increased nutritional value of diets enriched by the global exchange of food crops and animals.

Migration Alongside disease pathogens and plant and animal species, the Columbian exchange also involved the spread of human populations through transoceanic migration, whether voluntary or forced. During the period from 1500 to 1800, the largest contingent of migrants consisted of enslaved Africans transported involuntarily to South American, North American, and Caribbean destinations. A smaller but still sizable migration involved Europeans who traveled to the Americas and settled in lands depopulated by infectious and contagious diseases. During the nineteenth century, European peoples traveled in massive numbers mostly to the western hemisphere but also to south Africa, Australia, and Pacific islands where diseases had diminished indigenous populations, and Asian peoples migrated to tropical and subtropical destinations throughout much of the world. In combination, those migrations have profoundly influenced modern world history.

The Origins of Global Trade

The trading-post empires established by Portuguese, Dutch, and English merchants linked Asian markets with European consumers and offered opportunities for European mariners to participate in the carrying trade within Asia. European vessels transported Persian carpets to India, Indian cottons to southeast Asia, southeast Asian spices to India and China, Chinese silks to Japan, and Japanese silver and copper to China and India. By the late sixteenth century, European merchants were as prominent as Arabs in the trading world of the Indian Ocean basin.

Transoceanic Trade Besides stimulating commerce in the eastern hemisphere, the voyages of European merchant mariners encouraged the emergence of a genuinely global trading system. As Europeans established colonies in the Caribbean and the Americas, for example, trade networks extended to all areas of the Atlantic Ocean basin. European manufactured goods traveled west across the Atlantic in exchange for silver from Mexican and Peruvian mines and agricultural products such as sugar and tobacco, both of which were in high demand among European consumers. Trade in human beings also figured in Atlantic commerce. European textiles, guns, and other manufactured goods went south to west Africa, where merchants exchanged them for African slaves, who then went to the tropical and subtropical regions of the western hemisphere to work on plantations.

The Manila Galleons The experience of the Manila galleons illustrates the early workings of the global economy in the Pacific Ocean basin. For 250 years, from 1565 to 1815, Spanish galleons—sleek, fast, heavily armed ships capable of carrying large cargoes—regularly plied the waters of the Pacific Ocean between Manila in the Philippines and Acapulco on the west coast of Mexico. From Manila they took Asian luxury goods to Mexico and exchanged them for silver. Most of the precious metal made its way to China, where a thriving domestic economy demanded increasing quantities of silver, the basis of Chinese currency. In fact, the demand for silver was so high in China that European merchants exchanged it for Chinese gold, which they later traded profitably for more silver as well as luxury goods in Japan. Meanwhile, some of the Asian luxury goods from Manila remained in Mexico or went to Peru, where they contributed to a comfortable way of life for Spanish ruling elites. Most, however, went overland across Mexico and then traveled by ship across the Atlantic to Spain and European markets.

Environmental Effects of Global Trade As silver lubricated growing volumes of global trade, pressures fell on several animal species that had the misfortune to become prominent commodities on the world market. Fur-bearing animals came under particularly intense pressure, as hunters sought their pelts for sale to consumers in China, Europe, and North America. During the seventeenth century, an estimated two hundred to three hundred thousand sable pelts flowed annually from Siberia to the global market, and during the eighteenth century, more than sixteen million North American beaver pelts fed consumers' demands for fur hats and cloaks. Wanton hunting of fur-bearing animals soon drove many species into extinction or near-extinction, permanently altering the environments they had formerly inhabited. Quite apart from fur-bearing animals, early modern hunters harvested enormous numbers of deer, codfish, whales, walruses, seals, and other species as merchants

This is an artist's rendering of a Spanish galleon. Galleons were large, multidecked, highly stable and maneuverable sailing ships used by Europeans for war or commerce. The Spanish and the Portuguese built the largest types for their profitable overseas trade.

PART 5

sought to supply skins, food, oil, ivory, and other animal products to global consumers.

By the late sixteenth century, conditions favored the relentless human exploitation of the world's natural and agricultural resources, as European mariners had permanently linked the world's port cities and created global trading networks. During the next two centuries, the volume of global trade expanded, as English, Dutch, French, and other merchants contributed to the development of global markets. During the seventeenth century, for example, Dutch merchants imported, among other commodities, wheat from south Africa, cowry shells from India, and sugar from Brazil. The wheat fed domestic consumers, who increasingly worked as merchants, bankers, or manufacturers rather than as cultivators. English, Dutch, and other merchants eagerly purchased the cowry shells—which served as currency in much of sub-Saharan Africa—and exchanged them for slaves destined for plantations in the western hemisphere. The sugar went on the market at Amsterdam and found its way to consumers throughout Europe. During the eighteenth century, world trade became even more intricate as mass markets emerged for commodities such as coffee, tea, sugar, and tobacco. By 1750 all parts of the world except Australia participated in global networks of commercial relations in which European merchant mariners played prominent roles.

in perspective

Global commercial and biological exchanges arose from the efforts of European mariners to explore the world's waters and establish sea lanes that would support long-distance trade. Their search for sea routes to Asia led them to the western hemisphere and the vast expanse of the Pacific Ocean. The geographic knowledge that they accumulated enabled them to link the world's regions into a finely articulated network of trade. But commercial exchange was not the only result of this global network. Food crops, animal stocks, disease pathogens, and human migrants also traveled the sea lanes and dramatically influenced societies throughout the world. Transplanted crops and animal species led to improved nutrition and increasing populations throughout the eastern hemisphere. Epidemics sparked by unfamiliar disease pathogens ravaged indigenous populations in the Americas and the Pacific islands. Massive migrations of human communities transformed the social and cultural landscape of the Americas and encouraged increased mingling of the world's peoples. The European voyages of exploration, transoceanic trade networks, and the Columbian exchange pushed the world's regions toward interdependence and global integration. ●

CHRONOLOGY	
1394–1460	Life of Prince Henry the Navigator of Portugal
1488	Bartolomeu Dias's voyage around the Cape of Good Hope into the Indian Ocean
1492	Christopher Columbus's first voyage to the western hemisphere
1497–1499	Vasco da Gama's first voyage to India
1500	Establishment of Portuguese trading post in Calicut, India
1519–1522	Ferdinand Magellan's circumnavigation of the world
1565–1575	Spanish conquest of the Philippines
1619	Establishment of Batavia by the Dutch on the island of Java
1756–1763	Seven Years' War
1768–1780	Captain James Cook's voyages in the Pacific Ocean

For Further Reading

David R. Abernathy. *The Dynamics of Global Dominance: European Overseas Empires, 1415–1980.* New Haven, 2000. A survey of the rise and decline of European overseas empires during a period of more than five hundred years.

Rene J. Barendse. *The Arabian Seas.* Eastgate, N.Y., 2002. A path-breaking and complex work that emphasizes the long predominance of Asia in the world economy.

Francisco Bethencourt and Diogo Curto, eds. *Portuguese Overseas Expansion.* New York, 2007. A collection of essays provides an overview of Portuguese maritime expansion between 1400 and 1800.

K. N. Chaudhuri. *Trade and Civilisation in the Indian Ocean: An Economic History from the Rise of Islam to 1750.* Cambridge, 1985. A brilliant analysis that places the European presence in the Indian Ocean in a larger historical context.

———. *The Trading World of Asia and the English East India Company, 1660–1760.* Cambridge, 1978. The best study of the English East India Company and its role in world trade.

Carlo Cipolla. *Guns, Sails, and Empires: Technological Innovation and the Early Phases of European Expansion, 1400–1700.* New York, 1965. A well-written study of the naval and military technology available to European mariners.

Christopher Columbus. *The Diario of Christopher Columbus's First Voyage to America.* Trans. by Oliver Dunn and James E. Kelley Jr. Norman, Okla., 1989. A careful translation.

Alfred W. Crosby. *The Columbian Exchange: Biological and Cultural Consequences of 1492.* Westport, Conn., 1972. Focuses on early exchanges of plants, animals, and diseases between Europe and America.

———. *Ecological Imperialism: The Biological Expansion of Europe, 900–1900.* Cambridge, 1986. An important study that examines the establishment of European biological species in the larger world.

Philip D. Curtin. *Cross-Cultural Trade in World History.* New York, 1984. Focuses on the roles of cross-cultural brokers in facilitating trade between different societies.

Stephen Frederic Dale. *Indian Merchants and Eurasian Trade, 1600–1750.* Cambridge, 1994. Scholarly analysis of Indian merchant communities trading in Russia, Persia, and central Asia in early modern times.

Andre Gunder Frank. *ReORIENT: Global Economy in the Asian Age.* Berkeley, 1998. Important and challenging analysis of global economic integration in the early modern world.

Jonathan L. Israel. *Dutch Primacy in World Trade, 1585–1740.* Oxford, 1989. A thorough examination of the Dutch seaborne empire at its height.

Michael Khodarkovsky. *Where Two Worlds Meet: The Russian State and the Kalmyk Nomads, 1600–1771.* Ithaca, 1992. One of the first major studies to look at Russian imperial expansion in Siberia through the eyes of colonized peoples.

Pablo E. Perez-Mallaina. *Spain's Men of the Sea: Daily Life on the Indies Fleet in the Sixteenth Century.* Trans. by Carla Rahn Phillips. Baltimore, 1988. Recounts shipboard life in vivid detail.

William H. McNeill. *Plagues and Peoples.* Garden City, N.Y., 1976. Examines the effects of infectious and contagious diseases in world history.

David Ormrod. *The Rise of Commercial Empires: England and the Netherlands in the Age of Mercantilism, 1650–1770.* New York, 2003. An important contribution to an understanding of European imperialism and colonialism that focuses on the issues surrounding Dutch decline and British ascendancy.

Anthony Pagden. *European Encounters with the New World: From Renaissance to Romanticism.* New Haven, 1993. Scholarly examination of early European responses to the peoples, societies, and environments they encountered in the Americas.

John H. Parry. *The Age of Reconnaissance.* Berkeley, 1982. Reliable and readable survey of European expansion.

M. N. Pearson. *The Portuguese in India.* Cambridge, 1987. A brief, lively discussion of the early Portuguese empire in India.

William D. Phillips Jr. and Carla Rahn Phillips. *The Worlds of Christopher Columbus.* Cambridge, 1992. The best general study of Christopher Columbus.

Antonio Pigafetta. *Magellan's Voyage: A Narrative Account of the First Circumnavigation.* 2 vols. Trans. by R. A. Skelton. New Haven, 1969. Valuable account by a crewman on Magellan's circumnavigation of the world.

Kenneth Pomeranz. *The Great Divergence: China, Europe, and the Making of the Modern World Economy.* Princeton, 2000. Pathbreaking scholarly study that illuminates the economic history of the early modern world through comparison of economic development in Asian and European lands.

——— and Steven Topik. *The World That Trade Created: Society, Culture, and the World Economy, 1400 to the Present.* Armonk, N.Y., 1999. Informative articles arguing the fundamental importance of trade and commerce in world history, both as a precursor to globalization and as a historically transformative force.

John F. Richards. *The Unending Frontier: An Environmental History of the Early Modern World.* Berkeley, 2003. Thoroughly explores the environmental effects of the global historical processes that shaped the early modern world.

Stuart B. Schwartz, ed. *Implicit Understandings: Observing, Reporting, and Reflecting on the Encounters between Europeans and Other Peoples in the Early Modern Era.* Cambridge, 1994. Fascinating collection of essays by specialists on cross-cultural perceptions in early modern times.

Yuri Slezkine. *Arctic Mirrors: Russia and the Small Peoples of the North.* Ithaca, 1994. Thoughtful analysis of Russian relations with the hunting, fishing, and herding peoples of Siberia.

Sanjay Subrahmanyam. *The Career and Legend of Vasco da Gama.* Cambridge, 1997. The best critical study of the famous Portuguese mariner.

———. *The Portuguese Empire in Asia, 1500–1700: A Political and Economic History.* London, 1993. A sophisticated analysis of the Portuguese trading-post empire.

Hugh Thomas. *Rivers of Gold: The Rise of the Spanish Empire, from Columbus to Magellan.* New York, 2003. Detailed narrative of a brief period in Spain's imperial outreach.

James D. Tracy, ed. *The Political Economy of Merchant Empires: State Power and World Trade, 1350–1750.* Cambridge, 1991. Essays on the interconnections between political, military, and commercial relationships in early modern times.

———. *The Rise of Merchant Empires: Long-Distance Trade in the Early Modern World, 1350–1750.* Cambridge, 1990. Essays by specialists on global trade in early modern times.

Immanuel Wallerstein. *The Modern World-System.* 3 vols. New York, 1974. A controversial but influential interpretation of global political and economic development in modern times.

Merry E. Wiesner-Hanks. *Christianity and Sexuality in the Early Modern World: Regulating Desire, Reforming Practice.* London, 2000. Pioneering comparative study of Christian sexuality in global context.

The Transformation of Europe

chapter 23

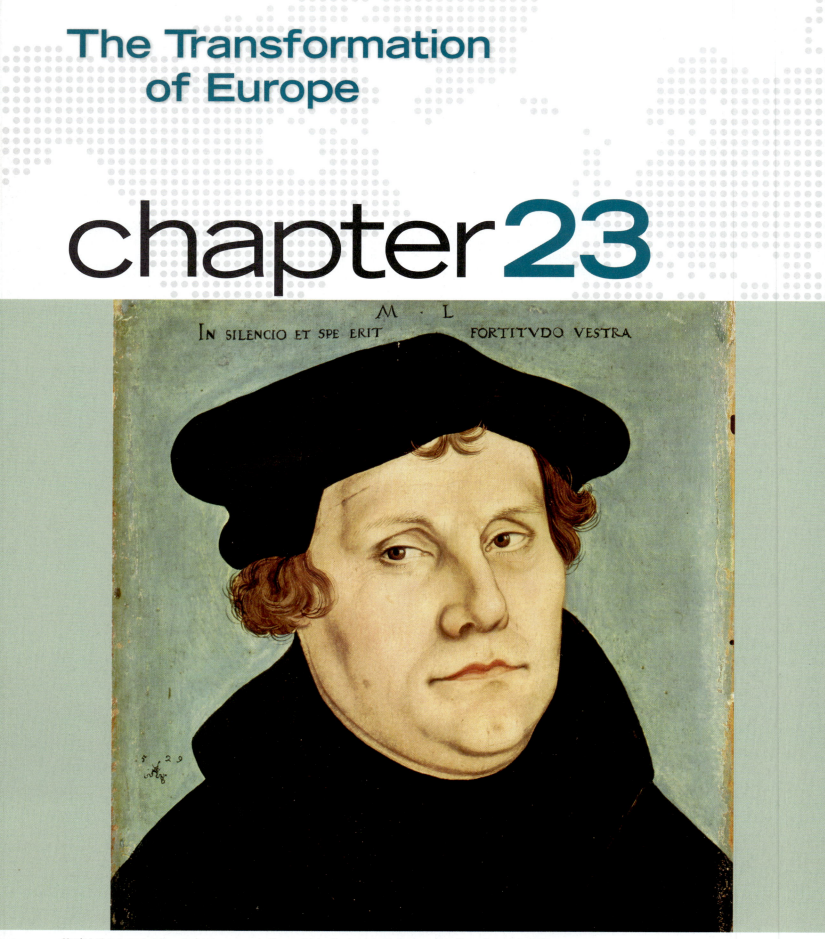

M · L

IN SILENCIO ET SPE ERIT FORTITVDO VESTRA

Martin Luther at age forty-two, depicted as a conscientious and determined man by the German painter Lucas Cranach in 1525.

EYEWITNESS:
Martin Luther Challenges the Church

In 1517 an obscure German monk posed a challenge to the Roman Catholic church. Martin Luther of Wittenberg denounced the church's sale of indulgences, a type of pardon that excused individuals from doing penance for their sins and thus facilitated their entry into heaven. Indulgences had been available since the eleventh century, but to raise funds for the reconstruction of St. Peter's basilica in Rome, church authorities began to market indulgences aggressively in the early sixteenth century. From their point of view, indulgences were splendid devices: they encouraged individuals to reflect piously on their behavior while also bringing large sums of money into the church's treasury.

To Martin Luther, however, indulgences were signs of greed, hypocrisy, and moral rot in the Roman Catholic church. Luther despised the pretentiousness of church authorities who arrogated to themselves powers that belonged properly to God alone: no human being had the power to absolve individuals of their sins and grant them admission to heaven, Luther believed, so the sale of indulgences constituted a huge fraud perpetrated on an unsuspecting public. In October 1517, following academic custom of the day, he offered to debate publicly with anyone who wished to dispute his views, and he denounced the sale of indulgences in a document called the *Ninety-Five Theses*.

Luther did not nail his work to the church door in Wittenberg, although a popular legend credited him with that heroic gesture, but news of the *Ninety-Five Theses* spread instantly: within a few weeks, printed copies were available throughout Europe. Luther's challenge galvanized opinion among many who resented the power of the Roman church. It also drew severe criticism from religious and political authorities seeking to maintain the established order. Church officials subjected Luther's views to examination and judged them erroneous, and in 1520 Pope Leo X excommunicated the unrepentant monk. In 1521 the Holy Roman emperor Charles V, a devout Roman Catholic, summoned Luther to an assembly of imperial authorities and demanded that he recant his views. Luther's response: "I cannot and will not recant anything, for it is neither safe nor right to act against one's conscience. Here I stand. I can do no other. God help me. Amen."

Martin Luther's challenge held enormous religious and political implications. Though expelled from the church, Luther still considered himself Christian—indeed, he considered his own faith true Christianity—and he held religious services for a community of devoted followers. Wittenberg became a center of religious dissent, which by the late 1520s had spread through much of Germany and Switzerland. During the 1530s dissidents known as Protestants—because of their protest against the established order—organized movements also in France, England, the Low Countries, and even Italy and Spain. By mid-century Luther's act of individual rebellion had mushroomed into the Protestant Reformation, which shattered the religious unity of western Christendom.

For all its unsettling effects, the Protestant Reformation was only one of several powerful movements that transformed European society during the early modern era. Another was the consolidation of strong centralized states, which took shape partly because of the Reformation. Between the sixteenth and the eighteenth centuries, monarchs in western Europe took advantage of religious quarrels to tighten control over their societies. By curbing the power of the nobility, expanding royal authority, and increasing control over their subjects, they built states much more powerful than the regional monarchies of the middle ages. By the mid-eighteenth century, some rulers had concentrated so much power in their own hands that historians refer to them as absolute monarchs.

Alongside religious conflict and the building of powerful states, capitalism and early modern science also profoundly influenced western European society in early modern times. Early capitalism pushed European merchants and manufacturers into unrelenting competition with one another and encouraged them to reorganize their businesses in search of maximum efficiency. Early modern science challenged traditional ways of understanding the world and the universe. Under the influence of scientific discoveries, European intellectuals sought an entirely rational understanding of human society as well as the natural world, and some sought to base European moral, ethical, and social thought on science and reason rather than Christianity.

Thus between 1500 and 1800, western Europe underwent a thorough transformation. Although the combination of religious, political, social, economic, intellectual, and cultural change was unsettling and often disruptive, it also strengthened European society. The states of early modern Europe competed vigorously and mobilized their human and natural resources in effective fashion. By 1800 several of them had become especially powerful, wealthy, and dynamic. They stood poised to play major roles in world affairs during the nineteenth and twentieth centuries.

THE FRAGMENTATION OF WESTERN CHRISTENDOM

In the third century C.E., Christian missionaries began to spread their faith from the Mediterranean basin throughout Europe, and by 1000 C.E. Christianity had established a foothold as far north as Scandinavia and Iceland. Although the peoples of western Europe spoke different languages, ate different foods, and observed different customs, the church of Rome provided them with a common religious and cultural heritage. During the sixteenth and seventeenth centuries, however, revolts against the Roman Catholic church shattered the religious unity of western Europe. Followers of Martin Luther and other Protestant reformers established a series of churches independent of Rome, and Roman Catholic leaders strengthened their own church against the challengers. Throughout early modern times, religious controversies fueled social tensions.

The Protestant Reformation

Roots of Reform The Protestant Reformation dates from the early sixteenth century, but many of the underlying conditions that prompted reformers to challenge the authority of the Roman Catholic church had existed for hundreds of years. Over the course of centuries, the church and its top officials had become deeply embroiled in the political affairs of western Europe. But political intrigues, combined with the church's growing wealth and power, also fostered greed and corruption, which undermined the church's spiritual authority and made it vulnerable to criticism. The blatant hedonism and crass materialism of church officials only further emphasized the perceived betrayal of Christian ideals. Although the church continued to enjoy the loyalty of most Christians, it faced a disapproval of its abuses that became increasingly strident in the decades before 1517. Alongside such criticism came a growing demand for a more personal involvement with the divine. Efforts by church authorities to eliminate pre-Christian traditions and alternative kinds of spirituality only intensified the desire among laypeople for forms of devotion that would connect them more directly with God than the church allowed. Martin Luther coalesced these expressions of religious discontent into a powerful revolt against the church.

Martin Luther Martin Luther (1483–1546) attacked the sale of indulgences as an individual, but he soon attracted enthusiastic support from others who resented the policies of the Roman church. Luther was a prolific and talented writer, and he published scores of works condemning the Roman church. His cause benefited enormously from the printing press, which had first appeared in Europe in the mid-fifteenth century. A sizable literate public inhabited European cities and towns, and readers eagerly consumed printed works on religious as well as secular themes. Printed editions of Luther's writings appeared throughout Europe and sparked spirited debates on indulgences and theological issues. His supporters and critics took their own works to the printers, and religious controversies kept the presses busy churning out pamphlets and treatises for a century and more.

Luther soon moved beyond the issue of indulgences: he attacked the Roman church for a wide range of abuses and called for thorough reform of Christendom. He advocated the closure of monasteries, translation of the Bible from Latin into vernacular languages, and an end to priestly authority, including the authority of the pope himself. When opponents pointed out that his reform program ran counter to church policy, he rejected the authority of the church hierarchy and proclaimed that the Bible was the only source of Christian religious authority.

Luther's works drew an enthusiastic popular response, and in Germany they fueled a movement to reform the church along the lines of Luther's teachings. Lay Christians flocked to hear Luther preach in Wittenberg, and several princes of the Holy Roman Empire warmed to Luther's views—partly because of personal conviction but partly also because religious controversy offered opportunities for them to build their own power bases. During the 1520s and 1530s, many of the most important German cities—Strasbourg, Nuremberg, and Augsburg, among others—passed laws prohibiting Roman Catholic observances and requiring all religious services to follow Protestant doctrine and procedures.

Reform outside Germany By the mid-sixteenth century, about half the German population had adopted Lutheran Christianity, and reformers had launched Protestant movements and established alternative churches in other lands as well. By the late 1520s the prosperous cities of Switzerland—Zurich, Basel, and Geneva—had fledgling Protestant churches. The heavily urbanized Low Countries also responded enthusiastically to Protestant appeals. Protestants appeared even in Italy and Spain, although authorities in those lands handily suppressed their challenge to the Roman church.

In England a Reformation took place for frankly political as well as religious reasons. Lutherans and other Protestants worked to build a following in England from the 1520s, but they faced stout government resistance until King Henry VIII (reigned 1509–1547) came into conflict with the pope. Henry wanted to divorce his wife, who had not borne a male heir, but the pope refused to allow him to do so. Henry's response was to sever relations with the Roman church and make himself Supreme Head of the Anglican church—an English pope, as it were. While Henry reigned, the theology of the English church changed little, but under pressure of reformers, his successors replaced Roman Catholic with Protestant doctrines and rituals. By 1560 England had permanently left the Roman Catholic community.

John Calvin Meanwhile, an even more influential Reformation was taking shape in France and the French-speaking parts of Switzerland. The initiator was a French lawyer, John Calvin (1509–1564), who in the 1530s converted to Protestant Christianity. Because the French monarchy sought to suppress Protestants, Calvin slipped across the border to French-speaking Geneva in Switzerland. There he organized a Protestant community and worked with local officials to impose a strict code of morality and discipline on the city. Calvin also composed an influential treatise, *Institutes of the Christian Religion* (first published in 1536 and frequently reprinted with revisions), that codified Protestant teachings and presented them as a coherent and organized package.

Calvin's Geneva was not only a model Protestant community but also a missionary center. Calvinist missionaries were most active in France, where they attracted strong interest in the cities, but they ventured also to Germany, the Low Countries, England, Scotland, and even distant Hungary. They established churches in all these lands and worked for reform along Protestant lines. They were most successful in the Netherlands and Scotland. By the late sixteenth century, Lutherans, Anglicans, and Calvinists together had built communities large enough that a return to religious unity in western Christendom was inconceivable.

The Catholic Reformation

Partly in response to the Protestant Reformation, Roman Catholic authorities undertook an enormous reform effort within their own church. To some extent their efforts represented a reaction to Protestant success. Yet Roman Catholic authorities also sought to define points of doctrine so as to clarify differences between Roman and Protestant churches, to persuade Protestants to return to the Roman church, and to deepen the sense of spirituality and religious commitment in their own community. Taken together, their efforts constituted the Catholic Reformation.

The Council of Trent Two institutions were especially important for defining the Catholic Reformation and advancing its goals—the Council of Trent and the Society of Jesus.

The Council of Trent was an assembly of bishops, cardinals, and other high church officials who met intermittently between 1545 and 1563 to address matters of doctrine and reform. Drawing heavily on the works of the thirteenth-century scholastic theologian St. Thomas Aquinas, the council defined the elements of Roman Catholic theology in detail. The council acknowledged that abuses had alienated many people from the Roman church, and it took steps to reform the church. The council demanded that church authorities observe strict standards of morality, and it required them to establish schools and seminaries in their districts to prepare priests properly for their roles.

St. Ignatius Loyola

While the Council of Trent dealt with doctrine and reform, the Society of Jesus went on the offensive and sought to extend the boundaries of the reformed Roman church. The society's founder was St. Ignatius Loyola (1491–1556), a Basque nobleman and soldier who in 1521 suffered a devastating leg wound that ended his military career. While recuperating he read spiritual works and popular accounts of saints' lives, and he resolved to put his energy into religious work. In 1540, together with a small band of disciples, he founded the Society of Jesus.

The Society of Jesus

Ignatius required that members of the society, known as Jesuits, complete a rigorous and advanced education. They received instruction not only in theology and philosophy but also in classical languages, literature, history, and science. As a result of that preparation—and their unswerving dedication to the Roman Catholic church—the Jesuits made extraordinarily effective missionaries. They were able to outargue most of their opponents and acquired a reputation for discipline and determination. They often served as counselors to kings and rulers and used their influence to promote policies that benefited the Roman church. They also were the most prominent of the early Christian missionaries outside Europe: in the wake of the European reconnaissance of the world's oceans, Jesuits at-

Under inspiration of the Catholic Reformation, many devout individuals sought mystic union with God. One of the most famous of the mystics was St. Teresa of Avila (in Spain), who founded a strict order of nuns and often experienced religious visions. A famous sculpture by the Italian artist Gianlorenzo Bernini depicts St. Teresa in an ecstatic trance accompanied by an angel.

tracted converts in India, China, Japan, the Philippines, and the Americas, thus making Christianity a genuinely global religion.

Witch-Hunts and Religious Wars

Europeans took religion seriously in the sixteenth century, and religious divisions helped to fuel social and political conflict. Apart from wars, the most destructive violence that afflicted early modern Europe was the hunt for witches, which was especially prominent in regions such as the Rhineland where tensions between Protestants and Roman Catholics ran high.

Like many other peoples, Europeans had long believed that certain individuals possessed unusual powers to influence human affairs or discover secret information such as the identity of a thief. During the late fifteenth century, theologians developed a theory that witches derived their powers from the devil. According to that theory, witches made agreements to worship the devil in exchange for supernatural powers, including the ability to fly through the night on brooms, pitchforks, or animals. Theorists believed that the witches regularly flew off to distant places to attend the "witches' sabbath," a gathering that featured devil worship, lewd behavior, and the concoction of secret potions, culminating in sexual relations with the devil himself.

Witch-Hunting

Although the witches' sabbath was sheer fantasy, fears that individuals were making alliances with the devil sparked an intensive hunt for witches. Witchcraft became a convenient explanation for any unpleasant turn of events—failure of a crop, outbreak of a fire, an unexpected death, or inability to conceive a child. About 110,000 individuals underwent trial as suspected witches during the sixteenth and seventeenth centuries, and about 45,000 of them died either by hanging or by burning at the stake. As a rule, church courts tried large numbers of witches, but they usually imposed nonlethal penalties such as excommunication or imprisonment. It was secular courts that condemned and executed the vast majority of witches.

Witches and Gender Gender played an important role in the witch-hunts. Men were among the victims, and in places such as Finland they actually exceeded the number of women accused of witchcraft. Most convicted witches were women, however. Indeed, women may have accounted for 85 percent or more of the condemned. Many of the women were poor, old, single, or widowed—individuals who lived on the margins of their societies and were easy targets for accusers, since they had few protectors. Witch-hunting was mostly a European affair, but it also spread to European colonies in the Americas. The most intense witch-hunt in the Americas took place in seventeenth-century New England, where a population of about 100,000 colonists tried 234 individuals for witchcraft and executed 36 of them by hanging.

By 1700 the fear of witches had largely diminished. Accusations, trials, and executions occurred only sporadically thereafter. The last legal execution for witchcraft in Europe took place in Switzerland in 1782. For the better part of two centuries, however, the intermittent pursuit of witches revealed clearly the stresses and strains that afflicted European society during early modern times.

Religious Wars Religious tensions even led to outright war between Protestant and Roman Catholic communities. Religious wars racked France for thirty-six years (1562–1598), for example, and they also complicated relations between Protestant and Roman Catholic states. In 1588 King Philip II of Spain (reigned 1556–1598) attempted to force England to return to the Roman Catholic church by sending the Spanish Armada—a huge flotilla consisting of 130 ships and 30,000 men—to dethrone the Protestant Queen Eliza-beth. The effort collapsed, however, when English forces disrupted the Spanish fleet by sending blazing, unmanned ships into its midst. Then a ferocious gale scattered Spanish vessels throughout the North Sea.

Religious convictions also aggravated relations between the Netherlands and Spain by fueling the revolt of the Dutch provinces from their overlord, the king of Spain. In 1567 Philip sent an army to tighten his control over the provinces and to suppress the Calvinist movement there. Resistance escalated into a full-scale rebellion. By 1610 the seven northern provinces (the modern Netherlands) had won their independence and formed a republic known as the United Provinces, leaving ten southern provinces (modern Belgium) under Spanish and later Austrian rule until the late eighteenth century.

The Thirty Years' War The religious wars culminated in a massive continental conflict known as the Thirty Years' War (1618–1648). The war opened after the Holy Roman emperor attempted to force his Bohemian subjects to return to the Roman Catholic church, and the main battleground was the emperor's territory in Germany. Other parties soon entered the fray, however, and by the time the war ended, Spanish, French, Dutch, German, Swedish, Danish, Polish, Bohemian, and Russian forces had taken part in the conflict.

The motives that prompted these states to enter the war were sometimes political or economic, but religious differences complicated the other issues and made them more difficult to resolve. Regardless of the motives, the Thirty Years' War was the most destructive European conflict before the twentieth century. Quite apart from violence and brutalities committed by undisciplined soldiers, the war damaged

Henry Fuseli's 1783 painting offers a dramatic depiction of three witches. The painter based his image on the three witches who appear in William Shakespeare's play *Macbeth*. He titled his painting "The Weird Sisters" or "The Three Witches." Which physical features identify these women as "weird" witches?

A la fin ces Voleurs infames et perdus ,
Comme fruits malheureux a cet arbre pendus

Monstrent bien que le crime (horrible et noire engeance)
Est luy mesme instrument de honte et de vengeance ,

Et que cest le Destin des hommes vicieux
Desprouuer tost ou tard la iustice des Cieux . 1)

The Thirty Years' War offered abundant opportunity for undisciplined mercenary soldiers to prey on civilian populations. Only rarely, as in the mass hanging depicted in this engraving of 1633, did soldiers receive punishment for their criminal acts.

economies and societies throughout Europe and led to the deaths of about one-third of the German population. The destructiveness of the Thirty Years' War raised questions about the viability of Europe as a region of strong, independent, well-armed, and intensely competitive states.

THE CONSOLIDATION OF SOVEREIGN STATES

Although fundamentally a religious movement, the Reformation had strong political implications, and centralizing monarchs readily made use of religious issues in their efforts to strengthen their states and enhance their authority. Ruling elites had their own religious preferences, and they often promoted a Protestant or Roman Catholic cause out of personal conviction. Religious controversies also offered splendid opportunities for ambitious subordinates who built power bases by appealing to particular religious communities. Over the long run, centralizing monarchs profited most from religious controversy generated by the Reformation. While the Holy Roman Empire fell into disarray because of political and religious quarrels, monarchs in other lands augmented their revenues, enhanced their authority, and created powerful sovereign states. After the devastation of the Thirty Years' War, rulers of these states devised a diplomatic system that sought to maintain order among the many independent and competitive European states.

The Attempted Revival of Empire

After the dissolution of the Carolingian empire in the ninth century C.E., there was no effective imperial government in western Europe. The so-called Holy Roman Empire emerged in the tenth century, but its authority extended only to Germany and northern Italy, and even there the emperors encountered stiff opposition from powerful princes and thriving cities. During the early sixteenth century, it seemed that Emperor Charles V (reigned 1519–1556) might establish the Holy Roman Empire as the preeminent political authority in Europe, but by midcentury it was clear that there would be no revival of empire. Thus, unlike China, India, and Ottoman lands in southwest Asia and north Africa, early modern Europe developed as a region of independent states.

Charles V After 1438 the Habsburg family, with extensive dynastic holdings in Austria, dominated the Holy Roman Empire. Through marriage alliances with princely and royal families, the Habsburgs accumulated rights and titles to lands throughout Europe and beyond. Charles V inherited authority over the Habsburgs' Austrian domains as well as the duchy of Burgundy (including the wealthy provinces of the Low Countries) and the kingdom of Spain (including its possessions in Italy and the Americas). When he became emperor in 1519, he acquired authority over Germany, Bohemia, Switzerland, and parts of northern Italy. His empire stretched from Vienna in Austria to Cuzco in Peru.

Imperial Fragmentation In spite of his far-flung holdings, Charles did not extend his authority throughout Europe or even establish a lasting imperial legacy. Throughout his reign Charles had to devote much of his attention and energy to the Lutheran movement and to imperial princes who took advantage of religious controversy to assert their independence. Moreover, Charles did not build an administrative structure for his empire but, instead, ruled each of his lands according to its own laws and customs. He was able to draw on the financial resources of wealthy lands such as the Low Countries and Spain to maintain a powerful army. Yet Charles did not have the ambition to extend his authority by military force, but used his army mostly to put down rebellions.

Foreign Challenges Foreign difficulties also prevented Charles from establishing his empire as the arbiter of Europe. The prospect of a powerful Holy Roman Empire struck fear in the kings of France, and it caused concern among the sultans of the Ottoman empire as well. Charles's holdings surrounded France, and the French kings suspected that the emperor wanted to absorb their realm and extend his authority throughout Europe. To forestall that possibility, the French kings created every obstacle they could for Charles. Even though they were staunch Roman Catholics, they aided German Lutherans and encouraged them to rebel. The French kings even allied with the Muslim Ottoman Turks against the emperor.

MAP 23.1

Sixteenth-century Europe.
Note the extent of Habsburg territories and the wide boundaries of the Holy Roman Empire.

With such powerful territories, what prevented the Habsburgs from imposing imperial rule on most of Europe?

For their part, the Ottoman sultans did not want to see a powerful Christian empire threaten their holdings in eastern Europe and their position in the Mediterranean basin. With the encouragement of the French king, Turkish forces conquered Hungary in 1526, and three years later they even laid siege briefly to Vienna. Moreover, during the early sixteenth century Ottoman forces imposed their rule beyond Egypt and embraced almost all of north Africa. By midcentury, Turkish holdings posed a serious threat to Italian and Spanish shipping in the Mediterranean.

Thus numerous domestic and foreign problems prevented Charles V from establishing his vast empire as the supreme political authority in Europe. His inability to suppress the Lutherans was especially disappointing to Charles, and in 1556, after agreeing that imperial princes and cities could determine the religious faith observed in their jurisdictions, the emperor abdicated his throne and retired to a monastery in Spain. His empire did not survive intact. Charles bestowed his holdings in Spain, Italy, the Low Countries, and the Americas on his son, King Philip II of Spain, while his brother Ferdinand inherited the Habsburg family lands in Austria and the imperial throne.

The New Monarchs

In the absence of effective imperial power, guidance of public affairs fell to the various regional states that had emerged during the middle ages. The city-states of Italy were prominent because of their economic power: since the eleventh century they had been Europe's most important centers of trade, manufacturing, and finance. The most powerful European states, however, were the kingdoms of England, France, and Spain. During the late fifteenth and sixteenth centuries, rulers of these lands, known as the "new monarchs," marshaled their resources, curbed the nobility, and built strong centralized regimes.

Finance   The new monarchs included Henry VIII of England, Louis XI and Francis I of France, and Fernando and Isabel of Spain. All the new monarchs sought to enhance their treasuries by developing new sources of finance. The French kings levied direct taxes on sales, households, and the salt trade. A new sales tax dramatically boosted Spanish royal income in the sixteenth century. For fear of provoking rebellion, the English kings did not introduce new taxes, but they increased revenues by raising fines and fees for royal services. Moreover, after Henry VIII severed ties between the English and Roman churches, he dissolved the monasteries and confiscated church wealth in England. This financial windfall enabled Henry to enhance royal power by increasing the size of the state and adding to its responsibilities. After the English Reformation, for example, the state provided poor relief and support for orphans, which previously had been responsibilities of churches and monasteries.

State Power   With their increased income the new monarchs enlarged their administrative staffs, which enabled them to collect taxes and implement royal policies more reliably than before. The French and Spanish monarchs also maintained standing armies that vastly increased their power with respect to the nobility. Their armies with thousands of infantrymen were too large for individual nobles to match, and they equipped their forces with cannons that were too expensive for nobles to purchase. The English kings did not need a standing army to put down the occasional rebellion that flared in their island realm and so did not go to the expense of supporting one. Yet they too increased their power with respect to the nobles by subjecting them to royal justice and forcing them to comply with royal policy.

The debates and disputes launched by the Protestant Reformation helped monarchs increase their power. In lands that adopted Protestant faiths—including England, much of Germany, Denmark, and Sweden—rulers expropriated the monasteries and used church wealth to expand their powers. That option was not open to Roman Catholic kings, but Protestant movements provided them with a justification to mobilize resources, which they used against political as well as religious adversaries.

The Spanish Inquisition   The Spanish Inquisition was the most distinctive institution that relied on religious justifications to advance state ends. Fernando and Isabel founded the Spanish Inquisition in 1478, and they obtained papal license to operate the institution as a royal agency. Its original task was to ferret out those who secretly practiced Judaism or Islam, but Charles V charged it with responsibility also for detecting Protestant heresy in Spain. Throughout the late fifteenth and sixteenth centuries, however, the Spanish Inquisition served political as well as religious purposes. Moreover, its reach extended well beyond the Iberian peninsula. Just as the fear of witchcraft crossed the Atlantic Ocean and inspired witch-hunts in England's North American colonies, concerns about heresy also made their way to the western hemisphere, where inquisitors worked to protect Spanish colonies from heretical teachings.

Inquisitors had broad powers to investigate suspected cases of heresy. Popular legends have created an erroneous impression of the Spanish Inquisition as an institution running amok, framing innocent victims and routinely subjecting them to torture. In fact, inquisitors usually observed rules of evidence, and they released many suspects after investigations turned up no sign of heresy. Yet, when they detected the scent of heresy, inquisitors could be ruthless. They sentenced hundreds of victims to hang from the gallows or burn at the stake and imprisoned many others in dank cells for extended periods of time. Fear of the inquisition intimidated many into silence, and a strict Roman Catholic orthodoxy prevailed in Spain. The inquisition deterred nobles from adopting Protestant views out of political ambition, and it used its influence on behalf of the Span-

INQVISITION

When the Spanish Inquisition detected traces of Protestant heresy, the punishment could be swift and brutal. In this engraving of about 1560, a large crowd observes the execution of heretics (top right) by burning at the stake.

ish monarchy. From 1559 to 1576, for example, inquisitors imprisoned the archbishop of Toledo—the highest Roman Catholic church official in all of Spain—because of his political independence.

Constitutional States

During the seventeenth and eighteenth centuries, as they sought to restore order after the Thirty Years' War, European states developed along two lines. Rulers in England and the Netherlands shared authority with representative institutions and created constitutional states, whereas monarchs in France, Spain, Austria, Prussia, and Russia concentrated power in their own hands and created a form of state known as absolute monarchy.

Constitutional States
The island kingdom of England and the maritime Dutch republic did not have written constitutions specifying the powers of the state, but during the seventeenth century they evolved governments that claimed

limited powers and recognized rights pertaining to individuals and representative institutions. Their constitutional states took different forms: in England a constitutional monarchy emerged, whereas the Netherlands produced a republic based on representative government. In neither land did constitutional government come easily into being: in England it followed a civil war, and in the Netherlands it emerged after a long struggle for independence. In both lands, however, constitutional government strengthened the state and provided a political framework that enabled merchants to flourish as never before in European experience.

The English Civil War
Constitutional government came to England after political and religious disputes led to the English civil war (1642–1649). From the early seventeenth century, the English kings had tried to institute new taxes without approval of the parliament, which for more than three centuries had traditionally approved new levies. While royal financial policies generated political tensions, religious disagreements aggravated matters further. As Anglicans, the kings supported a church with relatively ornate ceremonies and a hierarchy of bishops working under authority of the monarchs themselves. Meanwhile, however, many of the boldest and most insistent voices within parliament belonged

In this contemporary painting, the executioner holds up the just-severed head of King Charles I of England. The spectacle of a royal execution overcomes one woman, who faints (at bottom). How does the image of a beheaded king reflect the ongoing political changes in Europe?

to zealous Calvinists known as Puritans because they sought to purify the English church of any lingering elements, such as ornate ceremonies and a hierarchy of bishops, suggestive of Roman Catholic Christianity. By 1641, King Charles I and parliament were at loggerheads, unable to cooperate or even communicate effectively with each other. Both sides raised armies. In the conflicts that followed, parliamentary forces under the leadership of Oliver Cromwell (1599–1658) captured Charles, tried him for tyranny, and in an act that shocked all of Europe, marched him up on a platform and beheaded him in 1649.

The Glorious Revolution

In the absence of a king, Cromwell's Puritan regime took power but soon degenerated into a disagreeable dictatorship, prompting parliament to restore the monarchy in 1660. King and parliament, however, soon resumed their conflicts. The issue came to a head in a bloodless change of power known as the Glorious Revolution (1688–1689), when parliament deposed King James II and invited his daughter Mary and her Dutch husband, William of Orange, to assume the throne. The resulting arrange-

ment provided that kings would rule in cooperation with parliament, thus guaranteeing that nobles, merchants, and other constituencies would enjoy representation in government affairs.

The Dutch Republic

As in England, a potent combination of political and religious tensions led to conflict from which constitutional government emerged in the Netherlands. In the mid-sixteenth century, authority over the Low Countries, including modern-day Belgium as well as the Netherlands, rested with King Philip II of Spain. In 1567 Philip, a devout Roman Catholic, moved to suppress an increasingly popular Calvinist movement in the Netherlands—a measure that provoked large-scale rebellion against Spanish rule. In 1579 a group of Dutch provinces formed an anti-Spanish alliance, and in 1581 they proclaimed themselves the independent United Provinces. Representative assemblies organized local affairs in each of the provinces, and on this foundation political leaders built a Dutch republic. Spain did not officially recognize the independence of the United Provinces until the end of the Thirty Years' War in 1648, but the Dutch republic was effectively organizing affairs in the northern Low Countries by the early seventeenth century.

In many ways, the constitutional governments of England and the Dutch republic represented historical experiments. Apart from the Roman republic in classical times and a few Italian city-states of the medieval and Renaissance eras, European peoples had little experience with representative government. In their responses to political crises, popular leaders in both England and the Netherlands found it possible to mobilize support by appealing to the political and religious interests of broad constituencies and making a place for them in the government. The result was a pair of states that effectively harnessed popular support and used it to magnify state power.

In both England and the Dutch republic, merchants were especially prominent in political affairs, and state policy in both lands favored maritime trade and the building of commercial empires overseas. The constitutional states allowed entrepreneurs to pursue their economic interests with minimal interference from public authorities, and during the late seventeenth and eighteenth centuries, both states experienced extraordinary prosperity as a result of those policies. Indeed, in many ways the English and Dutch states represented an alliance between merchants and rulers that worked to the benefit of both. Merchants supported the state with the wealth that they generated through trade—

especially overseas trade—while rulers followed policies that looked after the interests of their merchants.

Absolute Monarchies

Whereas constitutional states devised ways to share power and authority, absolute monarchies found other ways to increase state power. Absolutism stood on a theoretical foundation known as the divine right of kings. This theory held that kings derived their authority from God and served as "God's lieutenants upon earth." There was no role in divine-right theory for common subjects or even nobles in public affairs: the king made law and determined policy. Noncompliance or disobedience merited punishment, and rebellion was a despicable act tantamount to blasphemy. In fact, absolute monarchs always relied on support from nobles and other social groups as well, but the claims of divine-right theory clearly reflected efforts at royal centralization.

The most conspicuous absolutist state was the French monarchy. The architect of French absolutism was a prominent church official, Cardinal Richelieu, who served as chief minister to King Louis XIII from 1624 to 1642. Richelieu worked systematically to undermine the power of the nobility and enhance the authority of the king. He destroyed nobles' castles and ruthlessly crushed aristocratic conspiracies. As a counterweight to the nobility, Richelieu built a large bureaucracy staffed by commoners loyal to the king. He also appointed officials to supervise the implementation of royal policy in the provinces. Finally, Richelieu attacked French Calvinists, who often allied with independent nobles, and destroyed their political and military power, although he allowed them to continue observing their faith. By midcentury France was under control of a tightly centralized absolute monarchy.

The Sun King The ruler who best epitomized royal absolutism was King Louis XIV (reigned 1643–1715), who once reportedly declared that he was himself the state: *"l'état, c'est moi."* Known as *le roi soleil* ("the sun king"), Louis surrounded himself with splendor befitting one who ruled by divine right. During the 1670s he built a magnificent residence at **Versailles,** a royal hunting lodge near Paris, and in the 1680s he moved his court there. Louis's palace at Versailles was the largest building in Europe, with 230 acres of formal gardens and 1,400 fountains. Because Louis did not want to wait years for saplings to grow, he ordered laborers to dig up 25,000 fully grown trees and haul them to Versailles for transplanting.

The sun king was the center of attention at Versailles. Court officials hovered around him and tended to his every need. All prominent nobles established residences at Versailles for their families and entourages. Louis strongly encouraged them to live at court, where he and his staff

Although best known as Louis XIII's "first minister," Cardinal Richelieu also gained fame for his patronage of the arts. Most notably, he founded the Académie Française, the learned society responsible for matters pertaining to the French language.

Versailles (vehr-SEYE)

The French painter Hyacinthe Rigaud, renowned for his portrait paintings of the royalty and nobility of Europe, created this vision of Louis XIV. Louis' reign, from 1643 to his death in 1715, lasted seventy-two years, three months, and eighteen days, and is the longest documented reign of any European monarch.

Absolutism in Russia Louis XIV was not the only absolute monarch of early modern Europe: Spanish, Austrian, and Prussian rulers embraced similar policies. The potential of absolutism to increase state power was particularly conspicuous in the case of Russia, where tsars of the Romanov dynasty (1613–1917) tightly centralized government functions. (*Tsar,* sometimes spelled *czar,* is a Russianized form of the term *caesar,* which Russian rulers borrowed from Byzantine emperors, who in turn had borrowed it from the classical Roman empire to signify their imperial status.) The Romanovs inherited a state that had rapidly expanded its boundaries since the mid-fourteenth century. Building on the foundation of a small principality around the trading city of Moscow, by 1600 Russia had become a vast empire extending from the Arctic seas in the north to the Caspian Sea in the south, with an increasing presence in the tundra and forests of Siberia as well.

Peter I Most important of the Romanov tsars was Peter I (reigned 1682–1725), widely known as Peter the Great, who inaugurated a thoroughgoing process of state transformation. Peter had a burning desire to make Russia, a huge but underpopulated land, into a great military power like those that had recently emerged in western Europe. In pursuit of that goal, he worked to transform Russia on the model of western European lands. In 1697–1698 he led a large party of Russian observers on a tour of Germany, the Netherlands, and England to learn about western European administrative methods and military technology. His traveling companions often behaved crudely by western European standards: they consumed beer, wine, and brandy in quantities that astonished their hosts, and King William III sent Peter a bill for damages done by his entourage at the country house where they lodged in England. (Among other things, Peter had ruined the gardens by having his men march through them in military formation.)

Upon return to Moscow, Peter set Russia spinning. He reformed the army by offering better pay and drafting peasants who served for life as professional soldiers. He provided his forces with extensive training and equipped them with modern weapons. He ordered aristocrats to study mathematics and geometry so that they could calculate how to aim cannons accurately, and he began the construction of a navy with an eye toward domination of the Baltic and other northern seas. He also overhauled the government bureaucracy to facilitate tax collection and improve administrative efficiency. His transformation of Russia even involved a cosmetic makeover, as he commanded his aristocratic subjects to wear western European fashions and ordered men to shave their traditional beards. These measures, which were extremely unpopular among conservative Russians, provoked spirited protest among those who resented the influence of western European ways. Yet Peter insisted on observance of his policies—to the point that he reportedly went into the streets and personally hacked the beards off

could keep an eye on them, and ambitious nobles gravitated there anyway in hopes of winning influence with the king. Louis himself was the arbiter of taste and style at Versailles, where he lavishly patronized painters, sculptors, architects, and writers whose creations met with his approval.

While nobles living at Versailles mastered the intricacies of court ritual and attended banquets, concerts, operas, balls, and theatrical performances, Louis and his ministers ran the state. In effect, Louis provided the nobility with luxurious accommodations and endless entertainment in exchange for absolute rule. From Versailles, Louis and his advisors promulgated laws and controlled a large standing army that kept order throughout the land. They also promoted economic development by supporting the establishment of new industries, building roads and canals, abolishing internal tariffs, and encouraging exports. Finally, they waged a series of wars designed to enlarge French boundaries and establish France as the preeminent power in Europe.

ΡΆΚΟλЬⲚИКЪ ГОВОРИТЪ
СЛЫШИ ЩЫΡЮⲖⲎⲎИКЪ
Я БОРОДЫ СТРИЧЬ НЕ
ХОЧУ ВОТЪ ГЛЕДИ Я НА
ТЕБЯ СКОРО КΑΡΔΥⲖЗΑΚΡΥ

ЦЫΡЮⲖⲎⲎИКЪ ХО
ЧЕТЪ ΡΆΚΟλЬⲚИКУ
БОРОДУ СТРИЧЬ.

Tsar Peter the Great, with a pair of shears, readies himself to remove the beard of a conservative noble. Peter had traveled widely in Europe, and he wanted to impose newer European customs on his subjects. That included being more cleanly shaved. Nobles wishing to keep their beloved beards had to pay a yearly tax to do so.

recalcitrants' faces. Perhaps the best symbol of his policies was St. Petersburg, a newly built seaport that Peter opened in 1703 to serve as a magnificent capital city and haven for Russia's fledgling navy.

Catherine II and the Limits of Reform The most able of Peter's successors was Catherine II (reigned 1762–1796), also known as Catherine the Great. Like Peter, Catherine sought to make Russia a great power. She worked to improve governmental efficiency by dividing her vast empire into fifty administrative provinces, and she promoted economic development in Russia's towns. For a while, she even worked to improve the conditions of Russia's oppressed peasantry by restricting the punishments that noble landowners could inflict on the serfs who worked their lands. She sought to eliminate common penalties such as torture, beating, and the mutilation of individuals by cutting off their noses, ears, or tongues.

Yet her interest in social reform cooled rapidly when it seemed to inspire challenges to her rule. She faced a particularly unsettling trial in 1773 and 1774, when a disgruntled former soldier named Yemelian Pugachev mounted a rebellion

This is a regal Russian portrait of the German-born empress of Russia, Catherine II. Although admired by many Russians as a source of national pride, she is also remembered as a ruthless ruler who affirmed autocracy and extended serfdom on a large scale.

in the steppe lands north of the Caspian Sea. Pugachev raised a motley army of adventurers, exiles, peasants, and serfs who killed thousands of noble landowners and government officials before imperial forces crushed the uprising. Government authorities took the captured Pugachev to Moscow in chains, beheaded him, quartered his body, and displayed his parts throughout the city as a warning against rebellion. Thereafter, Catherine's first concern was the preservation of autocratic rule rather than the transformation of Russia according to western European models.

Thus, in Russia as in other European lands, absolutist policies resulted in tight centralization and considerable strengthening of the state. The enhanced power that flowed from absolutism became dramatically clear in the period 1772 to 1797, when Austria, Prussia, and Catherine II's Russia picked the weak kingdom of Poland apart. In a series of three "partitions," the predatory absolutist states seized Polish territory and absorbed it into their own realms, ultimately wiping Poland entirely off the map. The lesson of the partitions was clear: any European state that hoped to

survive needed to construct an effective government that could respond promptly to challenges and opportunities.

The European States System

Whether they relied on absolutist or constitutional principles, European governments of early modern times built states much more powerful than those of their medieval predecessors. This round of state development led to difficulties within Europe, since conflicting interests fueled interstate competition and war. In the absence of an imperial authority capable of imposing and maintaining order in Europe, sovereign states had to find ways to resolve conflicts by themselves.

The Peace of Westphalia
The Thirty Years' War demonstrated the chaos and devastation that conflict could bring. In an effort to avoid tearing their society apart, European states ended the Thirty Years' War with the Peace of Westphalia (1648), which laid the foundations for a system of independent, competing states. Almost all the European states participated in drafting the Peace of Westphalia, and by the treaty's terms they regarded one another as sovereign and equal. They also mutually recognized their rights to organize their own domestic affairs, including religious affairs. Rather than envisioning imperial or papal or some other sort of supreme authority, the Peace of Westphalia entrusted political and diplomatic affairs to states acting in their own interests. European religious unity had disappeared, and the era of the sovereign state had arrived.

The Peace of Westphalia did not bring an end to war. Indeed, war was almost constant in early modern Europe. Most conflicts were minor affairs inaugurated by monarchs seeking to extend their authority to new lands or to reclaim territories seized by others, but they nevertheless disrupted local economies and drained resources. A few wars, however, grew to sizable proportions. Most notable among them were the wars of Louis XIV and the Seven Years' War. Between 1668 and 1713, the sun king sought to expand his borders east into Germany and to absorb Spain and the Spanish Netherlands into his kingdom. That prospect prompted England, the United Provinces, and Austria to mount a coalition against Louis. Later, the Seven Years' War (1756–1763) pitted France, Austria, and Russia against Britain and Prussia, and it merged with conflicts between France and Britain in India and North America to become a global war for imperial supremacy.

The Balance of Power
These shifting alliances illustrate the principal foundation of European diplomacy in early modern times—the balance of power. No ruler wanted to see another state dominate all the others. Thus, when any particular state began to wax strong, others formed coalitions against it. Balance-of-power diplomacy was risky business: it was always possible that a coalition might repress one strong state only to open the door for another. Yet, in playing balance-of-power politics, statesmen prevented the

building of empires and ensured that Europe would be a land of independent, sovereign, competing states.

Military Development Frequent wars and balance-of-power diplomacy drained the resources of individual states but strengthened European society as a whole. European states competed vigorously and sought to develop the most expert military leadership and the most effective weapons for their arsenals. States organized military academies where officers received advanced education in strategy and

tactics and learned how to maintain disciplined forces. Demand for powerful weapons stimulated the development of a sophisticated armaments industry that turned out ever more lethal products. Gun foundries manufactured cannons of increasing size, range, power, and accuracy as well as small arms that allowed infantry to unleash withering volleys against their enemies.

In China, India, and Islamic lands, imperial states had little or no incentive to encourage similar technological innovation in the armaments industry. These states possessed the forces and weapons they needed to maintain order within their boundaries, and they rarely encountered foreign threats backed up with superior armaments. In Europe, however, failure to keep up with the latest improvements in arms technology could lead to defeat on the battlefield and decline in state power. Thus Europeans continuously sought to improve

MAP 23.2

Europe after the Peace of Westphalia, 1648.
Compare this map with Map 23.1.

How have the boundaries of the Holy Roman Empire changed, and why?

their military arsenals, and as a result, by the eighteenth century European armaments outperformed all others.

EARLY CAPITALIST SOCIETY

While the Protestant Reformation and the emergence of sovereign states brought religious and political change, a rapidly expanding population and economy encouraged the development of capitalism, which in turn led to a restructuring of European economy and society. Technologies of communication and transportation enabled businessmen to profit from distant markets, and merchants and manufacturers increasingly organized their affairs with the market rather than local communities in mind.

Capitalism generated considerable wealth, but its effects were uneven and sometimes unsettling. Economic development and increasing prosperity were noticeable in western Europe, particularly England, France, Germany, and the Netherlands. Yet eastern Europe experienced much less economic ferment, as Poland and Russia increasingly became suppliers of grain and raw materials rather than centers of trade or production. Even in western Europe, early capitalism encouraged social change that sometimes required painful adjustments to new conditions.

Population Growth and Urbanization

American Food Crops
The foundation of European economic expansion in early modern times was a rapidly growing population, which reflected improved nutrition and decreasing mortality. The Columbian exchange enriched European diets by introducing new food crops to European fields and tables. Most notable of the introductions was the potato, which during the sixteenth and seventeenth centuries enjoyed the reputation of being an aphrodisiac. Although potatoes probably did not inspire much romantic ardor, they provided a welcome source of carbohydrates for peasants and laborers who were having trouble keeping up with the rising price of bread. From Ireland to Russia and from Scandinavia to the Mediterranean, cultivators planted potatoes and harvested crops that added calories to European diets. American maize also made its way to Europe. Maize, however, served mostly as feed for livestock rather than as food for human consumption, although peasants sometimes used cornmeal to make bread or porridges like polenta. Other American crops, such as tomatoes and peppers, added vitamins and tangy flavor to European diets.

While recently introduced American crops improved European diets, old diseases lost some of their ferocity. Smallpox continued to carry off about 10 percent of Europe's infants, and dysentery, influenza, tuberculosis, and typhus claimed victims among young and old, rich and poor alike. Yet better-nourished populations were better able to resist those maladies. Bubonic plague, a virulent epidemic killer during the fourteenth and fifteenth centuries, receded from European society. After its initial onslaught in the mid-fourteenth century, plague made periodic appearances throughout the early modern era. After the mid-seventeenth century, however, epidemics were rare and isolated events. The last major outbreaks of plague in Europe occurred in London in 1660 and Marseilles in 1720. By the mid-seventeenth century, epidemic disease was almost negligible as an influence on European population.

Population Growth
Although European birthrates did not rise dramatically in early modern times, decreasing mortality resulted in rapid population growth. In 1500 the population of Europe, including Russia, was about 81 million. During the sixteenth century, as Europe recovered from epidemic plague, the population rose to 100 million. The Thirty Years' War—along with the famine and disease that the war touched off—led to population decline from about 1620 to 1650, but by 1700 European population had rallied and risen to 120 million. During the next century it grew by an additional 50 percent to 180 million.

Urbanization
Rapid population growth drove a process of equally rapid urbanization. Some cities grew because rulers chose them as sites of government. Madrid, for example, was a minor town with a few thousand inhabitants until 1561 when King Philip II decided to locate his capital there. By 1600 the population of Madrid had risen to 65,000, and by 1630 it had reached 170,000. Other cities were commercial and industrial as well as government centers, and their numbers expanded along with the European economy. In the mid-sixteenth century, for example, the population of Paris was about 130,000, and London had about 60,000 inhabitants. A century later the population of both cities had risen to 500,000. Other European cities also experienced growth, even if it was not so dramatic as in Madrid, Paris, and London: Amsterdam, Berlin, Copenhagen, Dublin, Stockholm, Vienna, and others became prominent European cities during the early modern era.

Early Capitalism and Protoindustrialization

The Nature of Capitalism
Population growth and rapid urbanization helped spur a round of remarkable economic development. This economic growth coincided with the emergence of capitalism—an economic system in which private parties make their goods and services available on a free market and seek to take advantage of market conditions to profit from their activities. Whether they are single individuals or large companies, private parties own the land, machinery, tools, equipment, buildings, workshops, and raw materials needed for production. Private parties pursuing their own economic interests hire workers and decide for themselves what to produce: economic decisions are the prerogative of capitalist businessmen, not governments or social superiors. The center of a capitalist system is the market in which businessmen compete with one another, and the

forces of supply and demand determine the prices received for goods and services. If businessmen organize their affairs efficiently, they realize handsome profits when they place their goods and services on the market. Otherwise, they incur losses and perhaps even lose their businesses.

The desire to accumulate wealth and realize profits was by no means new. Ever since the introduction of agriculture and the production of surplus crops, some individuals and groups had accumulated great wealth. Indeed, for several thousand years before the early modern era, merchants in China, southeast Asia, India, southwest Asia, the Mediterranean basin, and sub-Saharan Africa had pursued commercial ventures in hopes of realizing profits. Banks, investors, and insurance underwriters had supported privately organized commercial ventures throughout much of the eastern hemisphere since the postclassical era (500–1500 C.E.).

Supply and Demand During early modern times, however, European merchants and entrepreneurs transformed their society in a way that none of their predecessors had done. The capitalist economic order developed as businessmen learned to take advantage of market conditions by building efficient networks of transportation and communication. Dutch merchants might purchase cheap grain from Baltic lands such as Poland or Russia, for example, store it in Amsterdam until they learned about a famine in

The Old Stock Exchange of Amsterdam, depicted here in a painting of the mid-seventeenth century, attracted merchants, investors, entrepreneurs, and businessmen from all over Europe. There they bought and sold shares in joint-stock companies such as the VOC and dealt in all manner of commodities traded in Amsterdam.

the Mediterranean, and then transport it and sell it in southern France or Spain. Their enormous profits fueled suspicions that they took advantage of those in difficulty, but their activities also supplied hungry communities with the necessities of life, even if the price was high.

Private parties organized an array of institutions and services to support early capitalism. Banks, for example, appeared in all the major commercial cities of Europe: they held funds on account for safekeeping and granted loans to merchants or entrepreneurs launching new business ventures. Banks also published business newsletters—forerunners of the *Wall Street Journal* and *Fortune* magazine—that provided readers with reports on prices, information about demand for commodities in distant markets, and political news that could have an impact on business. Insurance companies mitigated financial losses from risky undertakings such as transoceanic voyages. Stock exchanges arose in the major European cities and provided markets where investors could buy and sell shares in joint-stock companies and trade in other commodities as well.

Joint-Stock Companies Joint-stock companies were especially important institutions in early capitalist society. Large trading companies such as the English East India Company and its Dutch counterpart, the Vereenigde Oost-Indische Compagnie (VOC), spread the risks attached to expensive business enterprises and also took advantage of extensive communications and transportation networks. The trading companies organized commercial ventures on a larger scale than ever before. They were the principal foundations of the global economy that emerged in early modern times, and they were the direct ancestors of contemporary multinational corporations.

Politics and Empire Capitalism did not develop in a political vacuum. To the contrary, it emerged with the active support of government authorities who saw a capitalist order as the one best suited to their individual and collective interests. Merchants were especially influential in the affairs of the English and Dutch states, so it is not surprising that these lands adopted policies that were most favorable to capitalist enterprises throughout the early modern era. The English and Dutch states recognized individuals' rights to possess private property, enforced their contracts, protected their financial interests, and settled disputes between parties to business transactions. They also chartered joint-stock companies and authorized some of them to explore, conquer, and colonize distant lands in search of commercial opportunities. Thus early capitalism developed in the context of imperialism, as European peoples established fortified

An anonymous engraver depicts activity in a Dutch shipyard where workers build a massive, oceangoing sailing ship. In the seventeenth century, Dutch ships were inexpensive to operate, yet they accommodated abundant cargoes. What kinds of cargoes were Dutch ships likely to carry in this period?

trading posts in Asia and colonial regimes in both southeast Asia and the Americas. Indeed, imperial expansion and colonial rule were crucial for the development of capitalism, since they enabled European merchants to gain access to the natural resources and commodities that they distributed so effectively through their transportation networks.

Quite apart from its influence on trade and the distribution of goods, capitalism encouraged European entrepreneurs to organize new ways to manufacture goods. For centuries, craft guilds had monopolized the production of goods such as textiles and metalwares in European towns and cities. Guilds fixed prices and wages, and they regulated standards of quality. They did not seek to realize profits so much as to protect markets and preserve their members' places in society. As a result, they actively discouraged competition and sometimes resisted technological innovation.

Putting-out System Capitalist entrepreneurs seeking profits found the guilds cumbersome and inflexible, so they sidestepped them and moved production into the countryside. Instead of relying on urban artisans to produce cloth, for example, they organized a "putting-out system" by which they delivered unfinished materials such as raw wool to rural households. Men and women in the countryside would then spin the wool into yarn, weave the yarn into cloth, cut the cloth according to patterns, and assemble the pieces into garments. The entrepreneur paid workers for their services, picked up the finished goods, and sold them on the market. During the seventeenth and eighteenth centuries, entrepreneurs moved the production of cloth, nails, pins, pots, and many other goods into the countryside through the putting-out system.

Because rural labor was usually plentiful, entrepreneurs spent relatively little on wages and realized handsome profits on their ventures. The putting-out system represented an early effort to organize efficient industrial production. Indeed, some historians refer to the seventeenth and eighteenth centuries as an age of "protoindustrialization." The putting-out system remained a prominent feature of European society until the rise of industrial factories in the nineteenth century.

Social Change in Early Modern Europe

Capitalist economic development brought unsettling change to European lands. The putting-out system, for example, introduced considerable sums of money into the countryside. Increased wealth brought material benefits, but it also undermined long-established patterns of rural life. The material standards of rural life rose dramatically: peasant households acquired more cabinets, furnishings, and tableware, and rural residents wore better clothes, ate better food, and drank better wine. Individuals suddenly acquired incomes that enabled them to pursue their own economic interests and to become financially independent of their families and neighbors. When young adults and women began to earn their own incomes, however, many feared that they might slip out of the control of their families and abandon their kin who continued to work at agricultural tasks.

The putting-out system did not become a prominent feature of production in eastern Europe, but early capitalism prompted deep social change there as well as in lands to the west. Eastern Europe had few cities in early modern times, so in expansive agrarian states such as Poland, Bohemia, and Russia, most people had no alternative to working in the countryside. Landlords took advantage of this situation by forcing peasants to work under extremely harsh conditions.

Serfdom in Russia Russia in particular was a vast but sparsely populated empire with little trade or manufacturing. Out of a concern to retain the allegiance of the powerful nobles who owned most of Russia's land, the Romanov tsars restricted the freedoms of most Russian peasants and tied them to the land as serfs. The institution of serfdom had emerged in the early middle ages as a labor system that required peasants to provide labor services for landowners and prevented them from marrying or moving away without their landlords' permission. After the fifteenth century, serfdom gradually came to an end in western Europe. In eastern Europe, however, landowners and rulers tightened restrictions on peasants during the sixteenth century, and in Russia the institution of serfdom survived until the nineteenth century. In effect, the Romanovs won the support of the Russian nobles by ensuring that laborers would be available to work their estates, which otherwise would have been worthless. In 1649 the government promulgated a law code that provided for tight state control over the Russian labor force by establishing a rigid, castelike social order that sharply restricted both occupational and geographic mobility. The law of 1649 did not turn serfs into chattel slaves, but during the late seventeenth and eighteenth centuries, landlords commonly sold serfs to one another as if they were indeed private property. Under those conditions, landlords operated estates with inexpensive labor and derived enormous incomes from the sale of agricultural products on the market.

thinking about ENCOUNTERS

Capitalism and Overseas Expansion
In the early modern era, Europeans consolidated previous economic developments into a new and profitable system of capitalism, where the central organizing form became the market. Capitalism provided the key tools for more efficient forms of overseas expansion. What were the signal capitalist institutions that underpinned overseas endeavors? How in turn did imperial expansion promote the further growth of capitalism?

These arrangements played crucial roles in the emergence of capitalism. In the larger economy of early modern Europe, eastern European lands relied on serfs to cultivate grains and provide raw materials such as timber for export to western Europe, where merchants and manufacturers were able to employ free wage labor in building a capitalist economy. Already by the early sixteenth century, consumers in the Netherlands depended for their survival on grains imported from Poland and Russia through the Baltic Sea. Thus it was possible for capitalism to flourish in western Europe only because the peasants and semifree serfs of eastern Europe provided inexpensive foods and raw materials that fueled economic development. From its earliest days, capitalist economic organization had implications for peoples and lands far removed from the centers of capitalism itself.

Profits and Ethics Capitalism also posed moral challenges. Medieval theologians had regarded profit-making activity as morally dangerous, since profiteers looked to their own advantage rather than the welfare of the larger community. Church officials even attempted to forbid the collection of interest on loans, since they considered interest an unearned and immoral profit. But profit was the lifeblood of capitalism, and bankers were not willing to risk large sums of money on business ventures without realizing returns on their investments in the form of interest. Even as it transformed the European economy, capitalism found advocates who sought to explain its principles and portray it as a socially beneficial form of economic organization. Most important of the early apostles of capitalism was the Scottish philosopher Adam Smith (1723–1790), who held that society would prosper when individuals pursued their own economic interests.

Nevertheless, the transition to capitalist society was long and painful. When individuals abandoned the practices of their ancestors and declined to help those who had fallen on hard times, their neighbors readily interpreted their actions as expressions of selfishness rather than economic prudence. Thus capitalist economic practices generated deep social strains, which often manifested themselves in violence. Bandits plagued the countryside of early modern Europe, and muggers turned whole sections of large cities into danger zones. Some historians believe that witch-hunting activities reflected social tensions generated by early capitalism and that accusations of witchcraft represented hostility toward women who were becoming economically independent of their husbands and families.

The Nuclear Family In some ways, capitalism favored the nuclear family as the principal unit of society. For centuries European couples had mostly married late—in their mid-twenties—and set up independent households. Early capitalism offered opportunities for these independent families to increase their wealth by cultivating agricultural crops or producing goods for sale on the market. As nuclear families became more important economically, they also became more socially and emotionally independent. Love between a man and a woman became a more important consideration in the making of marriages than the interests of the larger extended families, and affection between parents and their children became a more important ingredient of family life. Capitalism did not necessarily cause these changes in family life, but it may have encouraged developments that helped to define the nature and role of the family in modern European society.

SCIENCE AND ENLIGHTENMENT

While experiencing religious, political, economic, and social change, western Europe also underwent intellectual and cultural transformation. Astronomers and physicists rejected classical Greek and Roman authorities, whose theories had dominated scientific thought during the middle ages, and based their understanding of the natural world on direct observation and mathematical reasoning. During the seventeenth and eighteenth centuries, they elaborated a new vision of the earth and the larger universe. Scholars relied on observation and mathematics to transform the natural sciences in a process known as the scientific revolution. The results of early modern science were so powerful that some European intellectuals sought to overhaul moral, social, and political thought by adapting scientific methods and relying on reason rather than traditional cultural authorities. Their efforts weakened the influence of churches in western Europe and encouraged the development of secular values.

The Reconception of the Universe

The Ptolemaic Universe Until the seventeenth century, European astronomers based their understanding of the universe on the work of the Greek scholar Claudius Ptolemy of Alexandria. About the middle of the second century C.E., Ptolemy composed a work known as the *Almagest* that synthesized theories about the universe. Ptolemy envisioned a motionless earth surrounded by a series of nine hollow, concentric spheres that revolved around it. Each of the first seven spheres had one of the observable heavenly bodies—the sun, the moon, Mercury, Venus, Mars, Jupiter, and Saturn—embedded in its shell. The eighth sphere held the stars, and an empty ninth sphere surrounded the whole cosmos and provided the spin that kept all the others moving. Beyond the spheres Christian astronomers located heaven, the realm of God.

Following Ptolemy, astronomers believed that the heavens consisted of matter unlike any found on earth. Glowing like perfect jewels in the night skies, heavenly bodies were composed of a pure substance that did not experience change or corruption, and they were not subject to the physical laws that governed the world below the moon. They followed perfect circular paths in making their revolutions around the earth.

sources from the past

Adam Smith on the Capitalist Market

Adam Smith devoted special thought to the nature of early capitalist society and the principles that made it work. In 1776 he published a lengthy book entitled An Inquiry into the Nature and Causes of the Wealth of Nations, *a vastly influential work that championed free, unregulated markets and capitalist enterprise as the principal ingredients of prosperity. Smith's optimism about capitalism sprang from his conviction that society as a whole benefits when individuals pursue their own economic interests and trade on a free market.*

Every individual is continually exerting himself to find out the most advantageous employment for whatever capital he can command. It is his own advantage, indeed, and not that of the society, which he has in view. . . .

As every individual, therefore, endeavours as much as he can both to employ his capital in the support of domestic industry, and so to direct that industry that its produce may be of the greatest value, every individual necessarily labours to render the annual revenue of the society as great as he can. He generally, indeed, neither intends to promote the public interest, nor knows how much he is promoting it. By preferring the support of domestic to that of foreign industry, he intends only his own security; and by directing that industry in such a manner as its produce may be of the greatest value, he intends only his own gain, and he is in this, as in many other cases, led by an invisible hand to promote an end which was no part of his intention. Nor is it always the worse for the society that it was no part of it. By pursuing his own interest he frequently promotes that of the society more effectually than when he really intends to promote it. I have never known much good done by those who affected to trade for the public good. It is an affectation, indeed, not very common among merchants, and very few words need be employed in dissuading them from it.

What is the species of domestic industry which his capital can employ, and of which the produce is likely to be of the greatest value, every individual, it is evident, can, in his local situation, judge much better than any statesman or lawgiver can do for him. The statesman, who should attempt to direct private people in what manner they ought to employ their capitals, would not only load himself with a most unnecessary attention, but assume an authority which could safely be trusted, not only to no single person, but to no council or senate whatever, and which would nowhere be so dangerous as in the hands of a man who had folly and presumption enough to fancy himself fit to exercise it.

To give the monopoly of the home market to the produce of domestic industry, in any particular art or manufacture, is in some measure to direct private people in what manner they ought to employ their capitals, and must, in almost all cases, be either a useless or a hurtful regulation. If the produce of domestic industry can be brought there as cheap as that of foreign industry, the regulation is evidently useless. If it cannot, it must generally be hurtful. It is the maxim of every prudent master of a family, never to attempt to make at home what it will cost him more to make than to buy. The tailor does not attempt to make his own shoes, but buys them of the shoemaker. The shoemaker does not attempt to make his own clothes, but employs a tailor. The farmer attempts to make neither the one nor the other, but employs those different artificers. All of them find it for their interest to employ their whole industry in a way in which they have some advantage over their neighbours, and to purchase with a part of its produce, or, what is the same thing, with the price of a part of it, whatever else they have occasion for.

For Further Reflection

■ To what extent do you think Adam Smith's analysis reflected the experiences of his own times, and to what extent did they represent universally valid observations?

Source: Adam Smith. *An Inquiry into the Nature and Causes of the Wealth of Nations.* Edinburgh: 1863, pp. 198–200.

Planetary Movement Although theoretically attractive, this earth-centered, or geocentric, cosmology did not mesh readily with the erratic movements of the planets—a term that comes from the Greek word *planetes,* meaning "wanderer." From the vantage point of the earth, the planets often followed regular courses through the skies, but they sometimes slowed down, stopped, or even turned back on their courses—motions that would be difficult to explain if the planetary spheres revolved regularly around the earth. Astronomers went to great lengths to explain planetary be-havior as the result of perfect circular movements. The result was an awkward series of adjustments known as epicycles—small circular revolutions that planets made around a point in their spheres, even while the spheres themselves revolved around the earth.

The Copernican Universe As astronomers accumulated data on planetary movements, most of them sought to reconcile their observations with Ptolemaic theory by adding increasing numbers of epicycles to their cosmic maps.

In 1543, however, the Polish astronomer Nicolaus Copernicus published a treatise, *On the Revolutions of the Heavenly Spheres,* that broke with Ptolemaic theory and pointed European science in a new direction. Copernicus argued that the sun rather than the earth stood at the center of the universe and that the planets, including the earth, revolved around the sun.

Compared with Ptolemy's earth-centered universe, this new sun-centered, or heliocentric, theory harmonized much better with observational data, but it did not receive a warm welcome. Copernicus's ideas not only challenged prevailing scientific theories but also threatened cherished religious beliefs. His theory implied that the earth was just another planet and that human beings did not occupy the central position in the universe. To some it also suggested the unsettling possibility that there might be other populated worlds in the universe—a notion that would be difficult to reconcile with Christian teachings, which held that the earth and humanity were unique creations of God.

The Scientific Revolution

Although it was unpopular in many quarters, Copernicus's theory inspired some astronomers to examine the heavens in fresh ways. As evidence accumulated, it became clear that the Ptolemaic universe simply did not correspond with reality. Astronomers based their theories on increasingly precise observational data, and they relied on mathematical reasoning to organize the data. Gradually, they abandoned the Ptolemaic in favor of the Copernican model of the universe. Moreover, some of them began to apply their analytical methods to mechanics—the branch of science that deals with moving bodies—and by the mid-seventeenth century accurate observation and mathematical reasoning dominated both mechanics and astronomy. Indeed, reliance on

In this seventeenth-century engraving, Galileo Galilei faces the Inquisition, a Roman Catholic institution that prosecuted individuals accused of a wide variety of crimes related to heresy. At a trial in 1633, the Inquisition found Galileo "vehemently suspect of heresy," forced him to recant Copernicanism, and placed him under house arrest for the remainder of his life.

observation and mathematics transformed the study of the natural world and brought about the scientific revolution.

Galileo Galilei The works of two scientists—Johannes Kepler of Germany and Galileo Galilei of Italy—rang the death knell for the Ptolemaic universe. Kepler (1571–1630) demonstrated that planetary orbits are elliptical, not circular as in Ptolemaic theory. Galileo (1564–1642) showed that the heavens were not the perfect, unblemished realm that Ptolemaic astronomers assumed but, rather, a world of change, flux, and many previously unsuspected sights. Galileo took a recently invented instrument—the telescope—turned it skyward, and reported observations that astonished his contemporaries. With his telescope he could see spots on the sun and mountains on the moon—observations that discredited the notion that heavenly bodies were smooth, immaculate, unchanging, and perfectly spherical. He also noticed four of the moons that orbit the planet Jupiter—bodies that no human being had ever before observed—and he caught sight of previously unknown distant stars, which implied that the universe was much larger than anyone had previously suspected.

In addition to his astronomical discoveries, Galileo contributed to the understanding of terrestrial motion. He designed ingenious experiments to show that the velocity of falling bodies depends not on their weight but, rather, on the height from which they fall. This claim brought him scorn from scientists who subscribed to scientific beliefs deriving from Aristotle. But it offered a better explanation of how moving bodies behave under the influence of the earth's gravitational pull. Galileo also anticipated the modern law of inertia, which holds that a moving body will continue to move in a straight line until some force intervenes to check or alter its motion.

Isaac Newton The new approach to science culminated in the work of the English mathematician Isaac Newton (1642–1727), who depended on accurate observation and mathematical reasoning to construct a powerful synthesis of astronomy and mechanics. Newton outlined his views on the natural world in an epoch-making volume of 1687 entitled *Mathematical Principles of Natural Philosophy*. Newton's work united the heavens and the earth in a vast, cosmic system. He argued that a law of universal gravitation regulates the motions of bodies throughout the universe, and he offered precise mathematical explanations of the laws that govern movements of bodies on the earth. Newton's laws of universal gravitation and motion enabled him to synthesize the sciences of astronomy and mechanics. They also allowed him to explain a vast range of seemingly unrelated phenomena, such as the ebb and flow of the tides, which move according to the gravitational pull of the moon, and the eccentric orbits of planets and comets, which reflect the gravi-

thinking about TRADITIONS

Science and the Enlightenment
Inspired by the advances in science, European intellectuals questioned long-standing beliefs concerning the nature and functioning of human society. What specific traditions did scientists and intellectuals challenge? How did religious tenets fare under such scrutiny?

tational influence of the sun, the earth, and other heavenly bodies. Until the twentieth century, Newton's universe served as the unquestioned framework for the physical sciences.

Newton's work symbolized the scientific revolution, but it by no means marked the end of the process by which observation and mathematical reasoning transformed European science. Inspired by the dramatic discoveries of astronomers and physicists, other scientists began to turn away from classical authorities and to construct fresh approaches to the understanding of the natural world. During the seventeenth and eighteenth centuries, anatomy, physiology, microbiology, chemistry, and botany underwent a thorough overhaul, as scientists tested their theories against direct observation of natural phenomena and explained them in rigorous mathematical terms.

Women and Science

In the sixteenth and seventeenth centuries, Europe's learned men challenged some of the most hallowed traditions concerning the nature of the physical universe and supplanted them with new scientific principles. Yet, when male scientists studied female anatomy, female physiology, and women's reproductive organs, they were commonly guided not by scientific observation but by tradition, prejudice, and fanciful imagination. William Harvey (1578–1657), the English physician who discovered the principles of the circulation of human blood, also applied his considerable talents to the study of human reproduction. After careful dissection and observation of female deer, chickens, and roosters, he hypothesized that women, like hens, served as mere receptacles for the "vivifying" male fluid. According to him, it was the male semen—endowed with generative powers so potent that it did not even have to reach the uterus to work its magic—from which the unfertilized egg received life and form. Anatomy, physiology, and limited reproductive function seemed to confirm the innate inferiority of women, adding a "scientific" veneer to the traditionally limited images, roles, and functions of women. With the arrival of printing, men were able to disseminate more widely those negative conclusions about women.

Émilie du Châtelet Despite prevailing critical attitudes, some women found themselves drawn to the new intellectual currents of the time. Women formulated their own

Émilie du Châtelet was perhaps the most exceptional female scientist of the Enlightenment. Although she had to contend with the conventional demands on women, she remained committed to her study of Newton and science.

theories about the natural world and published their findings. One of the most notable female scientists of her age was Émilie du Châtelet (1706–1749), a French mathematician and physicist. Long famous for being the mistress of the celebrated French intellectual Voltaire, she was in fact a talented intellectual and scientist in her own right. A precocious child, du Châtelet was apparently fluent in six languages at the age of twelve, and she benefited from having an unusually enlightened father who provided his rebellious daughter with an education more typical for boys. Her obvious intellectual abilities made her mother despair over her daughter's future, and her mother complained about a daughter who "flaunts her mind, and frightens away the suitors her other excesses have not driven off." Émilie du Châtelet nonetheless did marry, as was custom, and she had three children with her husband, the Marquis du Châtelet. She did this while also engaged in affairs of the intellect.

Du Châtelet established her reputation as a scientist with her three-volume work on the German mathematician Gottfried Leibniz (1646–1716) in 1740. Her crowning achievement, however, was her translation of Isaac Newton's monumental work *Principia Mathematica,* which has remained the standard French translation of the work. She did not simply render Newton's words into another language, however; rather, she explained his complex mathematics in graceful prose, transformed his geometry into calculus, and assessed the current state of Newtonian physics. She finished her work in the year of her death, at age forty-three, six days after giving birth to a child. Underscoring the difficulty of reconciling a woman's reproductive duties with her intellectual aspirations was her lover Voltaire's commentary. He declared in a letter to his friend Frederick II, King of Prussia (reigned 1740–1786), that du Châtelet was "a great man whose only fault was being a woman."

The Enlightenment

Newton's vision of the universe was so powerful and persuasive that its influence extended well beyond science. His work suggested that rational analysis of human behavior and institutions could lead to fresh insights about the human as well as the natural world. From Scotland to Sicily and from Philadelphia to Moscow, European and Euro-American thinkers launched an ambitious project to transform human thought and to use reason to transform the world. Like the early modern scientists, they abandoned Aristotelian philosophy, Christian theology, and other traditionally recognized authorities, and they sought to subject the human world to purely rational analysis. The result of their work was a movement known as the Enlightenment.

Science and Society Enlightenment thinkers sought to discover natural laws that governed human society in the same way that Newton's laws of universal gravitation and motion regulated the universe. Their search took different forms. The English philosopher John Locke (1632–1704) worked to discover natural laws of politics. He attacked divine-right theories that served as a foundation for absolute monarchy and advocated constitutional government on the grounds that sovereignty resides in the people rather than the state or its rulers. Indeed, he provided much of the theoretical justification for the Glorious Revolution and the establishment of constitutional monarchy in England. The Scottish philosopher Adam Smith turned his attention to economic affairs and held that laws of supply and demand determine what happens in the marketplace. The French nobleman Charles Louis de Secondat, better known as the Baron de Montesquieu (1689–1755), sought to establish a science of politics and discover principles that would foster political liberty in a prosperous and stable state.

The center of Enlightenment thought was France, where prominent intellectuals known collectively as *philosophes* ("philosophers") advanced the cause of reason. The philo-

Joseph Wright of Derby's painting entitled "A philosopher gives a lecture on the orrery" centers on a three-dimensional image of the cosmos (the orrery); his use of light offers a metaphor for the Enlightenment and natural philosophy.

sophes were not philosophers in the traditional sense of the term so much as public intellectuals. They addressed their works more to the educated public than to scholars: instead of formal philosophical treatises, they mostly composed histories, novels, dramas, satires, and pamphlets on religious, moral, and political issues.

Voltaire More than any other philosophe, François-Marie Arouet (1694–1778) epitomized the spirit of the Enlightenment. Writing under the pen name Voltaire, he published his first book at age seventeen. By the time of his death at age eighty-four, his published writings included some ten thousand letters and filled seventy volumes. With stinging wit and sometimes bitter irony, Voltaire championed individual freedom and attacked any institution sponsoring intolerant or oppressive policies. Targets of his caustic wit included

the French monarchy and the Roman Catholic church. When the king of France sought to save money by reducing the number of horses kept in royal stables, for example, Voltaire suggested that it would be more effective to get rid of the asses who rode the horses. Voltaire also waged a long literary campaign against the Roman Catholic church, which he held responsible for fanaticism, intolerance, and incalculable human suffering. Voltaire's battle cry was *écrasez l'infame* ("crush the damned thing"), meaning the church that he considered an agent of oppression.

Deism Some philosophes were conventional Christians, and a few turned to atheism. Like Voltaire, however, most of them were deists who believed in the existence of a god but denied the supernatural teachings of Christianity, such as Jesus' virgin birth and his resurrection. To the deists the universe was an orderly realm. Deists held that a powerful god set the universe in motion and established natural laws that govern it, but did not take a personal interest in its development or intervene in its affairs. In a favorite simile of the deists, this god was like a watchmaker who did not need

sourcesfromthepast

John Locke Claims People Are the Products of Their Environment

John Locke (1632–1704) was one of the leading intellectuals of his age. Although commonly recognized as an influential political theorist, he was also intensely curious about how humans acquired knowledge. In his seminal An Essay Concerning Human Understanding *(1690), Locke repudiates the prevailing view that knowledge—knowledge of certain moral truths or knowledge of the existence of God, for example—is innate, that is, imprinted on the human mind at birth. He argues instead that the foundation of all knowledge is sense experience (sensation), like the color of a flower, and awareness that one is thinking (reflection). These "ideas" provide the mind with knowledge.*

The way shown how we come by any knowledge, sufficient to prove it not innate. It is an established opinion amongst some men, that there are in the understanding certain innate principles; some primary notions, characters, as it were stamped upon the mind of man; which the soul receives in its very first being, and brings into the world with it. It would be sufficient to convince unprejudiced readers of the falseness of this supposition, if I should only show (as I hope I shall in the following parts of this Discourse) how men, barely by the use of their natural faculties, may attain to all the knowledge they have, without the help of any innate impressions; and may arrive at certainty, without any such original notions or principles. . . .

All ideas come from sensation or reflection. Let us then suppose the mind to be, as we say, white paper, void of all characters, without any ideas:—How comes it to be furnished? Whence comes it by that vast store which the busy and boundless fancy of man has painted on it with an almost endless variety? Whence has it all the materials of reason and knowledge? To this I answer, in one word, from Experience. In that all our knowledge is founded; and from that it ultimately derives itself. Our observation employed either, about external sensible objects, or about the internal operations of our minds perceived and reflected on by ourselves, is that which supplies our understandings with all the materials of thinking. These two are the fountains of knowledge, from whence all the ideas we have, or can naturally have, do spring.

The objects of sensation one source of ideas. First, our Senses, conversant about particular sensible objects, do con-

vey into the mind several distinct perceptions of things, according to those various ways wherein those objects do affect them. And thus we come by those ideas we have of yellow, white, heat, cold, soft, hard, bitter, sweet, and all those which we call sensible qualities; which when I say the senses convey into the mind, I mean, they from external objects convey into the mind what produces there those perceptions. This great source of most of the ideas we have, depending wholly upon our senses, and derived by them to the understanding, I call Sensation.

The operations of our minds, the other source of them. Secondly, the other fountain from which experience furnisheth the understanding with ideas is,—the perception of the operations of our own mind within us, as it is employed about the ideas it has got;—which operations, when the soul comes to reflect on and consider, do furnish the understanding with another set of ideas, which could not be had from things without. And such are perception, thinking, doubting, believing, reasoning, knowing, willing, and all the different actings of our own minds;—which we being conscious of, and observing in ourselves, do from these receive into our understandings as distinct ideas as we do from bodies affecting our senses. This source of ideas every man has wholly in himself; and though it be not sense, as having nothing to do with external objects, yet it is very like it, and might properly enough be called internal sense. But as I call the other Sensation, so I Call this Reflection, the ideas it affords being such only as the mind gets by reflecting on its own operations within itself.

For Further Reflection

■ What are the implications of Locke's claim for the development of human society that people are solely the products of their environment? How are those implications bound up with criticism of existing social structures?

Source: John Locke. *An Essay Concerning Human Understanding.* Kitchener, Ontario, Canada: Batoche Books, 1690, pp. 24, 73, 74. http://site.ebrary.com/lib/uhmanoa/Doc?id=2001993&ppg=24, 73, 74.

to interfere constantly in the workings of his creation, since it operated by itself according to rational and natural laws.

The Theory of Progress

Most philosophes were optimistic about the future of the world and humanity. They expected knowledge of human affairs to advance as fast as

modern science, and they believed that rational understanding of human and natural affairs would bring about a new era of constant progress. In fact, progress became almost an ideology of the philosophes, who believed that natural science would lead to greater human control over the world while rational sciences of human affairs would lead to indi-

Socially prominent women deeply influenced the development of Enlightenment thought by organizing and maintaining salons—gatherings where philosophes, scientists, and intellectuals discussed the leading ideas of the day. Though produced in 1814, this painting depicts the Parisian salon of Mme. Geoffrin (center left), a leading patron of the French philosophes, about 1775. In the background is a bust of Voltaire, who lived in Switzerland at the time.

vidual freedom and the construction of a prosperous, just, and equitable society.

The philosophes' fond wishes for progress, prosperity, and social harmony did not come to pass. Yet the Enlightenment helped to bring about a thorough cultural transformation of European society. It weakened the influence of organized religion, although it by no means destroyed institutional churches. Enlightenment thought encouraged the replacement of Christian values, which had guided European thought on religious and moral affairs for more than a millennium, with a new set of secular values arising from reason rather than revelation. Furthermore, the Enlightenment encouraged political and cultural leaders to subject society to rational analysis and intervene actively in its affairs in the interests of promoting progress and prosperity. In many ways, the Enlightenment legacy continues to influence European and Euro-American societies.

in perspective

During the early modern era, European society experienced a series of profound and sometimes unsettling changes. The Protestant Reformation ended the religious unity of western Christendom, and intermittent religious conflict disrupted European society for a century and more. Centralizing monarchs strengthened their realms and built a society of sovereign, autonomous, and intensely competitive states. Capitalist entrepreneurs reorganized the production and distribution of manufactured goods, and although their methods led to increased wealth, their quest for efficiency and profits clashed with traditional values. Modern science based on direct observation and mathematical explanations emerged as a powerful tool for the investigation of the natural world, and its influence extended even to thought about human affairs. Some people rejected traditional religious beliefs altogether and worked toward the construction of a new moral thought based strictly on science and reason. At just the time that European merchants, colonists, and adventurers were seeking opportunities in the larger world, European society was becoming more powerful, more experimental, and more competitive than ever before. ●

CHRONOLOGY

1473–1543	Life of Nicolaus Copernicus
1478	Foundation of the Spanish Inquisition
1483–1546	Life of Martin Luther
1491–1556	Life of Ignatius Loyola
1509–1547	Reign of King Henry VIII
1509–1564	Life of John Calvin
1517	Publication of the *Ninety-Five Theses*
1519–1556	Reign of Emperor Charles V
1540	Foundation of the Society of Jesus
1545–1563	Council of Trent
1556–1598	Reign of King Philip II
1564–1642	Life of Galileo Galilei
1571–1630	Life of Johannes Kepler
1588	Spanish Armada
1618–1648	Thirty Years' War
1632–1704	Life of John Locke
1642–1727	Life of Isaac Newton
1643–1715	Reign of King Louis XIV
1648	Peace of Westphalia
1689–1755	Life of the Baron de Montesquieu
1694–1778	Life of Voltaire
1706–1749	Life of Émilie du Châtelet
1723–1790	Life of Adam Smith

For Further Reading

Philip Benedict. *Christ's Churches Purely Reformed: A Social History of Calvinism.* New Haven, 2002. Impressive and very readable synthesis of the history of Calvinism and the general impact of the Protestant Reformation in Europe.

William J. Bouwsma. *John Calvin: A Sixteenth-Century Portrait.* New York, 1989. A penetrating examination of one of the principal Protestant reformers.

Fernand Braudel. *Civilization and Capitalism, 15th to 18th Century.* 3 vols. Trans. by S. Reynolds. New York, 1981–84. A rich analysis of early capitalist society by one of the greatest historians of the twentieth century.

Paul Dukes. *The Making of Russian Absolutism, 1613–1801.* 2nd ed. London, 1990. A succinct study of two disparate centuries, the seventeenth and eighteenth, and two influential tsars, Peter and Catherine.

Robert S. Duplessis. *Transitions to Capitalism in Early Modern Europe.* Cambridge, 1997. A valuable synthesis of research on early capitalism and protoindustrialization.

Elizabeth L. Eisenstein. *The Printing Press as an Agent of Change.* 2 vols. Cambridge, 1979. An insightful study that examines the significance of printing for the Protestant Reformation and the scientific revolution.

Patricia Fara. *Pandora's Breeches: Women, Science, and Power in the Enlightenment.* London, 2004. An engaging account of the contributions women made to science in the seventeenth and eighteenth centuries.

Peter Gay. *The Enlightenment: An Interpretation.* 2 vols. New York, 1966–69. A classic study making the case for the Enlightenment as a turning point in European cultural history.

Philip S. Gorski. *The Disciplinary Revolution: Calvinism and the Rise of the Early Modern State.* Chicago, 2003. Argues that the formation of strong European states was a result of religious and social control policies initiated by the Protestant Reformation.

Margaret Jacob. *The Cultural Meaning of the Scientific Revolution.* New York, 1989. Explores the larger cultural and social implications of early modern science.

Lisa Jardine. *Ingenious Pursuits: Building the Scientific Revolution.* New York, 1999. A close study of the messy context of the scientific revolution and of the ambiguous boundary between what have come to be thought of as the natural and the human sciences.

E. L. Jones. *The European Miracle: Environments, Economies, and Geopolitics in the History of Europe and Asia.* 2nd ed. Cambridge, 1987. Examines European politics and economic growth in comparative perspective.

———. *Growth Recurring: Economic Change in World History.* Oxford, 1988. Compares processes of economic growth in China, Europe, and Japan.

Leonard Krieger. *Kings and Philosophers, 1689–1789.* New York, 1970. A thoughtful analysis of European history during an age of absolutism and Enlightenment.

Thomas S. Kuhn. *The Structure of Scientific Revolutions.* 3rd ed. Chicago, 1997. An influential theoretical work that views scientific thought in larger social and cultural contexts.

Brian P. Levack. *The Witch-Hunt in Early Modern Europe.* New York, 1987. A compact but comprehensive survey of European witchcraft beliefs and pursuit of witches in the sixteenth and seventeenth centuries.

William H. McNeill. *The Pursuit of Power: Technology, Armed Force, and Society since A.D. 1000.* Chicago, 1982. Insightful analysis exploring the influence of sovereign states and early capitalism on military technology and organization.

Jerry Z. Muller. *The Mind and the Market: Capitalism in Modern European Thought.* New York, 2002. Broad history of the development of capitalism through the eyes of major European thinkers, including Adam Smith, Joseph Schumpeter, and Karl Marx.

Heiko A. Oberman. *Luther: Man between God and the Devil.* Trans. by E. Walliser-Schwartzbart. New Haven, 1989. A perceptive study of the first Protestant reformer by a foremost scholar.

Geoffrey Parker. *The Military Revolution: Military Innovation and the Rise of the West, 1500–1800.* Cambridge, 1988. A thoughtful essay on European military affairs in early modern times.

Kenneth Pomeranz. *The Great Divergence: China, Europe, and the Making of the Modern World Economy.* Princeton, 2000. Pathbreaking scholarly study that illuminates the economic history of the early modern world through comparison of economic development in Asian and European lands.

Roy Porter. *The Creation of the Modern World: The Untold Story of the British Enlightenment.* New York, 2000. An important work that returns the Enlightenment to Britain.

Eugene F. Rice Jr. and Anthony Grafton. *The Foundations of Early Modern Europe, 1460–1559.* 2nd ed. New York, 1994. Excellent introduction to political, social, economic, and cultural developments.

Jessica Riskin. *Science in the Age of Sensibility: The Sentimental Empiricists of the French Enlightenment.* Chicago, 2002. Study of the development of modern science not simply as a result of empiricism but also of sentimental, humanist sensibility.

Daniel Roche. *France in the Enlightenment.* Trans. by Arthur Goldhammer. Cambridge, Mass., 1998. Comprehensive account of the French Enlightenment and some of its most significant cultural, social, and political contexts.

Paolo Rossi. *The Birth of Modern Science.* Malden, Mass., 2001. Explores specific seventeenth-century value systems and traditions that were central to the rise of modern science.

Simon Schama. *The Embarrassment of Riches: An Interpretation of Dutch Culture in the Seventeenth Century.* New York, 1987. A marvelous popular study of the wealthy Dutch republic at its height.

Keith Thomas. *Religion and the Decline of Magic.* New York, 1971. A riveting analysis of popular culture in early modern times, especially strong on the explanation of magic and witchcraft.

James Van Horn Melton. *The Rise of the Public in Enlightenment Europe.* Cambridge, 2001. Work on the cultural aspects of the Enlightenment and the emergence of a public sphere in Britain, France, and German-speaking territories.

chapter 24

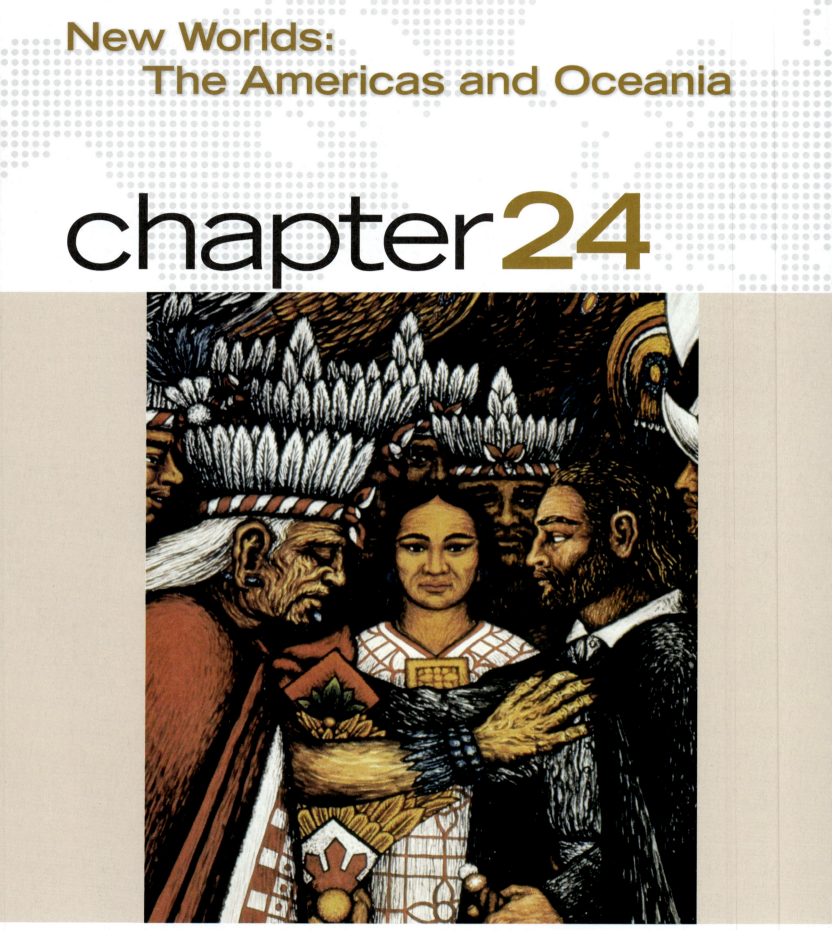

A mural by Tlaxala artist Desiderio Hernández Xochitiotzin depicts the central place of Doña Marina in facilitating encounters between Hernán Cortés (on the right) and the indigenous peoples of Mexico.

PART 5

EYEWITNESS:
The Mysterious Identity of Doña Marina

A remarkable young woman played a pivotal role in the Spanish conquest of Mexico. Originally called Malintzin, over the years she has come to be better known as Doña Marina, the name bestowed on her by Spanish forces. Doña Marina was born about 1500 to a noble family in central Mexico. Her mother tongue was Nahuatl, the principal language of the Aztec empire. When she was a girl, Doña Marina's family sent her to the Mexican coast as a slave, and her new family later passed her on to their neighbors in the Yucatan peninsula. During her travels she became fluent in Maya as well as her native Nahuatl language.

When Hernán Cortés arrived on the Mexican coast in 1519, his small army included a Spanish soldier who had learned the Maya language during a period of captivity in the Yucatan. But he had no way to communicate with the Nahuatl-speaking peoples of central Mexico until a Maya chieftain presented him with twelve young women, including Doña Marina, when he entered into an alliance with the foreigner. Doña Marina's linguistic talents enabled Cortés to communicate through an improbable chain of languages—from Spanish to Maya to Nahuatl and then back again—while making his way to the Aztec capital of Tenochtitlan. (Doña Marina soon learned Spanish and thus eliminated the Maya link in the linguistic chain.)

Doña Marina provided Cortés with intelligence and diplomatic as well as linguistic services. On several occasions she learned of plans by native peoples to overwhelm and destroy the tiny Spanish army, and she alerted Cortés to the danger in time for him to forestall an attack. Once, she was able to report the precise details of a planned ambush because she played along with an effort to bring her into the scheme. She also helped Cortés negotiate with emissaries from Tenochtitlan and other major cities of central Mexico. Indeed, in the absence of Doña Marina's services, it is difficult to see how Cortés's small band could have survived to see the Aztec capital.

Precisely because of her pivotal role in aiding Cortés and forwarding his invasion of the Aztec empire, Doña Marina earned another name commonly bestowed on her in Mexican history: La Malinche, or the traitor. The belief that she betrayed her people by collaborating with the Spanish underscored how native Americans faced many challenges and conflicts in their encounters with Europeans. Other subjects of the Aztec empire also chose to ally themselves with the Spanish given their disaffection from Aztec imperial rule, so Doña Marina represented the existing divisions within Mesoamerican society as well as the demonstrated bravery, intelligence, and survival skills of a woman often harshly treated. Because of her symbolic richness, she has likewise attained the status of mother of the Mexican peoples.

Apart from facilitating the Spanish conquest of the Aztec empire, Doña Marina played a role in the formation of a new society in Mexico. In 1522, one year after the fall of Tenochtitlan, she gave birth to a son fathered by Cortés, and in 1526 she bore a daughter to a Spanish captain whom she had married. Her offspring were not the first children born in the western hemisphere of indigenous and Spanish parentage, but they symbolize the early emergence of a mestizo population in Mexico. Doña Marina died soon after the birth of her daughter, probably in 1527, but during her short life she contributed to the thorough transformation of Mexican society.

Until 1492 the peoples of the eastern and western hemispheres had few dealings with one another. About 1000 C.E. Norse explorers established a short-lived colony in modern Newfoundland, and sporadic encounters between European fishermen and indigenous peoples of North America probably occurred before Christopher Columbus undertook his first voyage across the Atlantic Ocean. It is likely, too, that an occasional Asian or Austronesian mariner reached the Pacific coast of North or South America before 1492. Yet travel between the eastern hemisphere, the western hemisphere, and Oceania was too irregular and infrequent to generate interaction between peoples of different societies until the fifteenth century.

After 1492, however, the voyages of European mariners led to permanent and sustained contact between the peoples of the eastern hemisphere, the western hemisphere, and Oceania. The resulting encounters brought profound and often violent change to both American and Pacific lands. European peoples possessed powerful military weapons, horses, and sailing ships that provided them with technological advantages over the peoples they encountered in the Americas and the Pacific islands. Moreover, most Europeans also enjoyed complete or partial immunity to diseases that caused demographic disasters when introduced to the western hemisphere and Oceania. Because of their technological advantages and the wholesale depopulation that followed from epidemic diseases, European peoples were able to establish a presence throughout the Americas and much of the Pacific Ocean basin.

The European presence did not lead to immediate change in Australia and the Pacific islands, although it laid a foundation for dramatic and often traumatic change in the nineteenth and twentieth centuries. In the western hemisphere, however, large numbers of European migrants helped to bring about a profound transformation of American societies in early modern times. In Mexico and Peru, Spanish conquerors established territorial empires that were ruled from Spain. In Brazil, Portuguese entrepreneurs founded sugar plantations and imported African slaves to perform the heavy labor required for their operation. In North America, French, English, and Dutch fur traders allied with indigenous peoples who provided them with animal skins, and their more sedentary compatriots founded settler societies concentrating on the production of cash crops for export. Throughout the western hemisphere, peoples of European, African, and American ancestry interacted to fashion new worlds.

COLLIDING WORLDS

When European peoples first sought to establish their presence in the Americas, they brought a range of technology unavailable to the peoples they encountered in the western hemisphere. Even more important than European technology, however, were the divisions between indigenous peoples that Europeans were able to exploit and the effects of epidemic diseases that devastated native societies. Soon after their arrival in the western hemisphere, Spanish conquerors toppled the Aztec and Inca empires and imposed their own rule in Mexico and Peru. In later decades Portuguese planters built sugar plantations on the Brazilian coastline. French, English, and Dutch migrants displaced indigenous peoples in North America and established settler colonies under the rule of European peoples.

One of the earliest European depictions of Native Americans was this engraving of 1505. The caption informed readers that American peoples lived in communal society, where men took several wives but none had private possessions, and that they routinely smoked and consumed the bodies of slain enemies. How might such representations have shaped European ideas about native Americans?

The Spanish Caribbean

The Taíno The first site of interaction between European and American peoples was the Caribbean. When Spanish mariners arrived there, the Taíno (also known as Arawaks) were the most prominent people in the region. During the late centuries B.C.E., the ancestors of the Taíno had sailed in canoes from the Orinoco River valley in South America to the Caribbean islands, and by about 900 C.E. they had settled throughout the region. The Taíno cultivated manioc and other crops, and they lived in small villages under the authority of chiefs who allocated land to families and super- vised community affairs. They showed interest in the glass, beads, and metal tools that Spanish mariners brought as trade goods and offered little initial resistance to the visitors.

Spanish Arrival Christopher Columbus and his imme- diate followers made the island of Hispaniola (which em- braces modern Haiti and the Dominican Republic) the base of Spanish operations in the Caribbean. There, Spanish set- tlers established the fort of Santo Domingo, and the city, officially founded in 1498, became the capital of the Spanish Caribbean. Columbus's original plan was to build forts and trading posts where merchants could trade with local peo- ples for products desired by European consumers. Within a few years of Spanish arrival, however, it became clear that the Caribbean region offered no silks or spices for the Eu- ropean market. If Spanish settlers wanted to maintain their presence in the Caribbean, they would need to find some way to make a living.

The settlers first attempted to support their society by mining gold. Spanish settlers were too few in number to mine

sources from the past

First Impressions of Spanish Forces

As the Spanish army made its way to Tenochtitlan, Motecuzoma dispatched a series of emissaries to communicate with Cortés and learn his intentions. The following document, based on indigenous accounts but filtered through imperial Spanish sensibilities, suggested that Motecuzoma reacted with fright when presented with reports that were less than reassuring, since they focused on fearsome weapons and animals of the Spanish. Given the martial response of the Aztecs to the Spanish invasion, it seems highly unlikely that Motecuzoma or the Aztecs would have expressed terror in such a humiliating fashion.

And when [Motecuzoma] had heard what the messengers reported, he was terrified, he was astounded. . . .

Especially did it cause him to faint away when he heard how the gun, at [the Spaniards'] command, discharged [the shot]; how it resounded as if it thundered when it went off. It indeed bereft one of strength; it shut off one's ears. And when it discharged, something like a round pebble came forth from within. Fire went showering forth; sparks went blazing forth. And its smoke smelled very foul; it had a fetid odor which verily wounded the head. And when [the shot] struck a mountain, it was as if it were destroyed, dissolved. And a tree was pulverized; it was as if it vanished; it was as if someone blew it away.

All iron was their war array. In iron they clothed themselves. With iron they covered their heads. Iron were their swords. Iron were their crossbows. Iron were their shields. Iron were their lances.

And those which bore them upon their backs, their deer [that is, horses], were as tall as roof terraces.

And their bodies were everywhere covered; only their faces appeared. They were very white; they had chalky faces; they had yellow hair, though the hair of some was black. Long were their beards; they also were yellow. They were yellow-headed. [The black men's hair] was kinky, it was curly.

And their food was like fasting food—very large, white, not heavy like [tortillas]; like maize stalks, good-tasting as if of maize stalk flour; a little sweet, a little honeyed. It was honeyed to eat; it was sweet to eat.

And their dogs were very large. They had ears folded over; great dragging jowls. They had fiery eyes—blazing eyes; they had yellow eyes—fiery yellow eyes. They had thin flanks—flanks with ribs showing. They had gaunt stomachs. They were very tall. They were nervous; they went about panting, with tongues hanging out. They were spotted like ocelots; they were varicolored.

And when Motecuzoma heard all this, he was much terrified. It was as if he fainted away. His heart saddened; his heart failed him.

For Further Reflection

■ What did the Spanish and their indigenous allies hope to gain by presenting this image of Motecuzoma?

Source: Bernardino de Sahagún. *Florentine Codex: General History of the Things of New Spain,* 13 vols. Trans. by Arthur J. O. Anderson and Charles E. Dibble. Salt Lake City: University of Utah Press, 1950–82, 13:19–20. (Translation slightly modified.)

---

gold—and in any case they were not inclined to perform heavy physical labor—so the miners came largely from the ranks of the Taíno. Recruitment of labor came through an institution known as the **encomienda,** which gave Spanish *encomenderos* ("settlers") the right to compel the Taíno to work in their mines or fields. In return for labor, *encomenderos* assumed responsibility to look after their workers' health and welfare and to encourage their conversion to Christianity.

Conscription of Taíno labor was a brutal business. *Encomenderos* worked their charges hard and punished them severely when they did not deliver the expected quantities of gold or work sufficiently hard in the fields. The Taíno occasionally organized rebellions, but their bows, arrows, and slings had little effect against horse-mounted Spanish forces

wielding steel swords and firearms. By about 1515, social disruption and physical abuse had brought decline to Taíno populations on the large Caribbean islands—Hispaniola, Jamaica, Puerto Rico, and Cuba—favored by Spanish settlers.

Smallpox Serious demographic decline set in only after 1518, however, when smallpox reached the Caribbean region and touched off devastating epidemics among the peoples of the western hemisphere. To replace laborers lost to disease, *encomenderos* launched raiding parties to kidnap and enslave the Taíno and other peoples. This tactic exposed additional victims to introduced diseases and hastened the decline of indigenous populations.

Under pressure of epidemic disease, the native population of the Caribbean plummeted from about four million in 1492 to a few thousand in the 1540s. Native societies

---

encomienda (ehn-KOH-mee-ehn-dah)

themselves also passed out of existence. Only a few Taíno cultural elements survived: *canoe, hammock, hurricane, barbecue, maize,* and *tobacco* all derive from Taíno words, but the society that generated them had largely disappeared by the middle of the sixteenth century.

From Mining to Plantation Agriculture
Deposits of gold were thin in the Caribbean, but optimistic Spanish adventurers continued to seek treasure there for a century and more. After the mid-sixteenth century, however, when Spanish explorers located exceptionally rich sources of silver in Mexico and Peru, the Caribbean became a sleepy backwater of the Spanish empire. English pirates lurked in Caribbean waters hoping to intercept imperial fleets carrying American silver to Spain, but the region was not a center of production. Then, about the 1640s, French, English, and Dutch settlers began to flock to the Caribbean with the intention of establishing plantations. It became clear that even if the Caribbean islands lacked precious metals, they offered ideal conditions for the cultivation of cash crops, particularly sugar, which would fetch high prices in European markets. Later, tobacco also became a prime cash crop of the region. Meanwhile, because indigenous populations were extinct, planters lacked the labor they needed to operate their estates, so they imported several million slaves. By 1700 Caribbean society consisted of a small class of European administrators and large masses of African slaves.

The Conquest of Mexico and Peru

Spanish interest soon shifted from the Caribbean to the American mainland, where settlers hoped to find more resources to exploit. During the early sixteenth century, Spanish *conquistadores* ("conquerors") pressed beyond the Caribbean islands, moving west into Mexico and south into Panama and Peru. Between 1519 and 1521 Hernán Cortés and a small band of men brought down the Aztec empire in Mexico, and between 1532 and 1533 Francisco Pizarro and his followers toppled the Inca empire in Peru. Those conquests laid the foundations for colonial regimes that would transform the Americas.

In Mexico and Peru, Spanish explorers found societies quite different from those of the Caribbean islands. Both Mexico and Peru had been sites of agricultural societies, cities, and large states for more than a millennium. In the early fifteenth century, both lands fell under the sway of powerful imperial states: the Mexica people and their allies founded the Aztec empire that expanded to embrace most of Mesoamerica, while the Incas imposed their rule on a vast realm extending from modern Ecuador in the north to modern Chile in the south—the largest state South America had ever seen. The Aztec and Inca empires both had clear lines of political authority, and both had the means to mobilize massive populations, collect taxes or tribute to maintain their societies, and recruit labor for public works projects. (See chapter 20.)

Hernán Cortés
The conquest of Mexico began with an expedition to search for gold on the American mainland. In 1519 Cortés led about 450 soldiers to Mexico and made his way from Veracruz on the Gulf coast to the island city of Tenochtitlan, the stunningly beautiful Aztec capital situated in Lake Texcoco. They seized the emperor Motecuzoma II, who died in 1520 during a skirmish between Spanish forces and residents of Tenochtitlan. Aztec forces soon drove the conquistadores from the capital, and Cuauhtémoc (ca. 1502–1525)—the nephew and son-in-law of Motecuzoma—emerged as the last Aztec emperor. Cortés built a small fleet of ships, placed Tenochtitlan under siege, and in 1521 starved the city into surrender. Cuauhtémoc stood up to the torture Cortés inflicted upon him in an attempt to uncover the whereabouts of Aztec gold and treasures, but he did not escape the execution ordered by Cortés in 1525.

Steel swords, muskets, cannons, and horses offered Cortés and his soldiers some advantage over the forces they met and help to account for the Spanish conquest of the Aztec empire. Yet weaponry alone clearly would not enable Cortés's tiny force to overcome a large, densely populated society. Quite apart from military technology, Cortés's expedition benefited from divisions among the indigenous peoples of Mexico. With the aid of Doña Marina, the conquistadores forged alliances with peoples who resented domination by the Mexica, the leaders of the Aztec empire, and who reinforced the small Spanish army with thousands of veteran warriors. Native allies also provided Spanish forces with logistical support and secure bases in friendly territory.

Epidemic Disease
On the mainland, as in the Caribbean, epidemic disease aided Spanish efforts. During the siege of Tenochtitlan, smallpox raged through the city, killing inhabitants by the tens of thousands and fatally sapping the strength of defensive forces. Smallpox rapidly spread beyond the capital, raced through Mexico, and carried off so many people that Aztec society was unable to function. Only in the context of this drastic depopulation is it possible to understand the Spanish conquest of Mexico.

thinking about ENCOUNTERS

Conquest
Spaniards Hernán Cortés and Francisco Pizarro initiated the contacts with Mexico and Peru that resulted in the collapse of those previously strong imperial states. What was the nature of the initial relations between these Spaniards, the Aztecs, and the Incas? What factors altered the balance of power in these encounters?

This late-sixteenth-century painting idealized the Spanish conquest of the Aztec empire. Shown on the wall is Motecuzoma, captured by the Spaniards attacking his palace, and he is pleading with the Aztecs to surrender.

Francisco Pizarro Francisco Pizarro experienced similar results when he led a Spanish expedition from Central America to Peru. Pizarro set out in 1530 with 180 soldiers, later joined by reinforcements to make a force of about 600. The conquistadores arrived in Peru just after a bitter dispute between Huascar (1503–1532) and Atahualpa (ca. 1502–1533), two brothers within the Inca ruling house, and Pizarro's forces exploited the differences between those factions. Already by 1533 they had taken the Inca capital at Cuzco. Under pretext of holding a conference, they called the Inca ruling elites together, seized them, and killed most of them. They spared the Inca ruler Atahualpa until he had delivered a large quantity of gold to Pizarro. Then they strangled him and decapitated his body. The search for treasure continued after the end of Inca rule. Pizarro and his conquistadores looted gold and silver plaques from Cuzco's temples and public buildings, melted down statuettes fashioned from precious metals, and even filched jewelry and ornaments from the embalmed bodies of deceased Inca rulers.

Several considerations help to explain how Pizarro's tiny force was able to topple the Inca empire. Many subjects of the empire despised the Incas as overlords and tax collectors and put up little resistance to Pizarro's forces. Indeed, many allied with the Spanish invaders. Epidemic disease also discouraged resistance: smallpox had spread from Mexico and Central America to Peru in the 1520s, long before Pizarro's arrival, and had already taken a heavy toll among Andean populations. Pizarro and his army actually faced more threats from fresh Spanish interlopers than from native peoples. The conquest of Peru took longer than the conquest of Mexico, but by 1540 Spanish forces had established themselves securely as lords of the land.

Iberian Empires in the Americas

During the early days after the conquests, Cortés and Pizarro allocated lands and labor rights to their troops on their own authority. Gradually, however, the Spanish monarchy extended its control over the growing American empire, and

In this illustration from Peru-native Felipe Guaman Poma de Ayala's letter of complaint to the Spanish king—a record of grievances against Spanish overlords—conquistadores decapitate Atahualpa after executing him by strangulation in 1533.

by about 1570 the semiprivate regime of the conquistadores had given way to formal rule under the Spanish crown. Bureaucrats charged with the implementation of royal policy and the administration of royal justice replaced the soldiers of fortune who had conquered Mexico and Peru. The conquistadores did not welcome the arrival of the bureaucrats, but with the aid of Spanish lawyers, tax collectors, and military forces, royal officials had their way.

Spanish Colonial Administration

Spanish administrators established two main centers of authority in the Americas—Mexico (which they called New Spain) and Peru (known as New Castile)—each governed by a viceroy who was responsible to the king of Spain. In Mexico they built a new capital, Mexico City, on top of Tenochtitlan. In Peru they originally hoped to rule from the Inca capital of Cuzco, but they considered the high altitude unpleasant and also found the Andean city too inaccessible for their purposes. In 1535 they founded Lima and transferred the government to the coast where it was accessible to Spanish shipping.

The viceroys were the king's representatives in the Americas, and they wielded considerable power. The kings of Spain, attempting to ensure that their viceroys would

not build personal power bases and become independent, subjected them to the review of courts known as *audiencias* staffed by university-educated lawyers. The *audiencias* heard appeals against the viceroys' decisions and policies and had the right to address their concerns directly to the Spanish king. Furthermore, the *audiencias* conducted reviews of viceroys' performance at the end of their terms, and negative reviews could lead to severe punishment.

In many ways, Spanish administration in the Americas was a ragged affair. Transportation and communication difficulties limited the ability of viceroys to supervise their territories. In many regions, local administration fell to *audiencias* or town councils. Meanwhile, the Spanish monarchy exercised even less influence on American affairs than the viceroys. It often took two years for the central government in Spain to respond to a query from Mexico or Peru, and many replies simply asked for further information rather than providing firm directives. When viceroys received clear orders that they did not like, they found ways to procrastinate: they often responded to the king that "I obey, but I do not enforce," implying that with additional information the king would alter his decision.

New Cities

Spanish rule in the Americas led to the rapid establishment of cities throughout the viceroyalties. Like their compatriots in Spain, colonists preferred to live in cities even when they derived their income from the agricultural production of their landed estates. As the numbers of migrants increased, they expanded the territory under Spanish imperial authority and built a dense network of bureaucratic control based in recently founded cities. The jurisdiction of the viceroyalty of New Spain reached from Mexico City as far as St. Augustine in Florida (founded in 1565). Administrators in Lima oversaw affairs from Panama (founded in 1519) to Concepción (founded in 1550) and Buenos Aires (founded in 1536).

Portuguese Brazil

While Spanish conquistadores and administrators built a territorial empire in Mexico and Peru, Portuguese forces established an imperial presence in Brazil. The Portuguese presence came about by an odd twist of diplomatic convention. In 1494 Spain and Portugal signed the Treaty of Tordesillas, which divided the world along an imaginary north-south line 370 leagues west of the Azores and Cape Verde Islands. According to this agreement, Spain could claim any land west of that line, so long as it was not already under Christian rule, and Portugal gained the same rights for lands east of the line. Thus Portugal gained territory along the northeastern part of the South American continent, a region known as Brazil from the many brazilwood trees that grew along the coast, and the remainder of the western hemisphere fell under Spanish control.

The Portuguese mariner Pedro Alvares de Cabral stopped in Brazil briefly in 1500 while making a tack through the Atlantic Ocean en route to India. His compatriots did not

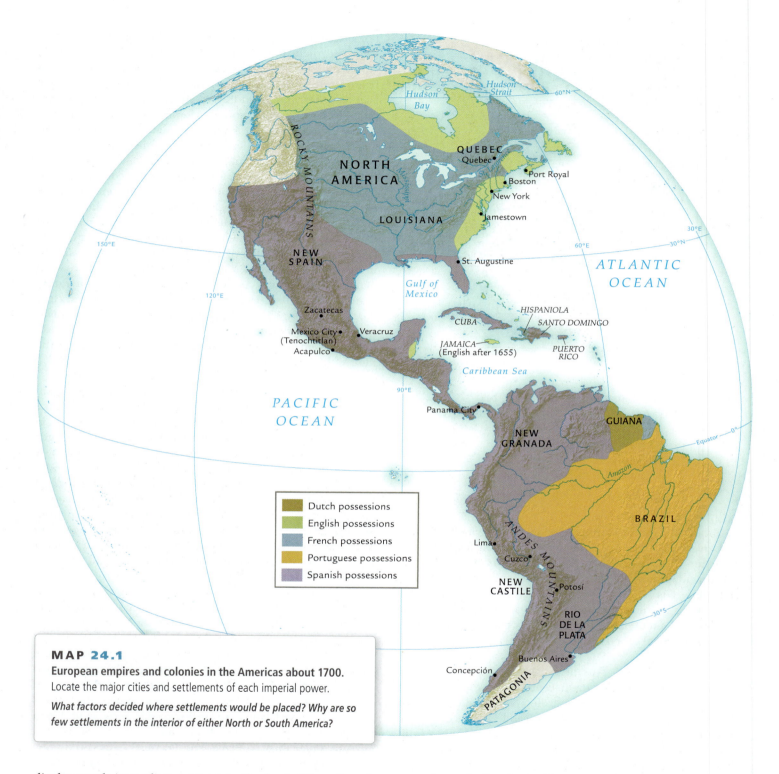

MAP 24.1

European empires and colonies in the Americas about 1700.
Locate the major cities and settlements of each imperial power.

What factors decided where settlements would be placed? Why are so few settlements in the interior of either North or South America?

display much immediate interest in the land. When French and Dutch mariners began to visit Brazilian shores, however, the Portuguese king decided to consolidate his claim to the land. He made vast land grants to Portuguese nobles in the expectation that they would develop and colonize their holdings, and later he dispatched a governor to oversee affairs and implement royal policy. Portuguese interest in Brazil rose dramatically after mid-century when entrepreneurs established profitable sugar plantations on the coast.

Colonial American Society   The cities of the Spanish and Portuguese empires became centers of European-style society in the Americas: the spires of churches and cathedrals defined their skylines, and Spanish and Portuguese were the languages of government, business, and society. Beyond the urban districts, however, indigenous ways of life persisted. In the Amazon basin and Paraguay, for example, native peoples produced little agricultural surplus, and there were no mineral deposits to attract European migrants. The few Spanish and Portuguese colonists who ventured to those regions learned to adapt to indigenous societies and customs: they ate bread made of manioc flour, made use of native hammocks and canoes, and communicated in the Guaraní and Tupí languages. Indeed, indigenous languages flourish even today throughout much of Latin America: among the more prominent are Nahuatl in Mexico, K´iché in Guatemala, Guaraní in Paraguay, and Quechua in the Andean highlands of Peru, Ecuador, and Bolivia.

Spanish and Portuguese peoples saw the western hemisphere more as a land to exploit and administer than as a place to settle and colonize. Nevertheless, sizable contingents of migrants settled permanently in the Americas. Between 1500 and 1800, upwards of five hundred thousand Spanish migrants crossed the Atlantic, alongside one hundred thousand Portuguese. Their presence contributed to the making of a new world—a world characterized by intense interaction between the peoples of Europe, Africa, and the Americas—in the western hemisphere.

Settler Colonies in North America

Throughout the sixteenth century, Spanish explorers sought opportunities north of Mexico and the Caribbean. They established towns, forts, and missions from modern Florida as far north as Virginia on the east coast of North America, and they scouted shorelines off Maine and Newfoundland. On the west coast they ventured into modern Canada and established a fort on Vancouver Island. By mid-century, French, English, and Dutch mariners sailed the North Atlantic in search of fish and a northwest passage to Asia, and by the early seventeenth century they were dislodging Spanish colonists north of Florida. Their search for a northwest passage proved fruitless, but they harvested immense quantities of fish from the cod-filled banks off Labrador, Newfoundland, Nova Scotia, and New England.

Foundation of Colonies More important, in the early seventeenth century explorers began to plant permanent colonies on the North American mainland. French settlers established colonies at Port Royal (Nova Scotia) in 1604 and Quebec in 1608, and English migrants founded Jamestown in 1607 and the Massachusetts Bay Colony in 1630. Dutch entrepreneurs built a settlement at New Amsterdam in 1623, but the colony did not remain long in Dutch hands: an English fleet seized it in 1664, rechristened it New York, and absorbed it into English colonial holdings. During the seventeenth and eighteenth centuries, French migrants settled in eastern Canada, and French explorers and traders scouted the St. Lawrence, Ohio, and Mississippi Rivers, building forts all the way to the Gulf of Mexico. Meanwhile,

English settlers established colonies along the east coast of the present-day United States of America.

Life in those early settlements was extremely difficult. Most of the settlers did not expect to cultivate food crops but, rather, hoped to sustain their communities by producing valuable commodities such as fur, pitch, tar, or lumber, if not silver and gold. They relied heavily on provisions sent from Europe, and when supply ships did not arrive as expected, they sometimes avoided starvation only because indigenous peoples provided them with food. In Jamestown, food shortages and disease became so severe that only sixty of the colony's five hundred inhabitants survived the winter of 1609–1610. Some settlers went so far as to disinter corpses and consume the flesh of their departed neighbors. One man even slaughtered and ate his wife.

Colonial Government The French and English colonies in North America differed in several ways from Spanish and Portuguese territories to the south. Whereas Iberian explorations had royal backing, private investors played larger roles in French and English colonial efforts. Individuals put up the money to finance expeditions to America, and they retained much more control over their colonies' affairs than did their Iberian counterparts. Although English colonies were always subject to royal authority, for example, they also maintained their own assemblies and influenced the choice of royal governors: there were no viceroys or *audiencias* in the North American colonies. At the conclusion of the Seven Years' War (1763), the French colony in Canada fell under British control, and it, too, soon acquired institutions of self-government.

Relations with Indigenous Peoples French and English colonies differed from Iberian territories also in their relationships with indigenous peoples. French and English migrants did not find large, centralized states like the Aztec and Inca empires. Nor did they encounter agricultural peoples living in densely settled societies. Although most of them spoke Algonquian, Iroquois, or Lakota languages, the peoples of eastern North America had formed dozens of distinct societies. Many of them practiced agriculture, but most also relied on hunting and consequently moved their villages frequently in pursuit of game. They did not claim ownership of precisely bounded territories, but they regularly migrated between well-defined regions.

When European settlers saw forested lands not bearing crops, they staked out farms and excluded the indigenous peoples who had frequently visited the lands during the course of their migrations. The availability of fertile farmland soon attracted large numbers of European migrants. Upwards of 150,000 English migrants moved to North America during the seventeenth century alone, and sizable French, German, Dutch, and Irish contingents joined them in the search for land.

European migrants took pains to justify their claims to American lands. English settlers in particular sought to

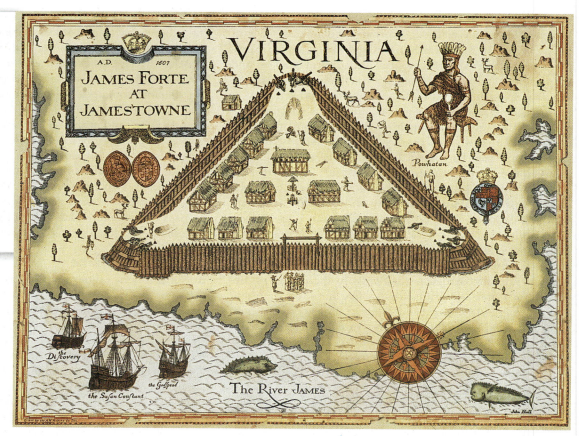

A painting of the English settlement at Jamestown in the early seventeenth century illustrates the precarious relations between European settlers and indigenous peoples. Note the heavy palisades and numerous cannons deployed within the fort, as well as the imposing figure of the native chief Powhatan depicted outside the settlement's walls.

provide legal cover for their expanding communities by negotiating treaties with the peoples whose lands they colonized. Quite apart from legal niceties, migrants also justified their occupation on the grounds that they made productive use of the land, whereas native peoples merely used it as a hunting park. In Europe, hunting was a pastime that only aristocratic and privileged classes could enjoy. Settlers did not recognize that hunting was a way of life, not a sport or a hobby, for the peoples of North America.

Conflict French and English settlers frequently clashed with native peoples who resented intrusions on their hunting grounds, but the conflicts differed from the campaigns of conquest carried out by the conquistadores in Mexico and Peru. English settlers negotiated rights to American lands by treaty, but native peoples did not appreciate the fine points of English law and frequently mounted raids on farms and villages. During an assault of 1622, for example, they massacred almost one-third of the English settlers in the Chesapeake region. Attacks on their communities brought reprisals from settlers, who ruthlessly destroyed the fields and villages of native peoples. Edward Waterhouse, who survived the raid of 1622, went so far as to advocate annihilation of the indigenous population: "Victorie may bee gained many waies: by force, by surprize, by [causing] famine [through]

burning their Corne, by destroying and burning their Boats, Canoes, and Houses, by breaking their fishing Weares [nets], by assailing them in their huntings, whereby they get the greatest part of their sustenance in Winter, by pursuing and chasing them with our horses, and blood-Hounds to draw after them, and Mastives [mastiffs] to teare them."

Indeed, a combination of epidemic disease and violent conflict dramatically reduced the indigenous population of North America in early modern times. In 1492 the native population of the territory now embraced by the United States was greater than five million, perhaps as high as ten million. By the mid-sixteenth century, however, smallpox and other diseases had begun to spread north from Mexico and ravage native societies in the plains and eastern woodlands of North America. Between 1600 and 1800 about one million English, French, German, Dutch, Irish, and Scottish migrants crossed the Atlantic and sought to displace native peoples as they pursued economic opportunities in North America. By 1800, indigenous peoples in the territory of the present-day United States numbered only six hundred thousand, as against almost five million settlers of European ancestry and about one million slaves of African ancestry. Although the settler colonies of North America differed markedly from the Iberian territorial empires to the south, they too contributed greatly to the transformation of the western hemisphere.

COLONIAL SOCIETY IN THE AMERICAS

The European migrants who flooded into the western hemisphere interacted both with the native inhabitants and with African peoples whom they imported as enslaved laborers. Throughout the Americas, relations between individuals of American, European, and African ancestry soon led to the emergence of mestizo populations. Yet European peoples and their Euro-American offspring increasingly dominated political and economic affairs in the Americas. They mined precious metals, cultivated cash crops such as sugar and tobacco, and trapped fur-bearing animals to supply capitalist markets that met the voracious demands of European and Asian consumers. Over time they also established their Christian religion as the dominant faith of the western hemisphere.

The Formation of Multicultural Societies

Mestizo Societies Although their influence reached the American interior only gradually, European migrants radically transformed the social order in the regions where they established imperial states or settler colonies. All European territories became multicultural societies where peoples of varied ancestry lived together under European or Euro-American dominance. Spanish and Portuguese territories soon became not only multicultural but ethnically mixed as well, largely because of migration patterns. Migrants to the Iberian colonies were overwhelmingly men: about 85 percent of the Spanish migrants were men, and the Portuguese migration was even more male-dominated than the Spanish. Because of the small numbers of European women, Spanish and Portuguese migrants entered into relationships with indigenous women, which soon gave rise to an increasingly *mestizo* ("mixed") society.

Most Spanish migrants went to Mexico, where there was soon a growing population of mestizos—those of Spanish and native parentage, like the children of Doña Marina. Women were more prominent among the migrants to Peru than to Mexico, and Spanish colonists there lived mostly in cities, where they maintained a more distinct community than did their counterparts in Mexico. In the colonial cities, Spanish migrants married among themselves and re-created a European-style society. In less settled regions, however, Spanish men associated with indigenous women and gave rise to mestizo society.

With few European women available in Brazil, Portuguese men readily entered into relations both with indigenous women and with African slave women. Brazil soon had large populations not only of mestizos but also of mulattoes born of Portuguese and African parents, *zambos* born of indigenous and African parents, and other combinations arising from these groups. Indeed, marriages between members of different racial and ethnic communities became common in colonial Brazil and generated a society even more thoroughly mixed than that of mestizo Mexico.

The Social Hierarchy In both Spanish and Portuguese colonies, migrants born in Europe known as ***peninsulares***, those who came from the Iberian peninsula, stood at the top of the social hierarchy, followed by ***criollos***, or *creoles*, those born in the Americas of Iberian parents. In the early days of the colonies, mestizos lived on the fringes of society. As time went on, however, the numbers of mestizos grew, and they became essential contributors to their societies, especially in Mexico and Brazil. Meanwhile, mulattoes, *zambos*, and others of mixed parentage became prominent groups in Brazilian society, although they were usually subordinate to European migrants, Euro-American creoles, and even mestizos. In all the Iberian colonies, imported slaves and conquered peoples stood at the bottom of the social hierarchy.

Sexual Hierarchies Race and ethnicity were crucial in shaping a person's position and role in colonial society. But

Indigenous Zapotec painter Miguel Mateo Maldonado y Cabrera (1695–1768) created this domestic portrait of a multicultural family in the viceroyalty of New Spain, today's Mexico. A Spanish man gazes at his Mexican Indian wife and their mestizo daughter.

---

peninsulares (pehn-IHN-soo-LAH-rayz)
criollos (kree-OH-lohs)

the defining factor in both Spanish and Portuguese America was the existence of a clear sexual hierarchy that privileged men. Women lived in a patriarchal world, where men occupied positions of power and delineated the boundaries of acceptable female behavior. Only when it came to punishing disobedient slaves did society ignore gender—both male and female slaves could count on the same harsh punishment, which usually took the form of flogging. To the extent that women did exercise power, most of it was informal and limited to the confines of the home.

Gender alone, however, did not explain the diverse experiences of women in colonial society. Commonly, the ratio of men to women in a given community either enhanced or limited women's choices. Women's experiences also varied with the degree of prosperity and the nature of the local economy. As women moved from childhood through marriage and motherhood, to being widows or "spinsters," their experiences and roles in society likewise underwent change. Race and class usually figured as powerful forces shaping women's lives. Women of European descent, though under strict patriarchal control and under pressure to conform to the stereotype of female dependence and passivity, sometimes used their elite position to their advantage. By necessity, women of color and low class became part of the colonial labor force, performing tasks closely tied to the commercialization of traditional female work such as food preparation, laundering, and weaving. Although poor, these women were freer to move about in public and to interact with others than were their elite counterparts. The most disadvantaged women were black, mulatta, and zamba slaves, who were required to perform hard physical tasks such as planting and cutting cane or working as laundresses.

North American Societies The social structure of the French and English colonies in North America differed markedly from that of the Iberian colonies. Women were more numerous among the French and especially the English migrants than in Spanish and Portuguese communities, and settlers mostly married within their own groups. French fur traders often associated with native women and generated *métis* (French for "mixed") in regions around forts and trading posts. In French colonial cities such as Port Royal and Quebec, however, liaisons between French and native peoples were less common.

Mingling between peoples of different ancestry was least common in the English colonies of North America. Colonists disdained the native peoples they encountered and regarded them as lazy heathens who did not recognize private property and did not exert themselves to cultivate the land. Later, they also scorned imported African slaves as inferior beings. Those attitudes fueled a virulent racism, as English settlers attempted to maintain sharp boundaries between themselves and peoples of American and African ancestry.

Yet even English settlers interacted with American and African peoples, and they readily borrowed useful cultural elements from other communities. They learned about American plants and animals, for example, and they used native terms to refer to unfamiliar animals such as raccoons and opossums or trees such as hickory and pecan. They adapted moccasins and deerskin clothes, and they gave up European military customs of marching in massed ranks and announcing their presence with drums and flying colors. From their slaves they borrowed African food crops and techniques for the cultivation of rice. Yet, unlike their Iberian neighbors to the south, the English settlers strongly discouraged relationships between individuals of different ancestry and mostly refused to accept or even acknowledge offspring of mixed parentage.

Mining and Agriculture in the Spanish Empire

From the Spanish perspective the greatest attractions of the Americas were precious metals, which drew thousands of migrants from all levels of Spanish society. The conquistadores thoroughly looted the easily accessible treasures of the Aztec and Inca empires. Ignoring the artistic or cultural value of artifacts, the conquerors simply melted down silver and gold treasures and fashioned them into ingots. Their followers opened mines to extract the mineral wealth of the Americas in more systematic fashion.

Silver Mining Gold was not the most abundant American treasure. Silver far outweighed gold in quantity and value, and much of Spain's American enterprise focused on its extraction. Silver production concentrated on two areas: the thinly populated Mexican north, particularly the region around Zacatecas, and the high, cold central Andes, particularly the stunningly rich mines of Potosí (present-day Bolivia). Both sites employed large numbers of indigenous laborers. Many laborers went to Zacatecas voluntarily as their home villages experienced the pressures of conquest and disease. Over time they became professional miners, spoke Spanish, and lost touch with the communities of their birth.

Meanwhile, Spanish prospectors discovered a large vein of silver near Potosí in 1545 and began large-scale mining there in the 1580s. By 1600 Potosí was a boomtown with a population of 150,000. Rapid growth created an explosive demand for labor. As in the Mexican mines, Spanish administrators relied mostly on voluntary labor, but they also adapted the Inca practice of requisitioning draft labor, known as the *mita* system, to recruit workers for particularly difficult and dangerous chores that free laborers would not accept. Under the *mita* system, Spanish authorities annually required each native village to send one-seventh of its male population to work for four months in the mines at Potosí. Draft laborers received payment for their work, but wages were very low, and the conditions of work were extremely harsh. Some *mita* laborers hauled heavy baskets of silver ore up steep mine shafts, while others worked with toxic mercury, which miners used to separate the silver from

Mining operations at Potosí in South America gave rise to a large settlement that housed miners and others who supplied food, made charcoal, fashioned tools, and supported the enterprise. In this illustration from the mid-1580s, llamas laden with silver ore descend the mountain (background) while laborers work in the foreground to crush the ore and extract pure silver from it.

its ore. Death rates of draft laborers were high, and many native men sought to evade *mita* obligations by fleeing to cities or hiding in distant villages. Thus, even though at any given moment draft laborers represented only about 10 percent of the workforce at Potosí, the *mita* system touched a large portion of the indigenous population and influenced settlement patterns throughout the Andean region.

The Global Significance of Silver
The mining industries of Mexico and Peru powered the Spanish economy in the Americas and even stimulated the world economy of early modern times. Silver produced profits for private investors and revenues for the crown. The Spanish government reserved a fifth of the silver production for itself. This share, known as the *quinto,* represented the principal revenue that the crown derived from its American possessions. American silver helped Spanish kings finance a powerful army and bureaucracy, but much of it also went well beyond Spain to lubricate the European and the larger world economies.

Most American silver made its way across the Atlantic to Spain and markets throughout Europe, and from there European merchants traded it for silk, spices, and porcelain in the markets of Asia. Some silver went from Acapulco on the west coast of Mexico across the Pacific to the Philippines in the Manila galleons, and from Manila it also made its way to Asian markets. No matter which direction it went or which oceans it crossed, American silver quickly traveled throughout the world and powerfully stimulated global trade.

The Hacienda
Apart from mining, the principal occupations in Spanish America were farming, stock raising, and craft production. The organization of mining industries created opportunities for cultivators, herders, and artisans to provision mining towns with food, wine, textiles, tools, furniture, and craft items. By the seventeenth century the most prominent site of agricultural and craft production in Spanish America was the estate, or hacienda, which produced foodstuffs for its own use as well as for sale to local markets in nearby mining districts, towns, and cities. The products of the hacienda were mostly of European origin: wheat, grapes, and meat from pigs and cattle were the most prominent agricultural products. Bordering the large estates were smaller properties owned by Spanish migrants or creoles as well as sizable tracts of land held by indigenous peoples who lived in native villages and practiced subsistence agriculture.

Labor Systems
The major source of labor for the haciendas was the indigenous population. Spanish conquerors first organized native workforces under the *encomienda* system. As originally developed in Spain during the era of the *reconquista* (see chapter 19), the *encomienda* system rewarded Spanish conquerors by allowing them to exact both

sources from the past

Captain James Cook on the Hawaiians

Spanish mariners may well have been the first Europeans to visit the Hawaiian Islands, but Captain James Cook made the earliest surviving record of a European visit. His journal entries for the first few days of his visit depict a thriving society closely related to those of Tahiti and other Polynesian islands.

[Monday, 19 January 1778] There were three and four men in each [canoe] and we were agreeably surprised to find them of the same nation as the people of Otahiete [Tahiti] and the other [Polynesian] islands we had lately visited. It required but very little address to get them to come along side, but we could not prevail upon any one to come on board; they exchanged a few fish they had in the Canoes for any thing we offered them, but valued nails, or iron above every other thing; the only weapons they had were a few stones in some of the Canoes and these they threw overboard when they found they were not [needed]. . . . As soon as we made sail the Canoes left us, but others came off from the shore and brought with them roasting pigs and some very fine [sweet] Potatoes, which they exchanged, as the others had done, for whatever was offered them; several small pigs were got for a sixpenny nail or two apiece, so that we again found our selves in the land of plenty. . . .

[Tuesday, 20 January 1778] The next morning we stood in for the land and were met by several Canoes filled with people, some of them took courage and ventured on board. I never saw Indians so much astonished at the entering a ship before, their eyes were continually flying from object to object, the wildness of their looks and actions fully expressed their surprise and astonishment at the several new objects before them and evinced that they never had been on board of a ship before. However the first man that came on board did not with all his surprise forget his own interest, the first moveable thing that came in his way was the lead and line, which he without asking any questions took to put into his Canoe and when we stopped him said "I am only going to put it into my boat" nor would he quit it till some of his countrymen spoke to him. . . .

As there were some venereal complaints on board both the Ships, in order to prevent its being communicated to these people, I gave orders that no Women, on any account whatever were to be admitted on board the Ships, I also forbid all manner of connection with them, and ordered that none who had the venereal upon them should go out of the ships. But whether these regulations had the desired effect or not time can only discover. . . .

[Wednesday, 21 January 1778] As soon as every thing was settled to my satisfaction, I . . . took a walk up the Valley, accompanied by Dr. Anderson and Mr. Webber, conducted by one of the Natives and attended by a tolerable train. Our guide proclaimed our approach and every one whom we met fell on their faces and remained in that position till we passed. This, as I afterwards understood, is done to their great chiefs. Our road lay in among the Plantations, which were chiefly of Taro, and sunk a little below the common level so as to contain the water necessary to nourish the roots. . . .

At the beach I found a great crowd and a brisk trade for pigs, fowls and roots which was carried on with the greatest good order, though I did not see a man that appeared of more consequence than another if there was they did not show themselves to us. . . . No people could trade with more honesty than these people, never once attempting to cheat us, either ashore or along side the ships. Some indeed at first betrayed a thievish disposition, or rather they thought they had a right to any thing they could lay their hand upon but this conduct they soon laid aside.

For Further Reflection

■ How does Cook's record of his first meeting with the Hawaiians compare and contrast with Christopher Columbus's account, presented earlier (in chapter 22), of his first encounter with indigenous American peoples?

Source: James Cook. *The Journals of Captain Cook.* Ed. by Philip Edwards. London: Penguin, 1999, pp. 530–34. (Translation slightly modified.)

in perspective

The Americas underwent thorough transformation in early modern times. Smallpox and other diseases sparked ferocious epidemics that devastated indigenous populations and undermined their societies. In the wake of severe depopulation, European peoples toppled imperial states, established mining and agricultural enterprises, imported enslaved African laborers, and founded colonies throughout much of the western hemisphere. Some indigenous peoples disappeared entirely as distinct groups. Others maintained their communities, identities, and cultural traditions but fell increasingly under the influence of European migrants and their Euro-American offspring. In Oceania only Guam and the Mariana

Islands felt the full effects of epidemic disease and migration in the early modern era. By the late eighteenth century, however, European and Euro-American peoples with advanced technologies had thoroughly explored the Pacific Ocean basin, and epidemic diseases traveled with them to Australia and the Pacific islands. As a result, during the nineteenth and twentieth centuries, Oceania underwent a social transformation similar to the one experienced earlier by the Americas. ●

CHRONOLOGY

1492	First voyage of Christopher Columbus to the western hemisphere
1494	Treaty of Tordesillas
1500	Brazil claimed for Portugal by Pedro Alvarez de Cabral
1518	Smallpox epidemic in the Caribbean
1519–1521	Spanish conquest of Mexico
1525	Execution of Cuauhtémoc
1532–1540	Spanish conquest of Peru
1545	Spanish discovery of silver near Potosí
1604	Foundation of Port Royal (Nova Scotia)
1607	Foundation of Jamestown
1608	Foundation of Quebec
1623	Foundation of New Amsterdam
1630	Foundation of the Massachusetts Bay Colony
1688	Smallpox epidemic on Guam
1754–1763	French and Indian war in North America
1763	Transfer of French Canadian possessions to British rule
1768–1779	Captain James Cook's exploration of the Pacific Ocean
1788	Establishment of first European colony in Australia

PART 5

For Further Reading

Rolena Adorno. *Guaman Poma: Writing and Resistance in Colonial Peru.* Austin, 2000. A native Andean, who came of age after the fall of the Inca empire, tells Philip III of Spain of the evils of colonialism and the need for reform.

Alvar Nuñez Cabeza de Vaca. *Castaways.* Trans. by F. M. López-Morillas. Berkeley, 1993. Translation of Cabeza de Vaca's account of his shipwreck and travels through what is now the southwestern United States to Mexico.

Colin G. Callaway. *New Worlds for All: Indians, Europeans, and the Remaking of Early America.* Baltimore, 1997. Scholarly synthesis examining interactions and cultural exchanges between European and indigenous American peoples.

William Cronon. *Changes in the Land: Indians, Colonists, and the Ecology of New England.* New York, 1983. Brilliant study concentrating on the different ways English colonists and native peoples in colonial New England used the environment.

Philip D. Curtin. *The Rise and Fall of the Plantation Complex: Essays in Atlantic History.* 2nd ed. Cambridge, 1998. Examines plantation societies and slavery as institutions linking lands throughout the Atlantic Ocean basin.

Bernal Díaz del Castillo. *The Conquest of New Spain.* Trans. by J. M. Cohen. Harmondsworth, 1963. A conveniently available translation of Bernal Díaz's account of the conquest of Mexico from the viewpoint of a soldier.

John H. Elliot. *Empires of the Atlantic World: Britain and Spain in America 1492–1830.* New Haven, 2006. Excellent comparative study of Spanish and English colonies in the Americas.

K. R. Howe. *Where the Waves Fall: A New South Sea Island History from First Settlement to Colonial Rule.* Honolulu, 1984. A thoughtful survey of Pacific islands history emphasizing interactions between islanders and visitors.

Frances A. Karttunen. *Between Worlds: Interpreters, Guides, and Survivors.* New Brunswick, N.J., 1994. Reflective essays on Doña Marina and others who served as translators or interpreters between their society and the larger world.

John E. Kicza. *Resilient Cultures: America's Native Peoples Confront European Colonization, 1500–1800.* Upper Saddle River, N.J., 2002. A comprehensive comparative study assessing the impact of colonization on indigenous American peoples as well as native influences on American colonial history.

Karen Ordahl Kupperman. *Indians and English: Facing Off in Early America.* Ithaca, 2000. Fascinating reconstruction of the early encounters between English and indigenous American peoples, drawing on sources from all parties to the encounters.

Miguel León-Portilla. *The Broken Spears: The Aztec Account of the Conquest of Mexico.* Rev. ed. Boston, 1992. Offers translations of indigenous accounts of the Spanish conquest of the Aztec empire.

Kathleen Ann Meyers. *Neither Saints nor Sinners: Writing the Lives of Women in Spanish America.* New York, 2003. Examines female self-representation through the life writings of six seventeenth-century women in Latin America.

Gary B. Nash. *Red, White, and Black: The Peoples of Early America.* 3rd ed. Englewood Cliffs, N.J., 1992. Outstanding survey of early American history focusing on the interactions between peoples of European, African, and American ancestry.

James Pritchard. *The French in the Americas, 1670–1730.* Cambridge, 2004. Valuable study of French settlers and imperial policies in the Americas.

Matthew Restall, Lisa Sousa, and Kevin Terraciano, eds. *Mesoamerican Voices: Native Language Writings from Colonial Mexico, Yucatan, and Guatemala.* Cambridge, 2005. Composed between the sixteenth and eighteenth centuries, this collection of texts offers access to an important historical source.

Susan Migden Socolow. *The Women of Colonial Latin America.* Cambridge, 2000. An introductory survey of the female experience in the colonial societies of Spain and Brazil.

David J. Weber. *Bárbaros: Spaniards and Their Savages in the Age of Enlightenment.* New Haven, 2005. Pathbreaking and nuanced study of how Spanish administrators tried to forge a more enlightened policy toward native peoples.

————. *The Spanish Frontier in North America.* New Haven, 1992. A comprehensive study of Spanish efforts to explore and colonize lands north of Mexico.

Richard White. *The Middle Ground: Indians, Empires, and Republics in the Great Lakes Region, 1650–1815.* Cambridge, 1991. Insightful study of relations between French, English, and indigenous peoples in the Great Lakes region.

and short—he experienced the great pressures of settlement and leadership and then died

The emperor Yongle designed the Forbidden City as a vast, walled imperial retreat in central Beijing. Here a sculptured lion guards the Forbidden City's Gate of Supreme Harmony.

gathered momentum as one city after another withdrew its loyalty from the Ming dynasty. To complicate matters further, Manchu forces invaded from the north in search of opportunities for expansion in China. In 1644, rebel forces captured the Ming capital at Beijing. Manchu invaders allied with an army loyal to the Ming, crushed the rebels, and recovered Beijing. The Manchus portrayed themselves as avengers who saved the capital from dangerous rebels, but they neglected to restore Ming rule. Instead, they moved their own capital to Beijing and simply displaced the Ming dynasty.

The Qing Dynasty

The Manchus When the Ming dynasty fell, Manchus poured into China from their homeland of Manchuria north of the Great Wall. The victors proclaimed a new dynasty, the Qing ("pure"), which ruled China until the early twentieth century (1644–1911).

The Manchus mostly were pastoral nomads, although many had turned to agriculture and settled in the rich farmlands of southern Manchuria. Their remote ancestors had traded with China since the Qin dynasty, and they had frequently clashed with their neighbors over land and resources in northern China and southern Manchuria. During the late sixteenth and early seventeenth centuries, an ambi-

tious chieftain named Nurhaci (reigned 1616–1626) unified Manchu tribes into a centralized state, promulgated a code of laws, and organized a powerful military force. During the 1620s and 1630s, the Manchu army expelled Ming garrisons in Manchuria, captured Korea and Mongolia, and launched small-scale invasions into China. After their seizure of Beijing in 1644, the Manchus moved to extend their authority throughout China. For almost forty years they waged campaigns against Ming loyalists and other rebels in southern China until by the early 1680s the Manchus had consolidated the Qing dynasty's hold throughout the land.

The establishment of the Qing dynasty was due partly to Manchu military prowess and partly to Chinese support for the Manchus. During the 1630s and 1640s, many Chinese generals deserted the Ming dynasty because of its corruption and inefficiency. Confucian scholar-bureaucrats also worked against the Ming, since they despised the eunuchs who dominated the imperial court. The Manchu ruling elites were schooled in Chinese language and Confucian thought, and they often enjoyed more respect from the scholar-bureaucrats than did the emperor and high administrators of the Ming dynasty itself.

The Manchus were careful to preserve their own ethnic and cultural identity. They not only outlawed intermarriage

MAP 26.2
The Qing empire, 1644–1911.
Compare this map with Map 26.1.

Why would the Qing emperors have wanted to incorporate such extensive territories in Mongolia and Tibet into their empire?

between Manchus and Chinese but also forbade Chinese from traveling to Manchuria and from learning the Manchurian language. Qing authorities also forced Chinese men to shave the front of their heads and grow a Manchu-style queue as a sign of submission to the dynasty.

Kangxi and His Reign Until the nineteenth century, strong imperial leadership muted tensions between Manchu rulers and Chinese subjects. The long reigns of two particularly effective emperors, Kangxi (1661–1722) and Qianlong (1736–1795), helped the Manchus consolidate their hold on China. Kangxi was a Confucian scholar as well as an enlightened ruler. He was a voracious reader and occasionally composed poems. He studied the Confucian classics and sought to apply their teachings through his policies. Thus, for example, he organized flood-control and irrigation projects in observance of the Confucian precept that rulers should look after the welfare of their subjects and promote agricul-

ture. He also generously patronized Confucian schools and academies.

Kangxi was also a conqueror, and he oversaw the construction of a vast Qing empire. He conquered the island of Taiwan, where Ming loyalists had retreated after their expulsion from southern China, and absorbed it into his empire. Like his predecessors of the Han and Tang dynasties, Kangxi sought to forestall problems with nomadic peoples by projecting Chinese influence into central Asia. His conquests in Mongolia and central Asia extended almost to the Caspian Sea, and he imposed a Chinese protectorate over Tibet. Kangxi's grandson Qianlong continued this expansion of Chinese influence. Qianlong sought to consolidate Kangxi's conquests in central Asia by maintaining military garrisons in eastern Turkestan (the territory now known as Xinjiang province in western China) and encouraging merchants to settle there in hopes that they would stabilize the region. Qianlong also made Vietnam, Burma, and Nepal vassal states of the Qing dynasty.

Qianlong and His Reign Qianlong's reign marked the height of the Qing dynasty. Like Kangxi, Qianlong was a sophisticated and learned man. He reportedly composed more than one hundred thousand poems, and he was a discriminating connoisseur of painting and calligraphy. During his long, stable, and prosperous reign, the imperial treasury bulged so much that on four occasions Qianlong cancelled tax collections. Toward the end of his reign, Qianlong paid less attention to imperial affairs and delegated many responsibilities to his favorite eunuchs. His successors continued that practice, devoting themselves to hunting and the harem, and by the nineteenth century the Qing dynasty faced serious difficulties. Throughout the reign of Qianlong, however, China remained a wealthy and well-organized land.

The Son of Heaven and the Scholar-Bureaucrats

Although Qing rulers usually appointed Manchus to the highest political posts, they relied on the same governmental apparatus that the Ming emperors had established. Both the Ming and the Qing dynasties presided over a tightly centralized state, which they administered through a bureaucracy staffed by Confucian scholars. For more than five hundred years, the autocratic state created by the Ming emperor Hongwu governed China's fortunes.

The Son of Heaven
If the emperor of China during the Ming and Qing dynasties was not quite a god, he certainly was more than a mere mortal. Chinese tradition held that he was the "Son of Heaven," the human being designated by heavenly powers to maintain order on the earth. He led a privileged life within the walls of the Forbidden City. Hundreds of concubines resided in his harem, and thousands of eunuchs looked after his desires. His daily activities were carefully choreographed performances in the form of inspections, audiences, banquets, and other official duties. Everything about his person and the institution he represented conveyed a sense of awesome authority. The imperial wardrobe and personal effects bore designs forbidden to all others, for instance, and the written characters of the emperor's name were taboo throughout the realm. Individuals who had the rare privilege of a personal audience with the emperor had to perform the kowtow—three kneelings and nine head knockings. Those who gave even minor offense faced severe punishment. Even the highest official could have his bare buttocks flogged with bamboo canes, a punishment that sometimes brought victims to the point of death.

Though painted in the nineteenth century, this portrait depicts Kangxi in his imperial regalia as he looked at about age fifty. Kangxi reigned for sixty-one years, making him the longest-ruling emperor in Chinese history.

The Scholar-Bureaucrats
Day-to-day governance of the empire fell to scholar-bureaucrats appointed by the emperor. With few exceptions these officials came from the class of well-educated and highly literate men known as the scholar-gentry. These men had earned academic degrees by passing rigorous civil service examinations, and they dominated China's political and social life.

Preparations for the examinations began at an early age. Sometimes they took place in local schools, which like the civil service examinations were open only to males. Wealthy families often engaged the services of tutors, who made formal education available also to girls. By the time students were eleven or twelve years old, they had memorized several thousand characters that were necessary to deal with the Confucian curriculum, including the *Analects* of Confucius and other standard works. They followed those studies with instruction in calligraphy, poetry, and essay composition. Diligent students also acquainted themselves with a large corpus of commentaries, histories, and literary works in preparing for civil service examinations.

Civil Service Examinations
The examinations consisted of a battery of tests administered at the district, provincial, and metropolitan levels. Stiff official quotas restricted the number of successful candidates in each examination—only three hundred students could pass metropolitan examinations—and students frequently took the examinations several times before earning a degree.

Writing the examinations was a grueling ordeal. At the appointed hour, candidates presented themselves at the examination compound. Each candidate brought a water pitcher, a chamber pot, bedding, food, an inkstone, ink, and brushes. After guards had verified their identities and searched them for hidden printed materials, the new arrivals proceeded along narrow lanes to a honeycomb of small, cell-like rooms barely large enough to accommodate one man and his possessions. Aside from a bench, a makeshift bed, and boards that served as a desk, the rooms were empty. For the next three days and two nights, the cramped rooms were home to the candidates, who spent all their time writing "eight-legged essays"—literary compositions with eight distinct sections—on questions posed by the examiners. There were

Qiu Ying, a prominent Chinese artist of the sixteenth century, captured this image of candidates who had taken the civil service exams as they waited at the wall where officials would post the scores.

no interruptions, nor was there any communication between candidates. If someone died during the examination period, officials wrapped his body in a straw mat and tossed it over the high walls that ringed the compound.

The Examination System and Chinese Society

The possibility of bureaucratic service—with prospects for rich social and financial rewards—ensured that competition for degrees was ferocious at all levels. As a result, cheating candidates and corrupt examiners occasionally compromised the system. Yet a degree did not ensure government service. During the Qing dynasty the empire's one million degree holders competed for twenty thousand official civil service positions. Those who passed only the district exams had few opportunities for bureaucratic employment and usually spent their careers "plowing with the writing brush"

by teaching in local schools or serving as family tutors. Those who passed the metropolitan examinations, however, could look forward to powerful positions in the imperial bureaucracy.

The examination system was a pivotal institution. By opening the door to honor, power, and rewards, the examinations encouraged serious pursuit of a formal education. Furthermore, since the system did not erect social barriers before its recruits, it provided an avenue for upward social mobility. Years of education and travel to examination sites were expensive, so candidates from wealthy families enjoyed advantages over others, but the exams themselves were open to all males regardless of age or social class. Finally, in addition to selecting officials for government service, the education and examination system molded the personal values of those who managed day-to-day affairs in imperial China.

By concentrating on Confucian classics and neo-Confucian commentaries, the examinations guaranteed that Confucianism would be at the heart of Chinese education and that Confucians would govern the state.

ECONOMIC AND SOCIAL CHANGES

By modeling their governmental structure on the centralized imperial states of earlier Chinese dynasties, the Ming and Qing emperors succeeded in their goal of restoring and maintaining traditional ways in China. They also sought to preserve the traditional hierarchical and patriarchal social order. Yet, while the emperors promoted conservative political and social policies, China experienced economic and social changes, partly as a result of influences from abroad. Agricultural production increased dramatically—especially after the introduction of new food crops from the Americas—and fueled rapid population growth. Meanwhile, global trade brought China enormous wealth, which stimulated the domestic economy by encouraging increased trade, manufacturing, and urban growth. These developments deeply influenced Chinese society and partly undermined the stability that the Ming and Qing emperors sought to preserve.

The Patriarchal Family

Filial Piety Moralists portrayed the Chinese people as one large family, and they extended family values to the larger society. Filial piety, for example, implied not only duties of children toward their fathers but also loyalty of subjects toward the emperor. Like the imperial government, the Chinese family was hierarchical, patriarchal, and authoritarian. The father was head of the household, and he passed leadership of the family to his eldest son. The veneration of ancestors, which the state promoted as a matter of Confucian propriety, strengthened the authority of the patriarchs by honoring the male line of descent in formal family rituals. Filial piety was the cornerstone of family values. Children had the duty to look after their parents' happiness and well-being, and a crucial obligation was to support parents in their old age. Young children heard stories of sons who went so far as to cut off parts of their bodies to ensure that their parents had enough to eat!

The social assumptions of the Chinese family extended into patrilineal descent groups such as the clan. Sometimes numbering into the thousands, clan members came from all social classes, though members of the gentry usually dominated a given clan. Clans assumed responsibilities that exceeded the capacities of the nuclear family, such as the maintenance of local order, organization of local economies, and provision for welfare. Clan-supported education gave poor but promising relatives the opportunity to succeed in the civil service examinations. The principal motives behind

thinking about TRADITIONS

Chinese Women
Women had for long centuries lived under the strictures of a Confucian society. How did Confucian ideals in the Ming and Qing dynasties affect attitudes about women? What did the practice of foot binding suggest about gender relations in late imperial China?

this charity were corporate self-interest as well as altruism. A government position brought prestige and prosperity to the entire clan, so educational support was a prudent investment. Finally, clans served as a means for the transmission of Confucian values from the gentry leaders to all social classes within the clan.

Gender Relations Within the family, Confucian principles subjected women to the authority of men. The subordination of females began at an early age. Chinese parents preferred boys over girls. Whereas a boy might have the opportunity to take the official examinations, become a government official, and thereby bring honor and financial reward to the entire clan, parents regarded a girl as a social and financial liability. After years of expensive upbringing, most girls would marry and become members of other households. Under those circumstances it was not surprising that life was precarious for newborn girls, who were the primary victims of infanticide.

During the Ming and Qing dynasties, patriarchal authority over females probably became tighter than ever before in China. Since ancient times, relatives had discouraged widows from remarriage, but social pressures increased during the Ming dynasty. Friends and relatives not only encouraged widows to honor the memory of their departed husbands but also heaped posthumous honors on those who committed suicide and followed their spouses to the grave.

Foot Binding Moreover, foot binding, a custom that probably originated in the Song dynasty, became exceptionally popular during the late Ming and Qing dynasties. Tightly constrained and even deformed by strips of linen, bound feet could not grow naturally and so would not support the weight of an adult woman. Bound feet were small and dainty, and they sometimes inspired erotic arousal among men. The practice of foot binding became most widespread among the wealthy classes, since it demonstrated an ability to support women who could not perform physical labor, but commoners sometimes bound the feet of especially pretty girls in hopes of arranging favorable marriages that would enhance the family's social standing.

Marriage itself was a contractual affair whose principal purpose was to continue the male line of descent. A bride

To encourage widows to remain unmarried, the Ming and Qing governments constructed arches in honor of those who remained chaste. These arches erected during the Qing dynasty still stand in Anhui province in the Yangzi River valley.

became a member of the husband's family, and there was no ambiguity about her position in the household. On her wedding day, as soon as she arrived at her husband's home, the bride performed ritual acts demonstrating subservience to her husband and her new family. Women could not divorce their husbands, but men could put aside their wives in cases where there was no offspring or where the wife was guilty of adultery, theft, disobedience to her husband's family, or even being too talkative.

Thus custom and law combined to strengthen patriarchal authority in Chinese families during the Ming and Qing dynasties. Yet, while family life continued to develop along traditional lines, the larger Chinese society underwent considerable change between the sixteenth and the eighteenth centuries.

Population Growth and Economic Development

China was a predominantly agricultural society, a fact that meshed agreeably with the Confucian view that land was the source of everything praiseworthy. The emperor himself acknowledged the central importance of agriculture by plowing the first furrow of the season. Yet only a small fraction of China's land is suitable for planting: even today only about 11 percent is in cultivation. To feed the country's large population, China's farmers relied on intensive, garden-style agriculture that was highly productive. On its strong agrarian foundation, China supported a large population and built the most highly commercialized economy of the preindustrial world.

American Food Crops By intensively cultivating every available parcel of land, Chinese peasants increased their yields of traditional food crops—especially rice, wheat, and millet—until the seventeenth century. Beginning about the mid-seventeenth century, as peasants approached the upper limits of agricultural productivity, Spanish merchants coming by way of the Philippines introduced American food crops to China. American maize, sweet potatoes, and peanuts permitted Chinese farmers to take advantage of soils that previously had gone uncultivated. The introduction of new crops increased the food supply and supported further population growth.

Population Growth In spite of recurring epidemic diseases such as plague, which claimed the lives of millions, China's population rose rapidly from 100 million in 1500 to 160 million in 1600. Partly because of rebellion and war, it fell to 140 million in the mid-seventeenth century, but returned to 160 million by 1700 and then surged to 225 million by 1750, thus registering a more than 40 percent increase in half a century. This rapid demographic growth set the stage for economic and social problems, since agricultural production could not keep pace with population over a long term. Acute problems did not occur until the nineteenth century, but per capita income in China began to decline as early as the reign of Qianlong.

While an increasing population placed pressure on Chinese resources, the growing commercial market offered opportunities for entrepreneurs. Because of demographic

A Ming-era vase painting depicts a woman weaving silk as an attendant pours tea. Silk and tea were among the exports China produced for global trade.

During the early fifteenth century, the Ming emperor Yongle sought to establish a Chinese presence in the Indian Ocean basin, and he sponsored a series of seven massive maritime expeditions (1405–1433) led by the eunuch admiral Zheng He. The Chinese fleets included as many as 317 vessels and 28,000 men. Zheng He called at ports from Java to Malindi, suppressed pirates in southeast Asian waters, intervened in local conflicts in Sumatra and Ceylon, intimidated local authorities with shows of force in southern Arabia and Mogadishu, and made China's presence felt throughout the Indian Ocean basin.

After the reign of Yongle, however, the Ming government withdrew its support for expensive maritime expeditions and even tried to prevent Chinese subjects from dealing with foreign peoples. In its effort to pacify southern China during the later seventeenth century, the Qing government tried to end maritime activity altogether. An imperial edict of 1656 forbade "even a plank from drifting to the sea," and in 1661 the emperor Kangxi ordered evacuation of the southern coastal regions. Those policies had only a limited effect—small Chinese vessels continued to trade actively in Japan and southeast Asian ports—and when Qing forces pacified southern China in the 1680s, government authorities rescinded the strictest measures. Thereafter, however, Qing authorities closely supervised the activities of foreign merchants in China. They permitted Portuguese merchants to operate only at the port of Macau, and British agents had to deal exclusively with the official merchant guild in Guangzhou.

While limiting the activities of foreign merchants, government policies also discouraged the organization of large-scale commercial ventures by Chinese merchants. In the absence of government approval, it was impossible, for example, to maintain shipyards that could construct large sailing ships like the mammoth, nine-masted treasure ships that Zheng He had led throughout the Indian Ocean. Similarly, it was impossible to organize large trading firms like the English East India Company or the Dutch VOC.

Trade and Migration to Southeast Asia Nevertheless, thousands of Chinese merchants worked either individually or in partnerships, plying the waters of the China seas to link China with global trade networks. Chinese merchants were especially prominent in Manila, where they exchanged silk and porcelain for American silver that came across the Pacific Ocean with the Manila galleons. They were also frequent visitors at the Dutch colonial capital of Batavia, where they supplied the VOC with silk and porcelain in exchange for silver and Indonesian spices. Entrepreneurial Chinese merchants ventured also to lands throughout southeast Asia—the Philippines, Borneo, Sumatra, Malaya, Thailand, and elsewhere—in search of exotic tropical products for Chinese consumers. Indeed, the early modern era was an age when merchants established a prominent Chinese presence throughout southeast Asia.

expansion, entrepreneurs had access to a large labor force that was both occupationally and geographically mobile, so they were able to recruit workers readily at low cost. After the mid-sixteenth century, the Chinese economy benefited also from the influx of Japanese and American silver, which stimulated trade and financed further commercial expansion.

Foreign Trade Global trade brought prosperity to China, especially during the early Qing dynasty. Chinese workers produced vast quantities of silk, porcelain, lacquerware, and tea for consumers in the Indian Ocean basin, central Asia, and Europe. The silk industry was especially well organized: weavers worked in workshops for regular wages producing fine satins and brocades for export. Chinese imports were relatively few: they included spices from Maluku, exotic products such as birds and animal skins from tropical regions, and small quantities of woolen textiles from Europe. Compensation for exports came most importantly in the form of silver bullion, which supported the silver-based Chinese economy and fueled manufacturing.

Economic growth and commercial expansion took place mostly in an atmosphere of tight government regulation.

sources from the past

Qianlong on Chinese Trade with England

Qing administrators tightly restricted foreign trade. Foreign merchants had to deal with government-approved agents outside the city walls of Guangzhou and had to depart as soon as they had completed their business. In 1793 a British diplomat representing King George III of England bestowed gifts on the emperor Qianlong and petitioned for the right to trade at ports other than Guangzhou. In a letter to King George, Qianlong outlined his views on Chinese trade with England. His letter also bespeaks clearly the importance of government policy for commerce and economic affairs in China.

You, O king, from afar have yearned after the blessings of our civilization, and in your eagerness to come into touch with our influence have sent an embassy across the sea bearing a memorandum. I have already taken note of your respectful spirit of submission, have treated your mission with extreme favor and loaded it with gifts, besides issuing a mandate to you, O king, and honoring you with the bestowal of valuable presents. . . .

Yesterday your ambassador petitioned my ministers to memorialize me regarding your trade with China, but his proposal is not consistent with our dynastic usage and cannot be entertained. Hitherto, all European nations, including your own country's barbarian merchants, have carried on their trade with our Celestial Empire at Guangzhou. Such has been the procedure for many years, although our Celestial Empire possesses all things in prolific abundance and lacks no product within its own borders. There was therefore no need to import the manufactures of outside barbarians in exchange for our own produce. But as the tea, silk, and porcelain which the Celestial Empire produces are absolute necessities to European nations and to yourselves, we have permitted, as a signal mark of favor, that trading agents should be established at Guangzhou, so that your wants might be supplied and your country thus participate in our beneficence. But your ambassador has now put forward new requests which completely fail to recognize our throne's principle to "treat strangers from afar with indulgence," and to exercise a pacifying control over barbarian tribes the world over. . . . Your England is not the only nation trading at Guangzhou. If other nations, following your bad example, wrongfully importune my ear with further impossible requests, how will it be possible for me to treat them with easy indulgence? Nevertheless, I do not forget the lonely remoteness of your island, cut off from the world by intervening wastes of sea, nor do I overlook your excusable ignorance of the usages of our Celestial Empire. I have consequently commanded my ministers to enlighten your ambassador on the subject, and have ordered the departure of the mission. . . .

If, after the receipt of this explicit decree, you lightly give ear to the representations of your subordinates and allow your barbarian merchants to proceed to Zhejiang and Tianjin, with the object of landing and trading there, the ordinances of my Celestial Empire are strict in the extreme, and the local officials, both civil and military, are bound reverently to obey the law of the land. Should your vessels touch the shore, your merchants will assuredly never be permitted to land or to reside there, but will be subject to instant expulsion. In that event your barbarian merchants will have had a long journey for nothing. Do not say that you were not warned in due time! Tremblingly obey and show no negligence! A special mandate!

For Further Reflection

■ What considerations might have prompted the Chinese government to take such a restrictive approach to foreign trade?

Source: J. O. P. Bland. *Annals and Memoirs of the Court of Peking.* Boston: Houghton Mifflin, 1914, pp. 325–31. (Translation slightly modified.)

Government and Technology China's economic expansion took place largely in the absence of technological innovation. During the Tang and Song dynasties, Chinese engineers had produced a veritable flood of inventions, and China was the world's leader in technology. Yet by early Ming times, technological innovation had slowed. Imperial armed forces adopted European cannons and advanced firearms for their own uses—thus borrowing forms of gunpowder technology that had originated in China and that Europeans had refined and improved—but little innovation in agricultural and industrial technologies occurred during the Ming and Qing dynasties.

Part of the explanation for the slowdown has to do with the role of the government. During the Tang and Song dynasties, the imperial government had encouraged technological innovation as a foundation of military and economic strength. In contrast, the Ming and Qing regimes favored political and social stability over technological innovation, which they feared would lead to unsettling change. Alongside government policy, the abundance and ready availability of skilled workers also discouraged technological innovation. When employers wanted to increase production, they found that hiring additional workers was less costly than making large investments in new technologies. In the short term this tactic maintained relative prosperity in China while keeping most of the population gainfully employed. Over the longer term, however, it ensured that China lost technological ground to European peoples, who embarked on a round of stunning technological innovation beginning about the mid-eighteenth century.

Gentry, Commoners, Soldiers, and Mean People

Privileged Classes Except for the emperor and his family, scholar-bureaucrats and gentry occupied the most exalted positions in Chinese society. Because of their official positions, the scholar-bureaucrats ranked slightly above gentry. Nevertheless, scholar-bureaucrats had much in common with the gentry: they came largely from gentry ranks, and after leaving government service they usually rejoined gentry society. The scholar-bureaucrats and gentry functioned as intermediaries between the imperial government and local society. By organizing water control projects and public security measures, they played a crucial role in the management of local society.

Scholar-bureaucrats and gentry were easy to identify. They wore distinctive clothing—black gowns with blue borders adorned with various rank insignia—and commoners addressed them with honorific terms. They received favorable legal treatment that reflected their privileged status. As a rule, commoners could not call members of privileged classes to appear as witnesses in legal proceedings. They also enjoyed immunity from corporal punishment and exemption from labor service and taxes.

Most of the gentry owned land, which was their major source of income. As long as they did not have to perform physical labor, some gentry also supplemented their income by operating pawn and rice shops. Many of them were also silent business partners of merchants and entrepreneurs. Their principal source of income, however, came from the government service to which only they had access by virtue of their

This late-eighteenth-century drawing depicts Chinese men treading the pole of a device that raises irrigation water. The men all wear the braided queue that Manchus required of Chinese men.

academic degrees. In contrast to landed elites elsewhere, who often lived on rural estates, China's gentry resided largely in cities and towns, where they tended to political, social, and financial affairs.

Working Classes Confucian tradition ranked three broad classes of commoners below the gentry: peasants, artisans or workers, and merchants. By far the biggest class consisted of peasants, a designation that covered everyone from day laborers to tenant farmers to petty landlords. Confucian principles regarded peasants as the most honorable of the three classes, since they performed honest labor and provided the food that supported the entire population.

The category of artisans and workers encompassed a wide spectrum of occupations. Despite their lower status, crafts workers, tailors, barbers, physicians, and workers in manufacturing plants generally enjoyed higher income than peasants did. Artisans and workers were usually employees of the state or of gentry and merchant families, but they also pursued their occupations as self-employed persons.

Merchants Merchants, from street peddlers to individuals of enormous wealth and influence, ranked at the bottom level of the Confucian social hierarchy. Because moralists looked upon them as unscrupulous social parasites, merchants enjoyed little legal protection, and government policy was always critically important to their pursuits. Yet Chinese merchants often garnered official support for their enterprises, either through bribery of government bureaucrats or through profit-sharing arrangements with gentry families. Indeed, the participation of gentry families in commercial ventures such as warehousing, money lending, and pawnbroking blurred the distinction between gentry and merchants. Merchants blurred the distinction further by providing their sons with an education that prepared them for government examinations, which in turn could result in promotion to gentry status and appointment to civil service positions.

The prominence of artisans and merchants pointed up the social and economic development of China since the time of Confucius. Although China was still a basically agri-

The elegant clothing of this Chinese merchant suggests the wealth and power of merchants in late imperial China.

cultural land, manufacturing and commerce had become much more economically important than in ancient times. As a result, those who could recognize and exploit opportunities had the potential to lead comfortable lives and even to climb into the ranks of the privileged gentry class. Yet Chinese merchants and artisans did not forge cooperative relationships with government authorities like the political-commercial alliances formed in the English and Dutch states in early modern times. Late Ming and Qing authorities permitted Chinese merchants to engage in small-scale commerce, and they allowed foreigners to trade through the official merchant guild in Guangzhou. Their principal concern, however, was to preserve the stability of a large agrarian society, not to promote rapid economic development through trade. Thus, unlike some of their European counterparts, Chinese authorities did not adopt policies designed to strengthen both merchants and the state by authorizing merchants to pursue their efforts aggressively in the larger world.

Lower Classes Beyond the Confucian social hierarchy were members of the military forces and the so-called mean people. Confucian moralists regarded armed forces as a wretched but necessary evil and attempted to avoid military dominance of society by placing civilian bureaucrats in the highest command positions, even at the expense of military effectiveness. The mean people included slaves, indentured servants, entertainers, prostitutes, and other marginal groups such as the "beggars of Jiangsu" and the "boat people of Guangdong."

THE CONFUCIAN TRADITION AND NEW CULTURAL INFLUENCES

The Ming and Qing emperors looked to Chinese traditions for guidance in framing their cultural as well as their political and social policies. They provided generous support for Confucianism, particularly in the form of neo-Confucianism articulated by the twelfth-century scholar Zhu Xi, and they ensured that formal education in China revolved around Confucian thought and values. Yet the Confucian tradition was not the only cultural alternative in Ming and Qing China. Demographic and urban growth encouraged the emergence of a vibrant popular culture in Chinese cities, and European missionaries reintroduced Roman Catholic Christianity to China and acquainted Chinese intellectuals with European science and technology as well.

Neo-Confucianism and Pulp Fiction

Imperial sponsorship of Chinese cultural traditions meant primarily support for the Confucian tradition, especially as systematized by the Song dynasty scholar Zhu Xi, the most prominent architect of neo-Confucianism. Zhu Xi combined the moral, ethical, and political values of Confucius with the logical rigor and speculative power of Buddhist philosophy. He emphasized the values of self-discipline, filial piety, and obedience to established rulers, all of which appealed to Ming and Qing emperors seeking to maintain stability in their vast realm. Cultural policies of the Ming and Qing dynasties made the neo-Confucian tradition the reigning imperial ideology from the fourteenth to the early twentieth century.

Confucian Education To promote Confucian values, the Ming and Qing emperors supported educational programs at several levels. They funded the Hanlin Academy, a research institute for Confucian scholars in Beijing, and maintained provincial schools throughout China where promising students could study for the civil service examinations. The exams themselves encouraged the cultivation of Confucian values, since they focused largely on Confucian texts and neo-Confucian commentaries.

Ming and Qing courts also provided generous funding for other projects emphasizing Chinese cultural traditions. The Ming emperor Yongle sponsored the compilation of the *Yongle Encyclopedia,* a vast collection of Chinese philosophical, literary, and historical texts that filled almost twenty-three thousand scrolls. During the Qing dynasty both Kangxi and Qianlong organized similar projects. Kangxi's *Collection of Books* was smaller than the *Yongle Encyclopedia,* but it was more influential because the emperor had it printed and distributed, whereas Yongle's compilation was available only in three manuscript copies. Qianlong's *Complete Library of the Four Treasuries* was too large to publish—it ran to 93,556 pamphlet-size volumes—but the emperor deposited manuscript copies in seven libraries throughout China.

Popular Culture While the imperial courts promoted Confucianism, a lively popular culture took shape in the cities of China. Most urban residents did not have an advanced education and knew little about Confucius, Zhu Xi, or other intellectual luminaries. Many of them were literate merchants, however, and they preferred entertainment and diversion more intellectually engaging than that found in local teahouses and wine shops. Popular novels met their needs.

Popular Novels Confucian scholars looked down on popular novels as crude fiction that had little to do with the realities of the world. Printing made it possible to produce books cheaply and in mass quantities, however, and urban residents eagerly consumed the fast-paced novels that flooded Chinese cities during the Ming and Qing eras. Many of the novels had little literary merit, but their tales of conflict, horror, wonder, excitement, and sometimes unconcealed pornography appealed to readers.

Yet many popular novels also offered thoughtful reflections on the world and human affairs. The historical novel *The Romance of the Three Kingdoms,* for example, explored the political intrigue that followed the collapse of the Han dynasty. *The Dream of the Red Chamber* told the story of cousins deeply in love who could not marry because of their families' wishes. Through the prism of a sentimental love story, the novel shed fascinating light on the dynamics of wealthy scholar-gentry families. In a different vein, *Journey to the West* dealt with the seventh-century journey to India of the famous Buddhist monk Xuanzang. In the popular novel, Xuanzang's traveling companion was a monkey with magical powers who among other things could jump 10,000 kilometers (6,215 miles) in

a single bound. While promoting Buddhist values, *Journey to the West* also made the trickster monkey a wildly popular and celebrated character in Chinese literature. As recently as 1987, Chinese-American novelist Maxine Hong Kingston adapted this character to modern times in her novel *Tripmaster Monkey.*

The Return of Christianity to China

Nestorian Christians had established churches and monasteries in China as early as the seventh century C.E., and Roman Catholic communities were prominent in Chinese commercial centers during the Yuan dynasty. After the outbreak of epidemic plague and the collapse of the Yuan dynasty in the fourteenth century, however, Christianity disappeared from China. When Roman Catholic missionaries returned in the sixteenth century, they had to start from scratch in their efforts to win converts and establish a Christian community.

Matteo Ricci The most prominent of the missionaries were the Jesuits, who worked to strengthen Roman Catholic Christianity in Europe and also to spread their faith abroad. Founder of the mission to China was the Italian Jesuit Matteo Ricci (1552–1610), who had the ambitious goal of converting China to Christianity, beginning with the Ming emperor Wanli. Ricci was a brilliant and learned man as well as a polished diplomat, and he became a popular figure at the Ming court. Upon arrival at Macau in 1582, Ricci immersed himself in the study of the Chinese language and the Confucian classics. He had a talent for languages, and his phenomenal memory enabled him to master the thousands of characters used in literary Chinese writing. By the time he first traveled to Beijing and visited the imperial court in 1601, Ricci was able to write learned Chinese and converse fluently with Confucian scholars.

Ricci's mastery of Chinese language and literature opened doors for the Jesuits, who then dazzled their hosts with European science, technology, and mechanical gadgetry. Ricci and his colleagues had an advanced education in mathematics and astronomy, and they were able to correct Chinese calendars that consistently miscalculated solar eclipses. The Jesuits also prepared maps of the world—with China placed diplomatically at the center—on the basis of geographic knowledge that Europeans had gained during their voyages

Italian Jesuit Matteo Ricci (left) with Xu Quangqi, his most famous Chinese disciple. Both men wear the distinctive gowns of educated, refined scholar-gentry. A distinguished scholar who held an appointment at the Hanlin Academy, Xu helped Ricci translate Euclid's geometrical works into Chinese.

through the world's seas. The Jesuits even supervised the casting of high-quality bronze cannons for Ming and early Qing armies.

Confucianism and Christianity

The Jesuits piqued Chinese curiosity also with mechanical devices. Finely ground glass prisms became popular because of their refraction of sunlight into its component parts. Harpsichords also drew attention, and Jesuits with musical talents often composed songs for their hosts. Most popular of all, however, were the devices that Chinese called "self-ringing bells"— spring-driven mechanical clocks that kept tolerably accurate time, chimed the hours, and sometimes even struck the quarter hours as well.

The Jesuits sought to capture Chinese interest with European science and technology, but their ultimate goal was always to win converts. They portrayed Christianity as a faith very similar to Chinese cultural traditions. Ricci, for example, wrote a treatise entitled *The True Meaning of the Lord of Heaven* in which he argued that the doctrines of Confucius and Jesus were very similar, if not identical. Over the years, according to Ricci, neo-Confucian scholars had altered Confucius's own teachings, so adoption of Christianity by Chinese would represent a return to a more pure and original Confucianism. The Jesuits also held religious services in the Chinese language and allowed converts to continue the time-honored practice of venerating their ancestors.

In spite of their tolerance, flexibility, and genuine respect for their hosts, the Jesuits attracted few converts in China. By the mid-eighteenth century, Chinese Christians numbered about 200,000—a tiny proportion of the Chinese population of 225 million. Chinese hesitated to adopt Christianity partly because of its exclusivity: for centuries, Chinese had honored Confucianism, Daoism, and Buddhism at the same time. Like Islam, though, Christianity claimed to be the only true religion, so conversion implied that Confucianism, Daoism, and Buddhism were inferior or even fallacious creeds—a proposition most Chinese were unwilling to accept.

End of the Jesuit Mission

Ultimately, the Roman Catholic mission in China came to an end because of squabbles between the Jesuits and members of the Franciscan and Dominican orders, who also sought converts in China. Jealous of the Jesuits' presence at the imperial court, the Franciscans and Dominicans complained to the pope about their rivals' tolerance of ancestor veneration and willingness to conduct Chinese-language services. The pope sided with the critics and in the early eighteenth century issued several proclamations ordering missionaries in China to suppress ancestor veneration and conduct services according to European standards. In response to that demand, the emperor Kangxi ordered an end to the preaching of Christianity in China. Although he did not strictly enforce the ban, the mission weakened, and by the mid-eighteenth century it had effectively come to an end.

The Roman Catholic mission to China did not attract large numbers of Chinese converts, but it nonetheless had important cultural effects. Besides making European science and technology known in China, the Jesuits made China known in Europe. In letters, reports, and other writings distributed widely throughout Europe, the Jesuits described China as an orderly and rational society. The Confucian civil service system attracted the attention of European rulers, who began to design their own civil service bureaucracies in the eighteenth century. The rational morality of Confucianism also appealed to the Enlightenment philosophes, who sought alternatives to Christianity as the foundation for ethics and morality. For the first time since Marco Polo, the Jesuits made firsthand observations of China available to Europeans and stimulated strong European interest in east Asian societies.

THE UNIFICATION OF JAPAN

During the late sixteenth and early seventeenth centuries, the political unification of Japan ended an extended period of civil disorder. Like the Ming and Qing emperors in China, the **Tokugawa** shoguns sought to lay a foundation for long-term political and social stability, and they provided generous support for neo-Confucian studies in an effort to promote traditional values. Indeed, the shoguns went even further than their Chinese counterparts by promoting conservative values and tightly restricting foreign influence in Japan. As in China, however, demographic expansion and economic growth fostered social and cultural change in Japan, and merchants introduced Chinese and European influences into Japan.

The Tokugawa Shogunate

From the twelfth through the sixteenth century, a *shogun* ("military governor") ruled Japan through retainers who received political rights and large estates in exchange for military services. Theoretically, the shogun ruled as a temporary stand-in for the Japanese emperor, the ultimate source of political authority. In fact, however, the emperor was nothing more than a figurehead, and the shogun sought to monopolize power. After the fourteenth century the conflicting ambitions of shoguns and retainers led to constant turmoil, and by the sixteenth century Japan was in a state of civil war. Japanese historians often refer to the sixteenth century as the era of *sengoku*—"the country at war."

Tokugawa Ieyasu

Toward the end of the sixteenth century, powerful states emerged in several regions of Japan, and a series of military leaders brought about the unification of the land. In 1600 the last of these chieftains, Tokugawa Ieyasu (reigned 1600–1616), established a military government known as the Tokugawa *bakufu* ("tent government,"

Tokugawa (TOH-koo-GAH-wah)

MAP 26.3
Tokugawa Japan, 1600–1867.
Consider Japan's position with regard to China, Korea, and Russia.

Would it have been easy or difficult to enforce the ban on foreign trade during most of the period?

since it theoretically was only a temporary replacement for the emperor's rule). Ieyasu and his descendants ruled the *bakufu* as shoguns from 1600 until the end of the Tokugawa dynasty in 1867.

The principal aim of the Tokugawa shoguns was to stabilize their realm and prevent the return of civil war. Consequently, the shoguns needed to control the ***daimyo*** ("great names"), powerful territorial lords who ruled most of Japan from their vast, hereditary landholdings. The 260 or so daimyo functioned as near-absolute rulers within their domains. Each maintained a government staffed by military subordinates, supported an independent judiciary, established schools, and circulated paper money. Moreover, after the mid-sixteenth century, many daimyo established relationships with European mariners, from whom they learned how to manufacture and use gunpowder weapons. During the last decades of the *sengoku* era, cannons and personal firearms had played prominent roles in Japanese conflicts.

daimyo (DEYEM-yoh)

Control of the Daimyo From the castle town of Edo (modern Tokyo), the shogun governed his personal domain and sought to extend his control to the daimyo. The shoguns instituted the policy of "alternate attendance," which required daimyo to maintain their families at Edo and spend every other year at the Tokugawa court. This policy enabled the shoguns to keep an eye on the daimyo, and as a side effect it encouraged daimyo to spend their money on lavish residences and comfortable lives in Edo rather than investing it in military forces that could challenge the *bakufu*. The shoguns also subjected marriage alliances between daimyo families to *bakufu* approval, discouraged the daimyo from visiting one another, and required daimyo to obtain permits for construction work on their castles. Even meetings between the daimyo and the emperor required the shogun's permission.

In an effort to prevent European influences from destabilizing the land, the Tokugawa shoguns closely controlled relations between Japan and the outside world. They knew that Spanish forces had conquered the Philippine Islands in the sixteenth century, and they feared that Europeans might jeopardize the security of the *bakufu* itself. Even if Europeans did not conquer Japan, they could cause serious problems by making alliances with daimyo and supplying them with weapons.

Control of Foreign Relations

Thus during the 1630s the shoguns issued a series of edicts sharply restricting Japanese relations with other lands that remained in effect for more than two centuries. The policy forbade Japanese from going abroad on pain of death and prohibited the construction of large ships. It expelled Europeans from Japan, prohibited foreign merchants from trading in Japanese ports, and even forbade the import of foreign books. The policy allowed carefully controlled trade with Asian lands, and it also permitted small numbers of Chinese and Dutch merchants to trade under tight restrictions at the southern port city of Nagasaki.

During the seventeenth century, Japanese authorities strictly enforced that policy. In 1640 a Portuguese merchant ship arrived at Nagasaki in hopes of engaging in trade in spite of the ban. Officials beheaded sixty-one of the party and spared thirteen others so that they could relate the experience to their compatriots. Yet authorities gradually loosened the restrictions, and the policy never led to the complete isolation of Japan from the outside world. Throughout the Tokugawa period, Japan carried on a flourishing trade with China, Korea, Taiwan, and the Ryukyu Islands, and Dutch merchants regularly brought news of European and larger world affairs.

Economic and Social Change

By ending civil conflict and maintaining political stability, the Tokugawa shoguns set the stage for economic growth in Japan. Ironically, peace and a booming economy encouraged social change that undermined the order that the *bakufu* sought to preserve.

Economic growth had its roots in increased agricultural production. New crop strains, new methods of water control and irrigation, and the use of fertilizer brought increased yields of rice. Production of cotton, silk, indigo, and sake also increased dramatically. In many parts of Japan, villages moved away from subsistence farming in favor of production for the market. Between 1600 and 1700, agricultural production doubled.

Population Growth

Increased agricultural production brought about rapid demographic growth: during the seventeenth century the Japanese population rose by almost one-third, from twenty-two million to twenty-nine million. Thereafter, however, Japan underwent a demographic transition, as many families practiced population control to maintain or raise their standard of living. Between 1700 and 1850 the Japanese population grew moderately, from twenty-nine

million to thirty-two million. Contraception, late marriage, and abortion all played roles in limiting population growth, but the principal control measure was infanticide, euphemistically referred to as "thinning out the rice shoots." Japanese families resorted to those measures primarily because Japan was land poor. During the seventeenth century, populations in some areas strained resources, causing financial difficulties for local governments and distress for rural communities.

The Tokugawa era was an age of social as well as demographic change in Japan. Because of Chinese cultural influence, the Japanese social hierarchy followed Confucian precepts in ranking the ruling elites—including the shogun, daimyo, and samurai warriors—as the most prominent and privileged class of society. Beneath them were peasants and artisans. Merchants ranked at the bottom, as they did in China.

Social Change

The extended period of peace ushered in by Tokugawa rule undermined the social position of the ruling elites. Since the twelfth century the administration of local affairs had fallen mostly to daimyo and samurai

Dutch sailing ships and smaller Japanese vessels mingle in Nagasaki harbor. Dutch merchants conducted their business on the artificial island of Deshima, at left.

warriors. Once Japan was stable, however, the interest of Tokugawa authorities was to reduce the numbers of armed professional warriors, so they pushed daimyo and samurai to become bureaucrats and government functionaries. They even encouraged daimyo and samurai to turn their talents to scholarship, a pursuit that their martial ancestors would have utterly despised. As they lost their accustomed place in society, many of the ruling elite also fell into financial difficulty. Their principal income came in the form of rice collected from peasant cultivators of their lands. They readily converted rice into money through brokers, but the price of rice did not keep pace with other costs. Moreover, daimyo and samurai lived in expensive and sometimes ostentatious style—particularly daimyo who sought to impress others with their wealth while residing at Edo in alternate years. Many of them became indebted to rice brokers and gradually declined into genteel poverty.

Meanwhile, as in China, merchants in Japan became increasingly wealthy and prominent. Japanese cities flourished throughout the Tokugawa era—the population of Edo approached one million by 1700—and merchants prospered handsomely in the vibrant urban environment. Rice dealers, pawnbrokers, and sake merchants soon controlled more wealth than the ruling elites did. Those who became especially wealthy sometimes purchased elite ranks or contracted marriages with elite families in efforts to improve their social standing. Others did not go to such lengths but won respect anyway, in spite of occupations that ranked low in the ideal Confucian social order.

Neo-Confucianism and Floating Worlds

Japan had gone to school in China, and the influence of China continued throughout the Tokugawa era. Formal education began with study of Chinese language and literature. As late as the nineteenth century, many Japanese scholars wrote their philosophical, legal, and religious works in Chinese. The common people embraced Buddhism, which had come to Japan from China, and Confucianism was the most influential philosophical system.

Neo-Confucianism in Japan
Like the Ming and Qing emperors in China, the Tokugawa shoguns promoted the neo-Confucianism of Zhu Xi. With its emphasis on filial piety and loyalty to superiors, neo-Confucianism provided a respectable ideological underpinning for the *bakufu*. The shoguns patronized scholars who advocated neo-Confucian views, which figured prominently in the educational curriculum. All those who had a formal education—including the sons of merchants as well as offspring of government officials—received constant exposure to neo-Confucian values. By the early eighteenth century, neo-Confucianism had become the official ideology of the Tokugawa *bakufu*.

Native Learning
Yet even with Tokugawa sponsorship, neo-Confucianism did not dominate intellectual life in Japan. Although most scholars recognized Japan's debt to Chinese intellectual traditions, some sought to establish a sense of Japanese identity that did not depend on cultural kinship with China. Particularly during the eighteenth century,

The courtesan district of Kyoto hummed with activity in the mid-seventeenth century. In this woodblock print, courtesans await clients behind the wooden grill while urban residents fill the streets.

A colored woodcut by Okumura Masanobu depicts the audience at a seventeenth-century kabuki theater. Enthusiastic actors often ran down wooden ramps and played their roles among the audience.

scholars of "native learning" scorned neo-Confucianism and even Buddhism as alien cultural imports and emphasized instead the importance of folk traditions and the indigenous Shinto religion for Japanese identity. Many scholars of native learning viewed Japanese people as superior to all others and xenophobically regarded foreign influence as perverse. They urged the study of Japanese classics and glorified the supposed purity of Japanese society before its adulteration by Chinese and other foreign influences.

While scholars of neo-Confucianism and native learning debated issues of philosophy and Japanese identity, the emergence of a prosperous merchant class encouraged the development of a vibrant popular culture. During the seventeenth and eighteenth centuries, an exuberant middle-class culture flourished in cities such as Kyoto, the imperial capital; Edo, Japan's largest city and home to bureaucrats and

daimyo; and Osaka, the commercial hub of the islands. In those and other cities, Japan's finest creative talents catered to middle-class appetites.

Floating Worlds The centers of Tokugawa urban culture were the *ukiyo* ("floating worlds"), entertainment and pleasure quarters where teahouses, theaters, brothels, and public baths offered escape from social responsibilities and the rigid rules of conduct that governed public behavior in Tokugawa society. In contrast to the solemn, serious proceedings of the imperial court and the *bakufu*, the popular culture of urban residents was secular, satirical, and even scatological. The main expressions of this lively culture were prose fiction and new forms of theater.

Ihara Saikaku (1642–1693), one of Japan's most prolific poets, helped create a new genre of prose literature, the "books of the floating world." Much of his fiction revolved around the theme of love. In *The Life of a Man Who Lived for Love,* for example, Ihara chronicled the experiences of a townsman who devoted his life, beginning at the tender age of eight, to a quest for sexual pleasure. Ihara's treatment of love stressed the erotic rather than the aesthetic, and the brief, episodic stories that made up his work appealed to literate urban residents who were not inclined to pore over dense neo-Confucian treatises.

Beginning in the early seventeenth century, two new forms of drama became popular in Japanese cities. One was *kabuki* theater, which usually featured several acts consisting of lively and sometimes bawdy skits where stylized acting combined with lyric singing, dancing, and spectacular staging. A crucial component of kabuki was the actor's ability to improvise and embellish the dialogue, for the text of plays served only as guides for the dramatic performance. The other new dramatic form was *bunraku,* the puppet theater. In bunraku, chanters accompanied by music told a story acted out by puppets. Manipulated by a team of three, each puppet could

thinking about ENCOUNTERS

Crucifixions in Japan

The Jesuits came to Japan in 1549 and enjoyed some success in their early efforts to convert the Japanese to Christianity. Their continued success over time had major repercussions for Japanese converts. How and why did the Tokugawa *bakufu* respond to this Christian influence? What measures did the Japanese government take to stem the conversions?

execute the subtlest and most intricate movements, such as brushing a tear from the eye with the sleeve of a kimono. Both kabuki and bunraku attracted enthusiastic audiences in search of entertainment and diversion.

Christianity and Dutch Learning

Christian Missions
Alongside neo-Confucianism, native learning, and middle-class popular culture, Christian missionaries and European merchants contributed their own distinctive threads to the cultural fabric of Tokugawa Japan. The Jesuit Francis Xavier traveled to Japan in 1549 and opened a mission to seek converts to Christianity. In the early decades of their mission, Jesuits experienced remarkable success in Japan. Several powerful daimyo adopted Christianity and ordered their subjects to do likewise. The principal interest of the daimyo was to establish trade and military alliances with Europeans, but many Japanese converts became enthusiastic Christians and worked to convert their compatriots to the new faith. By the 1580s about 150,000 Japanese had converted to Christianity, and by 1615 Japanese Christians numbered about 300,000.

Although Christians were only a tiny minority of the Japanese population, the popularity of Christianity generated a backlash among government officials and moralists seeking to preserve Japanese religious and cultural traditions. The Tokugawa shoguns restricted European access to Japan largely because of concerns that Christianity might serve as a cultural bridge for alliances between daimyo and European adventurers, which in turn could lead to destabilization of Japanese society and even threats to the bakufu. Meanwhile, Buddhist and Confucian scholars resented the Christian conviction that their faith was the only true doctrine. Some Japanese converts to Christianity themselves eventually rejected their adopted faith out of frustration because European missionaries refused to allow them to become priests or play leadership roles in the mission.

Anti-Christian Campaign
Between 1587 and 1639, shoguns promulgated several decrees ordering a halt to Christian missions and commanding Japanese Christians to renounce their faith. In 1612 the shoguns began rigorous enforcement

A seventeenth-century European painting provides an emotional representation of Franciscans being crucified in Nagasaki.

sources from the past

Fabian Fucan Rejects Christianity

Fabian Fucan was a Japanese Buddhist who converted to Christianity and entered the Jesuit order as a novice in 1586. In the early seventeenth century, however, his relations with the Jesuits soured, and he eventually left the order. In 1620 he composed a treatise entitled Deus Destroyed *that leveled a spirited attack at Christianity and its God ("Deus" in Latin). His work reveals deep concerns about European imperial expansion as well as Christian doctrine.*

I joined this creed at an early age; diligently, I studied its teachings and pursued its practices. Due to my stupidity, however, I was long unable to realize that this was a perverse and cursed faith. Thus fruitlessly I spent twenty years and more! Then one day I clearly perceived that the words of the adherents of Deus were very clever and appeared very near reason—but in their teaching there was little truth. So I left their company. Some fifteen years have passed since: every morning I have lamented my desertion of the Great Holy True Law [of Buddhism]; every evening I have grieved over my adherence to the crooked path of the barbarians. All that effort to no effect! But I had a friend who remonstrated with me, saying: "'If you have made a mistake, do not be afraid of admitting the fact and amending your ways' [a Confucian precept]. Here, this is the Confucians' golden rule of life—act on it! Before, you learned all about the cursed faith of Deus; take pen in hand now, commit your knowledge to writing, and counter their teachings. Not only will you thereby gain the merit of destroying wickedness and demonstrating truth; you will also supply a guide toward new knowledge."

All right. Though I am not a clever man, I shall by all means try to act on this advice. I shall gather the important points about the teachings of the Deus sect and shall skip what is not essential; my aim is to write concisely. Thus shall I mount my attack; and I shall call my volume DEUS DESTROYED. . . .

Japan is the Land of the Gods. The generations of our rulers have received the Imperial Dignity from [the gods] Amaterasu Omikami, through U-gaya-fuki-awsezu no Mikoto and his August Child Jimmu Tenno, who became the progenitor of our Hundred Kings. The Three Divine Regalia [symbols of rule received from the gods] became the protectors of the Empire, so that among all the customs of our land there is not one which depends not on the Way of the Gods. . . .

And this, the adherents of Deus plan to subvert! They bide their time with the intent to make all of Japan into their own sectarians, to destroy the Law of Buddha and the Way of the Gods. Because the Law of Buddha and the Way of the Gods are planted here, the Royal Sway also flourishes; and since the Royal Sway is established here the glory of the Buddhas and the gods does grow. And therefore the adherents of Deus have no recourse but to subvert the Royal Sway, overthrow the Buddhas and the gods, eliminate the customs of Japan, and then to import the customs of their own countries; thus only will advance the plot they have concocted to usurp the country themselves.

They have dispatched troops and usurped such countries as Luzon [the Philippines] and Nova Hispania [Mexico], lands of barbarians with nature close to animal. But our land by far surpasses others in fierce bravery; and therefore the ambition to diffuse their faith in every quarter and thus to usurp the country, even if it take a thousand years, has penetrated down to the very marrow of their bones. Ah!—but what a gloomy prospect awaits them! For the sake of their faith they value their lives less than trash, than garbage. *Martyr,* they call this. When a wise sovereign rules the Empire good is promoted and evil is chastised. Rewards promote good and punishments chastise evil. There is no greater punishment than to take away life; but the adherents of Deus, without even fearing that their lives be cut, will not change their religion. How horrible, how awful it is!

For Further Reflection

■ Discuss the various religious, cultural, historical, political, and social aspects of Fabian Fucan's attack on Christianity.

Source: George Elison. *Deus Destroyed: The Image of Christianity in Early Modern Japan.* Cambridge, Mass.: Harvard University Press, 1973, pp. 259–60, 283–84.

of those decrees. They tortured and executed European missionaries who refused to leave the islands as well as Japanese Christians who refused to abandon their faith. They often executed victims by crucifixion or burning at the stake, which Tokugawa authorities regarded as especially appropriate punishments for Christians. The campaign was so effective that even some European missionaries abandoned Christianity. Most notable of them was the Portuguese Jesuit Christovão Ferreira, head of the Jesuit mission in Japan, who gave up Christianity under torture, adopted Buddhism, and interrogated many Europeans who fell into Japanese hands in the mid-seventeenth century. By the late seventeenth century, the anti-Christian campaign had claimed tens of thousands of lives, and Christianity survived as a secret, underground religion observed only in rural regions of southern Japan.

Dutch Learning Tokugawa policies ensured that Christianity would not soon reappear in Japan, but they did not entirely prevent contacts between Europeans and Japanese. After 1639, Dutch merchants trading at Nagasaki became Japan's principal source of information about Europe and the world beyond east Asia. A small number of Japanese scholars learned Dutch in order to communicate with the foreigners. Their studies, which they called "Dutch learning," brought considerable knowledge of the outside world to Japan. After 1720, Tokugawa authorities lifted the ban on foreign books, and Dutch learning began to play a significant role in Japanese intellectual life.

European art influenced Japanese scholars interested in anatomy and botany because of its accurate representations of objects. Scholars translated Dutch medical and scientific treatises into Japanese and learned to draw according to the principles of linear perspective, which enabled them to prepare textbooks that were more accurate than the Chinese works they had previously used. European astronomy was also popular in Japan, since it enabled scholars to improve calendars and issue accurate predictions of eclipses and other celestial events. By the mid-eighteenth century, the Tokugawa shoguns themselves had become enthusiastic proponents of Dutch learning, and schools of European medicine and Dutch studies flourished in several Japanese cities.

in perspective

Both China and Japan controlled their own affairs throughout the early modern era and avoided the turmoil that afflicted societies in the Americas and much of sub-Saharan Africa. After driving the Mongols to the steppe lands of central Asia, rulers of the Ming dynasty built a powerful centralized state in China. They worked diligently to eradicate all vestiges of Mongol rule and restore traditional ways by reviving Chinese political institutions and providing state sponsorship for neo-Confucianism. In the interest of stability, authorities also restricted foreign merchants' access to China and limited the activities of Christian missionaries. The succeeding Qing dynasty pursued similar policies. The Ming and Qing dynasties both brought political stability, but China experienced considerable social and economic change in early modern times. American food crops helped increase agricultural production, which fueled rapid population growth, and global trade stimulated the Chinese economy, which improved the position of merchants and artisans in society. The experience of the Tokugawa era in Japan was much like that of the Ming and Qing eras in China. The Tokugawa *bakufu* brought political order to the Japanese islands and closely controlled foreign relations, but a vibrant economy promoted social change that enhanced the status of merchants and artisans. ●

CHRONOLOGY

1368–1644	Ming dynasty (China)
1368–1398	Reign of Hongwu
1403–1424	Reign of Yongle
1552–1610	Life of Matteo Ricci
1572–1620	Reign of Emperor Wanli
1600–1867	Tokugawa shogunate (Japan)
1616–1626	Reign of Nurhaci
1642–1693	Life of Ihara Saikaku
1644–1911	Qing dynasty (China)
1661–1722	Reign of Kangxi
1736–1795	Reign of Qianlong
1793	British trade mission to China

For Further Reading

Timothy Brook. *The Chinese State in Ming Society.* London and New York, 2004. An important collection of essays on commercialism and social networks, and the role they played in the development of a stable society.

———. *The Confusions of Pleasure: Commerce and Culture in Ming China.* Berkeley, 1998. Fascinating social and cultural analysis of Ming China focusing on the role of commerce as an agent of social change.

George Elison. *Deus Destroyed: The Image of Christianity in Early Modern Japan.* Cambridge, Mass., 1973. Scholarly study of the Jesuit mission in Japan and its end during the early Tokugawa era.

Mark C. Elliott. *The Manchu Way: The Eight Banners and Ethnic Identity in Late Imperial China.* Stanford, 2001. Important scholarly study focusing on relations between Manchus and Chinese during the Qing dynasty.

Benjamin A. Elman. *A Cultural History of Civil Examinations in Late Imperial China.* Berkeley, 2000. A meticulous study of one of the most important institutions in Chinese history.

Jacques Gernet. *China and the Christian Impact.* Trans. by J. Lloyd. Cambridge, 1985. A careful study of the Jesuit mission in China, concentrating on the cultural differences between Chinese and Europeans.

Harry D. Harootunian. *Things Seen and Unseen: Discourse and Ideology in Tokugawa Nativism.* Chicago, 1988. A challenging scholarly analysis of the efforts by Tokugawa thinkers to construct a distinctive Japanese identity.

Donald Keene. *The Japanese Discovery of Europe, 1720–1830.* Rev. ed. Stanford, 1969. A highly readable account of Japanese encounters with Europe by way of Dutch merchants.

Susan Mann and Yu-Ying Cheng, eds. *Under Confucian Eyes: Writings on Gender in Chinese History.* Berkeley, 2001. A rich anthology of primary texts documenting the lives of women in imperial China.

Ichisada Miyazaki. *China's Examination Hell: The Civil Service Examinations in Imperial China.* Trans. by Conrad Schirokauer. New Haven, 1981. Explores all aspects of the labyrinthine civil service examination system.

Susan Naquin and Evelyn S. Rawski. *Chinese Society in the Eighteenth Century.* New Haven, 1987. A lucid and well-organized discussion of Chinese social history.

Kenneth Pomeranz. *The Great Divergence: China, Europe, and the Making of the Modern World Economy.* Princeton, 2000. Pathbreaking scholarly study that illuminates the economic history of the early modern world through comparison of economic development in Asian and European lands.

Evelyn S. Rawski. *The Last Emperors: A Social History of Qing Imperial Institutions.* Berkeley, 1998. A nuanced study of the Manchu rulers and the politics of assimilation.

Jonathan D. Spence. *The Death of Woman Wang.* New York, 1978. Engaging reconstruction of life in rural China during the early Qing dynasty.

———. *Emperor of China: Self-Portrait of K'ang-Hsi.* New York, 1974. Outstanding introduction to the reign of Kangxi based partly on numerous documents, some written by the emperor himself.

Ronald P. Toby. *State and Diplomacy in Early Modern Japan: Asia in the Development of the Tokugawa Bakufu.* Princeton, 1984. An important study dealing with Japanese trade and relations with other lands under Tokugawa rule.

H. Paul Varley. *Japanese Culture.* 4th ed. Honolulu, 2000. Places the cultural history of the Tokugawa era in its larger historical context.

Arthur Waldron. *The Great Wall of China: From History to Myth.* Cambridge, 1990. Fascinating work that places the Great Wall of Ming China in the context of earlier efforts to build defensive walls.

chapter27

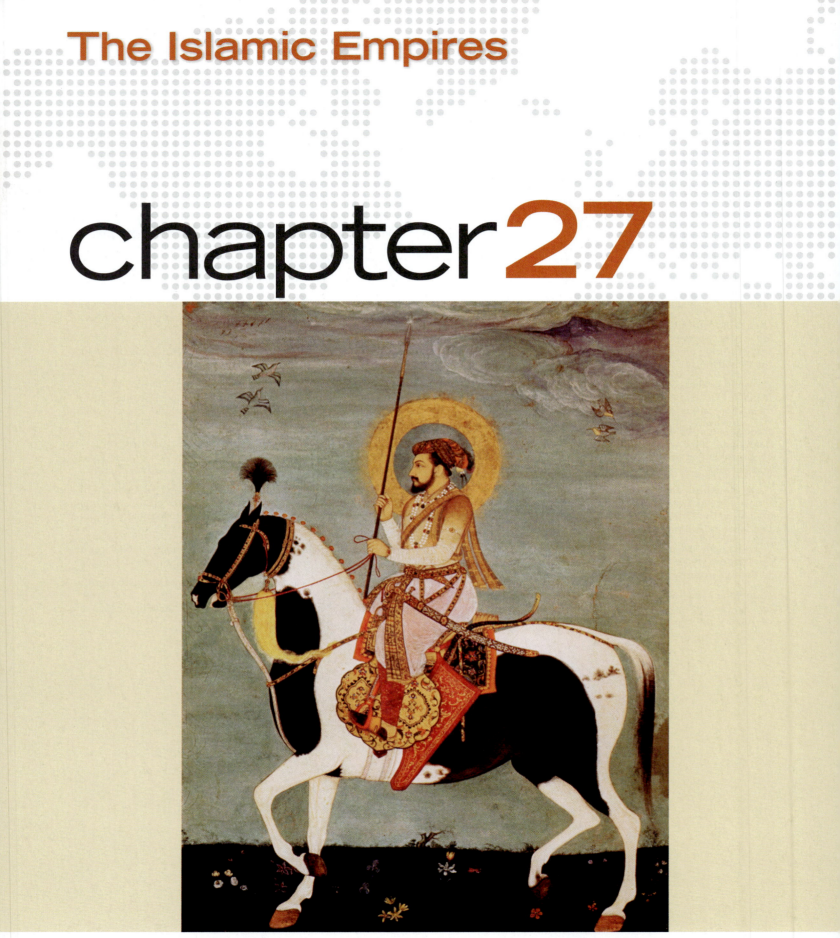

This equestrian portrait of Shah Jahan (reigned 1628–1658) is emblematic of the Mughal art promoted by Shah Jahan. Builder of the Taj Mahal, Shah Jahan here is shown in a rich and heroic light, symbolized by the ring of light, his clothing and weaponry, and the horse's exquisite appointments.

PART 5

EYEWITNESS:
Shah Jahan's Monument to Love and Allah

In 1635 Shah Jahan, the emperor of Mughal India, took his seat on the Peacock Throne. Seven years in the making, the Peacock Throne is probably the most spectacular seat on which any human being has rested. Shah Jahan ordered the throne encrusted with ten million rupees' worth of diamonds, rubies, emeralds, and pearls. Atop the throne itself stood a magnificent, golden-bodied peacock with a huge ruby and a fifty-carat, pear-shaped pearl on its breast and a brilliant elevated tail fashioned of blue sapphires and other colored gems.

Yet, for all its splendor, the Peacock Throne ranks a distant second among Shah Jahan's artistic projects: pride of place goes to the incomparable Taj Mahal. Built over a period of eighteen years as a tomb for Shah Jahan's beloved wife, Mumtaz Mahal, who died during childbirth in 1631, the Taj Mahal is a graceful and elegant monument both to the departed empress and to Shah Jahan's Islamic faith.

The emperor and his architects conceived the Taj Mahal as a vast allegory in stone symbolizing the day when Allah would cause the dead to rise and undergo judgment before his heavenly throne. Its gardens represented the gardens of paradise, and the four water channels running through them symbolized the four rivers of the heavenly kingdom. The domed marble tomb of Mumtaz Mahal represented the throne of Allah, and the four minarets surrounding the structure served as legs supporting the divine throne. Craftsmen carved verses from the Quran throughout the Taj Mahal. The main gateway to the structure features the entire text of the chapter promising that on the day of judgment, Allah will punish the wicked and gather the faithful into his celestial paradise.

The Peacock Throne and the Taj Mahal testify to the wealth of the Mughal empire, and the tomb of Mumtaz Mahal bespeaks also the fundamentally Islamic character of the ruling dynasty. But the Mughal empire, which ruled most of the Indian subcontinent for more than three hundred years, was not the only well-organized Islamic empire of early modern times. The Ottoman empire was a dynastic Muslim state centered in what is today Turkey. At the height of its power, it controlled a vast area from southeastern Europe to western Asia and North Africa. It was also the longest-lived of the Muslim empires, not disbanding until the early twentieth century. On the eastern borders of the Ottoman empire lay the ancient lands of Persia, where yet another Muslim empire emerged during the early sixteenth century. Ruled by the Safavid dynasty, this state never expanded far beyond its heartland of present-day Iran, but its Shiite rulers challenged the Sunni Ottomans for dominance in southwest Asia. The Safavid realm prospered from its place in trade networks linking China, India, Russia, southwest Asia, and the Mediterranean basin.

All three Islamic empires of early modern times had Turkish ruling dynasties. The Ottomans, Safavids, and Mughals came from nomadic, Turkish-speaking peoples of central Asia who conquered the settled agricultural lands of Anatolia, Persia, and India, respectively. All three dynasties retained political and cultural traditions that their ancestors had adopted while leading nomadic lives on the steppes, but they also adapted readily to the city-based agricultural societies that they conquered. The Ottoman dynasty made especially effective use of the gunpowder weapons that transformed early modern warfare, and the Safavids and the Mughals also incorporated gunpowder weapons into their arsenals. All three dynasties officially embraced Islam and drew cultural guidance from Islamic values.

During the sixteenth and early seventeenth centuries, the three Islamic empires presided over expansive and prosperous societies. About the mid-seventeenth century, however, they all began to weaken. Their waning fortunes reflected the fact that they had ceased to expand territorially and gain access to new sources of wealth. Instead, each empire waged long, costly wars that drained resources without bringing compensating benefits. The empires also faced domestic difficulties. Each of them was an ethnically and religiously diverse realm, and each experienced tensions when conservative Muslim leaders lobbied for strict observance of Islam while members of other communities sought greater freedom for themselves. Furthermore, the Islamic empires made little investment in economic and technological development. By the mid-eighteenth century, the Safavid empire had collapsed, and the Ottoman and Mughal realms were rapidly falling under European influence.

FORMATION OF THE ISLAMIC EMPIRES

By the sixteenth century, Turkish warriors had transformed the major Islamic areas of the world into vast regional empires. Three empires divided up the greater part of the Islamic world: the Ottoman empire, which was distinguished by its multiethnic character; the Safavid empire of Persia, which served as the center of Shiite Islam; and the Mughal empire, which had been imposed over a predominantly Hindu Indian subcontinent. The creation of these durable and powerful political entities brought to an end a century and a half of Muslim political disunity.

The Islamic empires began as small warrior principalities in frontier areas. They expanded at varying rates and with varying degrees of success at the expense of neighboring states. As they grew, they devised elaborate administrative and military institutions. Under the guidance of talented and energetic rulers, each empire organized an effective governmental apparatus and presided over a prosperous society.

The Ottoman Empire

Osman The Ottoman empire was an unusually successful frontier state. The term *Ottoman* derived from Osman Bey, founder of the dynasty that continued in unbroken succession from 1289 until the dissolution of the empire in 1923.

Osman was *bey* (chief) of a band of seminomadic Turks who migrated to northwestern Anatolia in the thirteenth century. Osman and his followers sought above all to become *ghazi*, Muslim religious warriors. In his encomium of the Ottomans, the poet Ahmadi described their ethos: "The Ghazi is the instrument of the religion of Allah, a servant of God who purifies the earth from the filth of polytheism; the Ghazi is the sword of God, he is the protector and the refuge of the believers. If he becomes a martyr in the ways of God, do not believe that he has died—he lives in beatitude with Allah, he has eternal life."

Ottoman Expansion The Ottomans' location on the borders of the Byzantine empire afforded them ample opportunity to wage holy war. Their first great success came in 1326 with the capture of the Anatolian city of Bursa, which became the capital of the Ottoman principality. Around 1352 they established a foothold in Europe when they seized the fortress of Gallipoli while aiding a claimant to the Byzantine throne. Numerous *ghazi*, many of them recent converts, soon flocked to join the Ottomans. The city of Edirne (Adrianople) became a second Ottoman capital and served as a base for further expansion into the Balkans. As warriors settled in frontier districts and pushed their boundaries forward, they took spoils and gathered revenues that enriched both the *ghazi* and the central government.

MAP 27.1

The Islamic empires, 1500–1800.

Locate the Ottoman capital of Istanbul, the Safavid capital of Isfahan, and the Mughal capital of Delhi.

What strategic or commercial purposes did each of these capitals fulfill, and how would their locations have aided or hindered imperial administration?

Bursa developed into a major commercial and intellectual center with inns, shops, schools, libraries, and mosques.

A formidable military machine drove Ottoman expansion. Ottoman military leaders initially organized *ghazi* recruits into two forces: a light cavalry and a volunteer infantry. As the Ottoman state became more firmly established, it added a professional cavalry force equipped with heavy armor and financed by land grants. After expanding into the Balkans, the Ottomans created a supremely important force composed of slave troops. Through an institution known as the *devshirme,* the Ottomans required the Christian population of the Balkans to contribute young boys to become slaves of the sultan. The boys received special training, learned Turkish, and converted to Islam. According to individual ability, they entered either the Ottoman civilian administration or the military. Those who became soldiers were known as Janissaries, from the Turkish *yeni cheri* ("new troops"). The Janissaries quickly gained a reputation for esprit de corps, loyalty to the sultan, and readiness to employ new military technology. Besides building powerful military forces, the Ottomans outfitted their forces with gunpowder weapons and used them effectively in battles and sieges.

Mehmed the Conqueror The capture of Constantinople in 1453 by Mehmed II (reigned 1451–1481)—known as Mehmed the Conqueror—opened a new chapter in Otto-

man expansion. With its superb location and illustrious heritage, Constantinople became the new Ottoman capital, subsequently known as Istanbul, and Mehmed worked energetically to stimulate its role as a commercial center. With the capture of the great city behind him, Mehmed presented himself not just as a warrior-sultan but also as a true emperor, ruler of the "two lands" (Europe and Asia) and the "two seas" (the Black Sea and the Mediterranean). He laid the foundations for a tightly centralized, absolute monarchy, and his army faced no serious rival. He completed the conquest of Serbia, moved into southern Greece and Albania, eliminated the last Byzantine outpost at Trebizond, captured Genoese ports in the Crimea, initiated a naval war with Venice in the Mediterranean, and reportedly hoped to cross the Strait of Otranto, march on Rome, and capture the pope himself. Toward the end of his life, he launched an invasion of Italy and briefly occupied Otranto, but his successors abandoned Mehmed's plans for expansion in western Europe.

Süleyman the Magnificent The Ottomans continued their expansion in the early sixteenth century when

Danube, and in 1529 subjected the Habsburgs' prized city of Vienna to a brief but nonetheless terrifying siege.

Under Süleyman the Ottomans also became a major naval power. In addition to their own Aegean and Black Sea fleets, the Ottomans inherited the navy of the Mamluk rulers of Egypt. A Turkish corsair, Khayr al-Din Barbarossa Pasha, who had challenged Spanish forces in Tunisia and Algeria, placed his pirate fleet under the Ottoman flag and became Süleyman's leading admiral. Thus Süleyman was able to challenge Christian vessels throughout the Mediterranean as well as Portuguese fleets in the Red Sea and the Indian Ocean. The Ottomans seized the island of Rhodes from the Knights of St. John, besieged Malta, secured Yemen and Aden, and even dispatched a squadron to attack the Portuguese fleet at Diu in India.

The Safavid Empire

In 1499 a twelve-year-old boy named Ismail left the swamps of Gilan near the Caspian Sea, where he had hidden from the enemies of his family for five years, to seek his revenge. Two years later he entered Tabriz at the head of an army and laid claim to the ancient Persian imperial title of shah. The young Shah Ismail (reigned 1501–1524) also proclaimed that the official religion of his realm would be Twelver Shiism, and he proceeded to impose it, by force when necessary, on the formerly Sunni population. Over the next decade he seized control of the Iranian plateau and launched expeditions into the Caucasus, Anatolia, Mesopotamia, and central Asia.

The Safavids For propaganda purposes, Shah Ismail and his successors carefully controlled accounts of their rise to power—and expediently changed the story when circumstances warranted. They traced their ancestry back to Safi al-Din (1252–1334), leader of a Sufi religious order in northwestern Persia. Sufism, a mystical belief and practice, formed an important Islamic tradition. The goal of a Sufi mystic, such as Safi al-Din, was to recover the lost intimacy between God and the human soul, and to find the truth of divine knowledge and love through a direct personal experience of God. The famous tomb and shrine of Safi al-Din at Ardabil became the home of Shah Ismail's family (named "Safavids" after the holy man himself), the headquarters of his religious movement, and the center of a determined, deliberate conspiracy to win political power for his descendants. The Safavids changed their religious preferences several times in the hope of gaining popular support before settling on a form of Shiism that appealed to the nomadic Turkish tribes moving into the area in the post-Mongol era.

Twelver Shiism Twelver Shiism held that there had been twelve infallible imams (or religious leaders) after Muhammad, beginning with the prophet's cousin and son-in-law Ali. The twelfth, "hidden," imam had gone into hiding around 874 to escape persecution, but the Twelver Shiites believed he was still alive and would one day return to take

Sultan Süleyman (center, on horse) leads Ottoman forces as they march on Europe. How does this illustration promote the power and prominence of Süleyman and his Ottoman forces?

sultan Selim the Grim (reigned 1512–1520) occupied Syria and Egypt. Ottoman imperialism climaxed in the reign of **Süleyman** the Magnificent (reigned 1520–1566). Süleyman vigorously promoted Ottoman expansion both in southwest Asia and in Europe. In 1534 he conquered Baghdad and added the Tigris and Euphrates valleys to the Ottoman domain. In Europe he kept the rival Habsburg empire on the defensive throughout his reign. He captured Belgrade in 1521, defeated and killed the king of Hungary at the battle of Mohács in 1526, consolidated Ottoman power north of the

Süleyman (SOO-lee-mahn)

sources from the past

Source: Ghislain de Busbecq. *The Turkish Letters of Ogier Ghislain de Busbecq*. Trans. by E. S. Foster. Oxford: Clarendon Press, 1927, pp. 209–14.

Ghislain de Busbecq's Concerns about the Ottoman Empire

Ogier Ghislain de Busbecq was a diplomat who traveled to Istanbul in 1555 as a representative of Habsburg King Ferdinand of Hungary and Bohemia to negotiate a border dispute between Ferdinand and Sultan Süleyman the Magnificent. In a series of four letters to a friend, Ghislain commented on Ottoman state, society, customs, and military forces. His observations left him deeply concerned about the prospects of Christian Europe in the event of conflict with the Ottoman realm.

The Sultan, when he sets out on a campaign, takes as many as 40,000 camels with him, and almost as many baggage-mules, most of whom, if his destination is Persia, are loaded with cereals of every kind, especially rice. Mules and camels are also employed to carry tents and arms and warlike machines and implements of every kind. . . . They are careful, however, to avoid touching the supplies which they carry with them as long as they are marching against their foes, but reserve them, as far as possible, for their return journey, when the moment for retirement comes and they are forced to retrace their steps through regions which the enemy has laid waste, or which the immense multitude of men and baggage animals has, as it were, scraped bare, like a swarm of locusts. It is only then that the Sultan's store of provisions is opened, and just enough food to sustain life is weighed out each day to the Janissaries and the other troops in attendance upon him. The other soldiers are badly off, if they have not provided food for their own use; most of them, having often experienced such difficulties during their campaigns—and this is particularly true of the cavalry—take a horse on a leading-rein loaded with many of the necessities of life. These include a small piece of canvas to use as a tent, which may protect them from the sun or a shower of rain, also some clothing and bedding and a private store of provisions, consisting of a leather sack or two of the finest flour, a small jar of butter, and some spices and salt; on these they support life when they are reduced to the extremes of hunger. They take a few spoonfuls of flour and place them in water, adding a little butter, and then flavour the mixture with salt and spices. This, when it is put on the fire, boils and swells up so as to fill a large bowl. They eat of it once or twice a day, according to the quantity, without any bread, unless they have with them some toasted bread or biscuit. They thus contrive to live on short rations for a month or even longer, if necessary. . . .

All this will show you with what patience, sobriety, and economy the Turks struggle against the difficulties which beset them, and wait for better times. How different are our soldiers, who on campaign despise ordinary food and expect dainty dishes (such as thrushes and beccaficoes) and elaborate meals. If these are not supplied, they mutiny and cause their own ruin; and even if they are supplied, they ruin themselves just the same. . . . I tremble when I think of what the future must bring when I compare the Turkish system with our own; one army must prevail and the other be destroyed, for certainly both cannot remain unscathed. On their side are the resources of a mighty empire, strength unimpaired, experience and practice in fighting, a veteran soldiery, habituation to victory, endurance of toil, unity, order, discipline, frugality, and watchfulness. On our side is public poverty, private luxury, impaired strength, spirit, lack of endurance and training; the soldiers are insubordinate, the officers avaricious; there is contempt for discipline; licence, recklessness, drunkenness, and debauchery are rife; and worst of all, the enemy is accustomed to victory, and we to defeat. Can we doubt what the result will be?

For Further Reflection

■ Why might Ghislain de Busbecq have assumed that conflict between Turkish and Habsburg forces was inevitable?

---

power and spread his true religion. Ismail's father had instructed his Turkish followers to wear a distinctive red hat with twelve pleats in memory of the twelve Shiite imams, and they subsequently became known as the *qizilbash* ("red heads"). Safavid propaganda also suggested that Ismail was himself the hidden imam, or even an incarnation of Allah. Although most Muslims, including most Shiites, would have regarded those pretensions as utterly blasphemous, the *qizilbash* enthusiastically accepted them, since they resembled traditional Turkish conceptions of leadership that associated military leaders with divinity. The *qizilbash* believed that Ismail would make them invincible in battle, and they became fanatically loyal to the Safavid cause.

Battle of Chaldiran Shah Ismail's curious blend of Shiism and Turkish militancy gave his regime a distinctive alongside smaller communities of Jains, Zoroastrians, Christians, and devotees of syncretic faiths such as Sikhism.

Christian Mission in India

Portuguese Goa became the center of a Christian mission in India. Priests at Goa sought to attract converts to Christianity and established schools that provided religious instruction for Indian children. In 1580 several Portuguese Jesuits traveled to the Mughal court at Akbar's invitation. They had visions of converting the emperor to Christianity and then spreading their faith throughout India, but their hopes went unfulfilled. Akbar received the Jesuits cordially and welcomed their participation in religious and philosophical discussions at his court, but he declined to commit to an exclusive faith that he thought would alienate many of his subjects.

Akbar's Divine Faith

Indeed, Akbar was cool even to his Islamic faith. In his efforts to find a religious synthesis that would serve as a cultural foundation for unity in his diverse empire, he supported the efforts of the early Sikhs, who combined elements of Hinduism and Islam in a new syncretic faith. He also attempted to elaborate his own "divine faith" that emphasized loyalty to the emperor while borrowing eclectically from different religious traditions. Akbar never explained his ideas systematically, but it is clear that they drew most heavily on Islam. The divine faith was strictly monotheistic, and it reflected the influence of Shiite and Sufi teachings. But it also glorified the emperor: Akbar even referred to himself as the "lord of wisdom," who would guide his subjects to understanding of the world's cre-

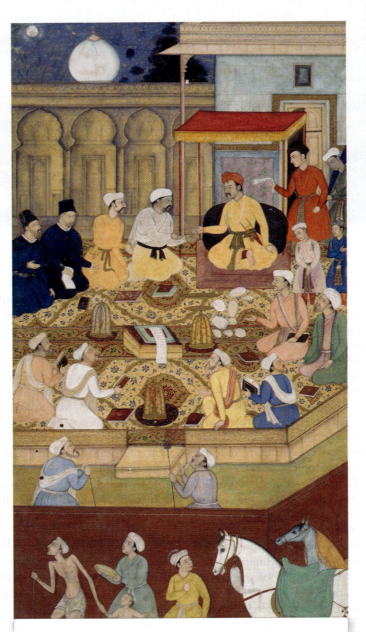

In a seventeenth-century painting, the emperor Akbar presides over discussions between representatives of various religious groups. Two Jesuits dressed in black robes kneel at the left.

ator god. The divine faith was tolerant of Hinduism, and it even drew inspiration from Zoroastrianism in its effort to bridge the gaps between Mughal India's many cultural and religious communities.

Status of Religious Minorities

The Islamic empires relied on a long-established model to deal with subjects who were not Muslims. They did not require conquered peoples to convert to Islam but extended to them the status of *dhimmi* ("protected people"). In return for their loyalty and payment of a special tax known as *jizya, dhimmi* communities retained their personal freedom, kept their property, practiced their religion, and handled their legal affairs. In the Ottoman empire, for example, autonomous religious communities known as *millet* retained their civil laws, traditions, and languages. *Millet* communities usually also assumed social and administrative functions in matters concerning birth, marriage, death, health, and education.

The situation in the Mughal empire was different, since its large number of religious communities made a *millet* system impractical. Mughal rulers reserved the most powerful military and administrative positions for Muslims, but in the day-to-day management of affairs, Muslims and Hindus cooperated closely. Some Mughal emperors sought to forge links between religious communities. Akbar in particular worked to integrate Muslim and Hindu elites. In an effort to foster communication and understanding among the different religious communities of his realm, he abolished the *jizya,* tolerated all faiths, and sponsored discussions and debates between Muslims, Hindus, Jains, Zoroastrians, and Christians.

thinking about TRADITIONS

Religious Diversity

An overarching feature of all three Islamic empires was the ethnic and religious diversity of the subject populations. What measures did the rulers of the Ottoman, Safavid, and Mughal states take to maintain harmony among the different ethnic and religious communities?

Promotion of Islam Policies of religious tolerance were not popular with many Muslims, who worried that they would lose their religious identity and that toleration might lead to their absorption into Hindu society as another caste. They therefore insisted that Mughal rulers create and maintain an Islamic state based on Islamic law. When Aurangzeb reached the Mughal throne in 1659, this policy gained strength. Aurangzeb reinstated the *jizya* and promoted Islam as the official faith of Mughal India. His policy satisfied zealous Muslims but at the cost of deep bitterness among his Hindu subjects. Tension between Hindu and Muslim communities in India persisted throughout the Mughal dynasty and beyond.

Cultural Patronage of the Islamic Emperors

As the empires matured, the Islamic rulers sought to enhance their prestige through public works projects and patronage of scholars. They competed to attract outstanding religious scholars, poets, artists, and architects to their courts. They lavished resources on mosques, palaces, government buildings, bridges, fountains, schools, hospitals, and soup kitchens for the poor.

Istanbul Capital cities and royal palaces were the most visible expressions of imperial majesty. The Ottomans beautified both Bursa and Edirne, but they took particular pride in Istanbul. Dilapidated and deserted after the conquest, it quickly revived and became a bustling, prosperous city of more than a million people. At its heart was the great Topkapi palace, which housed government offices, such as the mint, and meeting places for imperial councils. At its core was the sultan's residence with its harem, gardens, pleasure pavilions, and a repository for the most sacred possessions of the empire, including the mantle of the prophet Muhammad. Sultan Süleyman the Magnificent was fortunate to be able to draw on the talents of the architectural genius Sinan Pasha (1489–1588) to create the most celebrated of all the monuments of Istanbul. Sinan built a vast religious complex called the Süleymaniye, which blended Islamic and Byzantine architectural elements. It combined tall, slender minarets with large domed buildings supported by half domes in the style of the Byzantine church Hagia Sofia (which the Ottomans converted into the mosque of Aya Sofya).

Isfahan Shah Abbas made his capital, Isfahan, into the queen of Persian cities and one of the most precious jewels of urban architectural development anywhere in the world: its inhabitants still boast that "Isfahan is half the world." Abbas concentrated markets, the palace, and the royal mosque around a vast polo field and public square. Broad, shaded avenues and magnificent bridges linked the central city to its suburbs. Safavid architects made use of monumental entryways, vast arcades, spacious courtyards, and intricate, colorful decoration. Unlike the sprawling Ottoman and Mughal palaces, the Safavid palaces in Isfahan were relatively small and emphasized natural settings with gardens and pools. They were also much more open than Topkapi, with its series of

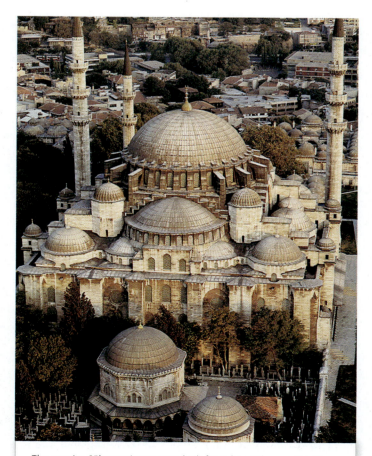

The massive Süleymaniye mosque built for Sultan Süleyman the Magnificent by the Ottoman architect Sinan Pasha in 1556.

Fatehpur Sikri, built by Akbar in the 1570s, commemorated the emperor's military conquests and housed the tomb of his religious guide. It included a palace, an audience hall where Akbar attended religious and philosophical debates, and a great mosque.

inner courts and gates. Ali Qapu, the palace on the square in Isfahan, had a striking balcony, and most of the palaces had large, open verandas. The point was not only to enable the shah to observe outside activities but also to emphasize his visibility and accessibility, qualities long esteemed in the Persian tradition of kingship.

To some extent, in accordance with steppe traditions, the early Mughals regarded the capital as wherever the ruler happened to camp. Yet they too came to sponsor urban development. Their work skillfully blended central Asian traditions with elements of Hindu architecture, and they built on a scale that left no doubt about their wealth and resources. They constructed scores of mosques, fortresses, and palaces and sometimes created entire cities.

Fatehpur Sikri The best example was Fatehpur Sikri, a city planned and constructed by Akbar that served as his capital from 1569 to 1585. It commemorated his conquest of the prosperous commercial province of Gujarat in a campaign that enabled Akbar to head off both Portuguese attacks and Ottoman intervention there. With its mint, records office, treasury, and audience hall, the new city demonstrated Akbar's strength and imperial ambitions. Fatehpur Sikri was also a private residence and retreat for the ruler, reproducing in stone a royal encampment with exquisite pleasure palaces where Akbar indulged his passions for music and conversation with scholars and poets. At yet another level, it was a dramatic display of Mughal piety and devotion, centered on the cathedral mosque and the mausoleum of Akbar's Sufi guru, Shaykh Salim Chisti. Despite their intensely Islamic character, many of the buildings consciously incorporated Indian elements such as verandas supported by columns and

decorations of stone elephants. Even the tomb of Shaykh Chisti bore some resemblance to a Hindu shrine. Unfortunately, Akbar selected a poor site for the city and soon abandoned it because of its bad water supply.

The Taj Mahal The most famous of the Mughal monuments—and one of the most prominent of all Islamic edifices—was the Taj Mahal. Shah Jahan had twenty thousand workers toil for eighteen years to erect the exquisite white marble mosque and tomb. He originally planned to build a similar mausoleum out of black marble for himself, but his son Aurangzeb deposed him before he could carry out the project. Shah Jahan spent his last years confined to a small cell with a tiny window, and only with the aid of a mirror was he able to catch the sight of his beloved wife's final resting place.

THE EMPIRES IN TRANSITION

The Islamic empires underwent dramatic change between the sixteenth and the eighteenth centuries. The Safavid empire disappeared entirely. In 1722 a band of Afghan tribesmen marched all the way to Isfahan, blockaded the city until its starving inhabitants resorted to cannibalism, forced the shah to abdicate, and executed thousands of Safavid officials as well as many members of the royal family. After the death of Aurangzeb in 1707, Mughal India experienced provincial rebellions and foreign invasions. By mid-century the subcontinent was falling under British imperial rule. By 1700 the Ottomans, too, were on the defensive: the sultans lost control over remote provinces such as Lebanon and Egypt, and throughout the eighteenth and nineteenth cen-

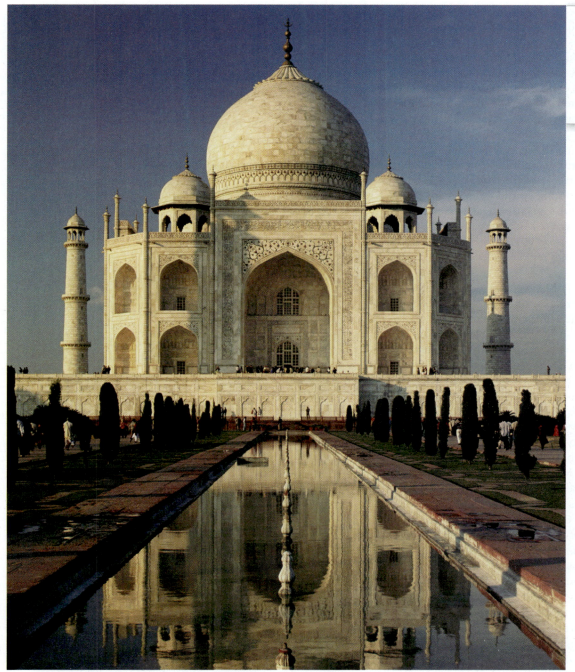

The Taj Mahal was a sumptuous mosque and tomb built between 1632 and 1649 by Shah Jahan in memory of his wife, Mumtaz Mahal.

turies European and Russian states placed political, military, and economic pressure on the shrinking Ottoman realm.

The Deterioration of Imperial Leadership

Strong and effective central authority was essential to the Islamic empires, and Muslim political theorists never tired of emphasizing the importance of rulers who were diligent, virtuous, and just. Weak, negligent, and corrupt rulers would allow institutions to become dysfunctional and social

order to break down. The Ottomans were fortunate in having a series of talented sultans for three centuries, and the Safavids and Mughals produced their share of effective rulers as well.

Dynastic Decline Eventually, however, all three dynasties had rulers who were incompetent or more interested in spending vast sums of money on personal pleasures than in tending to affairs of state. Moreover, all three dynasties faced difficulties because of suspicion and fighting among competing members of their ruling houses. The Ottomans sought to limit problems by confining princes in the palace, but that measure had several negative consequences. The princes had no opportunity to gain experience in government, but they were exposed to plots and intrigues of the various factions maneuvering to bring a favorable candidate to the throne. Notorious examples of problem rulers included Süleyman's successor Selim the Sot (reigned 1566–1574) and Ibrahim the Crazy (reigned 1640–1648), who taxed and spent to such excess that government officials deposed and murdered him. Several energetic rulers and talented ministers attempted to keep the government on track. Nonetheless, after the late seventeenth century, weak rule increasingly provoked mutinies in the army, provincial revolts, political corruption, economic oppression, and insecurity throughout the Ottoman realm.

Religious Tensions Political troubles often arose from religious tensions. Conservative Muslim clerics strongly objected to policies and practices that they considered affronts to Islam. Muslim leaders had considerable influence in the Islamic empires because of their monopoly of education and their deep involvement in the everyday lives and legal affairs of ordinary subjects. The clerics mistrusted the emperors' interests in unconventional forms of Islam such as Sufism, complained bitterly when women or subjects who were not Muslims played influential political roles, and protested any exercise of royal authority that contradicted Islamic law.

In the Ottoman empire, disaffected religious students often joined the Janissaries in revolt. A particularly serious threat came from the Wahhabi movement in Arabia, which denounced the Ottomans as dangerous religious innovators who were unfit to rule. Conservative Muslims fiercely protested the construction of an astronomical observatory in Istanbul and forced the sultan to demolish it in 1580. In 1742 they also forced the closure of the Ottoman printing press, which they regarded as an impious technology.

The Safavids, who began their reign by crushing Sunni religious authorities, fell under the domination of the very Shiites they had supported. Shiite leaders pressured the shahs to persecute Sunnis, non-Muslims, and even the Sufis who had helped establish the dynasty. Religious tensions also afflicted Mughal India. Already in the seventeenth century, the conservative Shaykh Ahmad Sirhindi (1564–1624) fearlessly rebuked Akbar for his policy of religious tolerance and his interest in other faiths. In the mid-eighteenth century, as he struggled to claim the Mughal throne, Aurangzeb drew on Sirhindi's ideas when he required non-Muslims to pay the poll tax and ordered the destruction of Hindu temples. Those measures inflamed tensions between the various Sunni, Shiite, and Sufi branches of Islam and also fueled animosity among Hindus and other Mughal subjects who were not Muslims.

Economic and Military Decline

In the sixteenth century, all the Islamic empires had strong domestic economies and played prominent roles in global trade networks. By the eighteenth century, however, domestic economies were under great stress, and foreign trade had declined dramatically or had fallen under the control of European powers. The Islamic empires were well on their way to becoming marginal lands that depended on goods produced elsewhere.

Economic Difficulties The high cost of maintaining an expensive military and administrative apparatus helped

All the Islamic empires fought numerous wars, many of which exhausted resources without adding to the productive capacities of the empires. This illustration depicts Ottoman forces (right) clashing with heavily armored Austrian cavalry near Budapest in 1540.

to bring about economic decline in the Islamic empires. As long as the empires were expanding, they were able to finance their armies and bureaucracies with fresh resources extracted from newly conquered lands. When expansion slowed, ceased, or reversed, however, they faced the problem of supporting their institutions with limited resources. The long, costly, and unproductive wars fought by the Ottomans with the Habsburgs in central Europe, by the Safavids and the Ottomans in Mesopotamia, and by Aurangzeb in southern India, exhausted the treasuries of the Islamic empires without making fresh resources available to them. As early as 1589 the Ottomans tried to pay the Janissaries in debased coinage and immediately provoked a mutiny. The next 150 years witnessed at least six additional military revolts.

As expansion slowed and the empires lost control over remote provinces, officials reacted to the loss of revenue by raising taxes, selling public offices, accepting bribes, or resorting to simple extortion. All those measures were counterproductive. Although they might provide immediate cash, they did long-term economic damage. To make matters worse, the governments viewed foreign trade as just another opportunity to bring in revenue. The Ottomans expanded the privileges enjoyed by foreign merchants, and the Mughals encouraged the establishment of Dutch and English trading outposts and welcomed the expansion of their business in India. Imperial authorities were content to have foreign traders come to them. None made serious efforts to establish commercial stations abroad, although Indian merchants organized their own private trading companies.

Military Decline As they lost initiative to western European peoples in economic and commercial affairs, the Islamic empires also experienced military decline because they did not seek actively to improve their military technologies. As early as the fifteenth century, the Ottomans had relied heavily on European technology in gunnery; indeed, the cannon that Mehmed the Conqueror used in 1453 to breach the defensive wall of Constantinople was the product of a Hungarian gun-founder. During the sixteenth and early seventeenth centuries, the Islamic empires

were able to purchase European weapons in large numbers and attract European expertise that kept their armies supplied with powerful gunpowder weapons. In 1605, for example, the cargo of an English ship bound for Anatolia included seven hundred barrels of gunpowder, one thousand musket barrels, five hundred fully assembled muskets, and two thousand sword blades, alongside wool textiles and bullion.

By about the mid-seventeenth century, European military technology was advancing so rapidly that the Islamic empires could not keep pace. None of the empires had a large armaments industry, so they had to rely on foreign suppliers. They still were able to purchase European weapons and expertise, but their arsenals became increasingly dated, since they depended on technologies that European peoples had already replaced. By the late eighteenth century, the Ottoman navy, which had long influenced maritime affairs in the Mediterranean, Red Sea, Persian Gulf, and Arabian Sea, was closing its shipbuilding operations and ordering new military vessels from foreign shipyards.

Cultural Conservatism

While experiencing economic and military decline, the Islamic empires also neglected cultural developments in the larger world. Europeans who visited the Islamic empires attempted to learn as much as possible about the language, religion, social customs, and history of the host countries. They published accounts of their travels that became extremely popular in their homelands, and they advocated serious study of Islamic lands. In the early seventeenth century, for example, the English scholar William Bedwell described Arabic as the only important language of trade, diplomacy, and religion from Morocco to the China seas.

Piri Reis To some extent, information also flowed in the other direction. During the sixteenth century, just as European mariners were scouting Atlantic waters, Ottoman mariners reconnoitered the Indian Ocean basin from east Africa to Indonesia—a project that reflected military concerns about European and other naval forces in the region. Ottoman geographers also manifested great interest in European

Ottoman cartographer Piri Reis drew on European charts when preparing this map of the Atlantic Ocean basin in 1513. Caribbean and South American coastlines are visible at left, while Iberian and west African coastlines appear in the upper right corner.

thinking about ENCOUNTERS

Islamic Mapmaking

Muslims evinced a generalized wariness about knowledge deriving from European contacts. One notable exception to this was Piri Reis, an Ottoman cartographer. Why did he draw on European sources for his maps? Why were maps seen as so strategically useful in an age of cross-cultural contacts?

knowledge of geography, some of which had considerable military value. The Ottoman admiral and cartographer Piri Reis produced several large-scale maps and a major navigational text, the *Book of Seafaring,* which drew on reports and maps from European mariners and explorers. Piri Reis even managed to consult a copy of a chart drawn by Christopher Columbus during his first voyage to the western hemisphere. Some of Piri Reis's maps included the Atlantic coast of North America and the lands visited by Columbus, which the cartographer probably learned about from Spanish sailors captured in naval conflicts with Ottoman forces.

Cultural Confidence Yet few Muslims traveled willingly to the infidel lands of "the Franks." Muslim rulers and their Muslim subjects were confident of their superiority and believed that they had nothing to learn from Europeans. As a result, most Muslims remained largely oblivious to European cultural and technological developments. Not until 1703 was there an attempt to introduce European scientific instruments such as the telescope into astronomical observatories. Then conservative Muslim clerics soon forced the removal of the foreign implements, which they considered impious and unnecessary.

The Printing Press The early experience of the printing press in the Islamic empires illustrates especially well the resistance of conservative religious leaders to cultural imports from western Europe. Jewish refugees from Spain introduced the first printing presses to Anatolia in the late fifteenth century. Ottoman authorities allowed them to operate presses in Istanbul and other major cities as long as they did not print books in the Turkish or Arabic language. Armenian and Greek printers soon established presses in the Ottoman realm and published books in their own languages. Not until 1729 did government authorities lift the ban on the printing of books in the Turkish and Arabic languages. During the next thirteen years, a Turkish press published seventeen books dealing mostly with history, geography, and language before conservative Muslims forced its closure in 1742. Only in 1784 did a new Turkish press open, and printing spread throughout the Ottoman empire soon thereafter.

Printing also caught on slowly in Mughal India. Jesuit missionaries in Goa published books, including translations of the Bible into Indian and Arabic languages, as early as the 1550s. Yet Mughal rulers displayed little interest in the press, and printing did not become prominent in Indian society until the establishment of British colonial rule in Bengal in the eighteenth century.

To some extent, aesthetic considerations stood in the way of the printing press: particularly in the Ottoman and Safavid empires, as in many other Muslim lands, scholars and general readers alike simply preferred elegant handwritten books to cheaply produced printed works, especially when the book in question was the Quran. Yet resistance to printing also reflected the concerns of conservative religious leaders that readily available printed books would introduce all manner of new and dangerous ideas to the public—indeed, that an active publishing industry might spread inconvenient questions about the organization of Muslim societies or even about the Islamic faith itself.

Thus, like imperial China and Tokugawa Japan, the Islamic empires resisted the introduction of cultural influences from western European societies. Rulers of the Islamic empires readily accepted gunpowder weapons as enhancements to their military and political power, but they and their subjects drew little inspiration from European religion, science, or ideas. Moreover, under the influence of conservative religious leaders, Islamic authorities actively discouraged the circulation of ideas that might pose unsettling challenges to the social and cultural order of the Islamic empires. Like the Ming, Qing, and Tokugawa rulers, the Ottoman, Safavid, and Mughal emperors preferred political and social stability to the risks that foreign cultural innovations might bring.

in perspective

Like China and Japan, the Islamic empires largely retained control of their own affairs throughout the early modern era. Ruling elites of the Ottoman, Safavid, and Mughal empires came from nomadic Turkish stock, and they all drew on steppe traditions in organizing their governments. But the rulers also adapted steppe traditions to the needs of settled agricultural societies and devised institutions that maintained order over a long term. During the sixteenth and seventeenth centuries, all the Islamic empires enjoyed productive economies that enabled merchants to participate actively in the global trade networks of early modern times. By the early eighteenth century, however, these same empires were experiencing economic difficulties that led to political and military decline. Like the Ming, Qing, and Tokugawa rulers in east Asia, the Islamic emperors mostly sought to limit foreign and especially European influences in their realms. The Islamic emperors ruled lands that were religiously and ethnically diverse, and most of them worried that the expansion of foreign religious and cultural traditions would threaten political and social stability. They allowed their subjects to practice faiths other than Islam, and the Mughal emperor Akbar even promoted a syncretic religion in hopes that it would defuse tensions between Hindus and Muslims. For the most part, however, rulers of the Islamic empires followed the advice of conservative Muslim clerics, who promoted Islamic values and fought the introduction of foreign cultural imports, such as the printing press and European science, that might undermine their authority. By the late eighteenth century, the Safavid empire had collapsed, and economic difficulties and cultural insularity had severely weakened the Ottoman and Mughal empires. ●

CHRONOLOGY	
1289–1923	Ottoman dynasty
1451–1481	Reign of Mehmed the Conqueror
1453	Ottoman conquest of Constantinople
1501–1524	Reign of Shah Ismail
1501–1722	Safavid dynasty
1514	Battle of Chaldiran
1520–1566	Reign of Süleyman the Magnificent
1526–1858	Mughal dynasty
1556–1605	Reign of Akbar
1588–1629	Reign of Shah Abbas the Great
1659–1707	Reign of Aurangzeb

For Further Reading

Esin Atil. *The Age of Sultan Süleyman the Magnificent.* Washington, D.C., 1987. Richly illustrated volume that emphasizes Süleyman's role as a patron of the arts.

Franz Babinger. *Mehmed the Conqueror and His Time.* Trans. by R. Manheim. Princeton, 1978. A magisterial biography of the sultan who conquered Constantinople.

Jonathan P. Berkey. *The Formation of Islam: Religion and Society in the Near East, 600–1800.* New York, 2002. Broad survey of the history of Islam and Islamic civilization.

Stephen Frederic Dale. *Indian Merchants and Eurasian Trade, 1600–1750.* Cambridge, 1994. Examines the workings of an Indian trading community that conducted business in Persia, central Asia, and Russia.

Suraiya Faroghi. *Towns and Townsmen of Ottoman Anatolia.* Cambridge, 1989. A valuable contribution to an understanding of the Ottoman domestic economy.

Carter Vaughn Findley. *The Turks in World History.* New York, 2005. A highly readable account that connects the two-thousand-year history of the Turkic peoples with larger global processes.

Dina Le Gall. *A Culture of Sufism: Naqshbandis in the Ottoman World, 1450–1700.* Albany, N.Y., 2005. Study of the cultural practices and religious beliefs of an important Sufi brotherhood.

Halil Inalçik. *The Ottoman Empire: The Classical Age, 1300–1600.* New York, 1973. A reliable survey by the foremost historian of the early Ottoman empire.

——— and Donald Quataert, eds. *An Economic and Social History of the Ottoman Empire, 1300–1914.* Cambridge, 1994. An exhaustive survey of Ottoman economic history.

Çemal Kafadar. *Between Two Worlds: The Construction of the Ottoman State.* Berkeley, 1995. Studies the origins and early development of the Ottoman empire.

Kemal H. Karpat. *The Politicization of Islam: Reconstructing Identity, State, Faith, and Community in the Late Ottoman State.* New York, 2001. Scholarly study of the Ottoman state's role in constructing Muslim identity.

Bernard Lewis. *The Muslim Discovery of Europe.* New York, 1982. An important study that charts Muslim interest in European affairs.

Bruce Masters. *The Origins of Western Economic Dominance in the Middle East: Mercantilism and the Islamic Economy in Aleppo, 1600–1750.* New York, 1988. A stimulating case study of an important trading city caught between a central government in chaos and European mercantile pressure.

David Morgan. *Medieval Persia, 1040–1797.* London, 1988. A brief and insightful survey that examines Persian history through the Safavid dynasty.

Leslie Pierce. *The Imperial Harem: Women and Sovereignty in the Ottoman Empire.* Oxford, 1993. Challenges many stereotypes about the role of women in the imperial Ottoman elite.

Gabriel Piterberg. *An Ottoman Tragedy: History and Historiography at Play.* Berkeley, 2003. Analysis of the Ottoman empire in the seventeenth century that also examines the evolution of Ottoman historiography.

John F. Richards. *The Mughal Empire.* Cambridge, 1993. A concise and reliable overview of Mughal history, concentrating on political affairs.

Roger Savory. *Iran under the Safavids.* Cambridge, 1980. A rich and authoritative survey of Safavid history, especially interesting for its views on Safavid origins, culture, and commercial relations.

Madeline Zilfi. *The Politics of Piety: The Ottoman Ulema in the Postclassical Age, 1600–1800.* Minneapolis, 1988. Examines the influence and changing role of the Ottoman religious leadership.

State of the World
Changing Views of the World, Changing Worldviews

Whether signaled by a young Mexican woman serving as an interpreter for Spanish conquerors or by the sounds of chiming clocks in China, novel cross-cultural experiences—on both an intimately human and a coldly technological level—symbolized the intense global transformations taking place in the early modern world. One of the most stunning alterations after 1500 involved the very way humans could now envision a world so perilously and profitably interconnected. Mariners and voyagers from as far afield as east Asia, the Ottoman empire, and western Europe charted the vast expanses of the world's oceans and opened up new human vistas on a world where two previously isolated hemispheres coexisted in an ever-tightening web of global interaction. Detailed maps of the Americas, Oceania, the Indian Ocean basin, and western Africa added to the world's cartographic knowledge and stood as two-dimensional emblems of this changed view of the world—and of the changed worldviews impelled by that new world understanding.

Few societies could withstand the impulses of change emanating from this new, globally intertwined world. Western Europeans in the vanguard of global voyaging in the early modern era consolidated their global influence by establishing empires and settler colonies in the Americas and by setting off a complex process of voluntary and forced human migrations that changed both the world and the worldviews of those involved. Indigenous Americans and Pacific Islanders suffered mass die-offs from epidemics and the consequent dimming of their strength, while the African slaves who replaced them as laborers likewise had their worldviews rudely adjusted during their forced migrations through the Atlantic Ocean basin. And, as the far-flung travels of Thomas Peters suggested, Africans experienced exposure to a complex mixture of worldviews shaped by indigenous African, American, and European ideologies. In this early modern era of interconnectedness, worldviews took on an increasingly cross-cultural cast.

The imperative to change in this era had both external global and internal cultural elements. This was nowhere more evident than in western European societies, where intercontinental outreach was matched by an internal questioning of traditions, whether religious, intellectual, or political. In the age of revolution after 1750, the external and internal pulses of change in Europe would collide and provide it with even more explosive global power. The prosperous societies in the early modern era, such as China, Japan, and the Islamic empires, succeeded in shielding their traditions and their worldviews from the intensifying impulses of change through much of this period. The chimes of those clocks in China, however, served as harbingers of a more deafening weapons technology that threatened imperial intrusion and the further altering of worldviews.

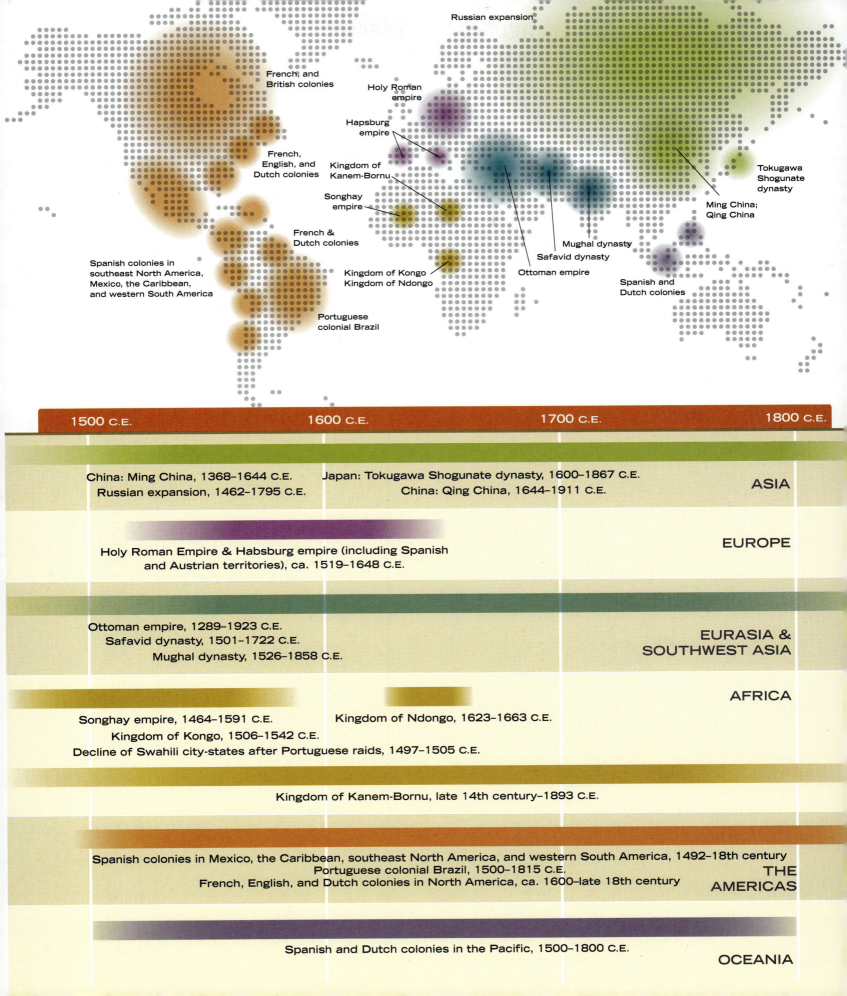

French, and
British colonies

Holy Roman
empire

Hapsburg
empire

Kingdom of
Kanem-Bornu

Songhay
empire

French,
English, and
Dutch colonies

Russian expansion

Tokugawa
Shogunate
dynasty

Ming China;
Qing China

French &
Dutch colonies

Spanish colonies in
southeast North America,
Mexico, the Caribbean,
and western South America

Kingdom of Kongo
Kingdom of Ndongo

Mughal dynasty

Safavid dynasty

Ottoman empire

Spanish and
Dutch colonies

Portuguese
colonial Brazil

| 1500 C.E. | 1600 C.E. | 1700 C.E. | 1800 C.E. |

ASIA

China: Ming China, 1368–1644 C.E.
Russian expansion, 1462–1795 C.E.

Japan: Tokugawa Shogunate dynasty, 1600–1867 C.E.
China: Qing China, 1644–1911 C.E.

EUROPE

Holy Roman Empire & Habsburg empire (including Spanish
and Austrian territories), ca. 1519–1648 C.E.

**EURASIA &
SOUTHWEST ASIA**

Ottoman empire, 1289–1923 C.E.
Safavid dynasty, 1501–1722 C.E.
Mughal dynasty, 1526–1858 C.E.

AFRICA

Songhay empire, 1464–1591 C.E.
Kingdom of Kongo, 1506–1542 C.E.
Decline of Swahili city-states after Portuguese raids, 1497–1505 C.E.

Kingdom of Ndongo, 1623–1663 C.E.

Kingdom of Kanem-Bornu, late 14th century–1893 C.E.

**THE
AMERICAS**

Spanish colonies in Mexico, the Caribbean, southeast North America, and western South America, 1492–18th century
Portuguese colonial Brazil, 1500–1815 C.E.
French, English, and Dutch colonies in North America, ca. 1600–late 18th century

OCEANIA

Spanish and Dutch colonies in the Pacific, 1500–1800 C.E.

glossary & pronunciation key

AH *a* sound, as in *car, father*
IH short *i* sound, as in *fit, his, mirror*
OO long *o* sound, as in *ooze, tool, crew*
UH short *u* sound, as in *up, cut, color*
A short *a* sound, as in *asp, fat, parrot*
EE long *e* sound, as in *even, meet, money*
OH long *o* sound, as in *open, go, tone*
EH short *e* sound, as in *ten, elf, berry*
AY long *a* sound, as in *ape, date, play*
EYE long *i* sound, as in *ice, high, bite*
OW diphthong *o* sound, as in *cow, how, bow*
AW diphthong *a* sound, as in *awful, paw, law*

Note on emphasis: Syllables in capital letters receive the accent. If there is no syllable in capitals, then all syllables get equal accent.

Abbasid (ah-BAH-sihd) Cosmopolitan Arabic dynasty (750–1258) that replaced the Umayyads; founded by Abu al-Abbas and reached its peak under Harun al-Rashid.

Abolitionism Antislavery movement.

Absolutism Political philosophy that stressed the divine right theory of kingship: the French king Louis XIV was the classic example.

Abu Bakr (ah-BOO BAHK-uhr) First caliph after the death of Muhammad.

Achaemenid empire (ah-KEE-muh-nid) First great Persian empire (558–330 B.C.E.), which began under Cyrus and reached its peak under Darius.

Aeschylus (ES-kuh-luhs) Greek tragedian, author of the *Oresteia*.

Age grades Bantu institution in which individuals of roughly the same age carried out communal tasks appropriate for that age.

Ahimsa (uh-HIM-suh) Jain term for the principle of nonviolence to other living things or their souls.

Ahura Mazda (uh-HOORE-uh MAHZ-duh) Main god of Zoroastrianism who represented truth and goodness and was perceived to be in an eternal struggle with the malign spirit Angra Mainyu.

Al-Andalus (al-ANN-duh-luhs) Islamic Spain.

Ali'i nui Hawaiian class of high chiefs.

Allah (AH-lah) God of the monotheistic religion of Islam.

Amon-Re (AH-muhn RAY) Egyptian god, combination of the sun god Re and the air god Amon.

Angkor (AHN-kohr) Southeast Asian Khmer kingdom (889–1432) that was centered on the temple cities of Angkor Thom and Angkor Wat.

Anti-Semitism Term coined in the late nineteenth century that was associated with a prejudice against Jews and the political, social, and economic actions taken against them.

Antonianism African syncretic religion, founded by Dona Beatriz, that taught that Jesus Christ was a black African man and that heaven was for Africans.

Apartheid (ah-PAHR-teyed) South African system of "separateness" that was implemented in 1948 and that maintained the black majority in a position of political, social, and economic subordination.

Appeasement British and French policy in the 1930s that tried to maintain peace in Europe in the face of German aggression by making concessions.

Arianism Early Christian heresy that centered on teaching of Arius (250–336 C.E.) and contained the belief that Jesus was a mortal human being and not coeternal with God; Arianism was the focus of Council of Nicaea.

Artha Hindu concept for the pursuit of economic well-being and honest prosperity.

Arthashastra (AR-thah-sha-strah) Ancient Indian political treatise from the time of Chandragupta Maurya; its authorship was traditionally ascribed to Kautalya, and it stressed that war was inevitable.

Aryans (AIR-ee-anns) Indo-European migrants who settled in India after 1500 B.C.E.; their union with indigenous Dravidians formed the basis of Hinduism.

Association of Southeast Asian Nations (ASEAN.) Regional organization established in 1967 by Thailand, Malaysia, Singapore, Indonesia, and the Philippines; the organization was designed to promote economic progress and political stability; it later became a free-trade zone.

Assyrians (uh-SEAR-ee-uhns) Southwest Asian people who built an empire that reached its height during the eighth and seventh centuries B.C.E.; it was known for a powerful army and a well-structured state.

Astrolabe Navigational instrument for determining latitude.

Aten Monotheistic god of Egyptian pharaoh Akhenaten (r. 1353–1335 B.C.E.) and a very early example of monotheism.

Audiencias Spanish courts in Latin America.

Australopithecus (ah-strah-loh-PITH-uh-kuhs) "Southern ape," oldest known ancestor of humans; it lived from around four million down to around one million years ago, and it could walk on hind legs, freeing up hands for use of simple tools.

Austronesians People who as early as 2000 B.C.E. began to explore and settle islands of the Pacific Ocean basin.

Avesta Book that contains the holy writings of Zoroastrianism.

Axum African kingdom centered in Ethiopia that became an early and lasting center of Coptic Christianity.

Aztec empire Central American empire constructed by the Mexica and expanded greatly during the fifteenth century during the reigns of Itzcoatl and Motecuzoma I.

Balfour Declaration British declaration from 1917 that supported the creation of a Jewish homeland in Palestine.

Bantu (BAN-too) African peoples who originally lived in the area of present-day Nigeria; around 2000 B.C.E. they began a centuries-long migration that took them to most of sub-Saharan Africa; the Bantu were very influential, especially linguistically.

Bedouins (BEHD-oh-ihnz) Nomadic Arabic tribespeople.

Benefice Grant from a lord to a vassal, usually consisting of land, which supported the vassal and signified the relationship between the two.

Berlin Conference Meeting organized by German chancellor Otto von Bismarck in 1884–1885 that provided the justification for European colonization of Africa.

Bezant Byzantine gold coin that served as the standard currency of the Mediterranean basin from the sixth through the twelfth century.

Bhagavad Gita (BUH-guh-vahd GEE-tuh) "Song of the Lord," an Indian short poetic work drawn from the lengthy *Mahabharata* that was finished around 400 C.E. and that expressed basic Hindu concepts such as karma and dharma.

Bhakti (BAHK-tee) Indian movement that attempted to transcend the differences between Hinduism and Islam.

Black Hand Pre–World War I secret Serbian society; one of its members, Gavrilo Princip, assassinated Austrian archduke Francis Ferdinand and provided the spark for the outbreak of the Great War.

Blitzkrieg German style of rapid attack through the use of armor and air power that was used in Poland, Norway, Denmark, Belgium, the Netherlands, and France in 1939–1940.

Bodhisattvas (BOH-dih-SAT-vuhs) Buddhist concept regarding individuals who had reached enlightenment but who stayed in this world to help people.

Bolshevik (BOHL-shih-vehk) Russian communist party headed by Lenin.

Bourgeoisie Middle class in modern industrial society.

Brahmins (BRAH-minz) Hindu caste of priests.

Brezhnev Doctrine Policy developed by Leonid Brezhnev (1906–1982) that claimed for the Soviet Union the right to invade any socialist country faced with internal or external enemies; the doc-trine was best expressed in Soviet invasion of Czechoslovakia.

Buddha (BOO-duh) The "enlightened one," the term applied to Siddhartha Gautama after his discoveries that would form the foundation of Buddhism.

Buddhism (BOO-diz'm) Religion, based on Four Noble Truths, associated with Siddhartha Gautama (563–483 B.C.E.), or the Buddha; its adherents desired to eliminate all distracting passion and reach nirvana.

Bunraku (boon-RAH-koo) Japanese puppet theater.

Byzantine Empire (BIHZ-ann-teen) Long-lasting empire centered at Constantinople; it grew out of the end of the Roman empire, carried the legacy of Roman greatness, and was the only classical society to survive into the early modern age; it reached its early peak during the reign of Justinian (483–565).

Caesaropapism Concept relating to the mixing of political and religious authority, as with the Roman emperors, that was central to the church-versus-state controversy in medieval Europe.

Cahokia (kuh-HOH-kee-uh) Large structure in modern Illinois that was constructed by the mound-building peoples; it was the third largest structure in the Americas before the arrival of the Europeans.

Caliph (KAL-ihf) "Deputy," Islamic leader after the death of Muhammad.

Capetian (cah-PEE-shuhn) Early French dynasty that started with Hugh Capet.

Capitalism An economic system with origins in early modern Europe in which private parties make their goods and services available on a free market.

Capitulation Highly unfavorable trading agreements that the Ottoman Turks signed with the Europeans in the nineteenth century that symbolized the decline of the Ottomans.

Carolingians Germanic dynasty that was named after its most famous member, Charlemagne.

Carthage Northern African kingdom, main rival to early Roman expansion, that was defeated by Rome in the Punic Wars.

Çatal Hüyük Important Neolithic settlement in Anatolia (7250–6150 B.C.E.).

Cathars Medieval heretics, also known as the Albigensians, who considered the material world evil; their followers renounced wealth and marriage and promoted an ascetic existence.

Catholic Reformation Sixteenth-century Catholic attempt to cure internal ills and confront Protestantism; it was inspired by the reforms of the Council of Trent and the actions of the Jesuits.

Caudillos (KAW-dee-ohs) Latin American term for nineteenth-century local military leaders.

Central Powers World War I term for the alliance of Germany, Austria-Hungary, and the Ottoman empire.

Chaghatai One of Chinggis Khan's sons, whose descendants ruled central Asia through the Chaghatai khanate.

Chan Buddhism (CHAHN BOO-diz'm) Influential branch of Buddhism in China, with an emphasis on intuition and sudden flashes of insight instead of textual study.

Chanchan (chahn-chahn) Capital of the pre-Incan, South American Chimu society that supported a large population of fifty thousand.

Chavín cult Mysterious but very popular South American religion (1000–300 B.C.E.).

Chimu Pre-Incan South American society that fell to Incas in the fifteenth century.

Chinampas Agricultural gardens used by Mexica (Aztecs) in which fertile muck from lake bottoms was dredged and built up into small plots.

Chivalry European medieval code of conduct for knights based on loyalty and honor.

Chola Southern Indian Hindu kingdom (850–1267), a tightly centralized state that dominated sea trade.

Chucuito Pre-Incan South American society that rose in the twelfth century and fell to the Incas in the fifteenth century.

City-state Urban areas that controlled surrounding agricultural regions and that were often loosely connected in a broader political structure with other city-states.

Cohong Specially licensed Chinese firms that were under strict government regulation.

Collectivization Process beginning in the late 1920s by which Stalin forced the Russian peasants off their own land and onto huge collective farms run by the state; millions died in the process.

COMECON The Council for Mutual Economic Assistance, which offered increased trade within the Soviet Union and eastern Europe; it was the Soviet alternative to the United States' Marshall Plan.

Communalism A term, usually associated with India, that placed an emphasis on religious rather than national identity.

Communism Philosophy and movement that began in middle of the nineteenth century with the work of Karl Marx; it has the same general goals as socialism, but it includes the belief that violent revolution is necessary to destroy the bourgeois world and institute a new world run by and for the proletariat.

Confucianism (kuhn-FYOO-shuhn-iz'm) Philosophy, based on the teachings of the Chinese philosopher Kong Fuzi (551–479 B.C.E.), or Confucius, that emphasizes order, the role of the gentleman, obligation to society, and reciprocity.

Congress of Vienna Gathering of European diplomats in Vienna, Austria, from October 1814 to June 1815. The representatives of the "great powers" that defeated Napoleon—Britain, Austria, Prussia, and Russia—dominated the proceedings, which aimed to restore the prerevolutionary political and social order.

Conquistadores (kohn-KEE-stah-dohr-ayz) Spanish adventurers such as Cortés and Pizarro who conquered Central and South America in the sixteenth century.

Constitutionalism Movement in England in the seventeenth century that placed power in Parliament's hands as part of a constitutional monarchy and that increasingly limited the power of the monarch; the movement was highlighted by the English Civil War and the Glorious Revolution.

Containment Concept associated with the United States and specifically with the Truman Doctrine during the cold war that revolved around the notion that the United States would contain the spread of communism.

Corporation A concept that reached mature form in 1860s in England and France; it involved private business owned by thousands of individual and institutional investors who financed the business through the purchase of stocks.

Corpus iuris civilis (KOR-puhs yoor-uhs sih-VEE-lihs) *Body of the Civil Law,* the Byzantine emperor Justinian's attempt to codify all Roman law.

Criollos (kree-OH-lohs) Creoles, people born in the Americas of Spanish or Portuguese ancestry.

Cross staff Device that sailors used to determine latitude by measuring the angle of the sun or the pole star above the horizon.

Cuneiform Written language of the Sumerians, probably the first written script in the world.

Daimyo (DEYEM-yoh) Powerful territorial lords in early modern Japan.

Dao Key element in Chinese philosophy that means the "way of nature" or the "way of the cosmos."

Daodejing (DOW-DAY-JIHNG) Book that is the fundamental work of Daoism.

Daoism (DOW-i'zm) Chinese philosophy with origins in the Zhou dynasty; it is associated with legendary philosopher Laozi, and it called for a policy of noncompetition.

Dar al-Islam The "house of Islam," a term for the Islamic world.

Declaration of Independence Drafted by Thomas Jefferson in 1776; the document expressed the ideas of John Locke and the Enlightenment, represented the idealism of the American rebels, and influenced other revolutions.

Declaration of the Rights of Man and the Citizen Document from the French Revolution (1789) that was influenced by the American Declaration of Independence and in turn influenced other revolutionary movements.

Decolonization Process by which former colonies achieved their independence, as with the newly emerging African nations in the 1950s and 1960s.

Deism (DEE-iz'm) An Enlightenment view that accepted the existence of a god but denied the supernatural aspects of Christianity; in deism, the universe was an orderly realm maintained by rational and natural laws.

Descamisados "Shirtless ones," Argentine poor who supported Juan and Eva Perón.

Détente A reduction in cold war tension between the United States and the Soviet Union from 1969 to 1975.

Devshirme Ottoman requirement that the Christians in the Balkans provide young boys to be slaves of the sultan.

Dharma (DAHR-muh) Hindu concept of obedience to religious and moral laws and order; also, the basic doctrine of Buddhism.

Dhimmi (dihm-mee) Islamic concept of a protected people that was symbolic of Islamic toleration during the Mughal and Ottoman empires.

Dhow Indian, Persian, and Arab ships, one hundred to four hundred tons, that sailed and traded throughout the Indian Ocean basin.

Diaspora People who have settled far from their original homeland but who still share some measure of ethnic identity.

Dionysus Greek god of wine, also known as Bacchus; Greek plays were performed in his honor.

Dravidians Peoples who produced the brilliant Harappan society in India, 3000–1500 B.C.E.

Dreadnoughts A class of British battleships whose heavy armaments made all other battleships obsolete overnight.

Duma Russian parliament, established after the Revolution of 1905.

Dutch learning European knowledge that reached Tokugawa Japan.

East India Company British joint-stock company that grew to be a state within a state in India; it possessed its own armed forces.

Eight-legged essay Eight-part essays that an aspiring Chinese civil servant had to compose, mainly based on a knowledge of Confucius and the Zhou classics.

Encomienda (ehn-KOH-mee-ehn-dah) System that gave the Spanish settlers *(encomenderos)* the right to compel the indigenous peoples of the Americas to work in the mines or fields.

Engenho Brazilian sugar mill; the term also came to symbolize the entire complex world relating to the production of sugar.

Enlightenment Eighteenth-century philosophical movement that began in France; its emphasis was on the preeminence of reason rather than faith or tradition; it spread concepts from the Scientific Revolution.

Epicureans (ehp-ih-kyoo-REE-uhns) Hellenistic philosophers who taught that pleasure—as in quiet satisfaction—was the greatest good.

Equal-field system Chinese system during the Tang dynasty in which the goal was to ensure an equitable distribution of land.

Essenes Jewish sect that looked for the arrival of a savior; they were similar in some of their core beliefs to the early Christians.

Etruscans (ih-TRUHS-kuhns) Northern Italian society that initially dominated the Romans; the Etruscans helped convey Greek concepts to the expanding Romans.

Eunuchs (YOO-nihks) Castrated males, originally in charge of the harem, who grew to play major roles in government; eunuchs were common in China and other societies.

European Community (EC) Organization of European states established in 1957; it was originally called the European Economic Community and was renamed the EC in 1967; it promoted economic growth and integration as the basis for a politically united Europe.

European Union Established by the Maastricht Treaty in 1993, a supranational organization for even greater European economic and political integration.

Fascism Political ideology and mass movement that was prominent in many parts of Europe between 1919 and 1945; it sought to regenerate the social, political, and cultural life of societies, especially in contrast to liberal democracy and socialism; fascism began with Mussolini in Italy, and it reached its peak with Hitler in Germany.

Five Pillars The foundation of Islam: (1) profession of faith, (2) prayer, (3) fasting during Ramadan, (4) almsgiving, and (5) pilgrimage, or hajj.

Five-year plans First implemented by Stalin in the Soviet Union in 1928; five-year plans were a staple of communist regimes in which every aspect of production was determined in advance for a five-year period; five-year plans were opposite of the free market concept.

Four Noble Truths The foundation of Buddhist thought: (1) life is pain, (2) pain is caused by desire, (3) elimination of desire will bring an end to pain, (4) living a life based on the Noble Eightfold Path will eliminate desire.

Front de Libération Nationale (FLN) The Algerian organization that fought a bloody guerrilla war for freedom against France.

Fulani (foo-LAH-nee) Sub-Saharan African people who, beginning in the seventeenth century, waged a series of wars designed to impose their own strict interpretation of Islam.

Gathas (GATH-uhs) Zoroastrian hymns believed to be compositions by Zarathustra.

Gauchos (GOW-chohz) Argentine cowboys, highly romanticized figures.

General Agreement on Tariffs and Trade (GATT) Free-trade agreement first signed in 1947; by 1994 it had grown to 123 members and formed the World Trade Organization (WTO).

Ghana (GAH-nuh) Kingdom in west Africa during the fifth through the thirteenth century whose rulers eventually converted to Islam; its power and wealth was based on dominating trans-Saharan trade.

Ghazi (GAH-zee) Islamic religious warrior.

Ghaznavids Turkish tribe under Mahmud of Ghazni who moved into northern India in the eleventh century and began a period of greater Islamic influence in India.

Gilgamesh Legendary king of the Mesopotamian city-state of Uruk (ca. 3000 B.C.E.), subject of the *Epic of Gilgamesh*, world's oldest complete epic literary masterpiece.

Glasnost (GLAHS-nohst) Russian term meaning "openness" introduced by Mikhail Gorbachev in 1985 to describe the process of opening Soviet society to dissidents and public criticism.

Globalization The breaking down of traditional boundaries in the face of increasingly global financial and cultural trends.

Global warming The emission of greenhouse gases, which prevents solar heat from escaping the earth's atmosphere and leads to the gradual heating of the earth's environment.

Golden Horde Mongol tribe that controlled Russia from the thirteenth to the fifteenth century.

Greater East Asia Co-Prosperity Sphere Japanese plan for consolidating east and southeast Asia under their control during World War II.

Great Game Nineteenth-century competition between Great Britain and Russia for the control of central Asia.

Great Zimbabwe Large sub-Saharan African kingdom in the fifteenth century.

Greenpeace An environmental organization founded in 1970 and dedicated to the preservation of earth's natural resources.

Guomindang (GWOH-mihn-dahng) Chinese nationalist party founded by Sun Yatsen (1866–1925) and later led by Jiang Jieshi; it has been centered in Taiwan since the end of the Chinese civil war.

Gupta (GOOP-tah) Indian dynasty (320–550 C.E.) that briefly reunited India after the collapse of the earlier Mauryan dynasty.

Hacienda (HAH-see-ehn-dah) Large Latin American estates.

Hagia Sophia (HAH-yah SOH-fee-uh) Massive Christian church constructed by the Byzantine emperor Justinian and later converted into a mosque.

Hajj (HAHJ) Pilgrimage to Mecca.

Hammurabi's Code (hahm-uh-RAH-beez) Sophisticated law code associated with the Babylonian king Hammurabi (r. 1792–1750 B.C.E.).

Harappan (hah-RAP-puhn) Early brilliant Indian society centered in Harappa and Mohenjo-daro.

Harijans "Children of God," Gandhi's term for the Untouchables.

Hebrews Semitic-speaking nomadic tribe influential for monotheistic belief in Yahweh.

Heian (HAY-ahn) Japanese period (794–1185), a brilliant cultural era notable for the world's first novel, Murasaki Shikibu's *The Tale of Genji*.

Hellenistic Era Phase in Greek history (328–146 B.C.E.), from the conquest of Greece by Philip of Macedon until Greece's fall to the Romans; this era was a more cosmopolitan age facilitated by the conquests of Alexander the Great.

Hieroglyphics (heye-ruh-GLIPH-iks) Ancient Egyptian written language.

Hijra Muhammad's migration from Mecca to Medina in 622, which is the beginning point of the Islamic calendar and is considered to mark the beginning of the Islamic faith.

Hinayana (HEE-nah-yah-nuh) Branch of Buddhism known as the "lesser vehicle," also known as Theravada Buddhism; its beliefs include strict, individual path to enlightenment, and it is popular in south and southeast Asia.

Hinduism Main religion of India, a combination of Dravidian and Aryan concepts; Hinduism's goal is to reach spiritual purity and union with the great world spirit; its important concepts include dharma, karma, and samsara.

Holocaust German attempt in World War II to exterminate the Jews of Europe.

Home front Term made popular in World War I and World War II for the civilian "front" that was symbolic of the greater demands of total war.

Hominid (HAWM-ih-nihd) A creature belonging to the family Hominidae, which includes human and humanlike species.

Homo erectus (HOH-MOH ee-REHK-tuhs) "Upright-walking human," which existed from two million to two hundred thousand years ago; *Homo erectus* used cleavers and hand axes and learned how to control fire.

Homo sapiens (HOH-MOH SAY-pee-uhns) "Consciously thinking human," which first appeared around two hundred fifty thousand years ago and used sophisticated tools.

Huitzilopochtli (wee-tsee-loh-pockt-lee) Sun god and patron deity of the Aztecs.

Hundred Days of Reform Chinese reforms of 1898 led by Kang Youwei and Liang Qichao in their desire to turn China into a modern industrial power.

Hyksos (HICK-sohs) Invaders who seized the Nile delta and helped bring an end to the Egyptian Middle Kingdom.

Iconoclasts (eye-KAHN-oh-klasts) Supporters of the movement, begun by the Byzantine Emperor Leo III (r. 717–741), to destroy religious icons because their veneration was considered sinful.

Ilkhanate (EEL-kahn-ate) Mongol state that ruled Persia after abolition of the Abbasid empire in the thirteenth century.

Imperialism Term associated with the expansion of European powers and their conquest and colonization of African and Asian societies, mainly from the sixteenth through the nineteenth century.

Inca empire Powerful South American empire that would reach its peak in the fifteenth century during the reigns of Pachacuti Inca and Topa Inca.

Indentured labor Labor source for plantations; wealthy planters would pay the laboring poor to sell a portion of their working lives, usually seven years, in exchange for passage.

Indo-Europeans Tribal groups from southern Russia who, over a period of millennia, embarked on a series of migrations from India through western Europe; their greatest legacy was the broad distribution of Indo-European languages throughout Eurasia.

Indra Early Indian god associated with the Aryans; Indra was the king of the gods and was associated with warfare and thunderbolts.

Intifada Palestinian mass movement against Israeli rule in the Gaza Strip and other occupied territories.

Investiture (ihn-VEHST-tih-tyoor) One aspect of the medieval European church-versus-state controversy, the granting of church offices by a lay leader.

Iroquois (EAR-uh-kwoi) Eastern American Indian confederation made up of the Mohawk, Oneida, Onondaga, Cayuga, and Seneca tribes.

Islam Monotheistic religion announced by the prophet Muhammad (570–632); influenced by Judaism and Christianity, Muhammad was considered the final prophet because the earlier religions had not seen the entire picture; the Quran is the holy book of Islam.

Jainism (JEYEN-iz'm) Indian religion associated with the teacher Vardhamana Mahavira (ca. 540–468 B.C.E.) in which every physical object possessed a soul; Jains believe in complete nonviolence to all living beings.

Jati Indian word for a Hindu subcaste.

Jizya (JIHZ-yuh) Tax in Islamic empires that was imposed on non-Muslims.

Joint-stock companies Early forerunner of the modern corporation; individuals who invested in a trading or exploring venture could make huge profits while limiting their risk.

Ka'ba (KAH-buh) Main shrine in Mecca, goal of Muslims embarking on the hajj.

Kabuki (kah-BOO-kee) Japanese theater in which actors were free to improvise and embellish the words.

Kama Hindu concept of the enjoyment of physical and sexual pleasure.

Kamikaze (KAH-mih-kah-zee) A Japanese term meaning "divine wind" that is related to the storms that destroyed Mongol invasion fleets; the term is symbolic of Japanese isolation and was later taken by suicide pilots in World War II.

Kanun (KAH-noon) Laws issued by the Ottoman Süleyman the Magnificent, also known as Süleyman Kanuni, "the Lawgiver."

Kapu Hawaiian concept of something being taboo.

Karma (KAHR-mah) Hindu concept that the sum of good and bad in a person's life will determine his or her status in the next life.

Khoikhoi South African people referred to pejoratively as the Hottentots by Europeans.

Kongo Central African state that began trading with the Portuguese around 1500; although their kings, such as King Affonso I (r. 1506–1543), converted to Christianity, they nevertheless suffered from the slave trade.

Koumbi-Saleh Important trading city along the trans-Saharan trade route from the eleventh to the thirteenth century.

Kshatriayas (KSHAHT-ree-uhs) Hindu caste of warriors and aristocrats.

Kulaks Land-owning Russian peasants who benefited under Lenin's New Economic Policy and suffered under Stalin's forced collectivization.

Kush Nubian African kingdom that conquered and controlled Egypt from 750 to 664 B.C.E.

Lamaist Buddhism (LAH-muh-ihst BOO-diz'm) Branch of Buddhism that was similar to shamanism in its acceptance of magic and supernatural powers.

La Reforma Political reform movement of Mexican president Benito Juárez (1806–1872) that called for limiting the power of the military and the Catholic church in Mexican society.

Latifundia (LAT-ih-FOON-dee-uh) Huge state-run and slave-worked farms in ancient Rome.

League of Nations Forerunner of the United Nations, the dream of American president Woodrow Wilson, although its potential was severely limited by the refusal of the United States to join.

Lebensraum (LAY-behnz-rowm) German term meaning "living space"; the term is associated with Hitler and his goal of carving out territory in the east for an expanding Germany.

Legalism Chinese philosophy from the Zhou dynasty that called for harsh suppression of the common people.

Levée en masse (leh-VAY on MASS) A term signifying universal conscription during the radical phase of the French revolution.

Lex talionis (lehks tah-lee-oh-nihs) "Law of retaliation," laws in which offenders suffered punishments similar to their crimes; the most famous example is Hammurabi's Laws.

Li (LEE) Confucian concept, a sense of propriety.

Linear A Minoan written script.

Linear B Early Mycenaean written script, adapted from the Minoan Linear A.

Luddites Early-nineteenth-century artisans who were opposed to new machinery and industrialization.

Machismo (mah-CHEEZ-moh) Latin American social ethic that honored male strength, courage, aggressiveness, assertiveness, and cunning.

Madrasas (MAH-drahs-uhs) Islamic institutions of higher education that originated in the tenth century.

Magyars (MAH-jahrs) Hungarian invaders who raided towns in Germany, Italy, and France in the ninth and tenth centuries.

Mahabharata (mah-hah-BAH-rah-tah) Massive ancient Indian epic that was developed orally for centuries; it tells of an epic civil war between two family branches.

Mahayana (mah-huh-YAH-nah) The "greater vehicle," a more metaphysical and more popular northern branch of Buddhism.

Majapahit (MAH-ja-PAHT) Southeast Asian kingdom (1293–1520) centered on the island of Java.

Mali (MAH-lee) West African kingdom founded in the thirteenth century by Sundiata; it reached its peak during the reign of Mansa Musa.

Manchus Manchurians who conquered China, putting an end to the Ming dynasty and founding the Qing dynasty (1644–1911).

Mandate of Heaven Chinese belief that the emperors ruled through the mandate, or approval, of heaven contingent on their ability to look after the welfare of the population.

Mandate system System that developed in the wake of World War I when the former colonies ended up mandates under European control, a thinly veiled attempt at continuing imperialism.

Manichaeism (man-ih-KEE-iz'm) Religion founded by the prophet Mani in the third century C.E., a syncretic version of Zoroastrian, Christian, and Buddhist elements.

Manor Large estates of the nobles during the European middle ages, home for the majority of the peasants.

Maori (mow-ree) Indigenous people of New Zealand.

Marae Polynesian temple structure.

Marathon Battlefield scene of the Athenian victory over the Persians in 490 B.C.E.

Maroons Runaway African slaves.

Marshall Plan U.S. plan, officially called the European Recovery Program, that offered financial and other economic aid to all European states that had suffered from World War II, including Soviet bloc states.

Mauryan empire Indian dynasty (321–185 B.C.E.) founded by Chandragupta Maurya and reaching its peak under Ashoka.

Maya (Mye-uh) Brilliant Central American society (300–1100) known for math, astronomy, and a sophisticated written language.

May Fourth Movement Chinese movement that began 4 May 1919 with a desire to eliminate imperialist influences and promote national unity.

Medes (meeds) Indo-European branch that settled in northern Persia and eventually fell to another branch, the Persians, in the sixth century B.C.E.

Meiji Restoration (MAY-jee) Restoration of imperial rule under Emperor Meiji in 1868 by a coalition led by Fukuzawa Yukichi and Ito Hirobumi; the restoration enacted western reforms to strengthen Japan.

Melaka (may-LAH-kah) Southeast Asian kingdom that was predominantly Islamic.

Mesopotamia Term meaning "between the rivers," in this case the Tigris and Euphrates; Sumer and Akkad are two of the earliest societies.

Mestizo (mehs-TEE-zoh) Latin American term for children of Spanish and native parentage.

Métis (may-TEE) Canadian term for individuals of mixed European and indigenous ancestry.

Millet An autonomous, self-governing community in the Ottoman empire.

Ming Chinese dynasty (1368–1644) founded by Hongwu and known for its cultural brilliance.

Minoan (mih-NOH-uhn) Society located on the island of Crete (ca. 2000–1100 B.C.E.) that influenced the early Mycenaeans.

Missi dominici (mihs-see doh-mee-nee-chee) "Envoys of the lord ruler," the noble and church emissaries sent out by Charlemagne.

Mithraism (MITH-rah-iz'm) Mystery religion based on worship of the sun god Mithras; it became popular among the Romans because of its promise of salvation.

Mochica (moh-CHEE-kuh) Pre-Incan South American society (300–700) known for their brilliant ceramics.

Moksha Hindu concept of the salvation of the soul.

Monotheism (MAW-noh-thee-iz'm) Belief in only one god, a rare concept in the ancient world.

Monroe Doctrine American doctrine issued in 1823 during the presidency of James Monroe that warned Europeans to keep their hands off Latin America and that expressed growing American imperialistic views regarding Latin America.

Mughals (MOO-guhls) Islamic dynasty that ruled India from the sixteenth through the eighteenth century; the construction of the Taj Mahal is representative of their splendor; with the exception of the enlightened reign of Akbar, the increasing conflict between Hindus and Muslims was another of their legacies.

Muhammad (muh-HAH-mehd) Prophet of Islam (570–632).

Muslim A follower of Islam.

Mycenaean (meye-seh-NEE-uhn) Early Greek society on the Peloponnese (1600–1100 B.C.E.) that was influenced by the Minoans; the Mycenaeans' conflict with Troy is immortalized in Homer's *Odyssey*.

Nara era Japanese period (710–794), centered on the city of Nara, that was the highest point of Chinese influence.

National Policy Nineteenth-century Canadian policy designed to attract migrants, protect industries through tariffs, and build national transportation systems.

NATO The North Atlantic Treaty Organization, which was established by the United States in 1949 as a regional military alliance against Soviet expansionism.

Ndongo (n'DAWN-goh) Angolan kingdom that reached its peak during the reign of Queen Nzinga (r. 1623–1663).

Neandertal (nee-ANN-duhr-tawl) Early humans (100,000 to 35,000 years ago) who were prevalent during the Paleolithic period.

Negritude (NEH-grih-tood) "Blackness," a term coined by early African nationalists as a means of celebrating the heritage of black peoples around the world.

Neo-Confucianism (nee-oh-kuhn-FYOO-shuhn-iz'm) Philosophy that attempted to merge certain basic elements of Confucian and Buddhist thought; most important of the early Neo-Confucianists was the Chinese thinker Zhu Xi (1130–1200).

Neolithic New Stone Age (10,000–4000 B.C.E.), which was marked by the discovery and mastery of agriculture.

Nestorian (neh-STOHR-ee-uhn) Early branch of Christianity, named after the fifth-century Greek theologian Nestorius, that emphasized the human nature of Jesus Christ.

New Economic Policy (NEP) Plan implemented by Lenin that called for minor free-market reforms.

Nirvana (nuhr-VAH-nuh) Buddhist concept of a state of spiritual perfection and enlightenment in which distracting passions are eliminated.

Noble Eightfold Path Final truth of the Buddhist Four Noble Truths that called for leading a life of balance and constant contemplation.

North American Free Trade Agreement (NAFTA) Regional accord established in 1993 between the United States, Canada, and Mexico; it formed world's second largest free-trade zone.

Nubia (NOO-bee-uh) Area south of Egypt; the kingdom of Kush in Nubia invaded and dominated Egypt from 750 to 664 B.C.E.

Oceania Term referring to the Pacific Ocean basin and its lands.

Olmecs Early Mesoamerican society (1200–100 B.C.E.) that centered on sites at San Lorenzo, La Venta, and Tres Zapotes and that influenced later Maya.

Oracle bones Chinese Shang dynasty (1766–1122 B.C.E.) means of foretelling the future.

Organization of African Unity (OAU) An organization started in 1963 by thirty-two newly independent African states and designed to prevent conflict that would lead to intervention by former colonial powers.

Organization of Petroleum Exporting Countries (OPEC) An organization begun in 1960 by oil-producing states originally for purely economic reasons but that later had more political influence.

Osiris Ancient Egyptian god that represented the forces of nature.

Ottoman empire Powerful Turkish empire that lasted from the conquest of Constantinople (Istanbul) in 1453 until 1918 and reached its peak during the reign of Süleyman the Magnificent (r. 1520–1566).

Paleolithic Old Stone Age, a long period of human development before the development of agriculture.

Palestinian Liberation Organization (PLO) Organization created in 1964 under the leadership of Yasser Arafat to champion Palestinian rights.

Paris Peace Accords Agreement reached in 1973 that marked the end of the United States' role in the Vietnam War.

Parsis (pahr-SEES) Indian Zoroastrians.

Parthians Persian dynasty (247 B.C.E.–224 C.E.) that reached its peak under Mithradates I.

Pater familias (PAH-tur fuh-MEE-lee-ahs) Roman term for the "father of the family," a theoretical implication that gave the male head of the family almost unlimited authority.

Patriarch (PAY-tree-ahrk) Leader of the Greek Orthodox church, which in 1054 officially split with the Pope and the Roman Catholic church.

Patricians Roman aristocrats and wealthy classes.

Pax Romana (pahks roh-MAH-nah) "Roman Peace," a term that relates to the period of political stability, cultural brilliance, and economic prosperity beginning with unification under Augustus and lasting through the first two centuries C.E.

Peninsulares (pehn-IHN-soo-LAH-rayz) Latin American officials from Spain or Portugal.

Perestroika (PAYR-eh-stroy-kuh) "Restructuring," a Russian term associated with Gorbachev's effort to reorganize the Soviet state.

Pharaohs (FARE-ohs) Egyptian kings considered to be gods on earth.

Plebians (plih-BEE-uhns) Roman common people.

Polis (POH-lihs) Greek term for the city-state.

Popol Vuh (paw-pawl vuh) Mayan creation epic.

Prehistory The period before the invention of writing.

Proletariat Urban working class in a modern industrial society.

Protestant Reformation Sixteenth-century European movement during which Luther, Calvin, Zwingli, and others broke away from the Catholic church.

Ptolemaic (TAWL-oh-may-ihk) Term used to signify both the Egyptian kingdom

founded by Alexander the Great's general Ptolemy and the thought of the philosopher Ptolemy of Alexandria (second century C.E.), who used mathematical formulas in an attempt to prove Aristotle's geocentric theory of the universe.

Putting-out system Method of getting around guild control by delivering unfinished materials to rural households for completion.

Qadi Islamic judge.

Qanat (kah-NAHT) Persian underground canal.

Qi (chee) Chinese concept of the basic material that makes up the body and the universe.

Qin (chihn) Chinese dynasty (221–207 B.C.E.) that was founded by Qin Shihuangdi and was marked by the first unification of China and the early construction of defensive walls.

Qing (chihng) Chinese dynasty (1644–1911) that reached its peak during the reigns of Kangxi and Qianlong.

Qizilbash (gih-ZIHL-bahsh) Term meaning "red heads," Turkish tribes that were important allies of Shah Ismail in the formation of the Safavid empire.

Quetzalcoatl (keht-zahl-koh-AHT'l) Aztec god, the "feathered serpent," who was borrowed originally from the Toltecs; Quetzalcoatl was believed to have been defeated by another god and exiled, and he promised to return.

Quinto (KEEN-toh) The one-fifth of Mexican and Peruvian silver production that was reserved for the Spanish monarchy.

Quipu (KEE-poo) Incan mnemonic aid comprised of different-colored strings and knots that served to record events in the absence of a written text.

Quran (koo-RAHN) Islamic holy book that is believed to contain the divine revelations of Allah as presented to Muhammad.

Ramayana (rah-mah-yah-nah) Ancient Indian masterpiece about the hero Rama that symbolized the victory of *dharma* (order) over *adharma* (chaos).

Rape of Nanjing Japanese conquest and destruction of the Chinese city of Nanjing in the 1930s.

Realpolitik (ray-AHL-poh-lih-teek) The Prussian Otto von Bismarck's "politics of reality," the belief that only the willingness to use force would actually bring about change.

Reconquista (ray-kohn-KEE-stah) Crusade, ending in 1492, to drive the Islamic forces out of Spain.

Reconstruction System implemented in the American South (1867–1877) that was designed to bring the Confederate states back into the union and also extend civil rights to freed slaves.

Romanov (ROH-mah-nahv) Russian dynasty (1610–1917) founded by Mikhail Romanov and ending with Nicholas II.

Rubaiyat (ROO-bee-aht) "Quatrains," famous poetry of Omar Khayyam that was later translated by Edward Fitzgerald.

Safavid (SAH-fah-vihd) Later Persian empire (1501–1722) that was founded by Shah Ismail and that became a center for Shiism; the empire reached its peak under Shah Abbas the Great and was centered on the capital of Isfahan.

Sakk Letters of credit that were common in the medieval Islamic banking world.

Saljuqs (sahl-JYOOKS) Turkish tribe that gained control over the Abbasid empire and fought with the Byzantine empire.

Samsara (sahm-SAH-ruh) Hindu term for the concept of transmigration, that is, the soul passing into a new incarnation.

Samurai (SAM-uhr-eye) A Japanese warrior.

Sasanids (suh-SAH-nids) Later powerful Persian dynasty (224–651) that would reach its peak under Shapur I and later fall to Arabic expansion.

Sati (SUH-TEE) Also known as *suttee,* Indian practice of a widow throwing herself on the funeral pyre of her husband.

Satraps (SAY-traps) Persian administrators, usually members of the royal family, who governed a satrapy.

Satyagraha (SAH-tyah-GRAH-hah) "Truth and firmness," a term associated with Gandhi's policy of passive resistance.

Scholasticism Medieval attempt of thinkers such as St. Thomas Aquinas to merge the beliefs of Christianity with the logical rigor of Greek philosophy.

Scientific racism Nineteenth-century attempt to justify racism by scientific means; an example would be Gobineau's *Essay on the Inequality of the Human Races.*

Seleucids (sih-LOO-sihds) Persian empire (323–83 B.C.E.) founded by Seleucus after the death of Alexander the Great.

Self-determination Belief popular in World War I and after that every people should have the right to determine their own political destiny; the belief was often cited but ignored by the Great Powers.

Self-Strengthening Movement Chinese attempt (1860–1895) to blend Chinese cultural traditions with European industrial technology.

Semitic (suh-miht-ihk) A term that relates to the Semites, ancient nomadic herders who spoke Semitic languages; examples of Semites were the Akkadians, Hebrews, Aramaics, and Phoenicians, who often interacted with the more settled societies of Mesopotamia and Egypt.

Sepoys Indian troops who served the British.

Serfs Peasants who, though not chattel slaves, were tied to the land and who owed obligation to the lords on whose land they worked.

Shamanism (SHAH-mah-niz'm) Belief in shamans or religious specialists who possessed supernatural powers and who communicated with the gods and the spirits of nature.

Shari'a (shah-REE-ah) The Islamic holy law, drawn up by theologians from the Quran and accounts of Muhammad's life.

Shia (SHEE-ah) Islamic minority in opposition to the Sunni majority; their belief is that leadership should reside in the line descended from Ali.

Shintoism (SHIHN-toh-iz'm) Indigenous Japanese religion that emphasizes purity, clan loyalty, and the divinity of the emperor.

Shiva (SHEE-vuh) Hindu god associated with both fertility and destruction.

Shogun (SHOH-gun) Japanese military leader who ruled in place of the emperor.

Shudras (SHOO-druhs) Hindu caste of landless peasants and serfs.

Siddhartha Gautama (sih-DHAR-tuh GOW-tau-mah) Indian *kshatriya* who achieved enlightenment and became known as the Buddha, the founder of Buddhism.

Sikhs (SIHKS) Adherents of an Indian syncretic faith that contains elements of Hinduism and Islam.

Silk roads Ancient trade routes that extended from the Mediterranean in the west to China in the east.

Social Darwinism Nineteenth-century philosophy, championed by thinkers such as Herbert Spencer, that attempted to apply Darwinian "survival of the fittest" to the social and political realm; adherents saw the elimination of weaker nations as part of a natural process and used the philosophy to justify war.

Socialism Political and economic theory of social organization based on the collective ownership of the means of production; its origins were in the early nineteenth century, and it differs from communism by a desire for slow or moderate change compared with the communist call for revolution.

Solidarity Polish trade union and nationalist movement in the 1980s that was headed by Lech Walesa.

Song (SOHNG) Chinese dynasty (960–1279) that was marked by an increasingly urbanized and cosmopolitan society.

Soviets Russian elected councils that originated as strike committees during the 1905 St. Petersburg disorders; they represented a form of local self-government that went on to become the primary unit of government in the Union of Soviet Socialist Republics. The term was also used during the cold war to designate the Soviet Union.

Spanish Inquisition Institution organized in 1478 by Fernando and Isabel of Spain to detect heresy and the secret practice of Judaism or Islam.

Srivijaya (sree-VIH-juh-yuh) Southeast Asian kingdom (670–1025), based on the island of Sumatra, that used a powerful navy to dominate trade.

Stateless societies Term relating to societies such as those of sub-Saharan Africa after the Bantu migrations that featured decentralized rule through family and kinship groups instead of strongly centralized hierarchies.

Stoics (STOH-ihks) Hellenistic philosophers who encouraged their followers to lead active, virtuous lives and to aid others.

Strabo (STRAH-boh) Greek geographer (first century C.E.).

Strategic Arms Limitations Talk (SALT) Agreement in 1972 between the United States and the Soviet Union.

Stupas (STOO-pahs) Buddhist shrines.

Sufis (SOO-fees) Islamic mystics who placed more emphasis on emotion and devotion than on strict adherence to rules.

Sui (SWAY) Chinese dynasty (589–618) that constructed the Grand Canal, reunified China, and allowed for the splendor of the Tang dynasty that followed.

Süleyman (SOO-lee-mahn) Ottoman Turkish ruler Süleyman the Magnificent (r. 1520–1566), who was the most powerful and wealthy ruler of the sixteenth century.

Sumerians (soo-MEHR-ee-uhns) Earliest Mesopotamian society.

Sundiata (soon-JAH-tuh) Founder of the Mali empire (r. 1230–1255), also the inspiration for the *Sundiata,* an African literary and mythological work.

Sunni (SOON-nee) "Traditionalists," the most popular branch of Islam; Sunnis believe in the legitimacy of the early caliphs, compared with the Shiite belief that only a descendant of Ali can lead.

Suu Kyi, Aung San (SOO KEY, AWNG SAHN) Opposition leader (1945–) in Myanmar; she was elected leader in 1990 but she was not allowed to come to power; she was a Nobel Peace Prize recipient in 1991.

Swahili (swah-HEE-lee) East African city-state society that dominated the coast from Mogadishu to Kilwa and was active in trade.

Taino (TEYE-noh) A Caribbean tribe who were the first indigenous peoples from the Americas to come into contact with Christopher Columbus.

Taiping rebellion (TEYE-pihng) Rebellion (1850–1864) in Qing China led by Hong Xiuquan, during which twenty to thirty million were killed; the rebellion was symbolic of the decline of China during the nineteenth century.

Taliban Strict Islamic organization that ruled Afghanistan from 1996 to 2002.

Tang Taizong (TAHNG TEYE-zohng) Chinese emperor (r. 627–649) of the Tang dynasty (618–907).

Tanzimat "Reorganization" era (1839–1876), an attempt to reorganize the Ottoman empire on Enlightenment and constitutional forms.

Temüjin (TEM-oo-chin) Mongol conqueror (ca. 1167–1227) who later took the name Chinggis Khan, "universal ruler."

Tenochtitlan (the-NOCH-tee-tlahn) Capital of the Aztec empire, later Mexico City.

Teotihuacan (tay-uh-tee-wah-KAHN) Central American society (200 B.C.E.–750 C.E.); its Pyramid of the Sun was the largest structure in Mesoamerica.

Teutonic Knights Crusading European order that was active in the Baltic region.

Third Rome Concept that a new power would rise up to carry the legacy of Roman greatness after the decline of the Second Rome, Constantinople; Moscow was referred to as the Third Rome during the fifteenth century.

Three Principles of the People Philosophy of Chinese Guomindang leader Sun Yatsen (1866–1925) that emphasized nationalism, democracy, and people's livelihood.

Tian (TEE-ehn) Chinese term for heaven.

Tikal (tee-KAHL) Maya political center from the fourth through the ninth century.

Timur-i lang (tee-MOOR-yee LAHNG) "Timur the Lame," known in English as Tamerlane (ca. 1336–1405), who conquered an empire ranging from the Black Sea to Samarkand.

Tokugawa (TOH-koo-GAH-wah) Last shogunate in Japanese history (1600–1867); it was founded by Tokugawa Ieyasu who was notable for unifying Japan.

Toltecs Central American society (950–1150) that was centered on the city of Tula.

Trail of Tears Forced relocation of the Cherokee from the eastern woodlands to Oklahoma (1837–1838); it was symbolic of U.S. expansion and destruction of indigenous Indian societies.

Triangular trade Trade between Europe, Africa, and the Americas that featured finished products from Europe, slaves from Africa, and American products bound for Europe.

Triple Alliance Pre–World War I alliance of Germany, Austria-Hungary, and Italy.

Triple Entente (ahn-TAHNT) Pre–World War I alliance of England, France, and Russia.

Truman Doctrine U.S. policy instituted in 1947 by President Harry Truman in which the United States would follow an interventionist foreign policy to contain communism.

Tsar (ZAHR) Old Russian term for king that is derived from the term *caesar.*

Twelver Shiism (SHEE'i'zm) Branch of Islam that stressed that there were twelve perfect religious leaders after Muhammad and that the twelfth went into hiding and would return someday; Shah Ismail spread this variety through the Safavid empire.

Uighurs (WEE-goors) Turkish tribe.

Ukiyo Japanese word for the "floating worlds," a Buddhist term for the insignificance of the world that came to

represent the urban centers in Tokugawa Japan.

Ulaanbaatar (OO-lahn-bah-tahr) Mongolian city.

Ulama Islamic officials, scholars who shaped public policy in accordance with the Quran and the *sharia.*

Umayyad (oo-MEYE-ahd) Arabic dynasty (661–750), with its capital at Damascus, that was marked by a tremendous period of expansion to Spain in the west and India in the east.

Umma (UM-mah) Islamic term for the "community of the faithful."

United Nations (UN) Successor to the League of Nations, an association of sovereign nations that attempts to find solutions to global problems.

Upanishads (oo-PAHN-ee-shahds) Indian reflections and dialogues (800–400 B.C.E.) that reflected basic Hindu concepts.

Urdu (OOR-doo) A language that is predominant in Pakistan.

Uruk (OO-rook) Ancient Mesopotamian city from the fourth millennium B.C.E. that was allegedly the home of the fabled Gilgamesh.

Vaishyas (VEYES-yuhs) Hindu caste of cultivators, artisans, and merchants.

Vaqueros (vah-KEHR-ohs) Latin American cowboys, similar to the Argentine gaucho.

Varna (VAHR-nuh) Hindu word for caste.

Varuna (vuh-ROO-nuh) Early Aryan god who watched over the behavior of mortals and preserved the cosmic order.

Vedas (VAY-duhs) "Wisdom," early collections of prayers and hymns that provide information about the Indo-European Aryans who migrated into India around 1500 B.C.E.; *Rig Veda* is the most important collection.

Velvet revolution A term that describes the nonviolent transfer of power in Czechoslovakia during the collapse of Soviet rule.

Venta, La (VEHN-tuh, lah) Early Olmec center (800–400 B.C.E.).

Venus figurines Small Paleolithic statues of women with exaggerated sexual features.

Vernacular (ver-NA-kyoo-lar) The language of the people; Martin Luther translated the Bible from the Latin of the Catholic church into the vernacular German.

Versailles (vehr-SEYE) Palace of French King Louis XIV.

Viet Minh North Vietnamese nationalist communists under Ho Chi Minh.

Vietnamization President Richard Nixon's strategy of turning the Vietnam War over to the South Vietnamese.

Vijayanagar (vee-juh-yah-NAH-gahr) Southern Indian kingdom (1336–1565) that later fell to the Mughals.

Vikings A group that raided the British Isles from their home at Vik in southern Norway.

Vishnu (VIHSH-noo) Hindu god, preserver of the world, who was often incarnated as Krishna.

Vodou (voh-DOW) Syncretic religion practiced by African slaves in Haiti.

Volksgeist (FOHLKS-geyest) "People's spirit," a term that was coined by the German philosopher Herder; a nation's volksgeist would not come to maturity unless people studied their own unique culture and traditions.

Volta do mar (VOHL-tah doh MAHR) "Return through the sea," a fifteenth-century Portuguese sea route that took advantage of the prevailing winds and currents.

Voltaire (vohl-TAIR) Pen name of French philosophe François-Marie Arouet (1694–1778), author of *Candide.*

Waldensians Twelfth-century religious reformers who criticized the Roman Catholic church and who proposed that the laity had the right to preach and administer sacraments; they were declared heretics.

Walesa, Lech (WAH-lehn-sah, LEHK) Leader of the Polish Solidarity movement.

Wanli (wahn-LEE) Chinese Ming emperor (r. 1572–1620) whose refusal to meet with officials hurried the decline of the Ming dynasty.

War Communism The Bolshevik policy of nationalizing industry and seizing private land during the civil war.

Warsaw Pact Warsaw Treaty Organization, a military alliance formed by Soviet bloc nations in 1955 in response to rearmament of West Germany and its inclusion in NATO.

Wind wheels Prevailing wind patterns in the Atlantic and Pacific Oceans north and south of the equator; their discovery made sailing much safer and quicker.

Witte, Sergei (VIHT-tee, SAYR-gay) Late-nineteenth-century Russian minister of finance who pushed for industrialization.

World Health Organization (WHO) United Nations organization designed to deal with global health issues.

World Trade Organization (WTO) An organization that was established in 1995 with more than 120 nations and whose goal is to loosen barriers to free trade.

Wuwei (woo-WAY) Daoist concept of a disengagement from the affairs of the world.

Xia (shyah) Early Chinese dynasty (2200–1766 B.C.E.).

Xianyang (SHYAHN-YAHNG) Capital city of the Qin empire.

Xiao (SHAYOH) Confucian concept of respect for one's parents and ancestors.

Xinjiang (shin-jyahng) Western Chinese province.

Xuanzang (SHWEN-ZAHNG) Seventh-century Chinese monk who made a famous trip to India to collect Buddhist texts.

Yahweh (YAH-way) God of the monotheistic religion of Judaism that influenced later Christianity and Islam.

Yangshao (YAHNG-show) Early Chinese society (2500–2200 B.C.E.).

Yangzi (YAHNG-zuh) River in central China.

Yongle (YAWNG-leh) Chinese Ming emperor (r. 1403–1424) who pushed for foreign exploration and promoted cultural achievements such as the *Yongle Encyclopedia.*

Young Turks Nineteenth-century Turkish reformers who pushed for changes within the Ottoman empire, such as universal suffrage and freedom of religion.

Yu (yoo) Legendary founder of the Xia dynasty (ca. 2200 B.C.E.).

Yuan (yoo-AHN) Chinese dynasty (1279–1368) that was founded by the Mongol ruler Khubilai Khan.

Yucatan (yoo-kuh-TAN) Peninsula in Central America, home of the Maya.

Yurts (yuhrts) Tents used by nomadic Turkish and Mongol tribes.

Zaibatsu (zeye-BAHT-soo) Japanese term for "wealthy cliques," which are similar to American trusts and cartels but usually organized around one family.

Zambos (ZAHM-bohs) Latin American term for individuals born of indigenous and African parents.

Zamudio, Adela (ZAH-moo-dee-oh, ah-DEH-lah) Nineteenth-century Bolivian poet, author of "To Be Born a Man."

Zarathustra (zar-uh-THOO-struh) Persian prophet (ca. sixth century B.C.E.) who founded Zoroastrianism.

Zemstvos (ZEHMST-voh) District assemblies elected by Russians in the nineteenth century.

Zen Buddhism Japanese version of Chinese Chan Buddhism, with an emphasis on intuition and sudden flashes of insight instead of textual study.

Zhou (JOH) Chinese dynasty (1122–256 B.C.E.) that was the foundation of Chinese thought formed during this period: Confucianism, Daoism, Zhou Classics.

Zhu Xi (ZHOO-SHEE) Neo-Confucian Chinese philosopher (1130–1200).

Ziggurats (ZIG-uh-rahts) Mesopotamian temples.

Zimbabwe (zihm-BAHB-way) Former colony of Southern Rhodesia that gained independence in 1980.

Zoroastrianism (zohr-oh-ASS-tree-ahn-iz'm) Persian religion based on the teaching of the sixth-century-B.C.E. prophet Zarathustra; its emphasis on the duality of good and evil and on the role of individuals in determining their own fate would influence later religions.

of the Royal Ontatio Museum © ROM (925.25.15a-b); **p. 449,** © Scala/Art Resource, NY; **p. 450T,** © Sylvain Grandadam/Photo Researchers, Inc.; **p. 450B,** © Scala/Art Resource, NY; **p. 452,** Courtesy Ryukoku University Library; **p. 453,** © Bibliotheque Nationale, Paris, France/ The Bridgeman Art Library; **p. 456,** World map engraving, 1532, Typus Comsmographicus Universalis by Münster, Sebastian. With permission of the Royal Ontario Museum © ROM (956.186.2); **p. 460L,** Library of Congress, Prints and Photographs Division (LC-USZC2-1687); **p. 460ML,** Fototeca Storica Nazionale/Getty Images; **p. 460MR,** © Creatas/PunchStock; **p. 460R,** © BananaStock/PunchStock.

PART 5

Photo Credits p. 462L, © Stapleton Collection/Corbis; **p. 462ML,** © Scala/ Art Resource, NY; **p. 462MR,** Benson Latin American Collection, General Libraries, University of Texas at Austin; **p. 462R,** © National Maritime Museum, London, #A1818; **p. 463L,** Peabody Essex Museum. Photo by Mark Sexton; **p. 463R,** © Francis G. Mayer/Corbis

CHAPTER 22

Text Credits p. 474, From *Diario of Christopher Columbus's First Voyage to America,* 1492–1493, translated and edited by Oliver C. Dunn and James E. Kelley, Jr. Published by the University of Oklahoma Press, 1989. Used by permission. **Photo Credits p. 464,** © Stapleton Collection/ Corbis; **p. 467,** © Bildarchiv Preussischer Kulturbesitz/Art Resource, NY; **p. 469,** © Germanisches Nationalmuseum, Nuremberg, Germany/ The Bridgeman Art Library; **p. 475,** © Stefano Bianchetti/Corbis; **p. 477T,** © HIP/Art Resource, NY; **p. 477B,** © National Maritime Museum, Greenwich, London; **p. 481,** © Maritiem Museum, Rotterdam. P-2161-31; **p. 482,** © Oregon Historical Society (OrHi 97421); **p. 486,** Peabody Museum, Harvard University (2004.24.29636); **p. 487,** © Stapleton Collection/Corbis; **p. 489,** © Bettmann/Corbis.

CHAPTER 23

Photo Credits pp. 492, 496, © Scala/Art Resource, NY; **p. 497,** © Erich Lessing/Art Resource, NY; **p. 498,** Anne S.K. Brown Military Collection, Brown University Library; **p. 501,** © Bibliotheque National de France, Paris; **p. 502,** © The Granger Collection, New York; **p. 503,** © The Art Archive/Corbis; **p. 504,** © Superstock/Getty Images; **p. 505,** © akg-images; **p. 506,** © The Art Archive/Corbis; **p. 509,** Amsterdam Historisch Museum (INV.NR.SA3025); **p. 510,** © The Granger Collection, New York; **p. 514,** © Stefano Bianchetti/Corbis; **p. 516,** © The Gallery Collection/Corbis; **pp. 517, 519,** © Erich Lessing/Art Resource, NY.

CHAPTER 24

Text Credits p. 526, Bernardino de Sahagún, *Florentine Codex: General History of the Things of New Spain,* 13 vols. Trans. By Arthur J. O. Anderson and Charles E. Dibble. Salt Lake City: University of Utah Press, 1950–82, 13:19–20. Used by permission; **p. 544,** James Cook, *The Journals of Captain Cook.* Ed. By Philip Edwards. London: Penguin, 1999. **Photo Credits p. 522,** Benson Latin American Collection, General Libraries, University of Texas at Austin; **p. 525,** © Spencer Collection, The New York Public Library, Astor, Lenox and Tilden Foundations/Art Resource, NY; **p. 528,** © The Gallery Collection/Corbis; **p. 529,** Biblioteca del ICI, Madrid, Spain/Index/The Bridgeman Art Library; **p. 532,** Courtesy of Whitehall-Robins Company, Photograph by Don Eiler; **p. 534,** © The Gallery Collection/Corbis; **p. 535,** Courtesy of the Hispanic Society of America, New York; **p. 536,** Det Kongelige Bibliothek, Copenhagen; **pp. 538, 539,** © Arents Collection, New York Public Library, Astor, Lenox and Tilden Foundations/Art Resource, NY; **p. 540,** © Christie's

Images/Corbis; **p. 543,** Honolulu Academy of Arts, Gift of the Honolulu Art Society, 1944 (12,161).

CHAPTER 25

Text Credits p. 554, Basil Davidson, *The African Past.* Boston: Little, Brown, 1964. Copyright © 1964 by Basil Davidson. Reprinted by permission of Curtis Brown, Ltd. **Photo Credits p. 548,** © National Maritime Museum, London, #A1818; **p. 551,** © The Art Archive/Bibliothèque Nationale Paris; **p. 553,** © Rare Books Division, New York Public Library, Astor, Lenox and Tilden Foundations/ Art Resource, NY; **p. 555,** From Description de l'Afrique by Olifert Dapper, 1686; **p. 557,** © Rare Books Division, New York Public Library, Astor, Lenox and Tilden Foundations/ Art Resource, NY; **p. 559,** © The British Museum; **p. 563,** © North Wind Picture Archives; **p. 564,** © Arents Collection, New York Public Library, Astor, Lenox and Tilden Foundations/ Art Resource, NY; **p. 565,** From Debret, *Voyages Pittoresque et Historiques au Bresil,* 1816–1831; **p. 567,** © Manuscripts, Archives and Rare Books Division, Schomberg Center for Research in Black Culture, New York Public Library, Astor, Lenox and Tilden Foundations/Art Resource, NY.

CHAPTER 26

Text Credits p. 591, George Elison, *Deus Destroyed: The Image of Christianity in Early Modern Japan.* Cambridge, Mass.: Harvard University, Council on East Asian Studies, 1973, pp. 259–60, 283–84. © 1973 The President and Fellows of Harvard College. **Photo Credits p. 570,** Peabody Essex Museum. Photo by Mark Sexton; **p. 574,** © Manfred Gottschalk/Workbook Stock/Getty Images; **p. 576,** © The Metropolitan Museum of Art/Art Resource, NY; **p. 577,** © National Palace Museum, Taipei, Taiwan, Republic of China; **p. 579,** © Dennis Cox/ChinaStock; **p. 580,** Golestan Palace, Tehran, Iran/© Giraudon/Bridgeman Art

index

588; population growth in, 587; social classes in, 587–88

Toltecs, 416–17, 417 (*map*)

tomatoes, 416, 604

tombs. *See* burials

Tonga, 428 (*map*), 429, 430, 432, 475; Cook in, 475, 476 (*map*)

tools, 291. *See also* technology

Topkapi palace (Istanbul), 607–8

Tordesillas, Treaty of (1494), 529

Tours, battle of (732 C.E.), 327, 333

trade: Abbasid dynasty and, 339; in Africa, trans-Saharan, 374–79, 376 (*map*); Arabia and, 260; Australia and, 428–29; in Aztec empire, 418–19; Byzantine empire and, 337–38; Caribbean, gold mining and, 525–26; in China, Qing dynasty, 580, 581 (*source document*); in China, Sui dynasty, 282–83; in China, Tang and Song dynasties, 288–90, 292–93, 294 (*source document*); cities and, 436–37; as crusade consequence, 412; France and, 399, 479 (*map*); global, origins of, 488–89; India and, 305–6, 311, 320; Islamic empires and, 270–72, 271 (*illus.*), 307–8, 605; Italy and, 399–400, 399 (*illus.*), 402 (*map*); as lure for exploration, 467–68; medieval Europe and, 399–400, 399 (*illus.*), 400 (*illus.*), 402 (*map*); Mongol empires and, 364; nomadic peoples and, 350, 355; in North America, 423, 462; Pacific islands and, 429, 543; patterns

of long-distance, 436–39; Pegolotti on, 401 (*source document*); sub-Saharan Africa and, 372, 374, 376 (*map*), 388; transoceanic, 488; triangular, 559–60, 560–61 (*map*); in western Europe, 339. *See also* fur trade; Indian Ocean basin trade; silk roads; slave trade, Atlantic; slave trade, Islamic; spice trade; *specific cities and countries*

trade winds, 469, 470–71 (*map*)

trading companies, 478–79, 510

trading post empires, 463, 476–79, 479 (*map*), 488; competition and conflict in, 483; Dutch, 477–78, 479 (*map*), 483; English, 477–78, 479 (*map*), 483; Portuguese trading posts, 476–77; Siberian, 483

translators, travelers and, 275

transportation: camel caravans, 270, 272, 374–75, 375 (*illus.*); in China, Tang dynasty, 284. *See also* horses; maritime technology; railroads; roads

travel and travel writing: Benjamin of Tudela, 341 (*source document*); Buzurg ibn Shahriyar, 305–6, 313; diplomatic missions, 364–65; Ibn Battuta, 380, 381 (*source document*), 384, 388, 435–36, 438–39 (*map*), 440–41, 441 (*source document*); al-Muqaddasi, 276 (*source document*); Polo, Marco, 323, 361 (*source document*), 362, 364, 391, 436, 437, 438–39 (*map*), 439, 440 (*illus.*); Suleiman, 294 (*source*

document); translators and, 275; William of Rubruck, 353, 356 (*source document*). *See also* historians; pilgrimages

trebuchets, 444

triangular trade, 559–60, 560–61 (*map*)

Tribute Money (Masaccio), 449 (*illus.*)

Tripmaster Monkey, (Kingston), 584

troubadours, 402–3, 403 (*illus.*), 442

The True Meaning of the Lord of Heaven (Ricci), 585

tsar, 450, 504

tuberculosis, 508

ibn Tughluq, Muhammad, Sultan of Delhi, 435

Tughril Beg, Saljuq ruler (eleventh century), 357

Tula (Mexico), 416, 417, 417 (*map*)

Tunisia, 267

Túpac Amaru rebellion, 536

Tupí language, 531

Turkana people, 561

Turkish peoples, 359 (*map*); Islam and, 267, 308, 356; migrations by, 354–58, 355 (*illus.*), 357 (*illus.*); Ottoman Turks, 329, 331, 358; Saljuq Turks, 268, 356, 357–58, 359 (*map*), 393; Uighurs, 286, 365. *See also* Anatolia; Ottoman empire

Twelver Shiism, 598–99

typhus, 508

Uighur Turks, 286, 365

ukiyo, 589

Ulaanbaatar (Mongol capital), 359

ulama, 268, 273

Umayyad dynasty (661–750), 265–66, 267, 270, 307

umma, 262, 264–65, 266

Union of South Africa. *See* South Africa

United East India Company. *See* VOC

United Kingdom. *See* Britain

United Provinces (Netherlands), 497, 502

United States (U.S.): abolition of slavery in, 568; American revolution, 549, 567

universities and higher education: *madrasas*, 273–74, 278; in medieval Europe, 404–5, 405 (*illus.*)

Upanishads, 317

Urban II, Pope (ca. 1035–1099), 411

U.S. *See* United States

Uzbeks, 600

Vanuatu, 475, 476 (*map*)

veiling of women, 272–73, 384

venereal diseases, 543

Venice (Italy), 448; bronze horses at St. Mark's basilica, 394 (*illus.*); Ottoman invasion of, 597; trade in, 399, 399 (*illus.*), 400, 402 (*map*)

Versailles, palace at, 503–4

viceroys, 529

Vienna, Ottoman attack on, 500, 598

Vietnam: Chams in, 321; China and, 282, 288, 299, 299 (*map*), 300 (*illus.*); Mongol invasion of, 362; under Qing dynasty, 575; under Tang dynasty, 285

Vijayanagar kingdom (1336–1565), 307 (*map*), 309–10, 310 (*illus.*), 601

Vikings, 334–37, 335 (*illus.*), 336 (*map*), 339

Vinland, 410

Viracocha (Inca deity), 427

Virgin Mary, 406, 406 (*illus.*)

Virgin of Guadalupe, 540, 540 (*illus.*)